DRUID MECHANICS PRESENTS:

Unreal Engine C++ the Ultimate Developer's Handbook

Learn C++ and Unreal Engine by Creating a Complete Action Game

Stephen Seth Ulibarri

Learn the fundamentals of the C++ programming language as well as Unreal Engine's code base for creating and packaging a complete hack and slash action game. Implement combat, AI and Behavior Trees, animation, gameplay mechanics, Interfaces and Delegates, collision and physics, ray casting, game saving, menu and HUD creation via UMG, and much more.

Courses by the Author

If you are a visual learner, the author of this book has created online video tutorials which you can take to solidify concepts related to game development and programming. The following courses are available on Udemy.com and can greatly enhance the knowledge you will gain in this book.

Learning C++

For a series covering the basics of the C++ programming language, take **Learn C++ for Game Development**, taught by Stephen Ulibarri. The course has over 12 hours of video content, and no programming experience in necessary. Theory is covered in classroom-style whiteboard talks, followed by hands-on application with coding examples. This course can be accessed with the following link:

https://www.udemy.com/course/learn-cpp-for-ue4-unit-1/

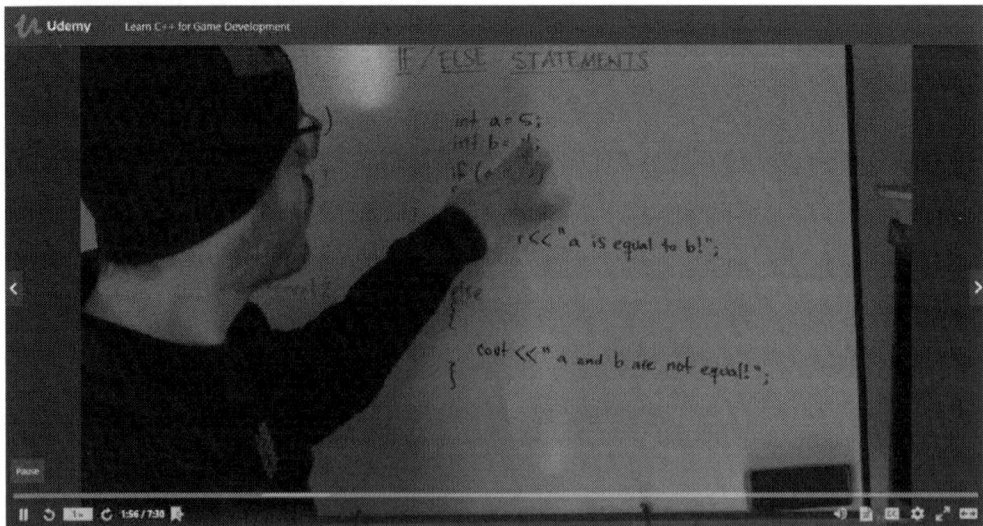

Learning Unreal Engine C++

For a series covering C++ programming in Unreal Engine, take **Unreal Engine C++ The Ultimate Developer Course**, taught by Stephen Ulibarri. The course has over 34 hours of video content, and you will create a complete video game, start to finish, and learn several valuable sources of free assets for your game. This course can be accessed with the following link:

https://www.udemy.com/course/unreal-engine-the-ultimate-game-developer-course/

Learning Unreal Blueprints

For a series covering Blueprints in Unreal Engine, take **Unreal Engine Blueprints - The Ultimate Developer Course**, taught by Stephen Ulibarri. The course has over 31 hours of video content, and you will create **three** complete video games, including a mobile game! Blueprints are used throughout the entire course. This course can be accessed with the following link:

https://www.udemy.com/course/unreal-engine-blueprints-the-ultimate-developer-course/

Follow Druid Mechanics for Updates!

Stephen Ulibarri continues to create tutorials and game development content on a regular basis. His works and updates can be found on the various social media platforms. Search for **Druid Mechanics** on Facebook, Twitter, Instagram, and YouTube.

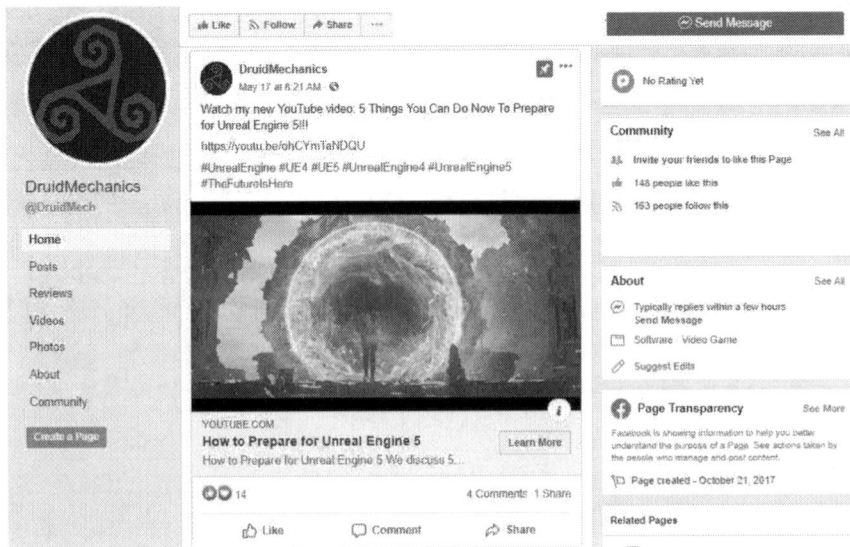

Unreal Engine C++ the Ultimate Developer's Handbook

Check **DruidMechanics** on Facebook for special coupons to Stephen's Udemy courses! Use the coupon codes announced on Druid Mechanics on Facebook for the lowest prices on the courses!

Download the Project File

The Project File for the game you will create in this book is available for download at https://github.com/DruidMech/UE4-Book-Repo.

Simply go to the above URL link and click **Clone or Download**, then select **Download Zip**. Once the *.zip* file downloads on your computer, extract its contents (right-click on it and select *Extract All…*), and you will have the Unreal Engine project file for the book.

Table of Contents

Unreal Engine C++ the Ultimate Developer's Handbook

Chapter 1 – An Overview of Unreal Engine

You are likely picking up this book because you want to program in Unreal Engine. If that is the case, this book has many incredibly interesting things in store for you. We will start at the beginning by answering the fundamental question: What is Unreal Engine? We will then dive right in by explaining how to get started downloading the engine and Visual Studio – an Integrated Development Environment (IDE) (or Xcode if you are on a Mac), which we will use while we program video games for Unreal Engine.

If you don't know C++, the programming language used in Unreal Engine, don't worry. This book will teach you C++, and you will have a valuable reference filled with examples of the C++ principles you will use as a game developer. Tab the book, put in bookmarks, post-it notes, and highlight it. It will serve you as a reference to check back on while you develop your games.

The same goes for the rest of the book. This book takes you through the process of creating a third-person action game, complete with character movement and combat, enemy artificial intelligence (using Unreal Engine's sophisticated Blackboard AI system), menu creation and much more. Throughout your game development career, you can refer back to the examples in this book to see how things are done when you create your own games.

If you wish to learn Unreal Engine 5, the principles in this book will still benefit you and apply. At the time of writing, Unreal Engine 5 has not yet been released, but Epic Games has announced that you can learn Unreal Engine 4 today and convert your project to Unreal Engine 5 whenever you're ready.

While working through the examples in this book, you will learn:

- Unreal Engine's class hierarchy system and why it is so useful and powerful (Chapter 2)

- How to create materials and lighting for your games (Chapter 3)

- How to program in C++, the industry standard language for games (Chapter 4)

- Creating Actors, the basic class you can place in the level (Chapter 5)

- Creating Pawns, classes which can be controlled with input (Chapter 6)

- Creating a functional game Character (Chapter 7)

- Physics and collisions (Chapter 8)

- Gameplay events, HUD and GUI elements (Chapter 9)

- Logging, debug messages, and line tracing (Chapter 10)

- Delegates and Interfaces (Chapter 11)

- AI and Unreal Engine's Behavior Tree system for Artificial Intelligence (Chapter 12)

- How to package a complete video game for production (Chapter 13)

You will finish this book with the skill set necessary to create complete video games. Most importantly, we will focus on the ability to figure out how to create gameplay mechanics using problem solving principles. It's not enough to just know how to create the project in this book. I want you to know how to apply these principles to any game you imagine. Not only should you understand how to apply the techniques in the examples provided, but you should be able to apply them to your own projects and creations, or problems presented to you in the games industry (or to your indie company).

About Unreal Engine

Unreal Engine is one of the most incredible software packages you will come across in modern times. The fact that you can download it and use it for free is just mind-blowing. Unreal Engine contains several software systems designed to handle the various components of video game development. To exhaustively cover all the capabilities of the engine would easily require several volumes. Game engines in general provide you with the tools and programs to help you customize and create a video game.

Unreal Engine was originally created by Epic Games to develop the Unreal Tournament video game series. Over the years, the engine went through several version overhauls, and has been improved and perfected at the hands of many top-tier developers. The game engine itself has become so well engineered that Epic Games decided to unleash it to the world at large. Now the engine has been used to create many AAA quality video games and the engine continually improves to keep up with the current advances in technology. The coming version, Unreal Engine 5 at the time of writing, promises some unprecedented features in video games, including global illumination and the ability to use multimillion or even billion polygon meshes at runtime.

The best way to prepare for Unreal Engine 5 is to do what you are doing now: Learn Unreal Engine 4! Transitioning to Unreal Engine 5 will be seamless, as they are designing it with forward compatibility in mind.

Now, we will dive into how to install the engine and the IDE onto our computer.

Installing Unreal Engine and Visual Studio

Installing Unreal Engine is simple:

1. Go to the Engine official website: www.unrealengine.com.

2. Create an account with Epic Games (it's free).

3. Once you login, you will have the option to download the engine for Mac or Windows. Make sure you download the correct version for your system.

You will also need an IDE (Integrated Development Environment). For Windows users, Microsoft Visual Studio is recommended. For Mac users, XCode is recommended. In the past, programming was done with simple text processors like Notepad. An IDE is a software application for programmers. IDEs usually contain a code editor, build automation tools, and a debugger among other features. We will be using Visual Studio in this book, and you can download it at https://visualstudio.microsoft.com/downloads/. The Community edition is free and is capable of meeting all of your coding needs for game development.

If you are a Mac user, you will need to download an IDE compatible for Mac such as XCode. You can download XCode at https://developer.apple.com/xcode/. All of the code in this book will still work for you, even though we are working the examples in Visual Studio.

When downloading and setting up your IDE, you will need to follow some guidelines for ensuring that you include all the appropriate modules for you to be able to program for Unreal Engine. For Visual Studio, you can find the steps for doing so at https://docs.unrealengine.com/en-US/Programming/Development/VisualStudioSetup/index.html. The Unreal Engine documentation is a valuable resource for you as a game developer using Unreal Engine.

When you download the engine, you also get the Epic Games Launcher, a useful tool that helps keep your Unreal Engine projects organized.

The Epic Games Launcher

The Epic Games Launcher is a powerful tool that provides you with an easy-to-use dashboard for managing your Unreal Engine projects. Various tabs to the left provide you with different domains for the Epic Games Launcher. You must select the **Unreal Engine** tab to access the Unreal Engine facilities. Once you have done so, you can see a set of tabs at the top of the Epic Games Launcher.

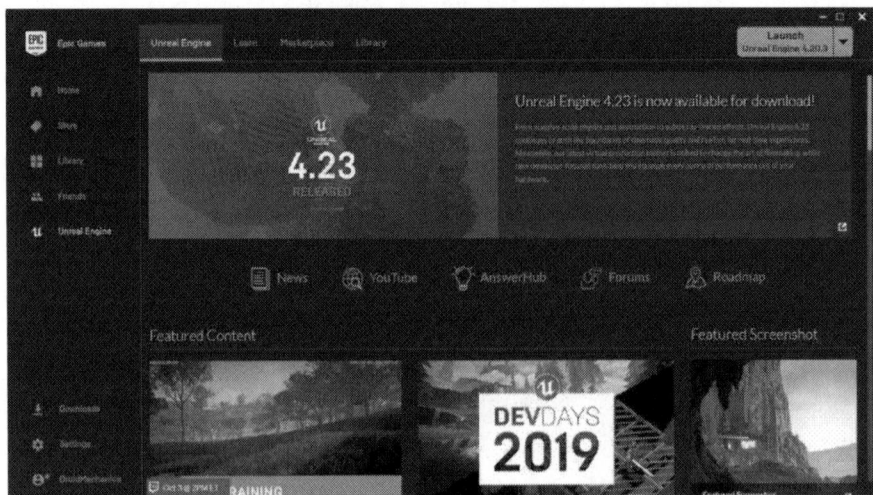

Figure 1.1: The Epic Games Launcher

Unreal Engine C++ the Ultimate Developer's Handbook

The **Unreal Engine** panel usually contains a news bulletin with the latest announcements relating to the engine. The **Learn** panel provides you with learning resources and Unreal Engine projects that you can download and learn from. The **Marketplace** allows you to buy game assets such as meshes and animations, sounds, particle effect systems and more. There is much content in the Unreal Engine Marketplace available for free, so spend some time browsing through this from time to time.

The **Library** tab will take you to a section where you can see the **Engine Versions** section, which shows which versions of Unreal Engine you currently have installed on your machine. The **My Projects** section shows the projects you have on your current machine. If this is your first time navigating to this window, you likely don't have any projects yet. Below this section is the **Vault**, where asset packages show up after you have downloaded them from the Marketplace.

Now that you're familiar with the Epic Games Launcher, you're ready to create your first game project!

Creating Your First Project

To create your first project, you will need to have a version of the engine installed on your computer.

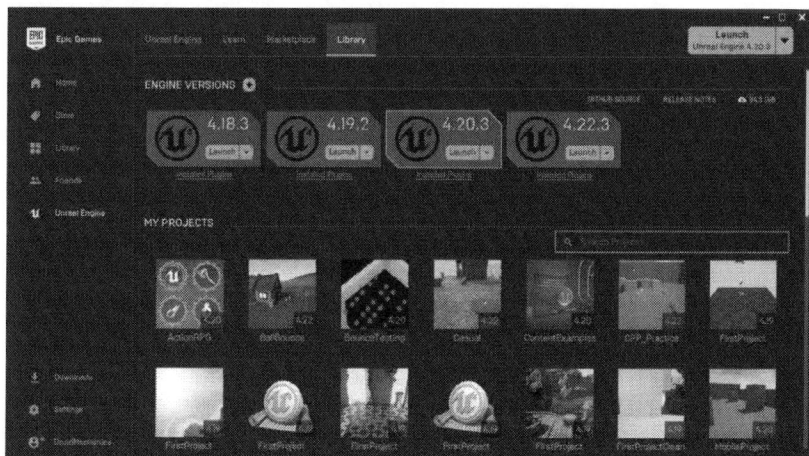

Figure 1.2: The Library Tab in the Epic Games Launcher

If you haven't installed a version, the following steps will guide you to do so.

1. Click on the **+** icon next to **Engine Versions** and select and engine version to install. Once installed, it will appear here in the Engine Versions section.

2. Click on the yellow **Launch** button.

3. The Unreal Editor will load and you will be presented with the **Project Browser**.

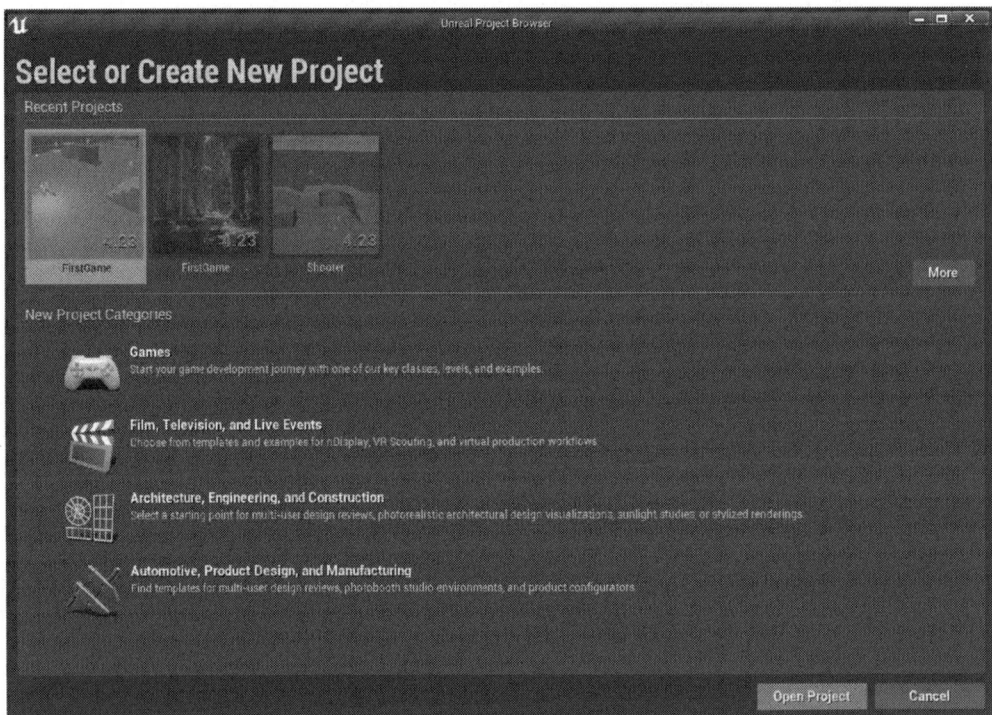

Figure 1.3: Unreal Project Browser

4. Here you have four options based on different categories for **Games**, **Film**, **Architecture**, or **Engineering**. Select **Games**.

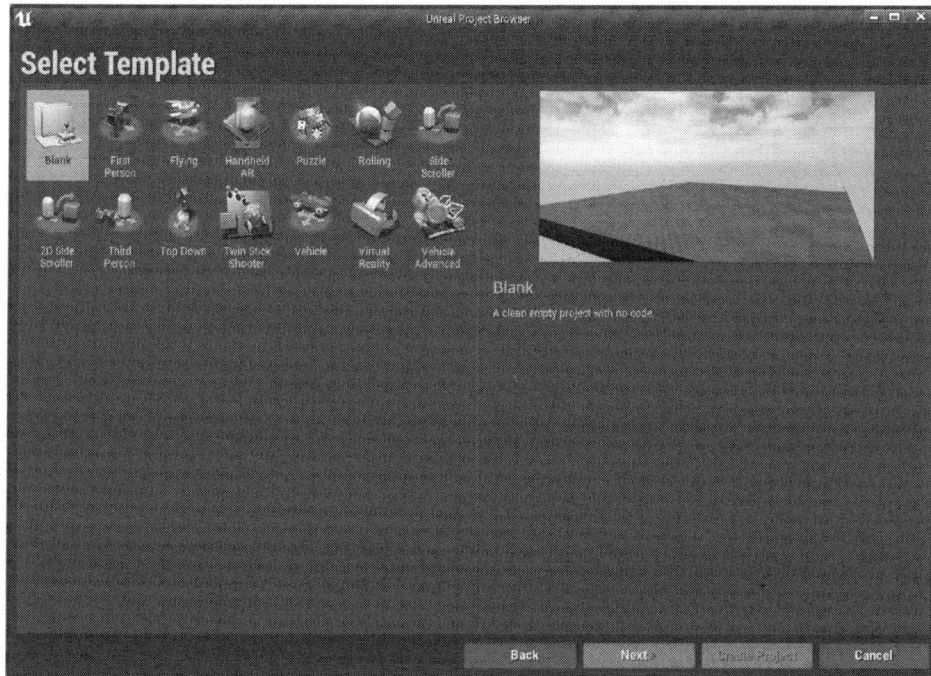

Figure 1.4: Selecting a New Project

5. You will have the option to create a blank project or a project based on a template. Template projects contain some functionality and assets already. This is so you can have an example of simple gameplay functionality and how it's made. For this reason, we will choose a template project. Select the **Third Person** and click **Next**.

6. From among the choices Select **C++**, **Maximum Quality**, **Raytracing Disabled**, **Desktop/Console**, and **With Starter Content**. This way, our project will contain some additional assets that we will use to design our levels.

7. Select a location for your project on your computer by selecting the folder.

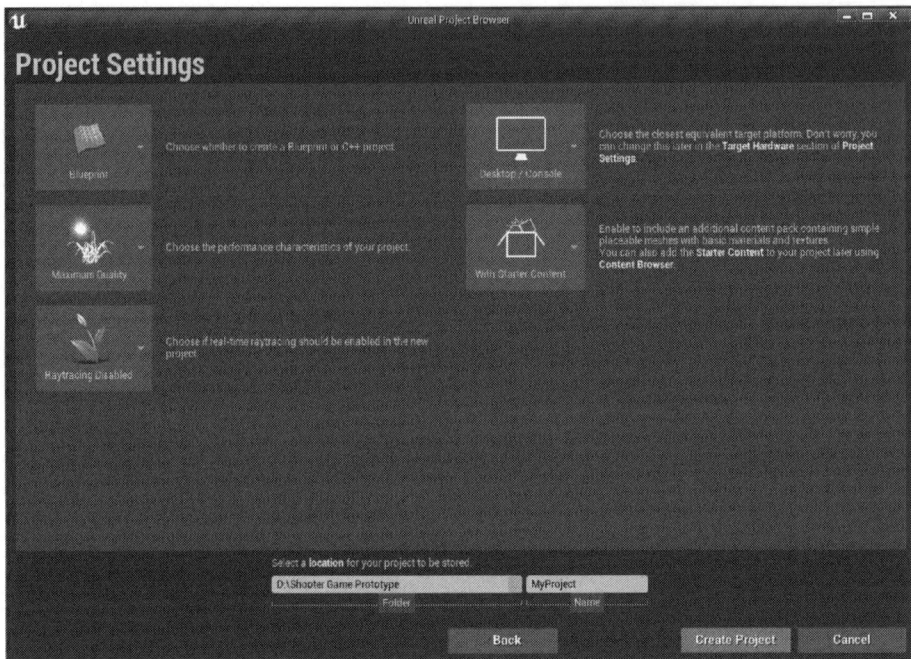

Figure 1.5: Selecting C++ for the Project

8. Choose a name for your project in the **Name** text box. It is important to give some consideration to the name of your project, because certain key classes in your game project will contain this name. For the purposes of this book, we will choose to name our project *FirstGame*. If you choose a different name, you will need to make accommodations to account for the discrepancies in your code as a result of having a different project name. To avoid confusion, it is recommended that you choose to name your project *FirstGame* in order to stay congruent with the code in this book.

9. Click **Create Project**. Unreal Engine will begin to construct the project file for you. Microsoft Visual Studio will automatically open and begin to construct the **Solution** – a project with the necessary files organized for a program to run – for your project. This will take some time. Do not close Visual Studio while it is still busy constructing the project.

10. When finished loading, Unreal Engine will open and you will be presented with the **Level Editor**.

Exploring the Level Editor

When you first open Unreal Engine, you are presented with the **Level Editor**.

Figure 1.6: The Level Editor

The **Level Editor** consists of several panels, each designed for a specific purpose:

- **Tab Bar** and **Menu Bar (1)**

- **Toolbar (2)**

- **Modes (3)**

- **Content Browser (4)**

- **Viewport (5)**

- **World Outliner (6)**

- **Details Panel (7)**

An explanation for each section is as follows:

Tab Bar and Menu Bar (1)

This is where you will see the tabs for the various windows you have open. Tabs can be docked up here for ease of use. By default, there is a tab for the current level which is open. It is labeled with the name of this level. The menu bar is similar to the menu bar in any windows application – it provides quick access to commonly used tools in the engine.

To the right of the Tab Bar, you will see a cap icon – clicking on this cap will bring up a Tutorials tab that gives you access to several walk-through tutorials in the engine on various topics. This can help you get up to speed more quickly. To the right of the cap icon, you will see the name of your current project. Hovering over this will result in a pop-up with various bits of information including the current version of the engine you are using.

To the right of this you have your standard minimize, maximize and close options.

Toolbar (2)

This provides a set of shortcut icons to commonly-used tools and operations. These are:

- **Save Current**: saves the current level

- **Source Control**: allows for a project to connect to source control if used

- **Content**: opens the **Content Browser** if it's not currently open

- **Marketplace**: Opens the Unreal Engine Marketplace

- **Settings**: Provides a quick dropdown to common settings

- **Blueprints**: Quick access to world blueprints such as the **Level Blueprint**

- **Cinematics**: Displays a list of Matinee and Level Sequence objects

- **Build**: Builds all Levels (precomputes lighting, generates navigation, updates brush models)

- **Compile**: Recompiles and reloads C++ code

- **Play**: Allows for the game to be play tested. Playing the game this way is commonly referred to as Play-In-Editor (PIE) mode.

- **Launch**: Launches the level like a standalone game

These utilities are accessible through the Tab Bar, but the icons make accessing them more convenient.

Modes (3)

This section contains different tool modes. Each mode contains a different set of tools for level editing. These modes are:

- **Place**: contains common objects you can place in the level such as meshes, lights, etc.

- **Paint**: provides painting facilities that let you procedurally paint in the level

- **Landscape**: provides tools for sculpting terrain in the level

- **Foliage**: provides tools for generating foliage based on mesh assets chosen from the **Content Browser**

- **Geometry Editing**: provides the ability to alter the vertices on mesh geometry

We will be selecting items from this panel from time to time. The **Place** mode is selected by default. Bringing an object from this menu is as simple as clicking on a selection and dragging it into the **Viewport**.

The Content Browser (4)

This is where you can import custom content and browse through that content in your game projects. Assets like meshes, sounds, materials, textures, and more can be seen here and chosen for use in the game.

Figure 1.7: Show or Hide the Sources Panel Icon

At the top-left of this panel, just under the green **Add New** button, there is an icon which you can hover over, shown in the left figure. A tool-tip will pop up that says "Show or hide the sources panel." Click on this, and you will get a hierarchical view of the folder structure for your game.

The Content folder is the highest level in the hierarchical folder structure for the content in your game. You can right-click on **Content** and select **New Folder** to create new folders in this hierarchical view. The **Content Browser** is highly searchable and filterable as well.

The **Content Folder** points to the directory with the same name in your project on your HDD. The game project exists there as an **Unreal Engine Project** file (.*uproject*) along with several key folders:

- **Binaries**: files compiled into machine language exist here, ready to be run by the computer

- **Config**: here exist configuration files that save the various settings in the engine

- **Content**: game assets exist here (this is the same **Content** folder in the **Content Browser**)

- **Saved**: Autosaves and backup information gets stored here

- **Source**: this is where all of the code exists

Along with these files, the solution (.*sln* if using Visual Studio) exists as well. This is the project that accesses all of the code in the **Source** folder.

Viewport (5)

This window provides the ability to see in the world and interact with objects in the level. Here you can move around, manipulate objects, and even play the game when selecting **Play** from the **Toolbar**. The **Viewport** also has many debugging tools built in such as stats, different view modes, as well as tools for changing the camera, snapping objects, etc.

World Outliner (6)

This panel provides a comprehensive list of all the objects in the currently-loaded map. You can select objects here and delete them, rename them, and group them together. Next to each item in the **World Outliner** is an eye icon. Clicking on this eye icon will result in the eye appearing closed. This affects the visibility of the object in the world. Some of the objects in the **World Outliner** are grouped into folders for organization. Multiple objects can be selected in the **World Outliner** and organized into a folder by selecting an object, holding shift to select other objects, then right-clicking and selecting *Move To -> Create New Folder*. This makes it easy to keep track of objects in a scene.

When you select an item in the **World Outliner**, it will be selected in the **Viewport**, as indicated by a yellow outline around the object. If you cannot see the item in the **Viewport**, you can focus on the selected item by hitting the *F* key. The view will zoom up to the item, wherever it is in the world, and place the item in the center of the **Viewport**.

Details Panel (7)

The **Details** panel is context sensitive, depending on what is selected in the world. For a given selected object, the **Details** panel is populated with default settings for that particular object.

If applicable, the **Details** panel will display **Transform** information for the selected object. A transform contains information regarding the location, rotation and scale of an object. Location, rotation, and scale are quantities, each of which have three components in the **Details** panel: X, Y and Z. The location of an object determines its coordinates in 3D space. The rotation of an object determines its orientation in the world. The scale of an object determines its size with respect to the X, Y and Z axes in space. More will be explained in this chapter on coordinate systems in the section titled **Coordinate Systems and Vectors.**

If the selected object has a **Static Mesh**, it will show up here in the **Details** panel. A Static Mesh is a piece of geometry. Static Meshes are different than skeletal meshes, which have skeleton information that is used to morph the mesh for animations. Static Meshes do not have skeleton information and cannot be morphed for animations, hence the term "static."

Any materials associated with the meshes on the selected object will also appear in the **Details** panel.

Meshes, materials, and other items that appear in the **Details** panel have a dropdown which allows you to change the asset used for that item. If the dropdown is grayed out, you may not change the asset assigned to that item. If it is not grayed out, you may change the asset. Under the dropdown are icons: an arrow, a magnifying glass, and, if the item is populated with a value, a bent yellow arrow.

Figure 1.8: The Arrow, Magnifying Glass, and Bent Yellow Arrow Icons

Note: this bent arrow will only be present if a property has been changed from default. The left-most arrow, when hovered, pops up a tool-tip that says "Use Selected Asset from **Content Browser**." If you click this while you have an asset selected in the **Content Browser**, that selected asset will be used to replace the asset assigned to this item in the **Details** panel. This will only occur if the item selected in the **Content Browser** is compatible with the type of asset for this item. The magnifying glass has a tool-tip that says "Browse to 'Asset_Name' in Content Browser." Clicking this will open the file location of that asset in the **Content Browser**. The tool-tip for the bent arrow says "Reset to Default Static Mesh: None" in the case of a Static Mesh item. Clicking the icon in this case will empty the item (set it to its default state) and the thumbprint icon will say "None".

The **Physics** section in the **Details** panel shows the physics settings for the object, if applicable. You can check or un-check *Simulate Physics* to enable or disable physics simulation for the given object. If your object does not need to participate in physics simulations for this game, it is wise to keep this checkbox un-checked. If you know it will participate in physics interactions such as collisions with other objects or falling due to the force of gravity, you will need to check this checkbox.

The **Collision** section in the **Details** panel shows the collision presets for this object if applicable. This is where you determine exactly how collisions will occur with this object and whether this object should collide, ignore or overlap other objects based on their Object Type.

The **Details** panel has a search bar, found just above the **Transform** rollout which allows you to find items quickly. This is used frequently by developers who don't wish to spend a lot of time scrolling through the **Details** panel in search of items.

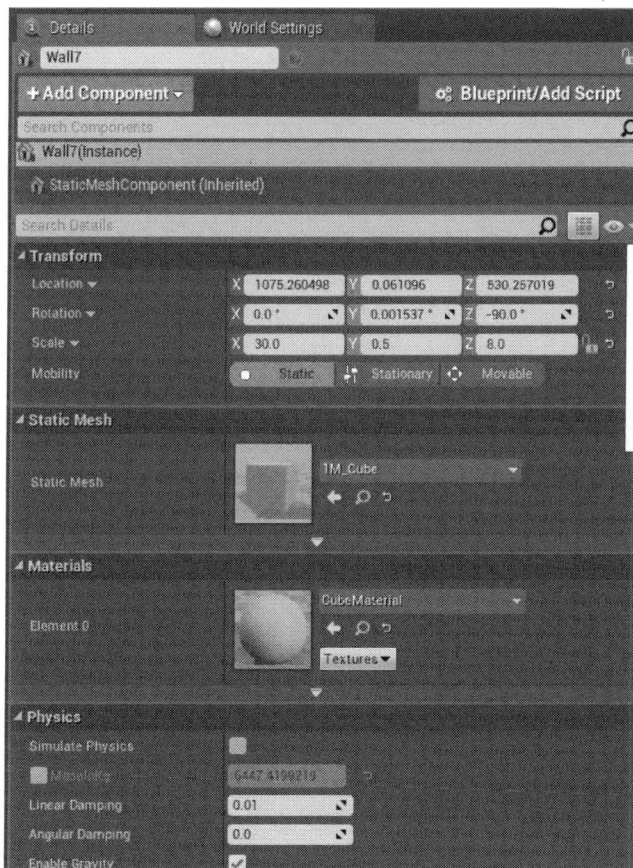

Figure 1.9: The Details Panel

You now have an understanding of the different panels in the **Level Editor**. Understanding what each panel provides for you is important for speeding up development workflow. These tools will come in handy every step of the way.

More on Unreal Engine's Editors

There are many editors in the engine and each one is designed to handle different functions. https://docs.unrealengine.com/en-US/GettingStarted/SubEditors/index.html shows all of the editors and explains each one.

Now that you know what the panels provide for you, it's time to learn how to create levels and maneuver through them.

Level Creation

When you create a new project, a default level is created. This level has the default name *ThirdPersonExampleMap* if you created a third person template project, which you can see in the Tab Bar.

You can create a new level by maneuvering to the Menu Bar and selecting *File -> New Level*. Here, you can select from among:

- **Default**: provides you with a handful of default objects in your new level including a floor platform, a sky sphere, a light source, and more

- **VR Basic**: a simple level designed for Virtual Reality projects

- **Empty Level**: creates a new level with literally nothing in it

Select **Default**. If you have changed anything in the current level, you will be asked if you wish to save your changes.

Once you create the new level, you will see the sky and floor platform among the other objects in the level. You can save the level by selecting *File -> Save Current As*. You will be presented with the option to choose where you would like your level to be saved in the project hierarchy. If you click on the *ThirdPersonCPP* dropdown on the left side of the window that pops up, you will see a *Maps* folder. If you click on this, you will see the

ThirdPersonExampleMap map. You can give your new map a name, or leave it at the default name provided, which will be *NewMap*. Click **Save**, and your new map will be saved in the same folder as *ThirdPersonExampleMap*. In the **Content Browser**, maneuver back to the *ThirdPersonCPP* folder, then the *Maps* folder, and double click on *ThirdPersonExampleMap*. The *ThirdPersonExampleMap* will open again.

You can play test the game by hitting the **Play** button from the **Toolbar**. You will still see the mouse icon and will need to click in the **Viewport** to gain control of the Character. Notice that the camera view now shows the back of the Character, and the Character is animated. Once you click in the **Viewport**, you will be able to control the camera with the mouse. This is because the template projects already have movement code built in. You can control the Character with the *W, A, S* and *D* keys. You can also use the arrow keys to control the Character and the camera without the use of the mouse. *Left* and *Right* control the camera and *Up* and *Down* control the Character. Hitting the *Space* key causes the Character to jump. Spend some time running around in the level to get used to the template project. When ready to stop, hit the *Escape* key on your keyboard.

This shows just how easy it is to create a new project in Unreal Engine and have a functional game project already working and ready to play. You've play-tested the example game in the template project. Now it's time for you to learn how to move around in the world through the **Viewport**.

Maneuvering in the World

We will now cover the basics of maneuvering throughout the level via the **Viewport**. If you click inside the **Viewport** with the left mouse button and drag the mouse from side to side, you will turn the camera. Notice the little red, blue and green widget at the bottom-left of the **Viewport**. This indicates the X, Y and Z directions of the world. Notice that you are changing the camera's orientation with respect to the X and Y directions, but the Z direction remains constant. Z represents the axis pointing upward. Left clicking and dragging the mouse forward and backward will result in moving the camera forward and backward in the level.

Right-clicking and dragging from side to side results in the same behavior as left-clicking and dragging side to side. Right-clicking and dragging forward and backward will result in looking up and down in the level. Notice that, as you do this, you will see the blue axis in the widget at the bottom-left of the **Viewport** changing as you change your orientation with respect to the Z axis.

Clicking both the left and right mouse buttons simultaneously while dragging the mouse from side to side will translate the camera left and right. Clicking and holding both left and right mouse buttons and dragging forward and backward will translate the camera up and down.

Using the above simple mouse maneuvering techniques allows you to explore the level and look at various areas of the map.

You can use the *Up, Down, Left,* and *Right* keyboard keys to translate throughout the world as well. If you are holding down either the left or the right mouse button, you can also use the *W, A, S* and *D* keys to do so as well. The *E* key will lift you straight up while the left or right mouse button is pressed, and the *Q* key will lower you straight down.

Holding the left or right mouse button and pressing the *C* key will zoom in. As soon as you release the mouse button, the zoom will return to normal. The *X* key likewise will result in zooming out. The scroll wheel scales the world, resulting in a change in camera speed (optionally, you can adjust the camera speed with icons at the top-right of the **Viewport**).

With the basics of maneuvering down, let's cover object manipulation.

Object Manipulation

All objects in the world are Actors. An Actor is an object that can be placed in a map (meshes, lights, cameras, etc.). Actors can be placed in the level by simply clicking and dragging them into the world from the **Content Browser** or the **Modes** panel.

Drag a light into the world by selecting the **Lights** tab in the **Modes** panel and finding a *Point Light* and dragging it in.

Objects in your game must be positioned and oriented so that the environment makes sense for the gameplay. Being able to move, rotate and scale objects will become natural and

reflexive as you design your levels and environments in

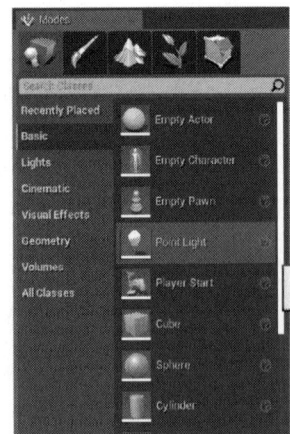

Figure 1.10: Adding a Point Light

Unreal Engine. Operations are performed on objects that are currently selected. Left-click on an object in the world to select it. With an object selected, holding the *SHIFT* key and left-clicking on another item will result in multiple object selection. *CTRL* and clicking on objects adds and

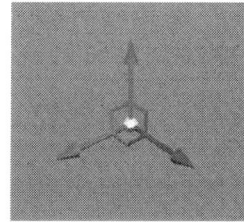

Figure 1.11: The Translation Gizmo

removes them from the current selection as well.

When you select an object, not only will it become outlined in yellow, but a 3D gizmo will appear at the center of the object. This gizmo will have a different appearance depending on the mode you are in for manipulating objects. The icons at the top-right of the **Viewport** allow you to change these modes. There are also hotkeys that allow you to switch between the modes: These are *W* for Translation Mode, *E* for Rotation Mode, and *R* for Scale Mode. The *Space* key cycles through them. We will now visit these modes in more detail.

Translation Mode

The *W* key is the hotkey for translating objects, or moving them around in space. Select an object in the world. If you hover the mouse cursor over the gizmo, it will highlight. There are three arrows, each one corresponding to one of the coordinate axis directions. You can hover over an individual arrow and click and drag to move the object in that particular direction. For example, if you click and drag while selecting the green arrow, the object will only move back and forth in the Y direction. If you look toward the center of the gizmo, lines protrude from the arrows to form squares which connect each pair of arrows. The square formed between the red and green arrows can be hovered over, resulting in both the red and the green arrows to highlight simultaneously. Clicking and dragging when this happens results in moving the object in both the X and Y directions at the same time. The object will move around in the world, but its elevation, or Z coordinate, will not change. While moving the object, you can glance over at its Location values in the **Details** panel and see its X and Y coordinate values changing but its Z coordinate will remain unchanged. You can use these squares at the center of the Translation Gizmo to select any pair of coordinate axes.

If snapping is enabled, you will be moving the object around in the world by discrete increments. You can tell if snapping is enabled if the snapping icon for that object manipulation mode is highlighted at the top-right of the **Viewport**. It is usually best practice to keep snapping enabled. If you need very granular movement, lower the snapping value to 1 cm.

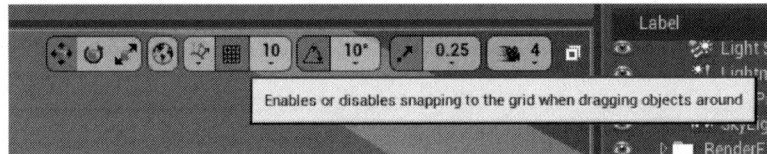

Figure 1.12: Enabling Snapping

Next to each snap icon for each mode is a number icon with a dropdown arrow. For translation, this number signifies how many units the object will translate through space with each snapping increment. These are in Unreal units which are centimeters by default. For rotation, these values are in degrees, and for scale, these values represent a fraction of the original scale (i.e. scaling an object by 0.5 results in the object being half as big as its original size).

The right-most icon at the top-right of the **Viewport** adjusts the camera speed. Raising this value will result in more rapid movement throughout the world when maneuvering through it.

Rotation Mode

With an object selected, you can switch to Rotation Mode by either clicking the appropriate icon at the top-right of the **Viewport** or hitting the *E* key. The Translation Gizmo will change to the Rotation Gizmo.

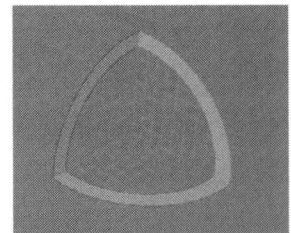

Figure 1.13: The Rotation Gizmo

Clicking on one of the curved segments and dragging the mouse will result in rotating the object about the corresponding axis. As you rotate the object, you will see the amount of rotation you are applying to the object in degrees.

Scale Mode

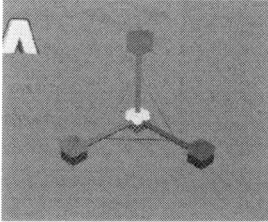

Figure 1.14: The Scale Gizmo

By selecting Scale Mode, either with the icon or with the hotkey, which is *R*, you will see the Scale Gizmo.

Clicking and dragging on one of the axes will scale the object in the corresponding direction. This is called non-uniform scaling.

You will notice that there are line segments protruding from each axis similar to those in the Translation Gizmo, only they form triangles rather than squares near the center of the gizmo. Hovering over these allow you to select multiple axes simultaneously. You can also hover over the center of the widget to uniformly scale the object in all three axes.

We now know how to translate, rotate, and scale objects in the world. However, when we perform these transformations, it is important to understand when we are doing so relative to the coordinate axes of the world versus those of the individual object. We will explore this distinction now.

Local vs. World Space

Each object in the world has its own relative orientation. This may or may not line up with the world directional axes. Select an object in the world, such as the cube in the image below. Enter Rotation Mode by hitting the *E* key and rotate the object roughly 45 degrees. Now hit the *W* key to enter Translation Mode. You will see the Translation Gizmo. You should notice that the transform gizmo no longer lines up with the edges of the cube. That's because we are currently working in world space, and the translation widget did not rotate along with the cube.

At the top-right of the **Viewport**, the fourth icon from the left, when hovered, says "Cycles the transform gizmo coordinate systems between world and local (object) space (Ctrl+)." Clicking on this icon will change the viewed coordinate system from world to local or vice versa for the selected object. Clicking the icon will change it from a cube to a world icon.

Figure 1.15: Using World Space

While the icon looks like a world, notice that the Translation Gizmo on the cube is aligned with the world gizmo at the bottom-left of the **Viewport**. This shows the global axis directions and translating the object will move it along these axes.

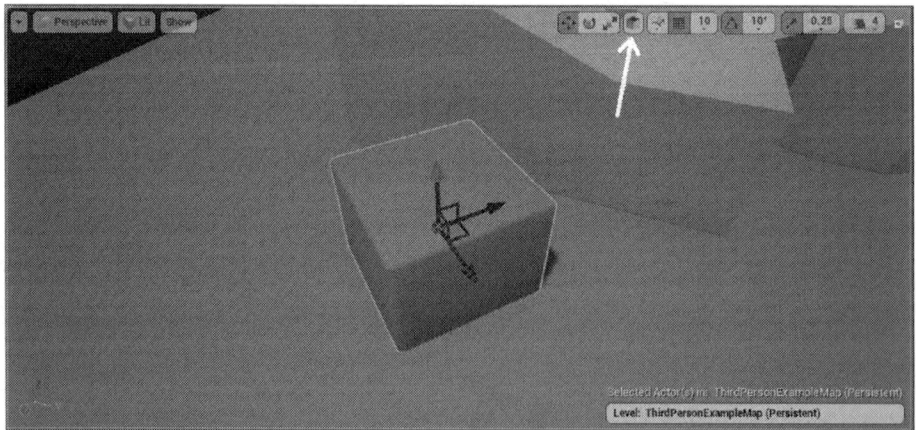

Figure 1.16: Using and Object's Local Space

While the icon looks like a cube, the Translation Gizmo will be aligned with the object's local orientation. Notice that the X-axis on the cube is not pointed in the same direction as the X-axis on the gizmo at the bottom-left of the screen. The Y-axis on the cube, likewise, is not matching the Y-axis on the world gizmo at the bottom-left of the screen.

The object's gizmo will not necessarily align with the gizmo at the bottom-left of the screen unless the object's orientation matches that of the world. Since we rotated this object, its gizmo and the gizmo at the bottom-left of the screen do not match. Translating the object in local mode will move the object along its own local axes and not the axes of the world.

It is important to understand the distinction between world and local coordinate systems and when it is appropriate to use each. If you wish to move an object along the X axis of the world, for example, you will want to be in world mode. If you wish to move an object along its own personal forward direction, you will want to use local mode for that object. For this reason, Unreal Engine contains many built-in functions for moving objects in the game according to their own local coordinate systems as well as other built-in functions for moving objects according to global space.

Multiple objects can be moved, rotated, or scaled together. When selecting multiple objects, the Gizmo appears at the center of the last object selected. This "center" may not be at the actual geometric center of the object if it has a mesh representation. This is because the origin of each individual object is determined when that mesh was created in a mesh creation software program.

Objects can be grouped together. With multiple objects selected, find one of them in the **World Outliner**. You will see that all of the selected objects will be highlighted there. Right-click on one of the selected items and select *Group*. The objects will be grouped together. This means that when you left-click to select one of them in the world, all of them will be selected simultaneously. The gizmo will then appear between the objects, at the midpoint between each object's local origin. You can then translate, rotate, or scale the selection and the group as a whole will be affected. To ungroup the objects, select the group and right-click on one of the objects in the **World Outliner** and select *Groups -> Ungroup*.

You now know how to maneuver through the world. You can also select objects and transform them via translation, rotation, and scale. Most importantly, you understand the difference between world and local transformations. This is important because when you are programming gameplay, you must know whether the changes you are applying to objects in code are relative to the world or to the objects themselves. Now that you understand changes to objects in the world, it's time to explore coordinate systems, how they work, and how vectors can be useful tools that describe geometrically significant attributes such as position in space.

Coordinate Systems and Vectors

So what exactly do we mean when we say things like "Coordinate Axis/Axes?" What is a coordinate system anyway? Game developers work extensively in 2D and 3D space and consequently must understand how to organize objects geometrically. We will now go into detail about coordinate systems and how they allow us to organize objects in the world and quantify their locations. We will also explore the concept of vectors and how they can be used as tools to quantify phenomena that have a direction and magnitude, as well as describe positions in a coordinate system.

Coordinates

Imagine yourself floating in space. Where you are, imagine a dot between your feet, and it's labeled with the number 0. Now begin to float straight forward. You leave the dot labeled 0 behind to remain at its original location. That dot shows you where you started. Between your feet, you have your own dot with its own label. This label shows you how far away you have traveled from the dot labeled 0. When you reach 1 unit away (we can use feet, meters, or any other unit we like... let's use feet for now), the dot between your feet shows a 1. The dot where you started still shows its 0. Let's give the dot with the 0 its own name. Since this dot is where we originated from, we'll call it the origin.

So you have floated 1 foot forward from the origin. You can continue to move forward if you like, and as you do, the number on your dot increases. You discover that you can float backwards, toward the origin. You can even reach it and keep going past it. As you pass it and keep floating backwards, you notice that your number becomes negative. Imagine that a red line appears, going through the origin. You are traveling forward and backward on this line.

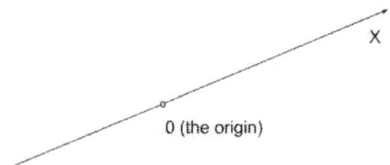

X

0 (the origin)

Figure 1.17: One Direction with an Origin

Since you can only travel back and forth in a single direction, your movement is said to be **one dimensional**. To name this dimension, we are going to call it **X**. As for the numerical value representing the distance you have traveled along this direction from the origin, we are going to call it your **X coordinate**. The red line on which you are traveling is called the **X-axis.** That way, if you say your X coordinate is -9.54, you have traveled 9.54 units (feet, in this case) in the negative X direction from the origin. With an origin and an X-axis, we have now created a **one-dimensional coordinate system**.

Now let's go back to the origin. You know you can move forward and backward. But so far, this is the only direction you've traveled. Imagine that you can now float sideways, to your right.

As soon as you start moving sideways, the dot between your feet suddenly gained a second number. Let's say you've traveled one foot to the right. The dot at your feet now says (0, 1). When you look at the origin, you notice that it too now has two numbers: (0, 0). As you travel to the right, this second number continues to increase while the first number remains 0. Imagine now that a green line has appeared, going through the origin and extending outwards, left and right, at a right-angle to the X-axis. This green line is the **Y-axis**. Because the Y-axis is at a right (90-degree) angle with the X-axis, it is said to be **perpendicular** to the X-axis. Another common term with the same meaning is **orthogonal**. As soon as you were able to travel in a direction orthogonal to your original axis, you were traveling in two dimensions. We have now expanded our one-dimensional coordinate system into a **two-dimensional coordinate system**.

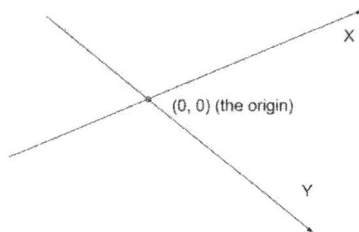

Figure 1.18: Two Dimensions

Now, you already realize that if you start at the origin and you move one foot in the positive Y direction, your Y-coordinate becomes 1. Your **coordinate pair** is (0, 1). From here, if you move one foot in the positive X direction, your X coordinate becomes 1, and your two-dimensional coordinates are (1, 1). Now you're off of the axis lines! You realize that you can move around, away from these lines, and your coordinates keep track of your position in XY space. We can call this space the **XY-plane**.

Notice while you are traveling that your coordinates may be positive or negative depending on which side of the axes you are. If your X-coordinate is positive, you're on one side of the Y-axis. But if your X-coordinate is negative, you're on the other side. Looking down at the XY-plane from above, you notice that the X and Y axes split the plane into four sections. These are called **quadrants**.

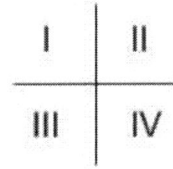

Figure 1.19: The Four Quadrants

So now you understand coordinate systems! We know that a 2D space has two directions, X and Y, and any point on the XY-plane can be described by its 2D coordinate pair, (x, y).

Now we're going to take this into the next dimension. Let's go back to the origin again.

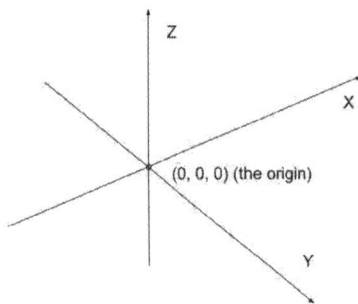

Now imagine that you can float straight up into the air! As soon as you do, you look down and see that the dot between your feet has suddenly gained a third number. As you raise a foot above the origin, your dot has the label (0, 0, 1). A blue line has now appeared as well, going through the origin and pointing upward and downward, orthogonal to **both** the X and Y axes. This is the Z axis, and we can also say that it is orthogonal to the XY-plane.

Figure 1.20: Three Dimensions

As you float downward and past the XY-plane, your Z coordinate becomes negative. Now you have a 3-component, triple-numbered coordinate value that represents your location in **3-dimensional space**. If you start at the origin and travel 2 feet in the positive X-direction, then 3 feet in the negative Y-direction, then 4 feet in the positive Z-direction, your location will be (2, -3, 4).

Now you can float around in any direction, and no matter where you go, your location can be represented by your 3D-coordinates! This three-dimensional space is separated into eight areas by the different planes formed by the axes. The areas are similar to the four quadrants of the XY-plane, however they are three-dimensional volumes and are sometimes referred to as **octants** (there are eight of them).

Now that you understand coordinate systems, it's time to visit another mathematical tool that allows you to have the power to represent positions in space among other things – the vector.

Vectors

Now that we understand coordinate systems, we can begin to discuss **vectors**. A **vector** is a mathematical quantity that has two descriptive characteristics: a **direction** and a **magnitude**.

If we look at the XY-plane, we can draw an arrow from the origin to a point in 2D space. Say this line is 5 feet long. We can let the length of this arrow represent its magnitude. Now because the arrow is pointing in a definite direction, and it has a definite magnitude (its length, which is 5), it qualifies as being a vector.

This vector can be described by an **ordered-pair** (4, 3) just like a location in space. In fact, if the tail of the vector is at the origin (and in this case, it is) the head of the vector *is* the location (4, 3). We can refer to this vector as the vector (4, 3) and this ordered pair is said to be its **components**.

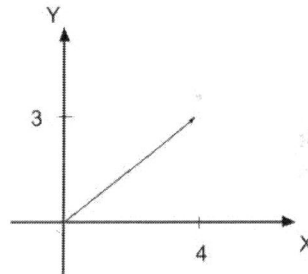

Figure 1.21: The Vector (4, 3)

Now, if we move the vector five units in the positive X direction and five units in the positive Y direction,

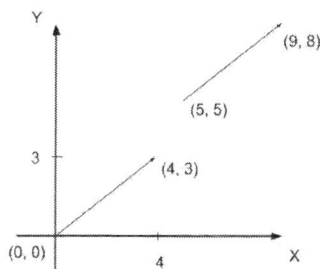

Figure 1.22: The Vector (4, 3) and the Same Vector, Moved

the tail of the vector will have a location (5, 5) and the head of the vector will have the location (9, 8).

If we know the starting point of the vector (its tail) and the end point of the vector (its head), how do we know what its characteristic ordered pair is? It turns out that we can calculate the vector's components from the coordinates of its head and tail.

We can obtain the characteristic components of the vector by doing a **component-wise subtraction** of the tail from the head. This means we will subtract the X coordinate of the tail from the X component of the head. The result will be the X component of the vector. Likewise we subtract the Y coordinate of the tail from the Y coordinate of the head. This results in the Y component of the vector. These calculations appear as follows:

$$X_{head} \; - \; X_{tail} = X_{vector}$$

$$Y_{head} \; - \; Y_{tail} = Y_{vector}$$

If we use the numbers for the moved vector, the math becomes:

$$9 - 5 = 4$$

$$8 - 5 = 3$$

The result, (4, 3), is the same ordered-pair as the original vector. Thus we know we performed our calculations correctly. This results in some important realizations.

We have seen that moving the vector from one location to another has not changed the vector. The vector with its tail at the origin and the vector with its tail at location (5, 5) are said to be the same vector. **Any two vectors are said to be equal if a component-wise comparison shows that their corresponding components are equal.**

We also now have the ability to calculate the vector from one point to another. Performing component-wise subtraction of any two points results in a vector from one point to the other. More specifically let the component-wise subtraction of point B from point A be represented as follows:

$$A - B = \; V_{B \to A}$$

In other words, component-wise subtraction of point **B** from point **A** equals the vector starting at **B** and ending at point **A**. The resulting vector is a vector whose tail is at the coordinates of **B** and whose head is at the coordinates of **A**.

Location coordinates can be described with vectors. If you are at a location in 3D space represented by the ordered triple (3, 4, 2), your position can be described by the vector whose tail is at the origin and whose head is at the point (3, 4, 2). A vector which represents a location is often referred to as a **location**

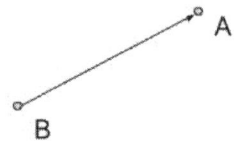

Figure 1.23: The Vector From B to A

vector.

You will often know the components of a vector but not its length. Conveniently, if you understand a few useful concepts, knowing the components is all you need. With the help of an ancient formula, you can calculate the length, or magnitude, of any vector.

Vector Magnitude

If you know the X, Y and Z components of a vector, you can calculate its magnitude (length). To understand how to do this, we use a mathematical formula called **The Pythagorean Theorem.** The Pythagorean Theorem involves the use of a **right triangle**, or a triangle which has a right angle (90 degrees) at one of its three corners. The side opposite the 90 degree angle is called its **hypotenuse**, and the other two sides are called its **legs**. We'll label the hypotenuse A and the two legs B and C in the following diagram.

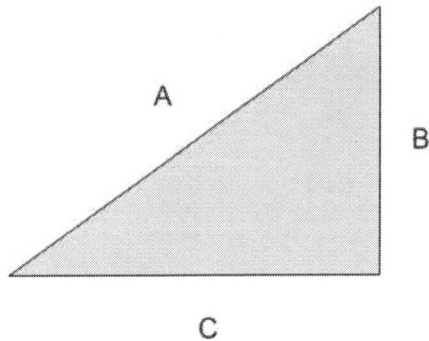

Figure 1.24: A Right Triangle

The Pythagorean Theorem states that:

$$A^2 = B^2 + C^2$$

Thus if we know two of the three sides, we can calculate the third side. Solving this equation for A gives us:

$$A = \pm\sqrt{B^2 + C^2}$$

Since we are concerned only with the length of A, the negative solution to this equation can be ignored.

A fundamental concept with vectors is that they can be decomposed into their constituent components. This means that a 2D vector such as (2, 3) is equivalent to the vector obtained by performing component-wise addition of vectors (2, 0) and (0, 3). These two vectors are the X and Y components of the vector, respectively. Now let's label the corners of the triangle mentioned previously, as follows:

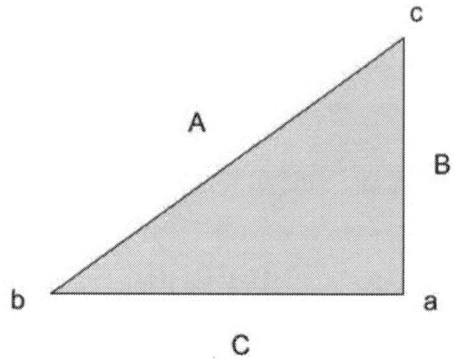

Figure 1.25: Right Triangle with Sides and Corners Labeled

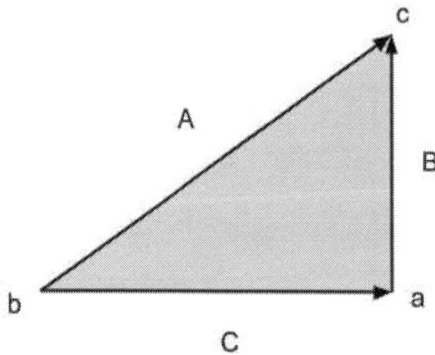

Figure 1.26: Right Triangle with vectors

Now imagine that we have a vector starting at **b** and ending at **c**. The length, or magnitude, of this vector is A. Imagine also that we have a vector starting at **b** and ending at **a**. The magnitude of this vector is C. Finally, imagine that we have a vector starting at **a** and ending at **c**. This vector has the magnitude B. If C is the length of the vector from **b** to **a**, then this vector's component representation is (C, 0). Likewise, if B is the length of the vector from **a** to **c**, then this vector's component representation is (0, B). If we use vector (component-wise) addition, these two add up to give (C, B) which is the vector from **b** to **c**, which has the length A.

This means that if we know the components of a vector, we know the lengths of the two legs of the right triangle formed by the triangle whose hypotenuse is the vector and whose legs are its X and Y components. For example, say we have a vector A, represented with components (4, 3), as shown:

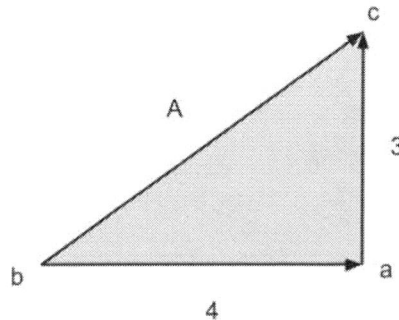

Figure 1.27: The (4, 3) Vector Decomposed into Components

We know that adding the vector from **b** to **a** with the vector from **a** to **c** gives us the vector from **b** to **c** with the length of A. Thanks to the Pythagorean Theorem, we can calculate the length of A as follows:

$$A = \sqrt{4^2 + 3^2} = \sqrt{16 + 9} = \sqrt{25} = 5$$

Since we can always break a vector down into its X and Y components, and because this vector can form a right triangle with these vectors, we can always use the Pythagorean Theorem to calculate its magnitude. In short, to get the length of a vector V use:

$$|V| = \sqrt{V_X{}^2 + V_Y{}^2}$$

Where $|V|$ is the magnitude of the vector and V_X and V_Y are its X and Y components, respectively.

You have used component-wise addition and subtraction (which will hereafter be referred to as vector addition and vector subtraction, respectively) to aid us in our calculations, but it turns out that addition and subtraction also has geometric significance for vectors.

Geometric Significance of Vector Addition and Subtraction

This also leads us to another important concept regarding vectors. We know that the vectors B and C formed by the two legs of the right triangle above can be added together to obtain A. As it turns out, this is a specific example of a general rule regarding vector addition. Observe the vectors to the right:

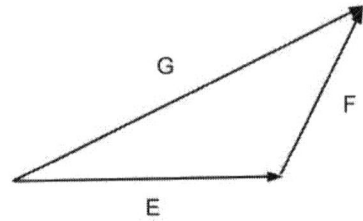

Figure 1.28: Vector Addition

The triangle formed by the vectors E, F and G is not a right triangle, thus the Pythagorean Theorem does not apply here. However, if we know the X and Y components of both E and F, and we perform vector addition on E and F, we will obtain the vector G. That is, if we take any vector F, placed such that its tail is at the head of another vector E, then performing vector addition of E and F will result in the vector G which is the vector whose tail is at the tail of E and whose head is at the head of F. In short,

$$E + F = G$$

Also, note that negating a vector (multiplying each of its components by -1) results in a vector pointed in exactly the opposite direction.

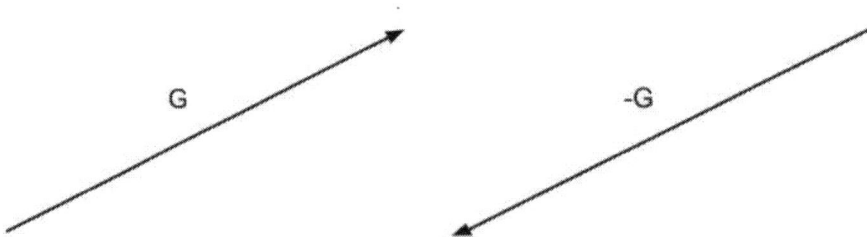

Figure 1.29: Negation of a Vector

And multiplying a vector by a scalar (a single value) will scale the vector by that number. Multiplying a vector by 0.5 will result in each of its components multiplied by 0.5 and the length of the vector itself will be half its original value. Feeling skeptical? Let's try this on the vector (4, 3). The length of (4, 3), as we saw above, is 5. Multiplying this vector by 0.5 results in (2, 1.5). The magnitude of this vector is calculated as follows:

$$\sqrt{2^2 + 1.5^2} = 2.5$$

which is exactly half of the length of the original vector, 5.

Vector subtraction works the same way as vector addition. Namely, it is performed component-wise. It also has geometric significance, similarly to vector addition. Suppose we want to subtract the vector F from E in the below diagram:

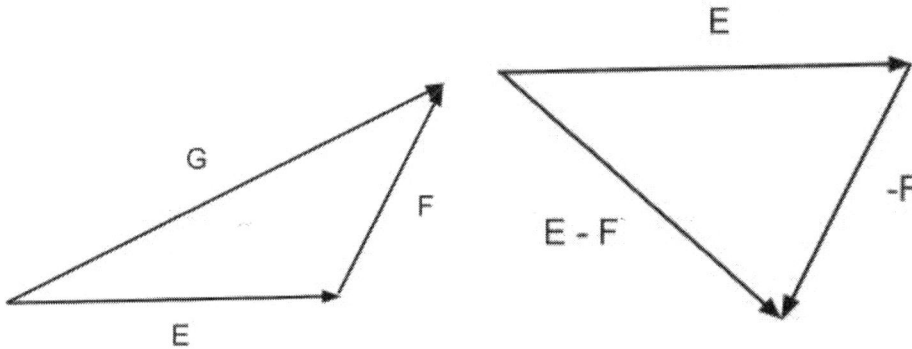

Figure 1.30: Adding Vectors E and F vs. Subtracting F from E

Subtracting F from E is equivalent to adding a negative F to E, so another way to look at E – F would be E + (-F).

Now that you understand the geometric significance of vector addition and subtraction, you can cleverly figure out directions and distances among objects in the world. This will come in handy quite often in the gameplay programming you will learn throughout this book.

Summary

In this chapter, we learned that we needed an IDE such as Visual Studio (or Xcode for Mac users) and downloaded Unreal Engine, and now have the tools necessary to begin developing games! We have taken a look at the Epic Games Launcher and seen how it can be used as a valuable resource. We have also created a project and learned how to maneuver through the world and manipulate objects. We have explored coordinate systems and vectors and touched on some basic vector mathematics. This has given us the ability to create game projects, edit levels and transform objects, and be able to represent them mathematically in 3D space.

Chapter 1 – An Overview of Unreal Engine

Now that we have the basics down, we are ready to dig deeper into the engine and start creating some code using Unreal Engine's powerful class hierarchy.

Chapter 2 – Creating Actors with Blueprints

Unreal Engine is structured such that those using it to make games have an incredible amount of power and control. The engine is written in the C++ programming language, and as a result, has a hierarchical nature. In programming, using a hierarchical structure to organize code is known as **object-oriented programming (OOP).** We will learn what that means and how it pertains to the idea of classes and how Unreal Engine utilizes this methodology to structure the engine. We will distinguish between Is-A versus Has-A relationships and what that means. Then we will open our project and create some basic Blueprints and give them components, variables and functions. To understand these concepts, we must start by exploring the Unreal Engine class hierarchy.

In this chapter, we will cover the following topics:

- The Unreal Engine Class Hierarchy

- Is-A vs. Has-A Relationships

- Components

- Variables

- Functions

Unveiling the Unreal Engine Class Hierarchy

Unreal Engine classes are organized according to a hierarchy. A class is a collection of properties such as variables (data) and functions (routines that run lines of code). A common analogy to classes in programming is one where we observe the animal kingdom. The class of creature called animal contains a set of characteristics all animals share. All animals must feed, for example. However there are more specific types of animal such as mammal or reptile. Since both mammal and reptile are animals, they both must feed. However mammals have fur, whereas reptiles have scales.

So while we can say that mammals and reptiles are both animals, we cannot say that all animals are mammals or all animals are reptiles. It is a one-way relationship. In other words, a mammal **is an** animal, but an animal **is not a** mammal (necessarily). The mammal class can be further sub-classed into more specific creatures. For example, there is the dog class and the cat class and this pattern can continue indefinitely. We have just described a hierarchy of classes (albeit without using proper biology terms, but hey, this isn't a biology book). You can see this hierarchy in the diagram below:

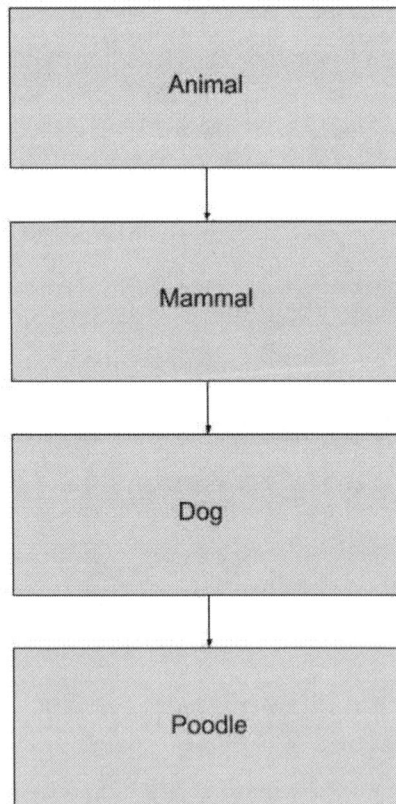

```
┌─────────────────────────┐
│                         │
│         Animal          │
│                         │
└─────────────────────────┘
             │
             ▼
┌─────────────────────────┐
│                         │
│         Mammal          │
│                         │
└─────────────────────────┘
             │
             ▼
┌─────────────────────────┐
│                         │
│          Dog            │
│                         │
└─────────────────────────┘
             │
             ▼
┌─────────────────────────┐
│                         │
│         Poodle          │
│                         │
└─────────────────────────┘
```

Figure 2.1: Inheritance Chain for Animals

The different classes in Unreal Engine are organized in the same way. At the top of the hierarchy is the Object class. There are classes even higher in the hierarchy than this, but this is as high as you need to concern yourself with for now. Below the Object class comes the Actor, then the Pawn, and from the Pawn comes the Character.

The Object Class

The `Object` class can be thought of as the animal class in the above example. It is the base class from which many other Unreal Engine classes are derived. It has basic capabilities that all Unreal Engine classes need, such as the ability to be kept track of by Unreal Engine's **reflection system**. In programming, reflection is the ability of a program to observe itself and keep track of its own state. Unreal's reflection system allows for **garbage collection** (automatic deletion of objects that are no longer being used), the ability to see C++ variables in the Unreal Engine editor via Blueprints and the **Details** panel, and more.

Because the `Object` class is so basic, it doesn't even have the capability of being placed in a level. In order to place an object in the level of your game, it must be at least derived from the `Actor` class.

The Actor Class

The `Actor` class is derived from the `Object` class. In the animal example, it can be thought of the as the mammal. It inherits traits from the `Object` class, such as being garbage collected, but it also has its own capabilities. Perhaps most importantly, it can be placed in the level.

The Actor class is filled with functions and variables that game developers would otherwise need to create themselves. Things like being able to access an Actor's location in space, destroy the Actor, spawn a new instance of the Actor... these are all features that are necessary for all items in the world to have. For this reason, the Actor and all classes that inherit from the Actor class get this functionality for free. The `Actor` class is the most common class that you will be using as a game developer in Unreal Engine.

The Pawn Class

The `Pawn` is derived from the `Actor` class. It has all of the capabilities of the `Actor` plus more. It can be possessed by a `Controller`, a special class that decides how user input will move a Pawn around in the game. Whereas Actors can be anything from static objects in the environment to props and destructible items, Pawns are meant for being controlled. This means receiving input from either a human with a Controller, mouse or keyboard, or from instructions provided by an AI (Artificial Intelligence). A game in Unreal Engine has a **Default Pawn**, or the Pawn designated for the player to control when the game starts. This can be specified by the developer. However, if a Default Pawn is not specified, one will be spawned automatically by the engine.

For more specialized behavior, we can go one step lower in the derivation chain, with the `Character`.

The Character Class

The `Character` class is derived from the `Pawn` class, so it too can be possessed by a `Controller`. The Character class also has some of its own specialized functionality appropriate for upright, typically walking or running Characters in game.

Characters get a default **Capsule Component** – a pill-shaped volume that encases the Character and handles most of the physics collisions for the Character. If the mesh itself were used for all of the in-game collisions for a Character, the computations would slow the frame rate down too much. Thus a simpler volume is used.

Characters have a **Character Movement Component**. This is a special class which contains many functions and variables related to controlling the Character in ways that typical game Characters require. Things like movement speed, acceleration rates, air control (the ability to control the Character's lateral movement while in midair) exist as properties on this component. Because the Character has a Character Movement Component, the Character Movement Component can easily be accessed through the `Character` class.

The similarity between the Unreal Engine class hierarchy and that of nature's animals can be seen in the diagram below:

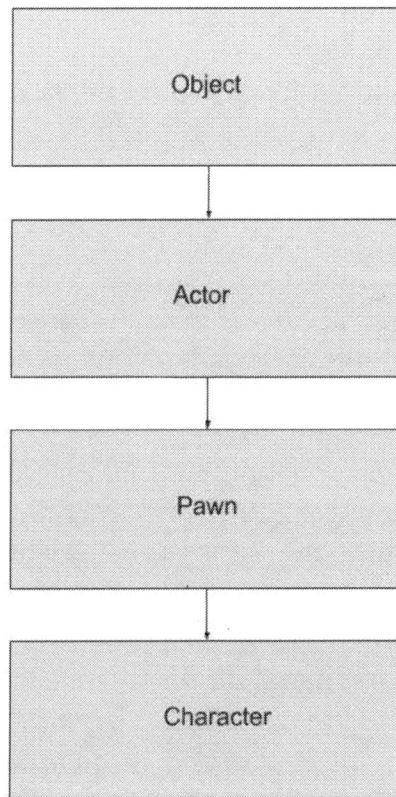

Figure 2.2: The Unreal Engine Hierarchy

So we see that Animals have both **is-a** relationships (a poodle is a dog) and **has-a** relationships (a dog has teeth, and a poodle **has** curly hair). But what implications do these relationships have on the Unreal Engine Hierarchy? What does it mean when we say that a `Character` is an `Actor` or a `Pawn` is an `Object`? We will now look what these relationships mean for code and the Unreal Engine class system.

Is-A vs. Has-A Relationships: Understanding the Difference

In programming, the terms **is-a** versus **has-a** relationships have very specific meanings. An **is-a** relationship is one in which a class is derived from a **parent** or **base** class (in programming, the terms **parent** and **base** are synonymous).

In a class hierarchy, a **child** or **derived** (the terms **child** and **derived** are also synonymous) class inherits qualities from its **parent** or **base** class. For example, an Actor is also an Object. A Pawn is also an Actor and an Object. A Character is a Pawn and an Actor and an Object. Thus if you perform some action that can only be performed on Actors, you can perform that action on Pawns and Characters because they too are Actors. However if you wish to perform an action that can only be performed on Characters, you cannot perform it on a Pawn because a Pawn is not a Character. So it is very important to understand the one-way nature of this inheritance relationship. Remember, all mammals are animals, but not all animals are mammals! A **has-a** relationship is when one class contains a variable which is the type of another class.

When one class contains other classes inside it, we call it **composition**. Composition allows a class to have functionality of another class by simply including a member of that class inside it. In Unreal Engine, a class will have **components** – instances of other classes inside it. An Actor will need to have a mesh to provide a visual representation of it in the world. Thus it will contain an object of the `StaticMesh` class, which is a member of the `Object` class. We learned previously that an `Object` doesn't even have the ability to be placed in the level. It can, however, be a member of a class that can. Thus `Actors` typically have `Object` components.

So we now see that there is a difference between a member of a class **being** a member of a higher class in the inheritance chain (**is-a** relationships) and **having** a member of another class (**has-a** relationships). But none of this has any real meaning until we actually create an object of a particular class. A class is a set of instructions, like the blueprint to a house. A blueprint to a house is not the house itself – it is a set of instructions telling the builder how to build the house. It isn't until the necessary equipment, materials and workers are assembled and get to work that a real house is made. Likewise, a class is simply a list of attributes (variables and functions) that describe what an object would look like if it were actually constructed. Once an object of the class is constructed, we say that we now have an **instance** of that particular class. So keep in mind the distinction between a class and an actual instance of that class. One exists as a template or set of instructions, and the other exists as an actual object in the world.

About Class Names

Notice the difference between the words object (all lowercase) and Object (capitalized). The former refers to an instance of a class that has been constructed in the game. The latter refers to the Object class, one of the classes in the Unreal Engine class hierarchy.

Now that we understand classes, inheritance hierarchies, is-a versus has-a relationships, and the difference between a class and an instance, it's time to start creating some classes (as well as creating some instances of them).

Components: Adding New Parts to an Actor

We will now get a chance to create some classes of our own and add components to them. Since the Object class is so basic that we can't even place one in the level, we are going to start with the Actor class instead. Just like the Actor class derives from the Object, we are going to create our own custom class that derives from Actor. To do this, follow these instructions:

1. In the **Content Browser**, right-click on the **Content** folder and select *New Folder*. Name it *Chapter2*.

2. Click on the green **Add New** button and select *Blueprint Class*.

3. Click on *Actor*.

4. Name your new Actor *FirstBlueprintActor*. Notice the asterisk at the bottom-left of the icon. This informs you that you haven't saved the item yet. Click **Save All.** The asterisk will go away.

5. Double-click on *FirstBlueprintActor*. This will open the **Blueprint Editor** for this class.

Notice that there are some panels in this editor that resemble those in the **Level Editor**. Many of them function in the same ways as the corresponding panel in the **Level Editor**. Notice however that you have two new panels to the left of the screen: the **Components** panel and the **My Blueprint** panel.

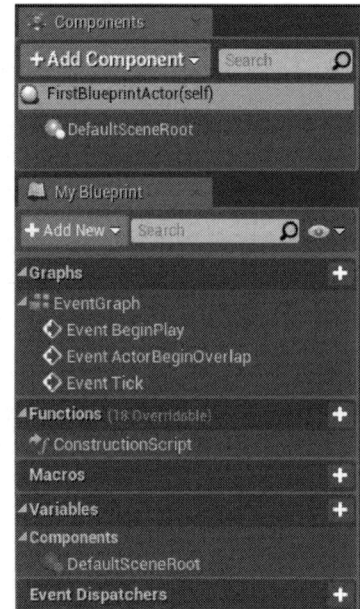

Figure 2.3: The Components and My Blueprint Tabs

These are described as follows:

- **Components**: lists the components that belong to this Actor.

- **My Blueprints:** shows Events, Functions and other relevant data for this Blueprint.

Just under **Add Component**, you will see the line *FirstBlueprintActor(self)*. Selecting this will select the Actor as a whole. Just under it is the *DefaultSceneRoot*. All Actors must have a Root Component and are provided one by default.

If you click on *DefaultSceneRoot*, the **Details** panel will now show properties of the *DefaultSceneRoot* itself. Notice in its **Transform** section it has a *Scale*, but no *Location* or *Rotation*. This is because it is the Root Component, and the location and rotation for components is relative to the root of the Actor. The **Details** panel appears as follows:

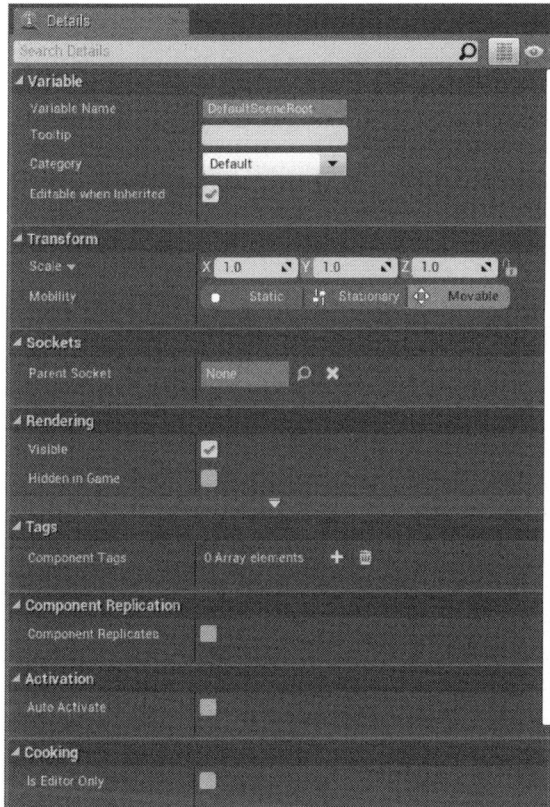

Figure 2.4: Details Panel of the DefaultSceneRoot Component

We now have an Actor class Blueprint. We can very easily add components to the Actor and attach them to each other in a hierarchy.

Adding a Component

Let's now add a component to our Actor:

1. In the **Components** panel, make sure *DefaultSceneRoot* is selected.

2. Click **Add Component**. A dropdown list will appear.

3. Find *Static Mesh* in the dropdown list and select it. This is a Static Mesh Component.

4. Name the Static Mesh Component *FirstBlueprintActorMesh*.

Notice that, with *FirstBlueprintActorMesh* selected, there are now **Location**, **Rotation**, and **Scale** in the **Transform** section of the **Details** panel. This is because *FirstBlueprintActorMesh* is not the Root Component, and thus it can have a location and rotation *relative* to the root. To explore this further, we need to give our Static Mesh Component a mesh.

The `StaticMeshComponent` class is derived from the `Object` class. It has its own properties in addition to those it inherits from `Object`. One of these properties is a *Static Mesh* property. We must give this Static Mesh property a value.

Adding a Static Mesh

1. With *FirstBlueprintActorMesh* selected, in the **Details** panel, find the **Static Mesh** section and notice the *Static Mesh* property. It has an empty icon that says "None" and a dropdown menu.

2. Select a Static Mesh to fill in the value for this empty variable. When you click the dropdown for this item, you will be presented only with items that are compatible with this item. For a Static Mesh, this consists only of Static Mesh items that exist in this project.

3. Select the Static Mesh called *SM_Couch*. The prefix "SM" is used as a convention in Unreal Engine to denote a Static Mesh. It is not required to name Static Meshes with this prefix, but doing so is a good idea, because it tells users the type of the asset and also makes it easier to search for it.

4. Once you select the *SM_Couch* asset, the icon for the Static Mesh property will show a thumbnail for the *SM_Couch* mesh. In the section below **Static Mesh** called **Materials**, the property *Element 0* will be populated with *M_Char*, the material asset for this mesh. This happens automatically, because the mesh

asset already had the material assigned to it. As you probably guessed, the "M" prefix stands for "Material."

5. Notice that the couch shows up in the **Viewport** for this Blueprint. Components that have visual representations such as meshes will show up here and be placed relative to the root. The local origin of this Actor is denoted by the white circle at the center of the **Viewport**. The gizmo at the bottom-left of the **Viewport** shows the directions of the **local** X, Y, and Z axes for this Actor.

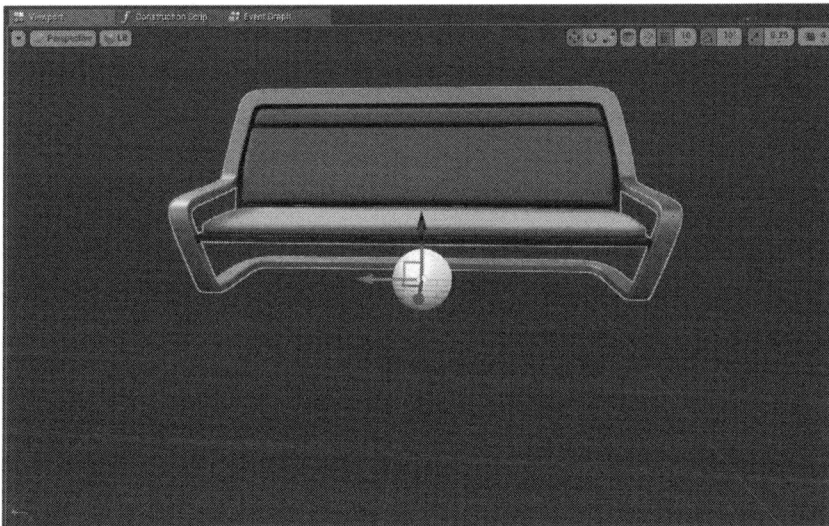

Figure 2.5: The Viewport for FirstBlueprintActor

6. The first item in the toolbar for this Blueprint is the **Compile** button. Its icon has now changed and has a question mark. This means that changes have been made to the Blueprint and it needs to be compiled. Click on the **Compile** button to compile the Blueprint and the question mark will turn into a check mark. Compiling a Blueprint manually like this rarely needs to be done, because once you press **Play** to play test the game, the engine will automatically compile the Blueprint.

Creating an Instance of FirstActor

We have created a class called *FirstBlueprintActor*, but we have not yet created an object (instance of the *FirstBlueprintActor* class). We will do so now.

1. Maneuver to the **Level Editor**. We will now place an instance of the *FirstBlueprintActor* class into our level. Doing so is as easy as clicking on the Blueprint icon for *FirstBlueprintActor* and dragging it into the level. Once you have done so, you have now created an instance of the *FirstBlueprintActor* class.

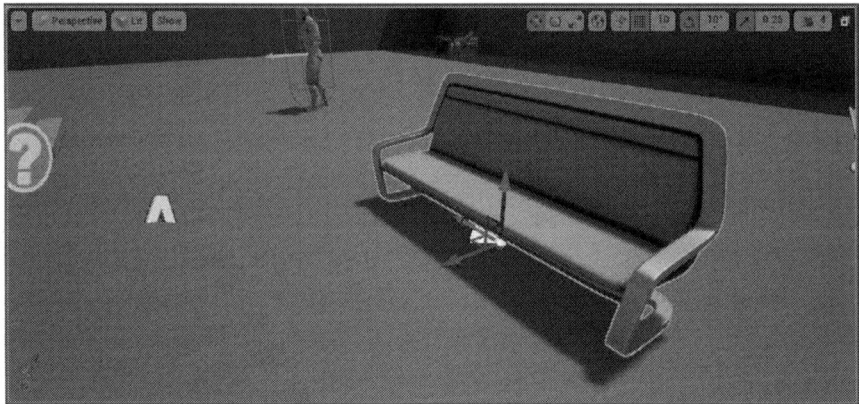

Figure 2.6: An Instance of the FirstBlueprintActor Class

6. Before you start rotating and positioning the couch, first take a look at its Translation Gizmo (with the *FirstBlueprintActor* selected, hit the *W* key to switch to Translation Mode).

7. Notice that the Translation Gizmo's X-axis is aligned with the X-axis of the world (as shown by the world Translation Gizmo at the bottom-left of the screen). We will be free to rotate and position the couch as we see fit later, but for now, keep the Actor aligned with the world axes.

We must now understand the difference between changing default properties on the Actor and changing properties on an instance of the Actor.

Transforming the Actor's Default Properties

We can alter the default properties of an Actor by changing them in its **Details** panel in the **Blueprint Editor**.

1. Maneuver back to the **Blueprint Editor**. In the **Components** panel, select *FirstBlueprintActorMesh*. With this component selected, we can transform the mesh in the **Viewport** using translation, rotation, and Scale Mode just like we did in the **Viewport** of the **Level Editor**. We can also change these values in the **Transform** section in the **Details** panel.

2. In this section, Change the Z component of the *Rotation* property to 90. Notice that the couch rotated by 90 degrees.

3. Maneuver back to the **Level Editor**. Now the couch is facing a different direction, but its transform gizmo **is still aligned with that of the world transform gizmo at the bottom-left of the screen.** This is because we didn't change the transform of the Actor. Rather, we changed the local rotation of one of its components (the Static Mesh Component).

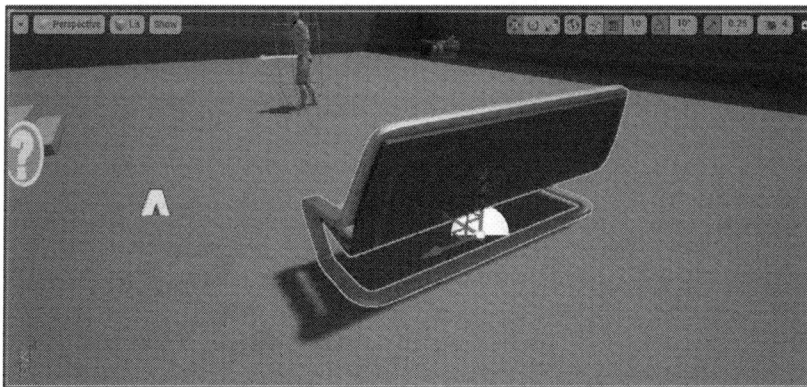

Figure 2.7: An Instance of FirstBlueprintActor with its Mesh Component Rotated 90 Degrees

Now go back into the **Blueprint Editor** and set the Z component of the *FirstBlueprintActorMesh* back to 0. This will be its default rotation. Let's see what

47

happens when we rotate the mesh on an instance of the *FirstBlueprintActor* class, rather than in the class defaults.

Transforming Properties on an Instance of the Actor

Now we will alter transform properties on the actual instance, rather than in the **Details** panel for the class Blueprint.

1. From within the **Level Editor**, notice that, as long as you have the instance of the *FirstBlueprintActor* selected, the **Details** panel is populated with data relevant to the instance. Just under the **Add Component** button is a **Search** bar. You can click the gray line just above the search bar to drag it down, exposing the components of this instance.

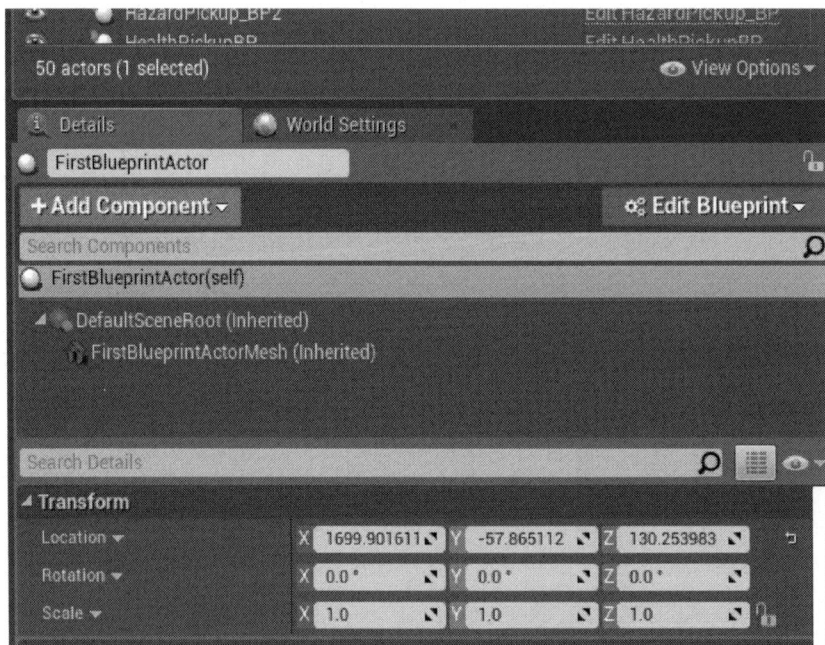

Figure 2.8: The Components of this Instance of FirstActor

2. With *FirstBlueprintActor(self)* selected in this section, the Actor as a whole is selected. Any transformations performed (Location, Rotation, and Scale changes) will be performed on the overall instance.

3. Select one of the components from this list, such as *FirstBlueprintActorMesh*. With this selected, you will no longer be applying changes to the overall Actor, but to the component itself.

4. Change the Z component of the Rotation to 90. You will notice that the couch rotates in the same manner as before. You may be tempted to think that we just applied the same exact change to the Actor, but we haven't.

We can understand the difference by dragging in a second instance of the *FirstBlueprintActor* class.

Figure 2.9: A Second Instance of the FirstActor class

Notice a difference? The new instance is in the original orientation, while the first instance is rotated. This is because in the **Blueprint Editor** for this class, the **default** value for the *FirstBlueprintActorMesh Rotation* property is (0, 0, 0). Whatever value we assign to it there, that is the value that new instances of the class will be created with when dragged into the world. Once in the world, we can further change properties on the instance, but these do not affect the class defaults for the Actor.

When we make changes to the transform of a component, these changes are applied to all the components attached to it. We can see this by selecting the second couch Actor and selecting the *DefaultSceneRoot* in the **Details** panel. We can then change the Y component of its *Scale* property to 0.5. The *FirstBlueprintActorMesh* will appear to shrink in the Actor's Y-direction. However if you select the *FirstBlueprintActorMesh* component, the Y component of its Scale property is still 1.0. Thus it is important to keep in mind that any changes to the transform of a component, including the Root Component, propagate to the attached components (children) of the altered component.

We will get plenty of practice with creating and manipulating components throughout the course of this book. Now it is time to explore the use of variables and functions in our Actor.

Variables

Variables are containers for data. An Object's transform (a structure containing a location, rotation, and scale) keeps these quantities stored in the form of variables. A variable has its own **data type**, a property that dictates the type and amount of data that can be stored in them. Typical data types are:

- **Integer**: a discrete, whole number such as 1, 2, 99, -120

- **Float**: a decimal value such as 1.23, 3.1416, 0.0

- **Boolean**: a variable with only two possible values: **True** or **False**

- **String:** a string of characters such as "MyActor" or "Sally"

The first three of the above data types are examples of what are known as **base** data types. They are basic types that help with calculations and decisions made at runtime by code. There can be more complex data types, known as **compound** data types, which are made up of the base data types. The String is an example of a compound data type. The String is an **array** – a sequence of variables strung together contiguously in memory – of characters. A **Vector** is another example of a compound data type. The Vector data type consists of three float values (one for each of the X, Y, and Z components). The Vector type actually contains functions as well as data. Classes themselves are considered custom data types. Thus a variable can be of an `Object` type, an `Actor` type, etc.

We will gain plenty of experience with data types throughout this course. To get our feet wet just a bit, we will now create a basic variable in our Actor Blueprint.

Creating Your First Variable

Creating variables in Blueprints is quite different from creating them in C++ code. We will now create a variable of the `float` data type.

1. Click **Add New** in the **My Blueprint** panel and select **Variable**. Your new variable will appear in the **Variables** section of the **My Blueprint** panel.

2. Name this variable *FirstVariable*. In the **Details** panel, you will see a **Variable** section. Here, you can see and change the **Variable Name**. Just below this, there is the **Variable Type** with a dropdown. By default, the variable is of Boolean type. In Blueprints, data types are color-coded, and you can see that the Boolean type is coded red.

3. Click the dropdown for **Variable Type**. The most common types along with their colors are displayed, as well as dropdowns for more complex types.

4. Choose the float type. In the **Details** panel, notice the section at the bottom titled **Default Value**. If you haven't compiled the Blueprint since you created the variable, it will say "Please compile the blueprint." Click the **Compile** icon. You will now see an option to provide a default value for the variable. In the case of the float type, this value is 0.0 unless you override it by filling in a value. Enter the value 100.0.

You have now created your first variable in Blueprints. You will create many variables throughout the course of this book, though you'll soon be creating variables in C++. For now, let's see how we can use this variable by making use of functions.

Functions

Functions are sets of code that will run when called upon by name. For this reason it is common to refer to the execution of a function as "calling" the function. Functions can be created in Blueprints as well as C++. We will create many functions throughout the course of this book. However, many functions already exist in the Unreal Engine code base. In order to be a good game programmer, it is necessary to know about the main functions involved in programming gameplay.

Creating a Function

The *BeginPlay* function exists in Blueprints as an **Event**. Events in Blueprints are red nodes that have output **Execution Pins.** Events respond to certain things that happen in the game such as overlaps and collisions. Once they are executed, the **flow of control** (the order in which a series of tasks are executed in code) initiates through the event node's output execution pin and enters into any series of nodes, each of which performs its own particular task.

Functions are nodes which contain their own functionality. Functions can be used and reused any number of times. They can take inputs and return output values.

BeginPlay is an event that gets executed once at the beginning of an object's lifetime. In the Actor we created, if the Actor is placed in the level, this event will be fired at the beginning of the game. To utilize the *BeginPlay* event, we must navigate to the Blueprint's **Event Graph**.

Just under the **Toolbar** are three tabs:

- **The Viewport:** shows the visible components of the Actor.

- **Construction Script:** Similar to the **Event Graph**, but any logic placed in this graph takes place before the game is started. It executes when an instance of this Actor is moved in the world or when one of its properties changes.

- **The Event Graph:** Contains Blueprint logic such as events and functions that respond to various things that happen in the game.

We will be utilizing the *BeginPlay* function in the **Event Graph**.

1. Click on the **Event Graph**. By Default, The *BeginPlay*, *ActorBeginOverlap*, and *Tick* events are visible but grayed out. This is because they are not yet being used. We will be using the *BeginPlay* event.

2. Left-click and drag from the white shape at the bottom-right of the *BeginPlay* node. A wire will come out. When you release the left mouse button, a menu will pop up. Search for *SetActorLocation*. The *SetActorLocation* function will appear. Click on it.

Figure 2.10: BeginPlay, SetActorLocation, and a Grayed-Out ActorBeginOverlap Event

3. The *SetActorLocation* node is an example of a function, as symbolized by the blue "**f**" symbol to the left of the function name. Notice several **input parameters**, or values at the left side of the node that can be inserted as input for the function (sometimes known as **arguments**). Take note of the two **return values** at the right side of the node: *Sweep Hit Result* and *Return Value*. These are values that the function provides when the function has finished executing.

4. The *Target* input parameter is a parameter of the Actor data type. Hover over the input parameters to see the types required. The *Target* parameter has a default value of "self" which means that the current Actor to which this function belongs is automatically **passed** (the term for inserting an input) into this function. Passing a different Actor into the function for the *Target* parameter would result in the function acting on that Actor instead.

5. *SetActorLocation* takes a target and a location. The *Sweep* and *Teleport* input parameters are of type Boolean (as indicated by their red color) and can be ignored for now. The *NewLocation* parameter is coded yellow because it is of type Vector. Create a Vector by right clicking on the graph and typing "make vector." Upon clicking *Make Vector* a new node is created. It has three float inputs and one Vector output. Float nodes can be inserted into the input pins.

In the **My Blueprint** panel, click on *FirstVariable* and drag it out onto the graph. Upon releasing, select Get *FirstVariable* and a node for the variable will appear.

6. Click on the green output pin and drag it out, connecting it to the green input pin for the Z input parameter on the *Make Vector* node.

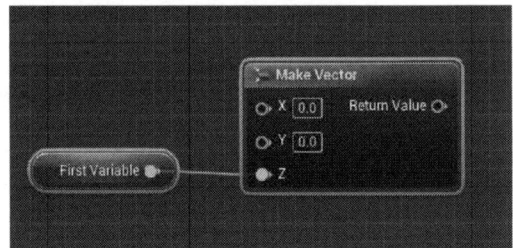

7. Now right-click on the graph area and type "GetActorLocation." Select the *GetActorLocation* node.

Figure 2.11: Creating a Vector for SetActorLocation

This returns the location of the Target (defaulted to self) in the form of a Vector.

8. Drag off of the yellow output pin from this node and type "+" and select *Vector + Vector* to create a node for adding two vectors.

9. Drag off of the yellow output node from the *Make Vector* node and plug it into the bottom input node for the *vector + vector* node.

10. Drag the output from the + node into the *New Location* input pin for *SetActorLocation*. The result should look as follows:

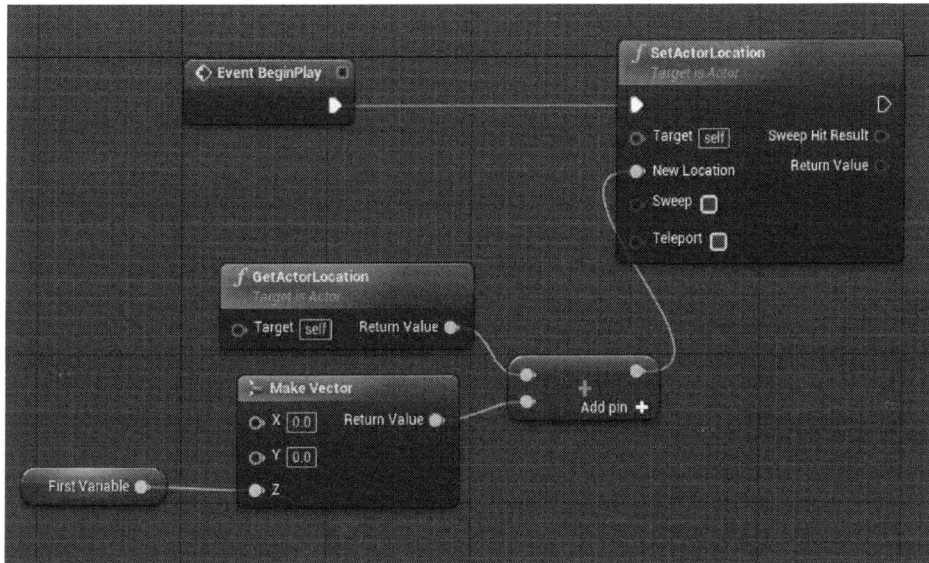

Figure 2.12: Calling SetActorLocation in BeginPlay

Now, at the start of the game, *BeginPlay* will execute, resulting in the *SetActorLocation* function being called. It will take the Vector passed in as an input and set the location of the Actor to the coordinates in the Vector.

Maneuver back to the **Level Editor** and press **Play**. The couches should be 100.0 units above their original locations.

We now have experience using a function in Blueprints by calling it upon execution of the *BeginPlay* event. Event *ActorBeginOverlap* executes whenever another Actor overlaps with the current Actor. Event *Tick* executes every frame (usually 60 to 120 times per second, depending on current computer performance). We will get experience with Overlap Events once we learn more about how overlapping works in Unreal Engine. We will also utilize the *Tick* function as we continue to learn more about programming in Unreal Engine with C++.

Summary

Now we understand the concept of classes and how they organize concepts in the Unreal Engine class hierarchy. We now know that objects of one type are also objects of their parent's type and can be used to derive child classes which inherit their properties. We have seen how we can add components to an Actor to give it properties such as mesh representations. Finally, we have learned how to create variables and use them when calling functions and implementing events such as the *BeginPlay* event. We are now familiar with the basics of the engine and can now visit some basics regarding its materials and lighting capabilities. We will familiarize ourselves with the **Materials Editor** and learn how to use it to create a custom material. We will also discover how Material Instances are useful for reusing data from an original material. We then will learn about lighting in Unreal Engine and how the various types of lights work.

Chapter 3 – Adding Materials and Lights

Materials and lights are the reason why the objects in a game world can be breathtaking. The difference between a smooth plastic surface and that of rough concrete in a game lies in its material. Materials contain information about the color of the object. They also contain information used by the rendering engine to affect how light reflects off of (or is absorbed by) the surface. The simulation of light in Unreal Engine results in realistic looking objects in the world.

The topics we will cover in this chapter include:

- **The Materials Editor**

- **Creating a Custom Material**

- **Material Instances**

- **Working with Lights in Unreal Engine**

We will first take a look at the Materials Editor and see how it can be used to create materials. We will also introduce Material Instances, which allow you to create a child of a particular material, inheriting its qualities while allowing for additional modifications. We will then visit the types of lights in Unreal Engine and learn how they behave during game simulation.

Working With the Material Editor

We will familiarize ourselves with the **Materials Editor** by looking at a material on a mesh. This will allow us to see how the material is designed and how the Materials Editor is used to apply textures and material channels.

In the **Viewport** of the **Level Editor**, click to select one of the couch Actors created in the previous chapter.

1. In the **Details** panel, select the *FirstActorMesh* component, just above *Search Details*.

Figure 3.1: Selecting the FirstBlueprintActorMesh Component

2. In the **Materials** section, notice *Element 0* is populated by *M_Chair*.

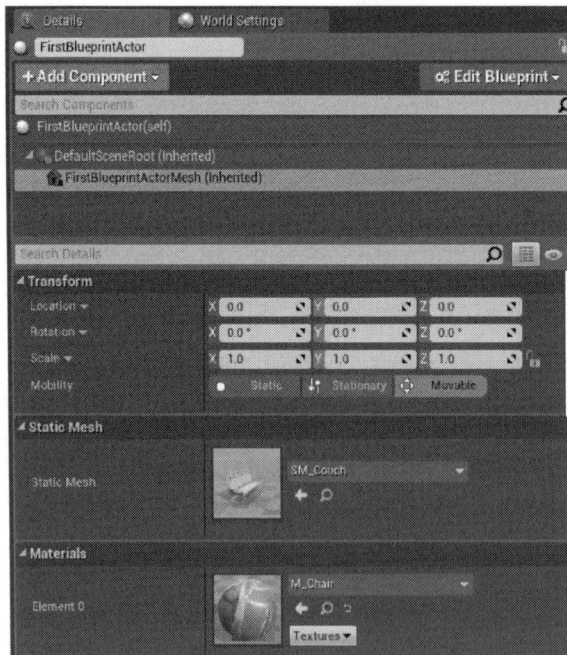

Figure 3.2: FirstBlueprintActorMesh Material Element 0

3. Let's take a look at this material. Click on the magnifying glass (*Browse To*) icon. The *M_Chair* material asset will show up in the **Content Browser**.

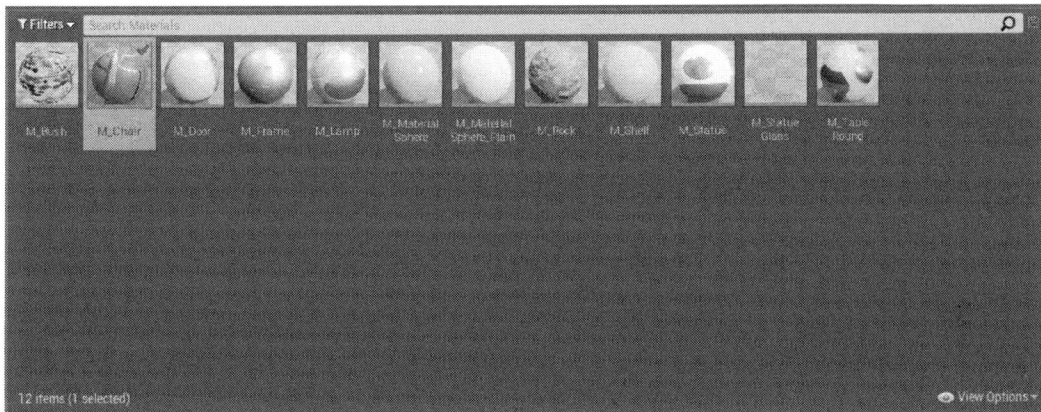

Figure 3.3: Browsing to the M_Chair Asset

This will open the location where *M_Chair* exists in the project. Notice there are other materials in this same folder. Double-click *M_Chair* to open it. The **Materials Editor** will open.

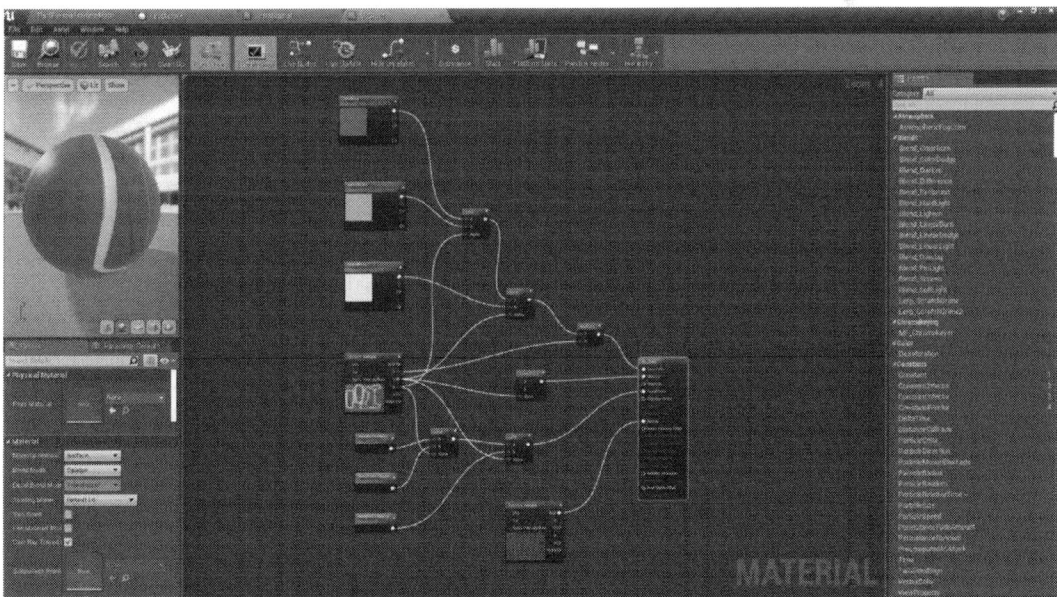

Figure 3.4: The Materials Editor for SM_Chair

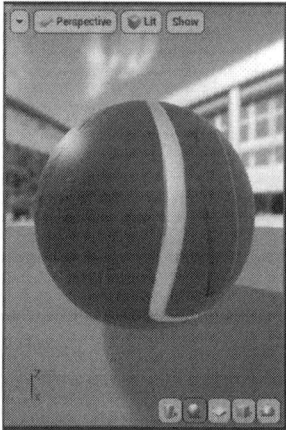

Figure 3.5: The Mini Viewport in the Materials Editor

4. Notice the small **Viewport** to the left of the screen above the **Details** panel.

This is where you can see a preview of the material as you create it, applied to the selected example mesh. By default, you will see a sphere. The Icons in the bottom-right of the **Viewport** allow you to change this example mesh.

5. Click on the cylinder. This will result in the material applied to an example cylinder as shown in **Figure 3.6**.

6. Click on the third icon. This will enable the plane preview mesh as shown in **Figure 3.6**.

7. The fourth icon enables a cube preview mesh as shown in **Figure 3.6**.

You may need to move the camera around to see the mesh straight on. To move the camera, hold the *ALT* key and left-click and drag in the **Viewport**. To zoom in/out, hold *ALT* and right-click and drag up/down.

Figure 3.6: Setting the Preview Mesh to a Plane and a Cylinder

8. The last icon allows you to select an arbitrary mesh to preview the material. Maneuver to the **Level Editor** and go to *Content -> StarterContent -> Shapes*. Select *Shape_Pipe_180*.

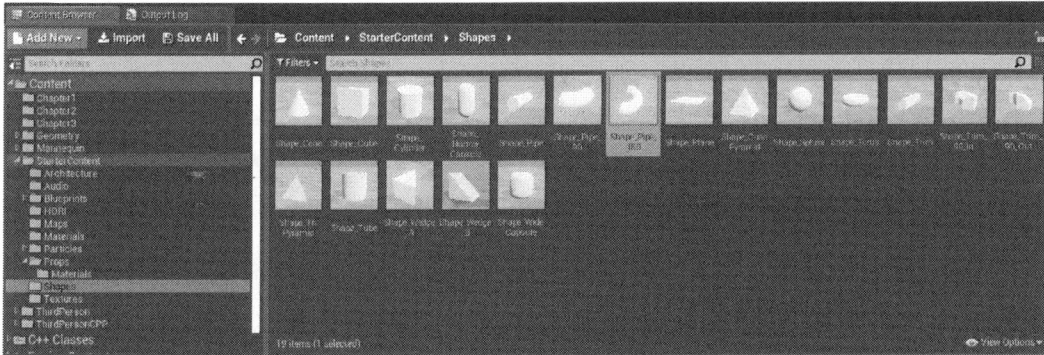

Figure 3.7: Selecting a Mesh from the Content Browser

With *Shape_Pipe_180* selected, maneuver back to the **Materials Editor** and select the fifth preview mesh icon:

Figure 3.8: Setting the Preview Mesh to a Pipe Mesh

9. Now let's bring our attention to the graph. Notice that all the nodes in this graph all funnel into the *M_Chair* node. This is the main node for the material. Each of these input pins represent different channels that make up the material.

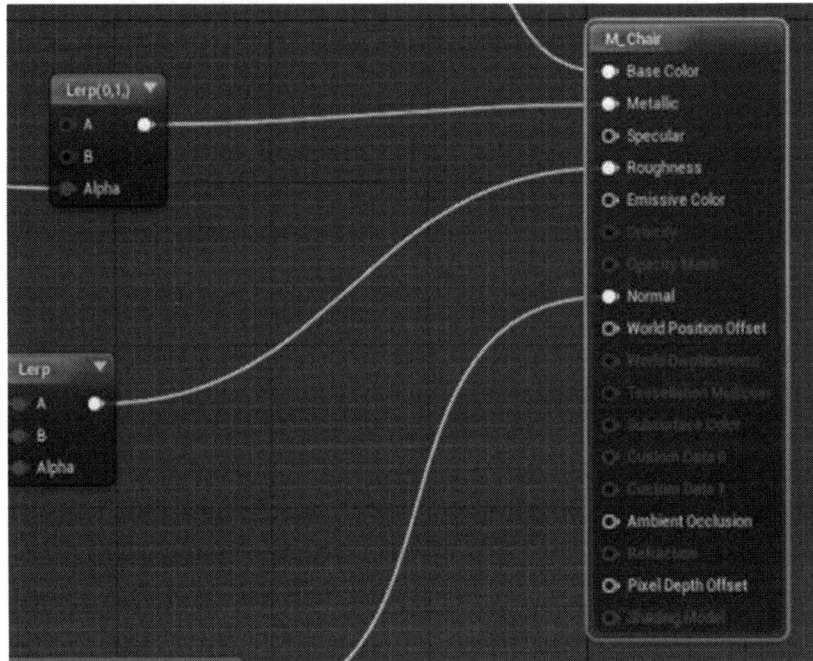

Figure 3.9: The Execution Wires all Funnel into M_Chair

As you can see, the many wires and nodes in the material graph can be complicated. Similar to the **Event Graph** for a Blueprint, the **Materials Editor** graph can contain nodes connected to each other via wires. Each node represents information that gets piped into the main node which is named after the material itself. This main node assembles all the data piped into it and constructs the final material, of which you can see a preview in the small **Viewport** to the left of the graph.

Now we will create our own custom material so we can understand more about how materials work.

Creating a Custom Material

The **Materials Editor** contains a graph similar to the **Event Graph** in the **Blueprint Editor** for Actors. We can use nodes to create a given material that can then be applied to various meshes in the game. We will now create a basic material from scratch and apply it to a mesh.

1. Click on the *Content* folder in the **Content Browser**. Right-click and create a new folder. Name it *Chapter3*.

2. In the *Chapter3* folder, right-click and select *Material*. A new asset Icon will appear in the *Chapter3* folder. Name it *FirstMaterial*.

3. Double-click the *FirstMaterial* icon to open the **Materials Editor**.

4. Click on the *Search* bar in the **Palette** panel at the right of the screen. Type "constant" and you will see items with *Constant* in their name. Click *Constant3Vector* and drag it out onto the graph. A node will appear labeled *0,0,0*.

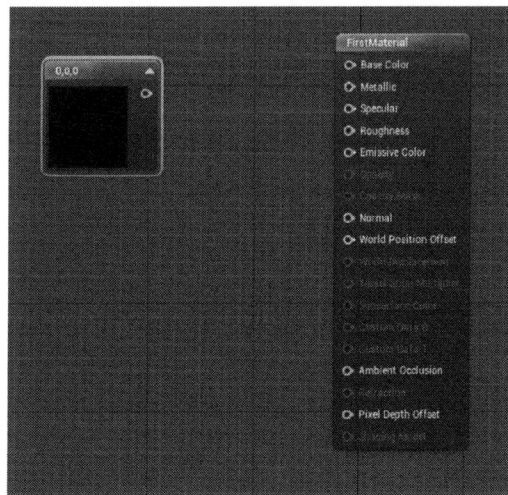

Figure 3.10: Adding a Constant3Vector

5. After adding a *Constant3Vector*, notice that the **Details** panel looks different. The property in the **Details** panel called *Constant* has a dropdown and you can set the values of the *R, G* and *B* components of this constant.

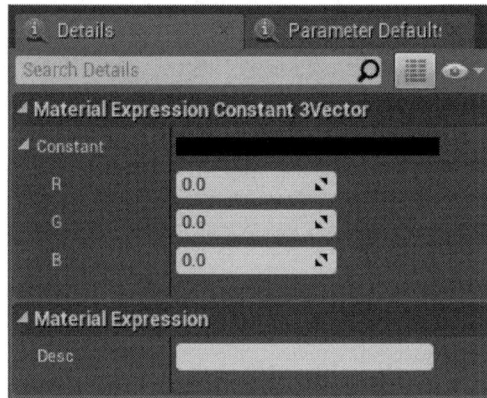

Figure 3.11: Details Panel for the Constant3Vector

6. Double click on the node labeled *0,0,0*. A **Color Picker** menu will pop up. Under **Advanced**, notice the *R, G,* and *B* values. These represent the red, green, and blue components of the vector.

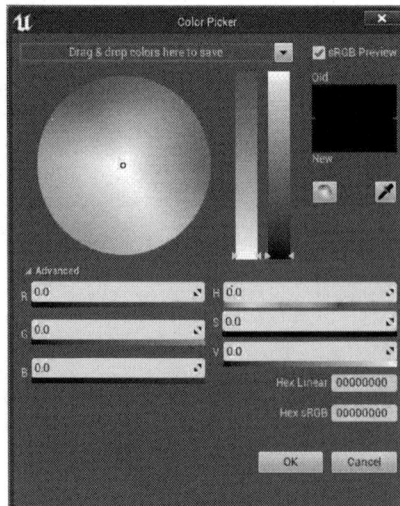

Figure 3.12: The Color Picker

Unreal Engine C++ the Ultimate Developer's Handbook

7. The two vertical strips to the right of the color circle are *Saturation* and *Value*, respectively. Click on the right strip (*Value*) and set it all the way up, where the indicator is at the top of the strip. If the value is all the way down, the color will be black. Click in the color circle and drag around until you find a color you like. Click **Okay**.

8. The *Constant3Vector* node will now show the color you chose. Drag from its output pin

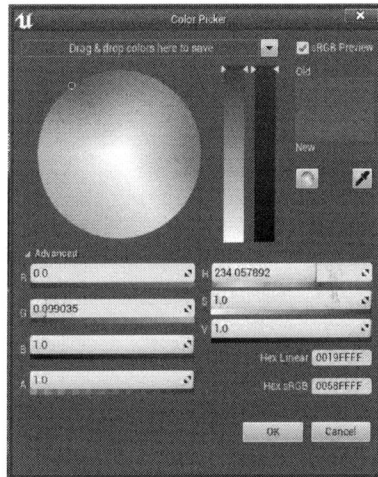

Figure 3.13: Color Picker with Saturation and Value All the Way Up

into the *Base Color* pin on the *FirstMaterial* node. This will pipe in the color associated with the vector to this material's *Base Color* channel. After a moment, the sphere in the **Viewport** will change to the color of our vector.

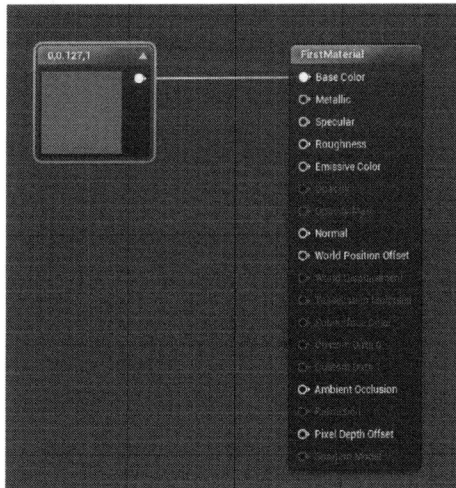

Figure 3.14: Plugging in the Constant3Vector to FirstMaterial

9. Click the **Save** icon.

10. Maneuver back to the **Level Editor**. In the **Modes** panel, click *Cube* and drag it into the world.

11. Click on the *FirstMaterial* icon in the **Content Browser** and drag it onto the mesh of the cube in the **Viewport**. The material will be applied to the cube mesh.

12. Look in the **Details** panel. Notice in the **Materials** section, *FirstMaterial* is applied to this cube. We could have set the material by changing this property in the **Details** panel directly.

Figure 3.15: Cube with FirstMaterial Applied

Now we know how to create a material and apply it to a mesh. So far, all we have added to our material is a **Base Color** property. Let's examine how a few of the other channels affect the material's appearance.

Exploring the Material Inputs

A material node takes several optional inputs that it uses to construct the overall appearance of the material. We will cover the most important of these, including:

- **Metallic**
- **Specular**
- **Roughness**
- **Emissive Color**
- **Normal**

We will start by exploring the effect the *Metallic* input has on the material.

Metallic

Using the *Metallic* input to our material node allows us to provide a value for the metallic channel of the material. Similarly to how we added a *Constant3Vector* to the graph and plugged it into the *Base Color* input for the material, we can create a constant and plug it into the *Metallic* input. *Metallic*, however, takes a single value (or a map of pixels), rather than a 3-component vector. We can get a single-valued constant by either searching for "constant" in the **Palette** or by holding down the *1* key and left-clicking in the graph. We will use the latter method in the following instructions as we add a value for the *Metallic* channel in our material.

1. Hold the *1* key and left-click on the graph to create a *Constant* node.

2. Drag the output of the *Constant* node into the *Metallic* input pin.

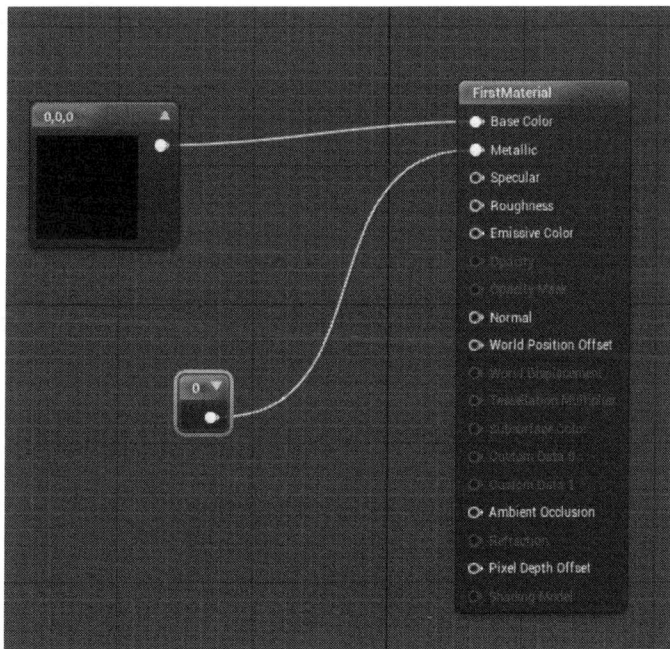

Figure 3.16: Plugging a Constant Node into Metallic

3. Change the *Value* property for the *Constant* node to 1.0 by making sure it is selected and entering 1.0 for the *Value* property in the **Details** panel.

4. Notice the change in the previewed material in the **Viewport**. Next to the **Save** and **Browse** icons in the tool bar, click on the **Apply** icon. This will apply the change to all meshes using this material in the world without saving the material.

5. Maneuver to the **Level Editor** and observe the change to the cube mesh in the world.

Metallic objects reflect light differently than non-metallic objects. While you can pick a value from 0.0 to 1.0 for the metallic channel, only a value of 0.0 or 1.0 is typically chosen, and seldom a value in between. This is because in reality objects are either metallic or they aren't, and to a material which is partially metallic is not realistic. Now we will examine the Specular channel.

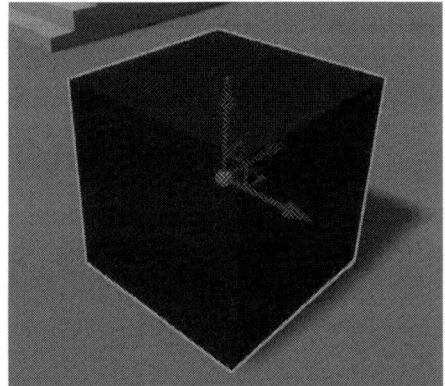

Figure 3.17: Cube Colored with a Metallic Value of 1.0

Specular

The Specular channel allows us to provide information regarding how shiny a material is. Specularity is typically a value between 0 and 1, with 0 resulting in no light reflectance and 1 reflecting the maximum amount of light.

Hold the *ALT* key while left-clicking on the output pin of the *Constant* node (or the input pin of the *Metallic* node) to break the connection. Connect it to the *Specular* input. While it is possible to input a scalar value to this channel, it is also possible to import a **specular map,** a 2D surface which contains grayscale information representing specular values on a per-pixel basis. This allows for a mesh to have reflective surfaces in some locations and non-reflective surfaces in others.

Adjust the value of the constant plugged into *Specular* to see the changes in the material. Below is an example of a specular value of 0.5:

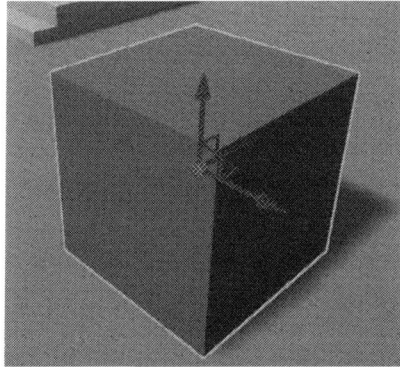

Figure 3.18: Cube with a Specular Value of 0.5

Now that we have seen how the specular channel behaves, let's take a look at roughness.

Roughness

Whereas the Specular channel determines how much light is reflected, the roughness channel determines the sharpness of the reflection. A high roughness value results in light scattered on the surface and the reflection is less prominent. With a low value for roughness, the reflection of the light source is sharp and defined. You can disconnect the *Constant* from the *Specular* channel and connect it to the *Roughness* channel and play with the values to see how the surface shininess is affected. The image below shows a roughness value of 0.0 applied to the preview mesh in the **Viewport** of the **Materials Editor**.

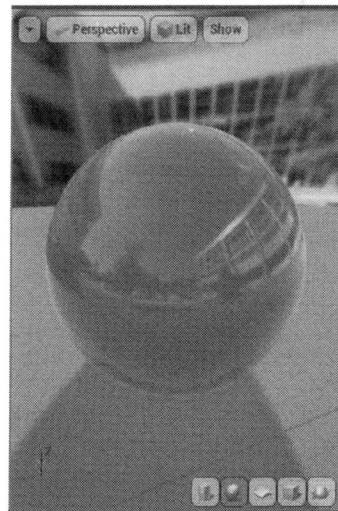

Figure 3.19: A Roughness Value of 0.0

As you can see, a round object such as a sphere shows reflections of the light source when the roughness value is low. This can be harder to notice on flat surfaces. Now that we have experimented with roughness, let's look at emissive color.

Emissive Color

This channel controls the parts of the material that will appear to glow. A
Constant3Vector can be inserted into this channel and the material will glow with the
color inserted. You can actually increase the value of the color piped into *Emissive Color*
by multiplying its value. We will increase the value of the *Constant3Vector* we used for
Base Color to demonstrate this.

1. Hold the *1* key and left-click in the graph to create a *Constant*.

2. Set the *Constant's* value to 10.

3. Drag off of the output pin from the *Constant3Vector* we already created and
   connected to *Base Color*. Upon releasing the left mouse button, type
   "multiply." Select *Multiply* to create a *Multiply* node.

Figure 3.20: Dragging off of the Constant3Vector and Typing Multiply

4. Drag off of the *Constant* and connect it to the *B* input. Connect the output of
   the *Multiply* to the *Emissive Color.*

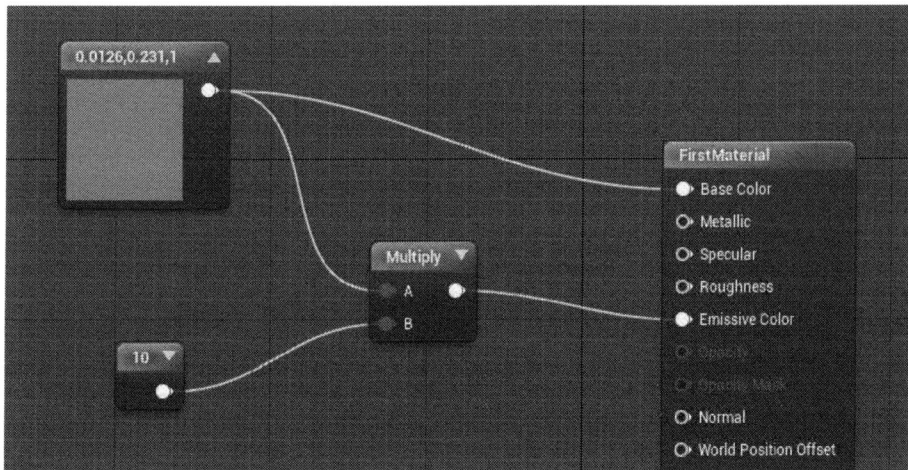

Figure 3.21: Plugging a Value into Emissive Color

We have now multiplied the *Constant3Vector* color by a value of 10 and used the result for the *Emissive Color* channel. The result is a brightly glowing material:

Figure 3.22: A Brightly Glowing Material

We have seen how using a value for the *Emissive Color* channel can make materials glow. Now it's time to visit one of the most important and widely used material channels: The normal channel.

Normal

The normal channel controls how light is reflected off of the surface. Normal maps are used to give the illusion of intricate detail on a flat surface. We will examine the effect of adding a normal map to our material.

1. Go to the **Content Browser** and click on the **Content** folder.

2. Next to **Filters**, type "M_" into the search bar.

3. Materials prefixed with *M_* will show up in the **Content Browser**. Double-click on *M_Concrete_Grime*. This is a concrete material that is included in the project because we chose to add starter content when creating the project.

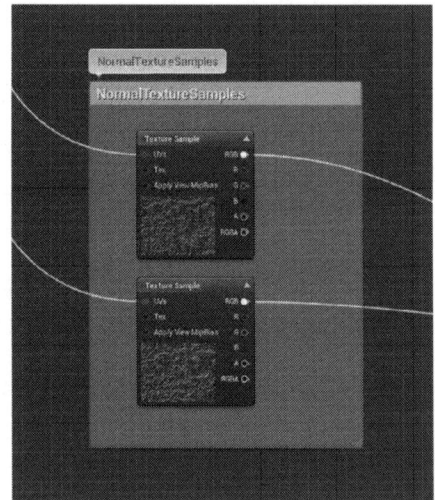

Figure 3.23: Normal Maps in the Concrete Texture

4. Find the section in the graph labeled *NormalTextureSamples*. Notice the nodes with the deep blue designs. Double click on one of these nodes.

5. You will be taken to the folder where the texture is located. It is called *T_Metal_Rust_N*. Double-click it to open it. This is what a normal map looks like.

6. In the **Content Browser**, click on *T_Metal_Rust_N* and drag it up to the *FirstMaterial* tab at the top of the editor. The *FirstMaterial* editor will open and you will be able to drag the icon onto the graph. It will show up as a *Texture Sample* node. Another way is to right-click in the graph and search for "texture sample" and to add a *Texture Sample* node. If a texture is selected in the

Content Browser, it will automatically set the *Texture* property to the selected texture. If not, you can select the *Texture Sample* node and change the *Texture* property in the **Details** panel.

7. Disconnect the pin going into the *Emissive Color* channel. Drag the *RGB* pin from the *Texture Sample* node into the *Normal* pin in the *FirstMaterial* node. Notice the change in the **Viewport**. Use *ALT* + left-click and drag to rotate the mesh sample in the **Viewport** so you can see the details of the material.

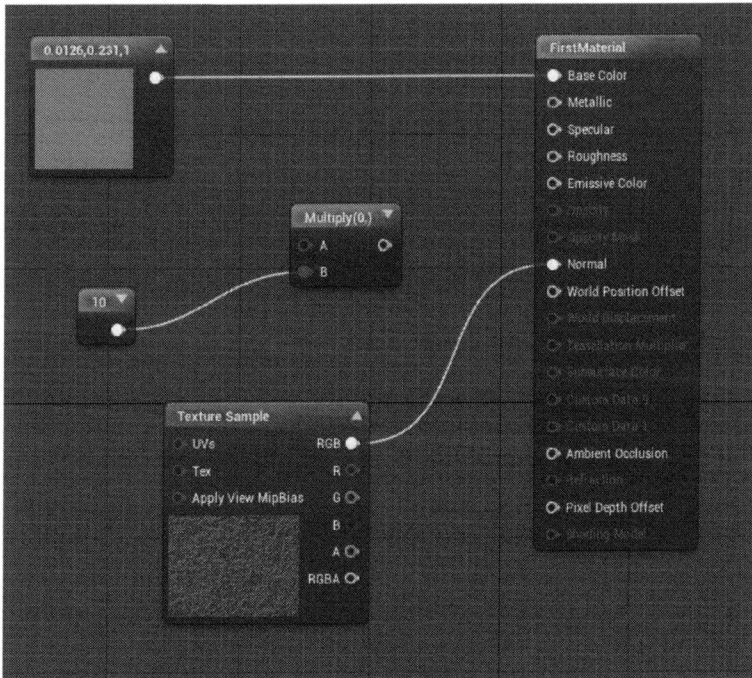

Figure 3.24: Adding a Normal Map

8. Click **Apply** in the tool bar and maneuver to the **Level Editor**. Notice the difference in the material of the cube now that the normal map is applied.

Figure 3.25: Normal Map Applied to the Cube

We now have some experience creating a basic material. We have seen how some of the channels work on a given material. To cover all the channels in depth would easily fill an entire book. For gameplay programmers, this is sufficient knowledge to continue at this point.

So now that we know how to create a material, it's time to learn how to make a **material instance**. Because creating materials can be time consuming, Unreal Engine created the idea of material instances to make things easier when multiple materials are needed. Material instancing is a method of creating a parent base material and being able to "instance" or make copies of that base material while being able to tweak and change parameters on the copies or instances.

Working with Material Instances

With material instances, the idea is to create a base parent material which will contain the properties inherited by the child materials or **instances**. In order for the instance to be able to change these properties, the properties must be **parameters.** Parameters are elements of a material specifically designed to be editable in instances of a material.

Converting a Node to a Parameter

If you search in the **Palette** search bar for "parameter," you will see all of the parameter types you can create in the **Materials Editor**. You can also convert nodes into parameters if their type is compatible. If you right-click on a node in the graph and you don't see a *Convert to Parameter* option, you cannot convert the node into a parameter. Now let's convert some values to parameters.

1. Right-click on the color vector we created for the *Base Color* channel. Select *Convert to Parameter*.

2. In the **Details** panel, a property called *Parameter Name* will pop up. Change the name to *Base Color*.

3. Right-click on the *Constant* value we created for the *Roughness* channel. Select *Convert to Parameter* and change its parameter name to *Roughness*.

4. Right-click on the *Texture Sample* we created for the *Normal* channel. Select *Convert to Parameter* and change its parameter name to *Normal Map*.

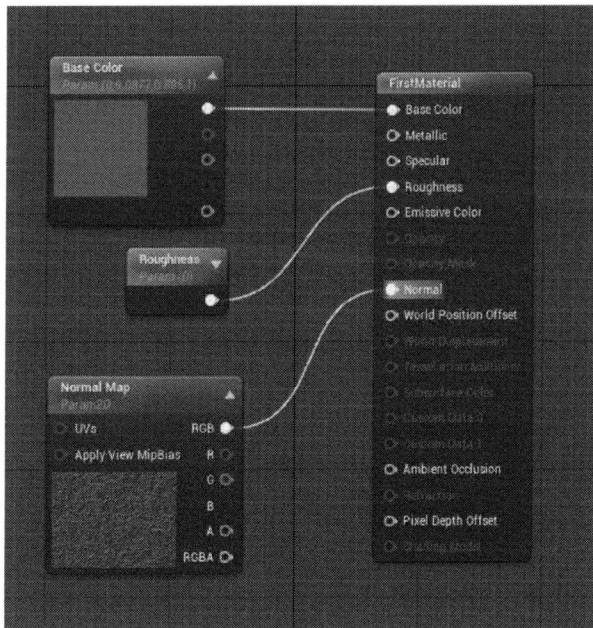

Figure 3.26: Material Parameters

Now that we have converted our nodes to parameters, it's time to create an instance of our *FirstMaterial*.

Creating a Material Instance

We will now create a material instance:

1. Maneuver to the *Chapter3* folder in the **Content Browser**. Right-click on *FirstMaterial* and select **Create Material Instance**.

2. Name the material instance *FirstInstance*.

3. Double-click the material instance to open it. In the **Details** panel, you should see a section called **Parameter Groups**. If you don't, you need to go back to *FirstMaterial* and compile the material by clicking **Apply**.

Figure 3.27: The FirstInstance Material Instance

4. Each of the parameters has a check box next to its name. If you wish to alter the properties of the parameters, you must check the check box in order to override those properties.

5. Create two more instances by right-clicking on *FirstMaterial* in the **Content Browser** and selecting **Create Material Instance**. Name them *FirstInstance2* and *FirstInstance3*.

6. Open *FirstInstance2*. Check the check boxes next to the parameters so you can override them.

7. Change the *Normal Map* parameter to *T_Metal_Steel_N*.

8. Change the *Roughness* parameter to a value of 0.5.

9. Change the *Base Color* to green by clicking on the color ribbon and selecting a color from the **Color Picker**.

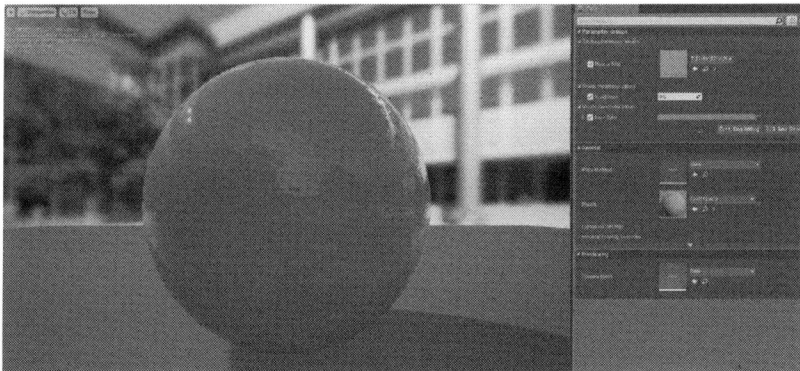

Figure 3.28: The FirstInstance2 Material Instance

10. Open *FirstInstance3*. Change the *Normal Map* to *T_ML_Aliminum01_N*.

11. Change the *Roughness* to a value of 0.25.

12. Change the color to yellow.

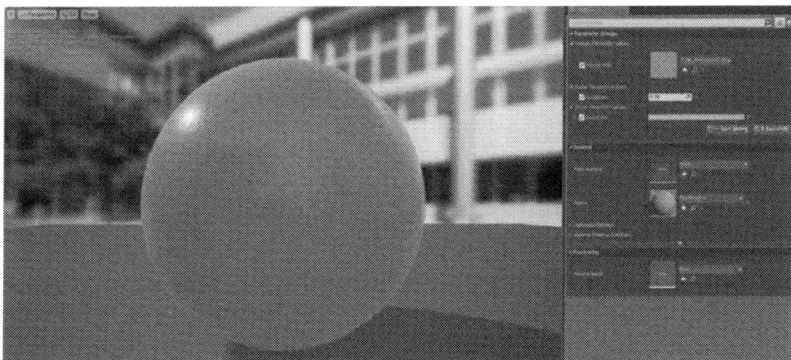

Figure 3.29: The FirstInstance3 Material Instance

13. In the **Level Editor**, with *Basic* selected in the **Modes** panel, drag two cubes into the world next to the original cube.

14. Apply *FirstInstance2to* one of the new cubes by clicking and dragging the material from the **Content Browser** onto the cube mesh. This is one way to apply a material instance to a mesh.

15. Select the other cube. Change its material in the **Details** panel by selecting *Element 0* under the **Materials** section and typing *FirstInstance3* into the search bar and selecting *FirstInstance3*. This is another way to apply a material instance to a mesh.

Figure 3.30: The Material Instances Applied to Meshes

We have now created three material instances based on the base material *FirstMaterial*! This is a very powerful skill to have, because some materials can be complicated and creating multiple versions of a material, each of which only have small variations in their properties, can be time consuming. With instances, parameters can be adjusted on instances in a fraction of the time it would require to create a completely new material.

The Power of Material Instances

We can now see an example of the power of using material instances by adding a new property to the parent material and seeing that property propagate to the children:

1. Open *FirstMaterial*. Duplicate the *Roughness* constant parameter by left-clicking on it and hitting *CTRL + W*.

2. Rename the new parameter *Specular*. Drag its pin into the *Specular* pin in *FirstMaterial*.

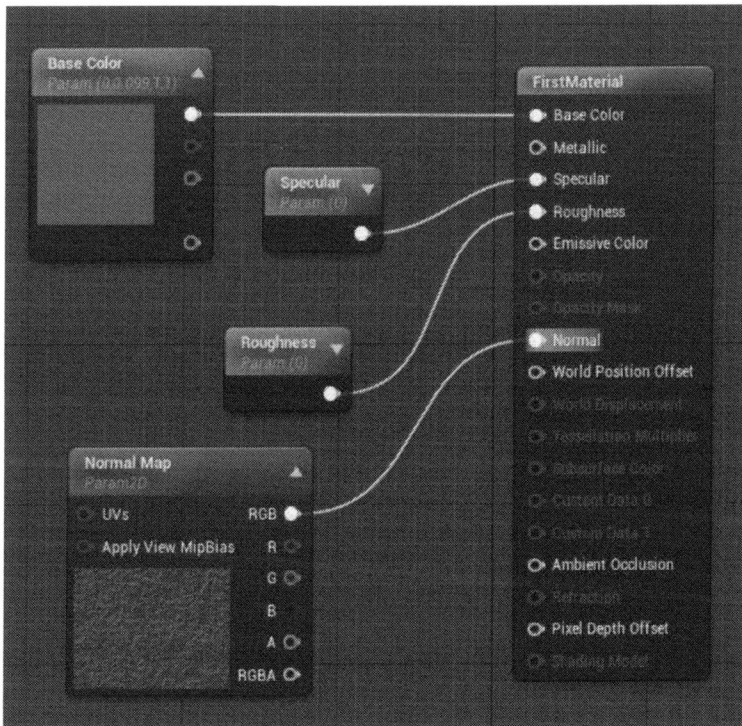

Figure 3.31: Adding a Specular Parameter to FirstMaterial

3. Click **Apply**.

4. Open each of the three material instances we created and now notice that the *Specular* property is there and can be altered. Set a new value for *Specular* by checking the check box and entering a value (or click and drag the number bar left or right to get a sliding-scale effect) and notice the material's specular properties change.

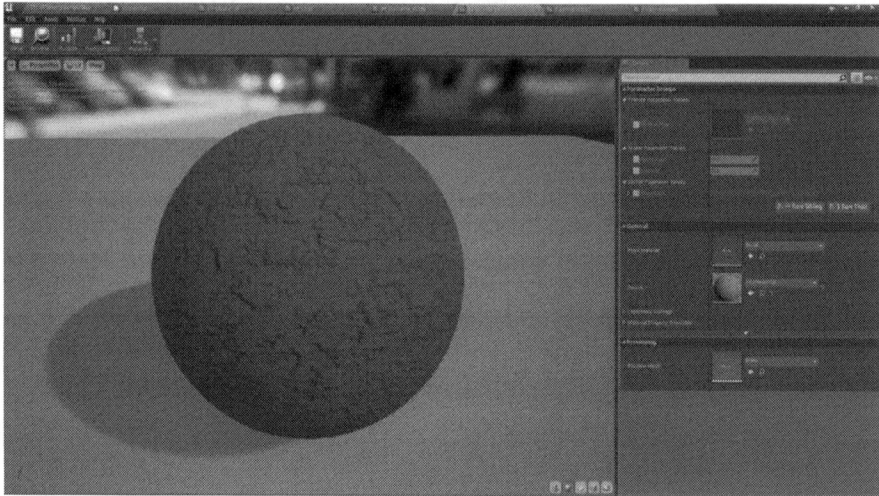

Figure 3.32: Material Instance with Parameters

This is an example of the power of using material instances. Any changes made to the parent material propagate to the children. This way, all instances that share a common parent can have new properties added to them simply by adding them to the parent material.

Material instances are also powerful for another reason. Their parameter values can be changed at runtime. This means you can change the appearance of a material instance during the game.

Now that we have experience creating materials and material instances, it's time to become familiar with the different types of lights available in Unreal Engine.

Working with Lights in Unreal Engine

Unreal Engine has several different types of lights with different properties. These include:

- **Point Light**
- **Spot Light**
- **Directional Light**
- **Sky Light**

Each type of light has a different effect on the game and is chosen for different reasons. We will now explore these light types and when to use them.

Point Light

The point light is a light that emanates from a single point in space. It radiates outward in all directions and has a single point of origin. We will now bring one into the world:

1. In the **Modes** panel, select **Lights**.

2. Drag a point light into the world.

3. Press *W* to enter translate mode and bring the light up to our three cubes we created previously. As you move the point light along the surface of the cubes, notice the shadows created by the normal maps.

Figure 3.33: A Point Light

In the **Details** panel for the point light, under the **Light** section, there are several properties for the light that can be altered. We will cover the main ones here:

- **Intensity**: sets the luminous intensity in units of candelas.

- **Light Color**: sets the color with an R, G, B component color value. You can click on the color ribbon to open the **Color Picker**.

- **Attenuation Radius**: This property bounds the light's visible influence. This radius is represented by a sphere which surrounds the light and can be seen when the light is selected. The larger the attenuation radius of a light, the more expensive it becomes to render.

- **Cast Shadows**: disabling this turns off shadows for the light, saving on performance.

Figure 3.34: The Attenuation Radius of a Point Light

Light Mobility

With the point light selected, notice in the **Transform** section of the **Details** panel that there is a *Mobility* property. This property can be one of three different options:

- **Static**: Static lights cannot move or change in the game.

- **Stationary**: Stationary lights cannot move in the game. They can change their intensity and color in the game, however.

- **Movable**: Movable lights can have their position, color, and intensity change in the game. This is the most computationally expensive setting for a light's mobility and should be used sparingly.

If a light doesn't need to be changed in game, setting its *Mobility* to *Static* will optimize performance. Light bulbs in the ceiling of a room in a building are typical candidates for a static point light. A candle sitting on a table may pulse and fade in intensity and thus a stationary light would be appropriate, because it doesn't need to move but it needs to change its intensity. A flashlight carried by a Character will require a movable light because it is being carried around in the level and it will be expected by the player that the light will dynamically cast shadows as it hits various items in the world.

As we have seen, we can change properties to customize the light source. Point lights are good for adding light to an area in your scene, but if you want the light to be more directional, other types of lights exist. We will now examine the spot light.

Spot Light

The spot light, in contrast to the point light, is directional. It can be oriented to point in a particular direction and its light takes the form of a cone. Outside this cone, the light has no influence.

Spot Lights actually have two cones which dictate the quality of the light emanated from them. These are the **Inner Cone** and the **Outer Cone**, respectively. The light from a spot light shines at maximum intensity on surfaces which lie inside the inner cone. The light intensity fades out towards the outer cone.

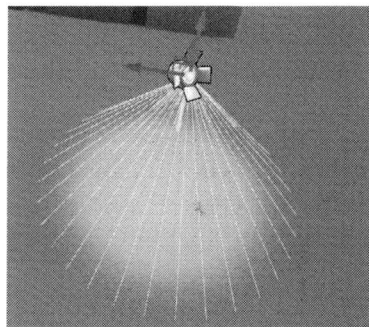

Figure 3.35: Light Fading from the Inner Cone to the Outer Cone

Figure 3.36: Increased Inner Cone Angle on a Spot Light

Bringing the *Inner Cone Radius* close to the *Outer Cone Radius* results in a harder edge on the light emanated from a spot light.

The spot light is also affected by the properties mentioned which affect point lights.

For some levels, you will want to have light that behaves more like the sun. This is where directional lights come into play.

Directional Light

The directional light is designed to simulate sunlight. The *First Person Example Map* already has a directional light in it by default. You can find it in the **World Outliner** under the **Lighting Folder**. It is named *Light Source*.

Although you can select a directional light and move it around in the level, this will not alter its effects on the world. The light emanates in a particular direction and does not have a definite source location. You can, however, alter its orientation. By selecting *Light Source* in the **World Outliner** and focusing on the light with the *F* key, you can rotate the directional light object with Rotation Mode by hitting the *E* key.

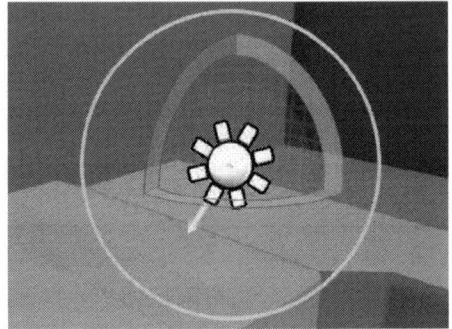

Figure 3.37: Changing the Orientation of a Directional Light

Rotating the directional light has the effect of changing the sun's position in the sky. Notice the shadows shift as you change the angles of the *X, Y,* and *Z* components of the directional light's *Rotation* property.

In addition to directional light, you can also influence the light of the scene based on the distant parts of your level using a sky light.

Sky Light

The sky light uses distant parts of the scene and uses that information to apply additional lighting to the level. Whether your level has mountains in the distance or rolling green hills, the sky light will use this information to influence the appearance of the map.

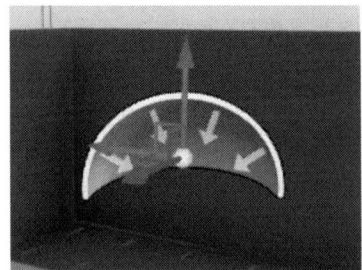

Figure 3.38: The Icon for a Sky Light

By default, the sky light is designed to construct the light from information captured from the scene. You can instead choose to use a **cube map**, an image designated to provide the lighting information used by the sky light.

We now have an understanding of the main types of lights used in Unreal Engine. A typical level has a directional light if it's in an outdoor setting. A sky light is also added to give additional lighting information to make the scene feel more realistic. Spot lights and point lights are added to scenes to illuminate the areas depending on the unique needs of the scene. A lamp may require a point light or a spot light to appear realistic and cast shadows by nearby objects.

It is important to understand the different light types and when to use them so that you can illuminate the level properly and draw the player's attention to the most important aspect of the game. You can come back to this section if you are unsure how to use lights in the different parts of the game while you are developing.

Summary

We have learned about materials and how to create them and apply them to meshes in our game. We have learned about material instances and how they can be utilized to save development time by reusing properties of a parent material on numerous instances of that material. We have created parameters that we can change on our individual material instances. We have also seen that adding properties to the parent material affects each instance, giving us the power to alter all of the instances which share a common parent. We have also looked at the main types of lights used in Unreal Engine and how to alter their properties. We have discussed the situations in which it is appropriate for using each type of light. Finally, we have discussed light mobility and how the various types of mobility affect the performance of the game.

We are now familiar with some of the visual aspects of Unreal Engine. This book, however, will be focusing on gameplay programming by utilizing the industry standard programming language for game performance: C++. In order for us to leverage the incredible power of Unreal Engine to create high fidelity video games, we must understand how to use this programming language. Get ready to take a deep dive straight into the world's most powerful programming language

Chapter 4 –C++ Programming Basics

In order to program games in Unreal Engine using C++, you must first learn the C++ programming language. While the C++ language is deep and rich with features, libraries and toolkits, the basics of the language are relatively simple. You must get the basics down before you can hope to understand the world of Unreal Engine C++, because the engine takes advantage of the features that make C++ known for its reliability and performance. A tradition for learning your first programming language involves creating your first program in which you learn how to do the most basic thing possible: print text to the screen. It has been the tradition that the first message a new programmer print to the screen is "Hello World!" We will follow this tradition.

In this chapter we will cover the following topics:

- Creating Your First Visual Studio Project

- Using Variables and Data Types

- Coding with Functions

- Using Macros and Symbols

- Working with Classes

- Inheritance

- Pointers

- Structs and Enums

- Flow Control

- Using Casting When Working With Objects

- Working with Templates

- Header Files

Technical Requirements

For this chapter, you will need a computer capable of running Microsoft Visual Studio (or Xcode, if you're using a Mac). At the time of writing this book, the hardware requirements for Visual Studio 2019 are:

- 1.8 GHz or faster processor. Quad-core or better recommended.

- 2 GB of RAM; 8 GB of RAM recommended.

- Hard disk space: Minimum of 800MB up to 210 GB of available space, depending on features installed; typical installations require 20-50 GB of free space.

- Hard disk speed: to improve performance, install Windows and Visual Studio on a solid state drive (SSD).

- Video card that supports a minimum display resolution of 720p (1280 by 720); Visual Studio will work best at a resolution of WXGA (1366 by 768) or higher.

You will need to download Microsoft Visual Studio (or Xcode, if you're using a Mac) to write, compile, run, and test your code.

Creating Your First Visual Studio Project

We will start by creating a project in Visual Studio. Make sure you have downloaded Visual Studio (or if you are using a Mac, Xcode). Open Visual Studio. You will be able to create a new project by going to *File -> New -> Project*. Call this project *HelloWorld*. To the right-hand side of the screen, you will see the **Solution Explorer**:

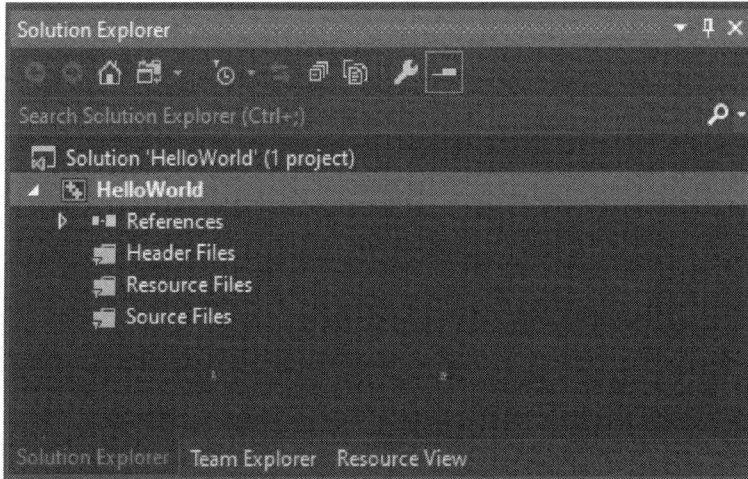

Figure 4.1: The Solution Explorer

Here, you will see the **source files** as you add them to the project. A source file is a file in which you will write code for your program. We will add our first source file to this project.

1. Right-click on *HelloWorld* in the **Solution Explorer**.

2. Select *Add -> New Item*.

3. Select *C++ File (.cpp)* and name the file *HelloWorldSource.cpp*.

4. Click *Add*.

The *HelloWorldSource.cpp* file will open and there will be a blue tab at the top left of the screen. You will also see your new source file in the **Solution Explorer** in the subfolder **Source Files**.

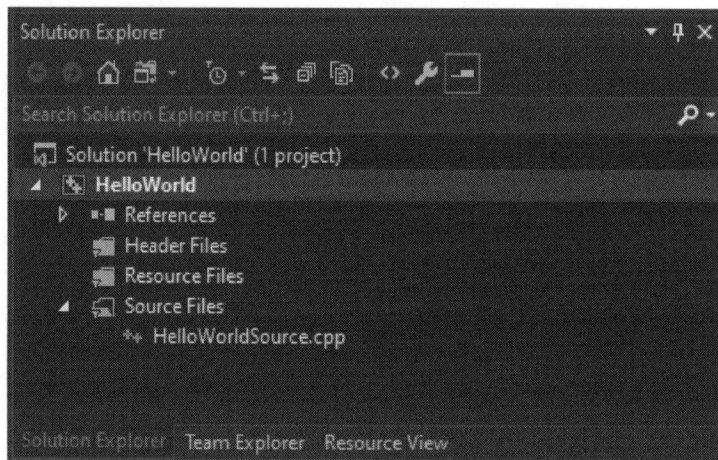

Figure 4.2: HelloWorldSource.cpp Added to Source Files

Notice that *HelloWorldSource.cpp* is empty. We're going to fix that by filling it with our first program!

Writing Your First Program

Your first program will be simple–it will print "Hello World!" to the screen. In order to do this, we will need to make use of some code that already exists. C++ comes with some code libraries built into the language. The aggregate of these built-in libraries is collectively called the C++ Standard Library. We will make use of some features of the C++ Standard Library to print text to the screen. In *HelloWorldSource.cpp*, add the following code.

```cpp
#include <iostream>
using namespace std;

int main()
{
    cout << "Hello World!\n";
    system("pause");

}
```

There are several things going on with this code. We will visit each item, one at a time.

The first line `#include <iostream>` is known as a **preprocessor directive.** The preprocessor is a program that scans over the code before compilation. When it encounters preprocessor directives, it performs certain actions depending on the type of directive. The `#include` directive tells the preprocessor to include another file called a **header** into this file. Header files contain code that is meant to be contained in other files. The header file we are including is called `iostream`. The `iostream` file is part of the C++ Standard Library and includes code that allows users to input and output streams of data. Since we wish to print text to the screen, we need to make use of `iostream` in order to output a stream of data in the form of text to the screen.

The next line `using namespace std;` makes use of the `using` keyword. This particular use of the `using` keyword allows us to use something called a **namespace.** A namespace can be thought of as a domain where certain names, or **identifiers**, are defined in code. In our case, we are interested in the identifier `cout`. The `cout` identifier exists in the `iostream` header file, inside the `std` namespace. Here, std is an abbreviation for "standard," as in Standard Library. Because `cout` exists within the `std` namespace, it will not be recognized by the compiler unless we specify that we are using that namespace.

After the second line, we have a line of white space. White space is ignored by the compiler and we can have as much of it in our code as we like.

Next, we have the **main function.** All C++ programs must have a main function. Without one, there would not be a designated starting point for when the program is run. When the program is run, lines of code are executed, one by one, starting with the first line inside of the main function's **function body**, designated by the opening and closing curly braces `{ }`. Once the end of the main function is reached, the program terminates. We will learn more about functions shortly, but for now, our description of them will be brief. All functions must return a value. The main function is no exception. Since all values in C++ have a data type, we must designate the type for the return value of each function we create. We have no intention of using the value returned by the main function, since the program will terminate when the end of the function is reached, and its return value is returned. Thus the arbitrary type `int` (the integer variable type) is designated to be main's return type.

All that's left to explain in the above code snippet are the two lines inside the body of the main function. The first of these,

```
cout << "Hello World!\n";
```

does the actual work of printing text to the screen. The `cout` identifier takes a string of characters and feeds them to an output data stream by making use of the $<<$ operator. In our case, the string of characters is `"Hello World!\n"`. These characters will be printed to the screen once the program is run, except for `\n`. This strange addition to the end of the string is called an **escape sequence**. When sending a string of characters to the output stream, escape sequences are recognized and trigger certain modifications to the string. The `\n` escape sequence is known as the **newline character**. Even though it looks like two characters, `\n` is considered a single character. It results in the text after it being printed on the next line, similarly to hitting the *RETURN* key on the keyboard when writing text in a word processor.

The last line inside the main function body is `system("pause");`. This command results in the program actually stopping at this line. Without it, the main function would reach its end after the `cout << "Hello World!\n";` line. Once the end of the main function is reached, the program terminates. This would not give us much time to see the fruits of our labor! Pausing the program allows us to see the text we printed to the screen. If you are using a Mac, `system("pause")` will not work. Instead, you can use `cin.get()`.

The last detail you probably noticed in this program is the usage of the semicolon. In the C++ language, the semicolon behaves like a period does in the English language. It tells the compiler that the current line of code is complete and any text that follows belongs to the next line. Lines of code are executed one at a time, so the compiler must know when one line ends and the next line begins. Lines of code are known as **statements** and perform some sort of action. Statements often contain **expressions**, pieces of code that specify an operation. The string of characters `"Hello World!\n"` is an expression, and the entire line `cout << "Hello World!\n";` is a statement.

We have seen that there is quite a lot involved in just a small amount of C++ code. Now that we have deconstructed our first program, it's time to see what happens when we actually compile and run it!

Compiling and Running Your Code

We have mentioned the compiler several times. But what exactly is the compiler? Why do we even need to compile our code, and what does it even mean to "compile" code?

C++ code, as cryptic as it may seem to a non-programmer, is actually closer to written English than machine language. It contains human-like words so that humans (at least the superior ones who can program) can read it. However, a machine cannot read C++ code. For this reason, C++ is called a **high-level programming language.** It is "high level" because it is closer to something humans can understand than machine language, which is said to be "low level." A **compiler** is a program that steps through each line of your code and converts it from *high level* to *low level* code.

There are actually several steps your code goes through before it is ready to be run. We have already mentioned the preprocessor, which scans the code for preprocessor directives and includes header files where it is told to do so. Compilation happens after this. Another program called a **linker** links the resulting code with other, pre-compiled code that may be needed (such as code from the standard library). This is a simplified explanation of the compilation process but for now it will suffice.

We can compile our program by going to **Build** in the menu bar, then selecting **Build Solution** (hotkey *CTRL + SHIFT + B*) or right-clicking on our solution name in the **Solution Explorer** and selecting **Build**.

Once we build the solution, the output window will show some results of the build process. If any mistakes were caught by the compiler, there will be errors in this window. If none were found, you should see something like this:

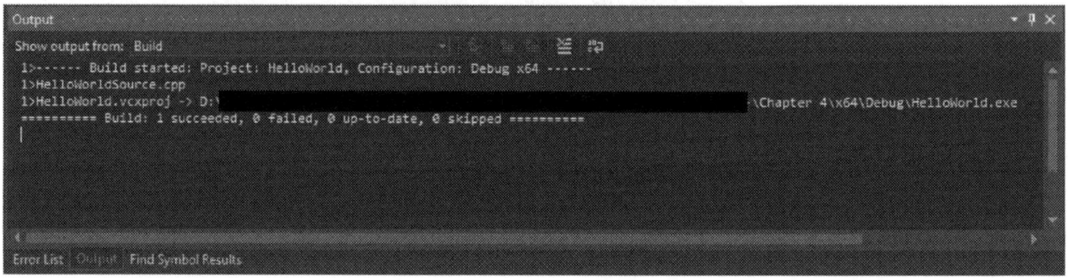

Figure 4.3: The Output Window

Once the project is compiled, we can now run our program! We can do so by going to **Debug** on the menu bar and selecting **Start Without Debugging** (hotkey *CTRL + F5*). Doing so will result in a console window popping up which should look like the following:

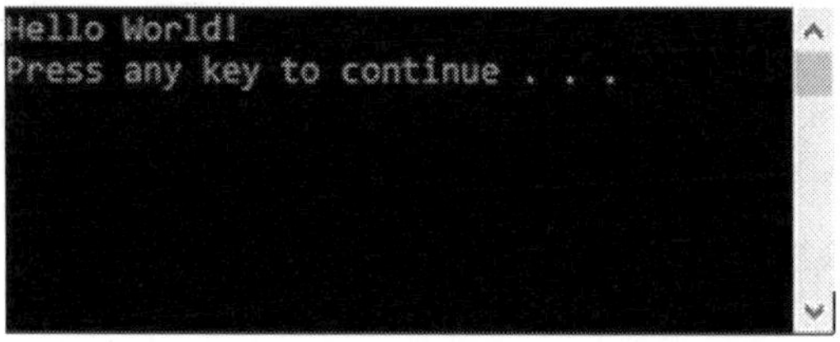

Figure 4.4: Your First Program – Hello World!

Congratulations! You are now officially a C++ programmer. Don't start celebrating just yet. You still have a way to go. You now understand how to create a Visual Studio project, add a source file to it, create a main function, include a header file, specify a namespace, print text to the screen using the cout command from the Standard Library, add a new line to your text with the \n escape sequence, pause the program using system("pause"), and run your program. Phew, that's a lot for your first lesson! The first lesson is always the hardest because all of these elements must come together to perform a task like printing text to the screen. From here on out though, lessons can come in smaller, bite-sized chunks.

Now that we've got our first program under our belts, let's visit some of the basics of programming. We'll start by revisiting the concept of data types, and learn their significance in C++, as well as how variables must specify the data type for the data they are designed to contain.

Using Variables and Data Types

All data in C++ has its own type. The type specifies the size of the data and how it is stored. C++ contains **base data types**, sometimes referred to as **primitive data types**, which are the basis for all constructs in the C++ programming language. Base data types and their associated sizes are as follows:

- Integer (4 bytes), keyword: `int`

- Character (1 byte) , keyword: `char`

- Boolean (1 byte) , keyword: `bool`

- Floating Point (4 bytes) , keyword: `float`

- Double Floating Point (8 bytes) , keyword: `double`

- Valueless or Void (no size) , keyword: `void`

- Wide Character (2 or 4 bytes) , keyword: `wchar_t`

These types are built into the C++ programming language. Each type has an associated size, which dictates how much memory can be used to store it. These sizes can vary depending on the system, but the above values are common. Memory exists in the form of **bits**. Each bit can hold one of two values: 0 or 1. Bits are grouped together into **bytes**. Eight bits make up one byte. Data of a particular type can be stored in a

variable. When a variable is created, its type must be declared. Once declared, the variable must hold only data of the specified type. A variable of the integer type cannot hold a value of the floating point type.

Declaring a variable is as simple as stating its data type, followed by the name of the variable. The data types are represented with their corresponding keywords in C++. Keywords for the above data types are listed next to their names and data sizes in the preceding bullet list.

Note on Variable Names and Keywords

You must not use keywords in C++ for variable names. If you type out a word in Visual Studio and it appears blue, it is a keyword. In addition, variable names must consist of letters, numbers, and underscores, and cannot begin with a number.

We can declare new variables of all the previously mentioned types (except for void, which is the lack of a value) just above the main function as follows. Add the following lines just above the main function:

```
int i;
char c;
bool b;
float f;
double d;
wchar_t w;
```

The above lines merely declare variables of the specified types. This means memory is set aside for their values according to the sizes reserved for their specified types. Because we did not assign values to these variables, they are automatically filled in with **default values**. We can see the values stored in each of our variables by printing them to the screen via the cout command. Add the following lines inside the main function, just under cout << "Hello World!\n";:

```
cout << i << endl;
cout << c << endl;
cout << b << endl;
cout << f << endl;
```

```
cout << d << endl;
cout << w << endl;
```

The endl command is also from iostream and exists in the std namespace. It results in a new line, similar to the \n character. Run the code above. You should see an output like the following:

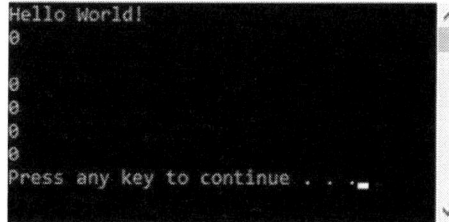

Figure 4.5: Printing the Default Values for our Variables

As you can see, the default values are 0 for each of the types except for c, which gets an empty value.

Values are assigned to variables via the **assignment operator**, which is the = sign. Assigning a value to a variable can be done upon declaration (on the same line as the variable declaration) or on a line after the declaration. Let's change the code in our source file to the following:

```
#include <iostream>
using namespace std;

int i = 1;
char c = 'C';
bool b;
float f;
double d;
wchar_t w;

int main()
{
        cout << "Hello World!\n";

        b = true;
```

```
f = 3.14;
d = 2.71828;
w = 'W';

i = 2;

cout << i << endl;
cout << c << endl;
cout << b << endl;
cout << f << endl;
cout << d << endl;
wcout << w << endl;

system("pause");
}
```

Notice that we assign values to the variables i and c on the lines in which they are declared. We gave values to the variables b, f, d, and w inside the main function. Look closely at the line following our definition of w. We overwrote the value of i! This is legal in C++. A variable which already has a value can be overwritten by simply using the assignment operator to give it a new value.

Note on Double vs. Single Quotes

The value we assigned to the character variable w is 'W' in single quotes. Careful not to use double quotes! Double quotes denote a string of characters, and single quotes denotes a single character.

Running the above code produces the following result:

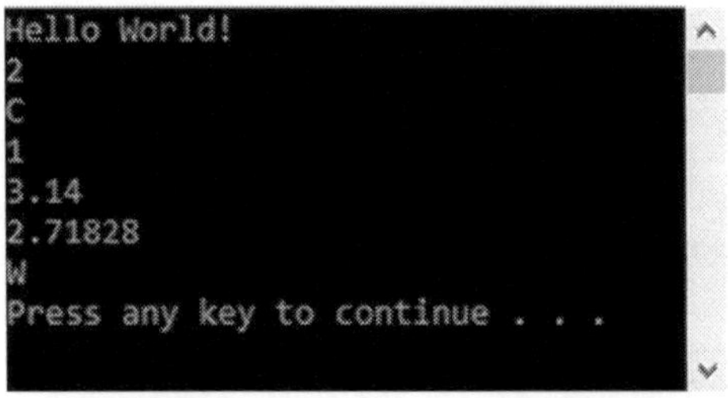

```
Hello World!
2
c
1
3.14
2.71828
W
Press any key to continue . . .
```

Figure 4.6: Printing the Values Assigned to our Variables

Notice that the value for `i` is 2, the value with which we overwrote it inside the main function. Also notice that we used the command `wcout` for `w` rather than `cout` because `w` is a variable of type `wchar_t`, or a wide character. Wide characters can accommodate for text with a larger encoding. Different forms of encoding allow for a larger selection of characters. For more information, search online for information on Character Encoding in your favorite search engine. Because `cout` is not designed to output wide characters, we must use `wcout`, which is designed to get the job done.

You may have also noticed that the value printed for `b` is 1. `cout` is designed to print a 1 for a Boolean if its value is `true` and a 0 if its value is `false`.

If you are the one to experiment, you may have attempted to assign a value to one of our new variables outside the main function, but not on the same line in which the variable was declared. If you did, you would have been met with a nice, friendly compilation error. This is because lines of code outside the main function (or any other function) are not actually run. Declaring variables is possible outside the main function and will exist globally (they will be accessible from the main function) and thus are called **global variables**, however if you wish to execute lines of code, they must be run, and code execution begins with the main function.

We now know how to create variables. We have seen that the data type for a variable must be declared upon the variable's creation. We have also seen that we can initialize a variable with a value as we create it (on the same line) with the assignment operator, or we can assign a value to it later. We have learned that a variable's value can be overwritten with a new value. Finally, we learned that lines of code outside the main function aren't actually run and attempting to overwrite the value of a variable outside the main function results in a compilation error.

Now that we're gotten our first taste of variable creation, it's time to take this journey one step further and dive into functions.

Coding with Functions

A function is a group of statements that execute in order to fulfill a specific task. Functions take zero or more parameters as input and return a single output value. Because values in C++ have data types, this return value must be specified when the function is **declared** or created. A function's name, parameters, and output type comprise its **signature**. Like variables, functions can be defined at the same location where they are declared, or they can be defined at another location.

Let's declare a new function. Just above the main function, add:

```
void Hello()
{
     cout << "Hello World!\n";

}
```

And replace the line `cout << "Hello World!\n";` with:

```
Hello();
```

Running this program produces the same exact output as before. The only difference is that we are using the `Hello` function to print text to the screen, rather than using `cout` directly. Executing a function with its name followed by `()` is referred to as **calling** the function.

Our function `Hello` does not return a value, so we gave it a `void` return type. Functions can accept values as input (we call these **parameters**) and return values as output. Let's create a function that takes input parameter values and returns an output value.

For one of our input values, let's make use of a **compound** data type–a data type made of one or more base data types. The C++ Standard Library contains a type called `string`. This type can store a string of characters such as "Hello World!" as opposed to the char and `wchar_t` types, which can only store a single character. A string such as "Hello World!" is known as a **string literal**–a series of characters treated as a single, constant value. The Standard Library's `string` type is a custom data type that provides us with the ability to store a string literal in a variable.

To be able to use the Standard Library's `string` type, we must include the `string` header file. Just under `#include <iostream>` add:

```
#include <string>
```

And just below the definition for the `Hello` function, let's create our new function:

```
string OutputData(string message, int _i, char _c, bool _b,
float _f, double _d, wchar_t _w);
```

Just to demonstrate that functions can be defined separately from their declaration, we will add the function definition just below (and outside) the main function. It may seem strange that this works, but if a function is declared without a definition, as long as it's defined somewhere else in the source file, the compiler will find it and match it with the declaration as long as the function signatures are the same. Just below the main function, add:

```
string OutputData(string message, int _i, char _c, bool
_b, float _f, double _d, wchar_t _w)
{
    cout << _i << endl;
    cout << _c << endl;
    cout << _b << endl;
    cout << _f << endl;
    cout << _d << endl;
    wcout << _w << endl;
    cout << message << endl;

    return message;
}
```

This function takes a `string`, an `int`, a `char`, a `bool`, a `float`, a `double`, and a `wchar_t` as input and returns a `string` as output. It also prints all of these input parameters to the screen before returning `message`, the input string **passed** (fed in as input) in. Notice we named our parameters starting with underscores, except for the string parameter. This is so they are not confused with the global variables we created outside the main function.

We can now replace all of the `cout` calls in our main function with just one call to the `OutputData` function. We can also take advantage of its return value by storing it in a variable. The main function should now look like this:

```
int main()
{
    Hello();

    b = true;
    f = 3.14;
    d = 2.71828;
```

```
w = 'W';

i = 2;

string retVal = OutputData ("Hello!", 42, 'B', false,
3.14, 4597.76, '*');

cout << "The value of retVal is: " << retVal << endl;

system ("pause");
}
```

We create a `string` variable called `retVal` (for return value) and assign it the value returned by the function `OutputData`. The flow of execution works from the right to the left – data is passed into the function's parentheses as a comma-separated list, and the program immediately jumps into the body of the function where it executes the lines of code there, one by one, until the function body reaches its end (the closing curly brace) and returns the value stored in `message`. This value is then assigned to the variable `retVal` via the use of the assignment operator, `=`. After the function prints all of the values passed in to the screen, we then use `cout` to print out the value stored in `retVal`, which will be the same value passed into `OutputData`. The result should appear as follows:

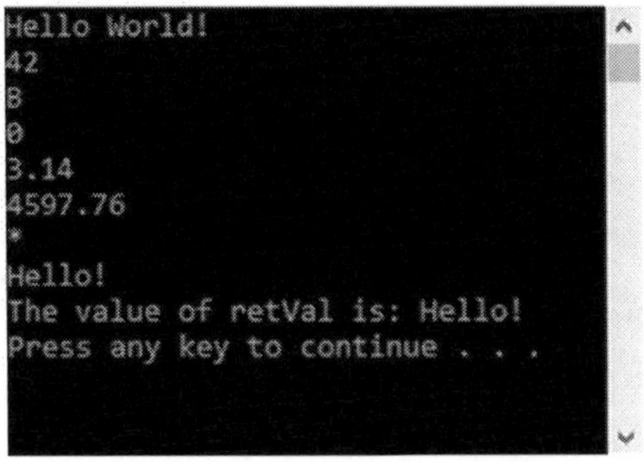

Figure 4.7: Results after creating the OutputData function

The call to `Hello` results in printing "Hello World!" to the screen. Inside the main function, in our call to the `OutputData` function, we passed in "Hello!", 42, 'B', false, 3.14, 4597.76, and '*'. Our function body dictated that the values be printed to the screen in order except for the `string` parameter `message`, which is passed in first and printed last. Finally, our function reaches its end with the return statement, returning the value stored in `message`. The flow of control jumps back to the `main` function, where the value returned from `OutputData` is assigned to `retVal`. We then use `cout` to print this value to the screen.

All functions must return a value. You may be wondering why not all functions contain a `return` statement. The reason for this is that functions which are of `void` return type don't require a `return` statement, although they can have them, as in the following line:

```
return;
```

Functions which return a non-`void` type must return a value compatible with that type. The only exception is the main function, in which you do not need to include a `return` statement. In older versions of C++, a return value of 0 was used, that is, the last line in the main function before its closing curly brace was:

```
return 0;
```

This can still be added to the main function, however if it is not added, it will be added for you automatically upon compilation.

One thing to consider with functions is that they create local copies of their input parameters. This means if you have a variable that exists outside the function, you cannot alter it by passing it into a function and expect the variable itself to be altered. This is due to the fact that all operations performed on the parameter inside the function are performed on the copy, and not the original variable. To be able to alter the actual variable, we must pass it in by **reference**.

Passing variables by reference

To alter a variable which exists outside a function, we must pass it in by reference. Observe the following program:

```
#include <iostream>
using namespace std;

void AddOne(int A)
{
```

```
        A = A + 1;
}

int main()
{
        int a = 1;
        cout << a << endl;
        AddOne(a);
        cout << a << endl;

        system("pause");

}
```

The output for the above is:

Figure 4.8: Attempt to Change External Variable

This is because we passed in the input parameter **by value**. The value 1 was copied into the local function parameter A and the addition of 1 was performed on the copy. Now, if we change the function signature to the following:

```
void AddOne(int& A)
```

We are passing in the variable A **by reference**. With this simple change, the output to the above program is:

Figure 4.9: Passing a Variable by Reference

As you can see, passing a variable in by reference makes the function more powerful. This also uses less memory because an additional variable doesn't need to be created for the copy.

References can be created outside of functions as well. For example, change the code in the main function to:

```
int a = 1;
int& a_ref = a;
cout << a << endl;
AddOne(a_ref);

cout << a << endl;
```

This results in the same output as that above, namely the value of a is altered from 1 to 2. This is because a_ref is a reference to a. References are aliases to other variables, and changing the reference changes the original variable, so be cautious of this when creating references.

We have now seen the power of functions. We have discovered that functions have an optional input parameter list and a non-optional return type, both of which must be specified upon a function's declaration. We've learned that the function's name, along with its parameter list and output type constitute its signature. We have seen that a function can be declared and defined all at once, or the definition can take place elsewhere in the code outside the main function. We then created a function that takes multiple input parameters and returns a string data type, a type included in the C++ Standard Library and available once the string header file is included. We also saw that we can pass variables into functions by reference to be able to actually change the value of the variable itself and avoid making a copy internal to the function. We also saw that references can be created outside of functions to have a variable which is an alias for another variable, and that changing the reference changes the original. Now that we've got the basics of functions down, we are ready to continue on to other features of the C++ language.

Using Macros and Symbols

Macros and symbols are a relic from the C programming language. There would be times where a programmer wanted a variable, but didn't want to be able to change (overwrite) its value. In other words, it was desired that the variable be **constant**. With modern C++, we have the const keyword:

```
const int i = 42;
```

The above statement declares a variable of type `const int` and assigns it a value of 42. A variable marked `const` cannot be changed. For this reason, it must be initialized with a value as soon as it's created (otherwise it would never be assigned a value).

Before `const` existed, programmers would define symbols in the following manner:

```
#define MY_CONSTANT 95
```

Anywhere in the code where `MY_CONSTANT` was used, the preprocessor would replace it with the value 95. Constants would typically be givens names in all caps to make it evident that they were constant when looking at code.

Occasionally you will encounter symbols such as these in C++ code. If curious, you can hover your mouse button over them and Visual Studio's **Intellisense** will show you its value. Intellisense is a feature of Visual Studio that makes life easier for programmers by providing features such as a tooltip popup like this, as well as auto-complete (offering to complete lines of code before you're done typing them).

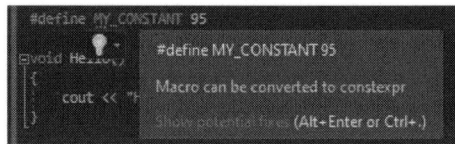

Figure 4.10: Intellisense Showing the Value of MY_CONSTANT

These symbols are sometimes referred to as **macros**. Macros can behave like functions as well, in that they can take inputs. Consider the following code:

```
#include <iostream>
using namespace std;

#define CUBE(b) b*b*b

int main()
{
    cout << CUBE(2) << endl;

    system("pause");
}
```

In the above code, we define the macro CUBE to multiply the input b by itself 3 times. The resulting output of the above code is:

Figure 4.11: Result of Using the CUBE Macro

It is generally recommended that you to use functions rather than macros. The reasons for this are that with macros, there is no type checking, whereas with functions, there is. This means that if you pass in an **argument** (the value passed into a function) which is not of the type designated for the input, a compilation error will result. Another reason to prefer functions over macros is that you can sometimes get unexpected results with macros. This is because macros are **preprocessed** whereas functions are **compiled.** In the above code, the preprocessor literally takes CUBE(2) and replaces it with 2*2*2 which results in the value 8 being printed to the screen. But suppose instead of CUBE(2) we use CUBE(1 + 1). In this case, the preprocessor replaces CUBE(1 + 1) with 1 + 1*1 + 1*1 + 1. Due to the order of operations (multiplication is carried out first, then addition) the resulting output is:

Figure 4.12: Erroneous Output from the CUBE Macro

This is clearly not the answer expected. The code was designed to perform a computation, yet in some cases the output is incorrect. This is known as a **bug**. Bugs like this can be prevented by using functions instead of macros for this type of computation. Consider the following function instead:

```
#include <iostream>
using namespace std;

float Cube(float f)
{
    return f * f * f;
```

```
}

int main()
{
      cout << Cube(1.f + 1.f) << endl;

      system("pause");
}
```

The output for the above code is:

Figure 4.13: Result from the Cube Function

The reason we get the correct output is because at runtime, the flow of execution jumps into the function, where the input parameter variable `f` is assigned the result of the addition `1.f + 1.f` (the f ensures that the value is a `float` and not a different data type). Once inside the function, `f` has the value 2 and the computation can be carried out correctly.

Notes on Type Conversion

It was ensured that the expression passed into the Cube function, `1.f + 1.f`, was a `float` value. Appending an `f` or a `d` after the decimal on a value designates it to be of `float` and `double` type, respectively. If an integer or a `double` were passed into the Cube function, the value would be *automatically converted* into a `float`. This phenomenon, known as **implicit type conversion**, happens automatically and without warning, so it's important to understand when it happens. If a `float` or `double` is converted to an `int`, numbers to the right of the decimal are dropped – resulting in the potential loss of data. In this case, the `float` or `double` is said to be **demoted** to an int. If an `int` is converted to a `float` or `double`, it is said to be **promoted**. Data can be lost in general when a larger type is converted to a smaller type (i.e. `double` to `float`, etc.) because the smaller type has less memory available to hold the information, so be aware of implicit type conversions.

We have learned about macros and symbols, and how they are a legacy from the C programming language and thus can still be used. We also learned that modern C++ contains the `const` keyword, which allows us to create constant variables which can never be changed. We learned that macros can behave similarly to functions in that they can take inputs. For small, simple operations, they can be more efficient than functions, since the preprocessor replaces each instance of them in code with their defined functionality. This prevents the flow of control from jumping out of the current location and into another (as happens with functions). We discussed how macros do not do type checking, whereas functions do. We discussed an example of how macros can produce unexpected (and incorrect) results, providing us with a good reason to use them with caution. Now that we have a solid understanding of macros and symbols, we are ready to tackle one of the most powerful features of the C++ language: classes.

Working with Classes

Classes are user-defined data types. We have already used a class – the Standard Library's `string` class. Classes can contain variables and functions. Since creating a class is equivalent to creating a new data type, classes can contain variables which are themselves other classes. Declaring a new class involves the use of the class keyword, as in the following program:

```cpp
#include <iostream>
#include <string>
using namespace std;

class Animal
{
public:
    string name;
    float hunger;
    void Call()
    {
        cout << name << " has a hunger value of " <<
hunger << endl;
    }
};
```

```
int main()
{
    Animal creature;
    creature.name = "Fido";
    creature.hunger = 10.f;
    creature.Call();

    system("pause");
}
```

The above code declares a new class called `Animal`. This data type contains variables, often referred to as **members** or **member variables** and a function. When a class contains functions, they are often referred to as **methods**.

Creating the class `Animal` is not the same as declaring a variable of the `Animal` data type. It is simply defining what the `Animal` class will look like once we actually create one, which we do inside the main function. We can access member variables and functions with the dot (.) operator.

You might have noticed the use of the `public` keyword. This is called an **access modifier** and it designates all code beneath it in the class to be publically accessible. This means it can be accessed from outside of the class, like we did in the main function by accessing the class's contents via the dot operator. **Private access** refers to when a class accesses its own member variables and methods from within the class, such as is done in the `Call` function. There is a third, less often used access modifier: `protected`. Variables and functions in a `protected` section can be accessed from within their own class, as well as from within classes derived from them. This is an oversimplification and you can learn more details about access modifiers online with a quick search. For this book, the use of `public` and `private` will suffice.

To protect variables so that they cannot be tampered with from outside the class, they can be placed in a `private` section. Then to alter those variables, functions can be created to access and modify them. To protect data in this manner is called **encapsulation**. Observe the following modifications to the code:

```
#include <iostream>
#include <string>
using namespace std;
```

```cpp
class Animal
{
public:
      Animal();
      Animal(string _name, float _hunger);

      void Call()
      {
            cout << name << " has a hunger value of " <<
hunger << endl;
      }

      void SetName(string _name);
      void SetHunger(float _hunger);

private:
      string name;
      float hunger;
};

int main()
{
      Animal creature;
      creature.SetName("Fido");
      creature.SetHunger(10.f);
      creature.Call();

      Animal critter("Spot", 9.f);
      critter.Call();

      system("pause");
}

Animal::Animal()
{
      name = "Default Name";
}

Animal::Animal(string _name, float _hunger)
```

```
{
    name = _name;
    hunger = _hunger;
}

void Animal::SetName(string _name) { name = _name; }
void Animal::SetHunger(float _hunger) { hunger = _hunger; }
```

In the above code, we have changed several things. Look first at the `private` section. Beneath it, we have the member variables `name` and `hunger`. This protects them from outside access. If we were to attempt to access them from within the main function with the dot operator, we would be met with an error. Instead, we created two functions, `SetName` and `SetHunger`. Because they set the values for these variables, functions like these are referred to as **setters**. Likewise, functions designed to return the value of a class's members are referred to as **getters**.

We declared two setters, `SetName` and `SetHunger`. Notice that we didn't define them in the class body this time. In order to define a method outside the class body, you must **fully qualify** it with the class name and the **scope resolution** (`::`) operator. We did this in the final two lines of the program, below and outside the main function. Placing the function definitions down here allows us to better organize our code. Notice also that we placed the function body on the same line as the function name. The C++ compiler counts this compact form as valid and it is sometimes used to save space.

Undoubtedly you noticed the two new functions called `Animal`. Classes have a special type of function named after the class itself. This is called the **constructor**. These do not require you to choose a designated data type upon declaration. The purpose of the constructor is to initialize the variables with values and execute any other code you wish to run upon the construction of the object. The constructor exists for all classes, whether you define one or not. If you do not, a **default constructor** is created automatically and populates default values for the member variables. Notice that we created two versions of the constructor: one with no input parameters, and one with two input parameters. Declaring the same function more than once with different input parameters is known as **function overloading**. The consequence of having two overloads of the constructor is that new `Animal` objects can be constructed in different ways depending on which constructor is used to construct them. The first `Animal` we created, `creature`, was constructed using the first `Animal` constructor. We then used the setters we created to set values for its `name` and `hunger` variables.

The second `Animal` we created, `critter`, was constructed using the second `Animal` constructor, using parentheses on the identifier we gave the object, `critter`. Inside the parentheses, we passed in values which the second overload of the `Animal` constructor used to assign values to the `name` and `hunger` variables, respectively.

Note on Overloading Functions

In order to create overloads of a function, the functions must share the same name, but differ either in the value types of their inputs, or in the number of input parameters. Simply having different return types is not sufficient for overloading.

We have seen that we can create our own custom data types via the use of the `class` keyword. We learned that classes can contain member variables and methods, accessible via the dot operator, and that access modifiers control whether or not we can access those variables and functions from outside the class. We learned that encapsulation is the technique of protecting member variables in their own `private` sections in the class and that creating functions to get or set them controls the manner in which they are accessed. We learned that functions can be defined outside the class by fully qualifying the name via the scope resolution operator. We learned that all classes have a special function called the constructor which handles the initialization code upon the creation of new variables of the corresponding class type. We saw that functions, the constructor included, can be overloaded by creating multiple versions of the same function with different inputs. Finally, we saw that function bodies can be placed on the same line as the function name in order to save space.

Congratulations! You have just learned one of the most useful concepts in the C++ programming language. Because classes allow us to create **objects** of custom types, their use is often referred to as **object-oriented programming**, or OOP. Languages that have this feature are called object-oriented languages, and being able to take advantage of this feature is a major reason why they are used. However, we haven't yet seen all the reasons why OOP is so powerful! A major benefit of OOP is the ability of one class to inherit properties from another—a phenomenon known as **inheritance**. Now that we understand the basics of classes, it's time to learn how inheritance works.

Passing Variables and Functions Down with Inheritance

In object-oriented programming, inheritance involves deriving one class from another. The **base class**, or **parent class**, contains functions and variables, and the **derived class**, or **child class**, inherits those functions and variables. The child class can then behave as the parent class for any new classes derived from it. This results in what is commonly referred to as an **inheritance chain** or **inheritance hierarchy**. Deriving a child class from a base class is quite simple. Observe the following classes:

```cpp
#include <iostream>
#include <string>

class P
{
public:
      void P_F();
};

class C : public P
{
public:
      void C_F();
};

int main()
{
      P p;
      C c;

      p.P_F();
      c.P_F();
      c.C_F();

      system("pause");
}

void P::P_F() { std::cout << "P Function()" << std::endl; }
void C::C_F() { std::cout << "C Function()" << std::endl; }
```

We created a parent class P, which has a `public` function P_F, which prints "P `Function()`" to the screen. We then derived a child class from P, called C, which has a similar function of its own. When using `cout` and `endl`, we prefixed them with `std` and the scope resolution operator (`::`) since we didn't use the line `using namespace std;` this time. Qualifying them with the name of the namespace and the scope resolution operator ensures that they are recognized as belonging to that namespace and thus accessible.

Output for the above program is:

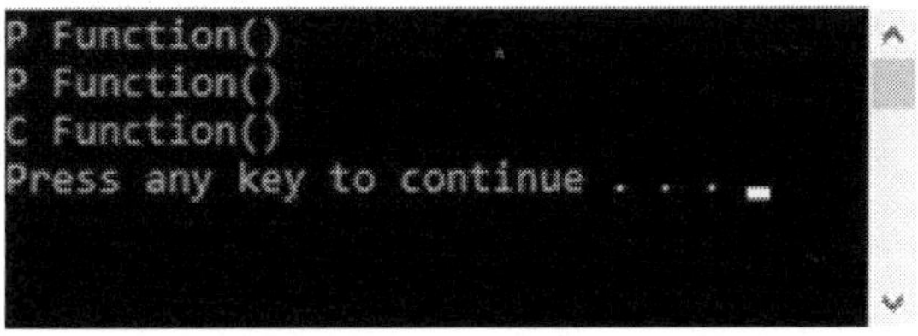

Figure 4.14: Parent and Child Classes in Action

As you can see, calling the parent function P_F from an object of the parent class P works as expected. We also see that calling the same function from the child class C also works, because C inherits the function from P. We then make a call to C_F, a function exclusive to C.

Suppose instead of C having its own function, we wish for C to have its own version of a function it inherited from P. This is called **function overriding** (not to be confused with function overloading) and is done by making the parent version of the function **virtual**. When a function is overridden, it is good practice to mark the function as an override as in the following example.

```
#include <iostream>
#include <string>

class P
{
public:
        P() { std::cout << "P()\n"; }
        P(std::string constructor_message) { std::cout <<
constructor_message << std::endl; }
```

```
        virtual void F(std::string message);
};

class C : public P
{
public:
        C() { std::cout << "C()\n"; }
        C(std::string constructor_message):
P(constructor_message) { }
        virtual void F(std::string message) override;
};

int main()
{
        std::cout << "Calling P() and C()\n\n";
        P p;
        C c;
        std::cout << std::endl;

        std::cout << "Calling overloads with strings:\n\n";
        P p_message("p_message");
        C c_message("c_message");
        std::cout << std::endl;

        std::cout << "Calling P.F() and C.F()\n\n";
        p.F("Calling F()");
        c.F("Calling F()");
        std::cout << std::endl;

        system("pause");
}

void P::F(std::string message) { std::cout << "P version:"
<< message << std::endl; }

void C::F(std::string message) { std::cout << "C version:"
<< message << std::endl; }
```

The output for the above function is:

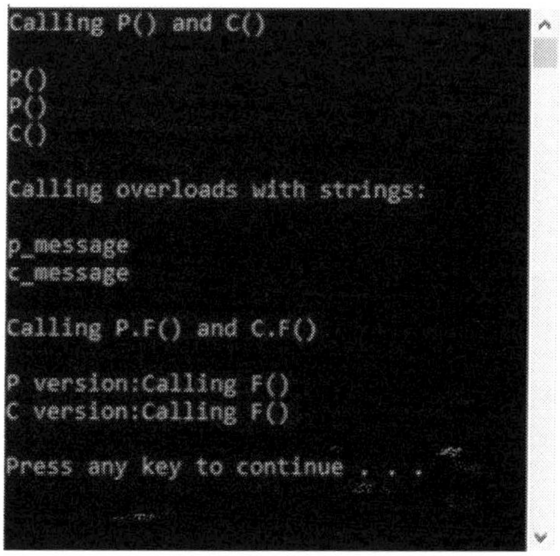

Figure 4.15: Overriding Functions

Notice a few important things. We created two overloads of the P constructor: one which takes no parameters and one which takes a string `constructor_message` which is printed to the screen. Likewise, C has two constructors, except C calls the parent version of the constructor by placing a colon (`:`) after the constructor's parentheses, before the opening curly brace of its body. When a colon is placed here, following the colon, you can call a parent version of the constructor. P has a function F, which takes a string as input and prints that string to the screen after printing "P version:" so we can see which version is calling the function. C overrides this function, and its version says "C version:" for the same reason.

Now let's observe some implications of the output. First, notice that the P constructor was called once when constructing the P object p. But then we see that it was called again before the C constructor was called, because "P()" was printed to the screen twice. This is because when we created the C object c, the parent version of the constructor was called **in addition** to the child version. This happens automatically and is something you must be aware of. If you wish to choose which version of the parent constructor gets called, you must specify which one by placing a colon after the constructor parentheses as we did with C's second constructor overload. We can see that when we created the P object p_message, we called P's second constructor because we passed in a string value, "p_message". We then created a C object called c_message, calling its second constructor by passing in the string value "c_message". Notice from the output that we chose for the second P constructor to be called upon the construction of C. Since this constructor overload for C does nothing in its body, this is the only result we see from c_message's construction. Finally, we call F on both p and c, respectively, and see that we get each class's version of the function.

We have now seen that a derived class can override functions it inherits from a base class when the base version is marked as virtual. We learned that the overridden version on the derived class should be marked as override to show that the function is indeed overriding a base version (the compiler will automatically consider it to be an override if it is not marked override). We have also seen that when a derived class is constructed, the base constructor is called automatically. We learned that we can specify which version of the base class gets called by placing a call to the particular override of the base constructor after a colon following the derived constructor's closing parentheses.

Now that we have an understanding of inheritance, we are ready to move on to the next major topic of the C++ programming language: pointers.

Pointers

Pointers are one of the most important topics in C++. With them, you can make programs run more efficiently, and thus, faster. Inefficient programming in games can affect the user experience. As a result, the use of pointers is routine when programming games, especially when programming in Unreal Engine. So what exactly is a pointer, anyway?

A **pointer** is a variable that holds an address. That's it. Every variable in your program represents data stored somewhere in the computer's memory, and each of these memory locations has an address. A pointer is simply a variable that holds an address in memory. Let's take a look at how we can use pointers in a program.

```
#include <iostream>
#include <string>

class A
{
```

```cpp
public:
    A();
    A(int i_data, float f_data);
    void F(std::string message);
    void SetIntData(int i_data) { int_data = i_data; }
    void SetFloatData(int f_data) { float_data = f_data; }
    void PrintData();
private:
    int int_data;
    float float_data;
};

int main()
{
    std::cout << "Creating an A object:\n\n";
    A a;
    a.SetIntData(9);
    a.SetFloatData(2.18);
    a.PrintData();

    std::cout << "\n\nCreating a pointer to an A
object:\n\n";
    A* A_ptr = &a;
    std::cout << "Calling F from the pointer:\n";
    (*A_ptr).F("Call F.");

    std::cout << "\nCalling methods using arrow
notation:\n\n";
    A_ptr->SetIntData(3);
    A_ptr->SetFloatData(4.99f);
    A_ptr->PrintData();

    std::cout << "Creating an A object dynamically:\n\n";

    A* a_dyn = new A(42, 9.587f);
    a_dyn->PrintData();
    delete a_dyn;

    std::cout << std::endl;
```

```
        system("pause");
}

A::A() { std::cout << "A()\n"; }
A::A(int i_data, float f_data): int_data(i_data),
float_data(f_data) { std::cout << "A()\n"; }
void A::F(std::string message) { std::cout << "A message: "
<< message << std::endl; }

void A::PrintData() { std::cout << "Int Data: " << int_data
<< " Float Data: " << float_data << std::endl; }
```

The output for the above program is shown below.

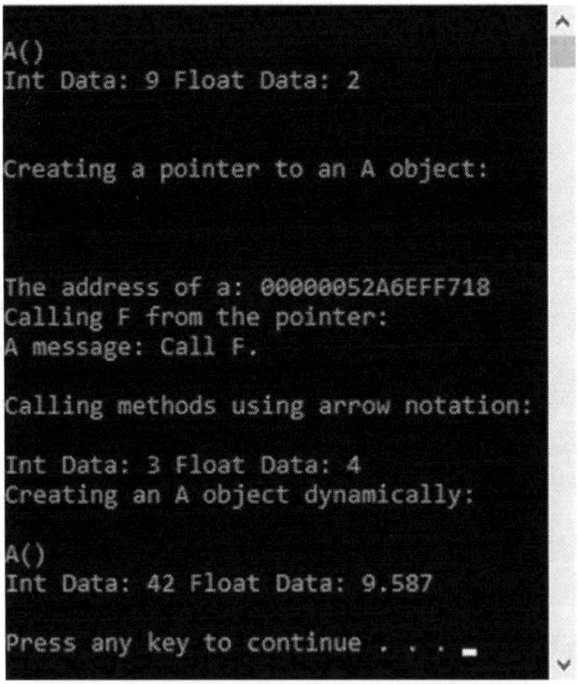

Figure 4.16: Output Showing the Use of Pointers

There are several things happening in the code above. Let's step through each one.

First, we created a class called A and gave it two constructor overloads. The first overload takes no arguments and sends "A()\n" to the cout command. The second constructor makes use of the colon (:) operator to initialize two variables. We have seen how we can specify which parent constructor overload is called by using this operator after the constructor parentheses, but now we see that we can initialize member variables this way as well.

We also created some member functions. F prints a message to the screen. SetIntData and SetFloatData set the private variables int_data and float_data, respectively. PrintData prints the values of these variables to the screen.

The first thing we do in the main function is create an A object called a. We call the setter functions to give its private members some values, then call PrintData to print them to the screen.

Next we create a pointer variable called A_ptr. The data type for this variable is A*, which we refer to as "A-star" or "pointer to A." To declare a variable of pointer type, you simply use the type with an asterisk (*) appended to it. We initialized this pointer variable with the address of a, using the address-of operator (&). We look at the value of this address by simply using cout and printing A_ptr to the screen.

Next, we **dereference** the pointer using the dereference operator (*). Whenever this operator is placed directly before a pointer, the pointer is **dereferenced**. This means the variable in that memory address is accessed. Once dereferenced, we can call functions on the a object, which we do when we call F with the dot operator. We had to place parentheses around the dereferenced pointer first, because the dot operator takes precedence over the dereference operator. This means the compiler will attempt to apply the dot operator to A_ptr first before applying the dereference operator. By placing parentheses around *A_ptr, we ensure that the dereference takes place first (operations inside parentheses are always carried out first), then the dot operator is applied.

Since dereferencing a pointer with the (*) operator requires that we place parentheses, the syntax looks a bit ugly. Since pointer dereferencing is so common, a more attractive way to access variables and functions in this way was created, and is known as **arrow**

notation. We use arrow notation to access `SetIntData`, `SetFloatData`, and `PrintData`. A more attractive alternative for an operation in a programming language is known as **syntactic sugar**.

Finally, we create a new pointer of type `A*` called `a_dyn`. Next, we create a new A object using the `new` keyword, and choose to construct it using the second constructor override, passing in initial values for `int_data` and `float_data`. Wait a minute, what's this `new` keyword? And why did we use the `delete` keyword two lines later?

The new and delete Keywords

In C++, there are two types of memory: memory on the **stack** and memory on the **heap**.

The stack is reserved for variables that we declare in an ordinary fashion, like all the variables we've declared so far. The memory for these variables is **allocated** (reserved) at compile time. In other words, the memory is set aside before the program even runs.

The heap is a separate space in memory where **dynamically allocated** variables are stored. This means that memory isn't set aside for these variables until the flow of execution hits the lines at which they are declared and constructed. If those lines are never reached, those objects are never created, and the memory is never used.

When we create variables using stack memory, they are created and deleted automatically. Objects exist within their own **scope**, determined by the curly braces in which they reside. Opening and closing curly braces denote a **block** – one or more statements that are treated like a single statement by the compiler. Once the end of a block is reached, any variables created on the stack within the block are said to go **out of scope**–they are deleted. The same cannot be said for variables created on the heap. When we create variables using heap memory, the memory isn't managed for us. The memory gets allocated on the stack and will stay allocated until we manually delete it. This is the reason for using the `delete` keyword.

Creating variables on the heap and not deleting them when they are no longer needed creates a **memory leak**. If heap memory runs out, the program will terminate. This is why it is so important to make sure heap-allocated memory is freed when it is no longer used.

When to Use Dynamic Memory Allocation

So when should we construct objects dynamically? Let's consider a game example. Suppose we have a creature in our game that should be created when our Character enters a room. If we created the creature on the stack, the memory would already be reserved at compile time. But if the Character never enters the room, that memory was reserved unnecessarily. If, on the other hand, we created the creature on the heap, the memory would only be allocated if the Character actually enters the room, thus leaving more memory for other variables in the program.

We now understand that a pointer is simply a variable that holds a memory address. We have seen how to declare a pointer using the * operator and how to access the address of a variable using the address-of operator (&). We learned how to dereference a pointer using the * operator at the beginning of the variable name, and saw that parentheses are needed to access its contents to ensure that the dereference operation occurs first. We also saw that using arrow notation is a more attractive way to access functions and variables via a pointer. Finally, we learned how to dynamically allocate memory using the `new` keyword, and that this variable is stored on the heap, whereas normal variables are stored on the stack. We learned that heap allocated memory must be freed using the `delete` keyword, whereas stack allocated memory is automatically managed for us, since variables are deleted once they go out of scope.

Now that we understand pointers, we can take a look at two more C++ concepts that will be useful in our journey as C++ programmers: `struct`s and `enum`s.

Structs and Enums

It's time to add two more tools to our tool belt: `struct`s and `enum`s! These concepts will broaden our capabilities as programmers. We will start with `struct`s.

Structs

A `struct` is a concept from the C programming language that survived when C++ was created. In the C++ programming language, the `struct` and the `class` are identical in every way except for one: the body of a `struct` is `public` by default, whereas the body of a `class` is `private` by default. That's it!

When to use a `class` versus when to use a `struct` is a matter of personal coding style, however in Unreal Engine, the typical convention is to use a `class` for big involved types such as things that need to be placed in the level, and to use a `struct` for small data structures which hold information. Since we have already covered class creation, we will skip `struct` creation, since the two entities behave the same in C++. We will now look at `enums`.

Enums

The word `enum` is short for enumeration. An `enum` is a set of named integer constants. Enums can be useful for naming states in a game. For example, your Character might have three movement states: idle, walking, and running. Instead of keeping an integer to represent its movement state, leaving it up to the programmer to remember which number corresponds to which state, an `enum` can make life much easier. Declare an `enum` as follows:

```
enum MovementStatus
{
    Idle,
    Walk = 43,
    Run

};
```

This `enum` contains three **enum constants**. These are named integer constants which automatically have values assigned to them. The first constant is assigned a value of 0 by default, and each subsequent constant gets 1 more than the previous one. Of course, you can assign values to them, as was done with the second constant, `Walk`. When you do this, the next `enum` constant will be assigned a value 1 higher than the previous, so Run will be assigned a value of 44.

Enums can be used to control whether or not a section of code is executed. We will make use of `enums` in this manner in the next section, when we learn about flow control.

Flow Control

In a C++ program, it is often not appropriate for every single line of code to run. Some code exists for performing an action in certain circumstances. When those circumstances don't occur, that code should not run. There are tools in the C++ language that allow us to determine which conditions should be met in order for certain parts of code to run. The art of doing so is referred to as **flow control**.

Working with if Statements

Certain code should run only when certain conditions are met. To check such a condition, the `if` statement is used. The `if` statement makes use of the `if` keyword, followed by parentheses. The condition to be checked goes inside the parentheses, and the following body (denoted by curly braces) is executed if the condition is met.

Every expression in C++ can be evaluated for its truth value. Numbers evaluate to `false` if their value is equal to 0. All other values evaluate to false. Comparison operators exist to determine conditions. With two comparable values A and B, the basic comparison operators are defined as follows:

Operator Name	Syntax	Definition
Equal to	A == B	Returns true if A is equal to B.
Not equal to	A != B	Returns true if A is not equal to B.
Less than	A < B	Returns true if A is less than B.
Greater than	A > B	Returns true if A is greater than B.
Less than or equal to	A <= B	Returns true if A is less than B. Also returns true if A is equal to B.
Greater than or equal to	A >= B	Returns true if A is greater than B. Also returns true if A is equal to B.

Table 4.1: Comparison Operators

We can execute code conditionally using the above operators as in the following program.

```cpp
#include <iostream>
#include <string>

enum MovementStatus
{
    Idle,
    Walk = 43,
    Run
};
```

```
int main()
{
    int A = 1;
    int B = 2;
    MovementStatus Movement = Idle;

    if (A == B)
    {
        std::cout << "This code will never run.\n\n";
    }

    if (Movement == Idle) { std::cout << "Movement is in
the Idle state.\n\n"; }
    if (A < B && Movement == Idle) { std::cout <<
"Movement is in the Idle state. A is also Less than
B.\n\n"; }
    if (A > B || Movement == Idle) { std::cout <<
"Movement is in the Idle state. A is also Less than
B.\n\n"; }

    system("pause");

}
```

The above program outputs:

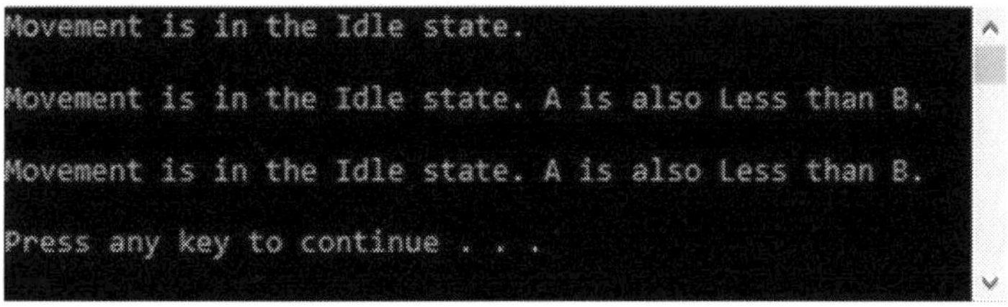

Figure 4.17: Flow Control Output

In the above program, we define an enum called MovementStatus containing three enum constants: Idle, Walk, and Run. In the main function, we declare two integers, A and B, and assign them the values 1 and 2, respectively. We then create a variable of type MovementStatus and initialize it with the value of Idle. We then use an if statement to see if A is equal to B. Since A and B are not equal, the expression A == B returns `false` and thus the `if` statement's body is never executed. The next two `if` statements are defined on single lines to save space. A and B are compared as well as `Movement`, which is compared with the `enum` constant `Idle`. Notice the new use of the `&&` and `||` operators, which are the AND and OR operators, respectively. The condition `A < B && Movement == Idle` will evaluate to `true` only if **both** expressions on the left and right of the `&&` operator evaluate to true. If one of these is false, the entire expression returns false. The condition `A > B || Movement == Idle` will return `true` if **either** of the expressions on the left and right of the `||` operator evaluate to true. This means one can evaluate to `true` and the other false, and the entire expression will still return true. The only way an OR comparison will evaluate to `false` is if **both** expressions to the left and right of it evaluate to false. Thus in the comparison made above, `A > B` is checked, which returns false, but `Movement == Idle` is also checked, which evaluates to true, therefore the `if` statement's body is executed.

Working with else and else if

The `else` keyword allows you to have a backup body that will run if the condition for the `if` statement fails. There can even be an additional condition checked in this case, by using the `if` keyword again, as in the following example.

```cpp
#include <iostream>
#include <string>

enum MovementStatus
{
    Idle,
    Walk = 43,
    Run
};

int main()
{
    int A = 1;
    int B = 2;
    MovementStatus Movement = Idle;

    if (A == B)
```

```
{
     std::cout << "This code will never run.\n\n";
}
else
{
     std::cout << "This code will run.\n\n";
}

if (Movement == Walk)
{
     std::cout << "Status of Movement is: Walk.\n\n";
}
else if (Movement == Run)
{
     std::cout << "Status of Movement is: Run.\n\n";
}
else
{
     std::cout << "Status of Movement is: Idle.\n\n";
}

system("pause");

}
```

The output for the above code is:

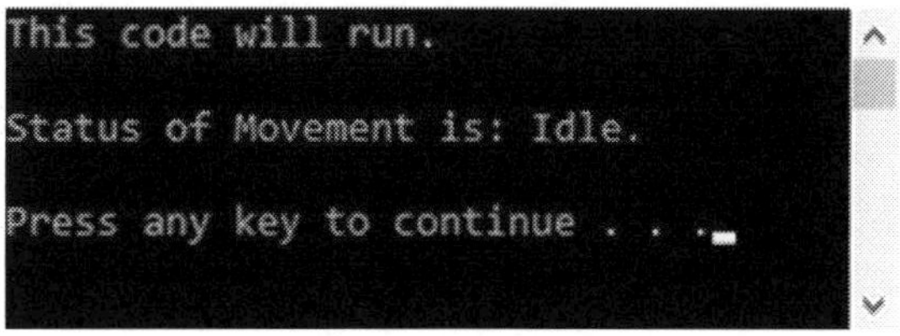

Figure 4.18: Using else and else if

This code checks to see if A is equal to B, which it is not. The else body is thus executed. Next, Movement is checked to see if it is equal to Walk, which it is not. It is then checked again to see if it is equal to Run. Since both of these conditions fail, the else body is executed.

The if, else, and else if statements aren't the only way to control the flow of execution. Another common way is to use loops. We will first take a look at the for loop and how it works.

Using the for Loop

A for loop allows us to execute a block of code a certain number of times. It looks like the following:

```
for (int i = 0; i < 10; i++)
{
     std::cout << i << std::endl;

}
```

This loop will result in the following output:

Figure 4.19: For Loop Output

As you can see, there are three separate statements in the for loop's parentheses. The first is where you can initialize the loop variable. You need not declare the loop variable here, but it is common to do so. The second statement is the loop condition. The loop will continue to be executed over and over until this statement evaluates to false, at which point the flow of control exits the loop and resumes after its ending curly brace. The third statement is where you can increment (or decrement) the loop variable. In the above example we use the **post-increment operator,** which results in the loop variable being increased by 1. Keep in mind that the loop condition is checked before the loop body is entered, so if it evaluates to false right off the bat, the loop body won't even execute once.

Notes on the Increment Operators

The post-increment operator applied to the integer i (as in i++) results in the following: First the value of i is returned, then the variable is incremented by 1. The pre-increment operator applied to the integer i (as in ++i) results in the following: first i is incremented by 1, then the value of i is returned. Either one can be used in the for loop's third statement in the parentheses, because the statement is completed before the next condition check. There exist **pre-decrement** and **post-decrement** (--) operators that behave similarly.

The for loop isn't the only kind of loop. Another is the while loop, which we will examine now.

Using the while Loop

The while loop will execute over and over until its loop condition evaluates to false. An example while loop is as follows:

```
while (i < 10)
{
    std::cout << i << std::endl;
    ++i;

}
```

The output for the above while loop is identical to that of the for loop mentioned above. As you can see, the same result can be achieved in different ways.

We now have several flow control tools we can use to dictate whether or not our lines of code will run and under which circumstances. This gives our programs more versatility and allows us to prevent the execution of expensive operations if they are not absolutely necessary.

Next we will learn about casting, an essential tool we will use frequently in our gameplay programming in Unreal Engine.

Using Casting When Working With Objects

When using an object-oriented programming language such as C++, we can be working with one type that is simultaneously another type. This is thanks to the phenomenon of inheritance and **is-a** relationships. The following example will make use of **casting**.

```cpp
#include <iostream>

class Parent
{
public:
    virtual void CallOut() { std::cout << "Parent
CallOut()\n\n"; }
};

class Child: public Parent
{
public:
    virtual void CallOut() override { std::cout << "Child
CallOut()\n\n"; }
};

class Grandchild : public Child
{
public:
    virtual void CallOut() override { std::cout <<
"Grandchild CallOut()\n\n"; }
};

int main()
{
    Parent* p = new Parent;
    Parent* c = new Child;
    Parent* g = new Grandchild;

    Parent* ObjectArray[3];
    ObjectArray[0] = p;
    ObjectArray[1] = c;
    ObjectArray[2] = g;

    for (int i = 0; i < 3; i++)
```

```
    {
        std::cout << "i = " << i << std::endl;
        Parent* P =
dynamic_cast<Parent*>(ObjectArray[i]);
        if (P) { P->CallOut(); }
        Child* C = dynamic_cast<Child*>(ObjectArray[i]);
        if (C) { C->CallOut(); }
        Grandchild* G =
dynamic_cast<Grandchild*>(ObjectArray[i]);
        if (G) { G->CallOut(); }
    }

    system("pause");

}
```

We have created an inheritance chain starting with `Parent`. `Child` inherits from `Parent`, and `Grandchild` inherits from `Child`.

We will now take advantage of a peculiar attribute of inheritance. Since a `Child` **is a** `Parent`, we can create a pointer of type `Parent*` and make it point to a `Child`. We can also make it point to a `Grandchild` since these two types are their own types in addition to the `Parent` type. So we have created three pointers of type `Parent*` and initialized them with the addresses of dynamically allocated objects of types `Parent`, `Child` and `Grandchild`, respectively.

Next we create an **array**. An array is simply a variable with multiple values, each of the same type. To declare an array, we simply declare the data type, in this case, `Parent*`, followed by the variable name, which in this case is `ObjectArray`. We must indicate how large the array will be upon its declaration using square brackets. Since our array will contain 3 elements, we used a 3 here. To access an array element, square brackets containing the index for the element are used. The array elements begin at 0 and end at 1 less than the number of elements in the array.

Notes on Indexing Array Elements Out of Bounds

If you attempt to access an element in an array at an index that doesn't exist in that array, you will get a compilation error. If a variable value is used to index an array and the array is indexed out of bounds, the program will typically crash.

We use square brackets to access the 0 through 2nd element of the array, setting their values with the assignment (=) operator. We then use a `for` loop and print the index to the screen for each value of `i` in the loop. After this, the real magic happens.

We use `dynamic_cast` to cast the array element to a particular type. Dynamic casting is a form of casting done at runtime. It takes a type in pointed brackets, followed by the object we are casting in parentheses. The object in the parentheses is checked for its type. If it has the **is-a** relationship with the type specified in pointy brackets, it is casted to that type. What is returned is the value of the object in the form of the type casted to. If the type specified in the pointy brackets is not a type with which the object has the **is-a** relationship, the cast will **fail**. When this happens, a **null pointer** (a pointer to nothing) is returned. When a null pointer is checked with an `if` statement, the `if` condition fails, and the `if` body is not executed.

The output for the above program is as follows.

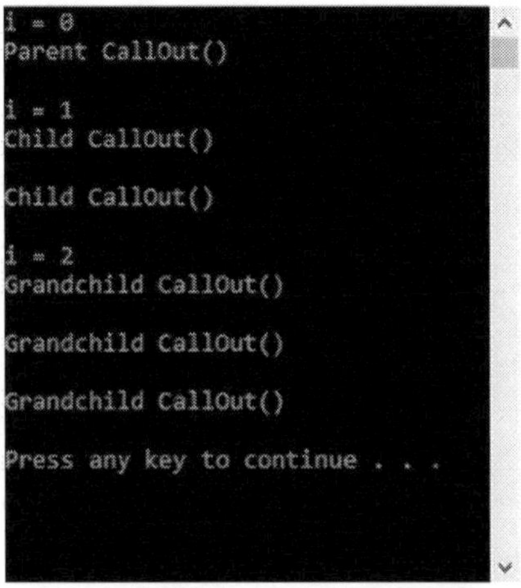

```
i = 0
Parent CallOut()

i = 1
Child CallOut()

Child CallOut()

i = 2
Grandchild CallOut()

Grandchild CallOut()

Grandchild CallOut()

Press any key to continue . . .
```

Figure 4.20: Casting in an Inheritance Chain

The first iteration of the loop, we are accessing the first element (element 0) of `ObjectArray`. The object pointed to by the `Parent*` pointer is of type `Parent`, so the cast to `Parent` succeeds and the check `if (P)` succeeds. The other two casts fail, and thus the `CallOut` function is only called once. The next iteration of the loop, we are accessing the second element (element 1). The object pointed to by the `Parent*` pointer is of type `Child`, so the first and second casts succeed and the third fails. Notice that when `CallOut` is called, the child version is called each time. This is because even though the first cast is to `Parent*`, the object itself is of type `Child`. It is the type of the object itself that determines which version of a virtual function is called, not the type of the pointer. This allows us to have an array of elements of type `Parent*` that point to various types in the inheritance hierarchy as long as the objects pointed to are `Parent` or lower on the chain. This behavior is referred to as **polymorphism**.

Polymorphism is very useful in object-oriented programming. It means we can loop through `ObjectArray` and call the `CallOut` function on each element and get the correct override based on the type of the object pointed to. We can do this by replacing the `for` loop with:

```
for (int i = 0; i < 3; i++)
{
    /*
    std::cout << "i = " << i << std::endl;
    Parent* P =
dynamic_cast<Parent*>(ObjectArray[i]);
    if (P) { P->CallOut(); }
    Child* C = dynamic_cast<Child*>(ObjectArray[i]);
    if (C) { C->CallOut(); }
    Grandchild* G =
dynamic_cast<Grandchild*>(ObjectArray[i]);
    if (G) { G->CallOut(); }
    */

    ObjectArray[i]->CallOut();

}
```

We have **commented out** the lines above `ObjectArray[i]->CallOut();` using /* to open the comment and */ to close it. Any code that is commented out will be ignored by the compiler. You can comment out single lines by placing a double slash (//) at the beginning of the line. This allows you to ignore certain sections in your code while developing. The results of the above `for` loop are:

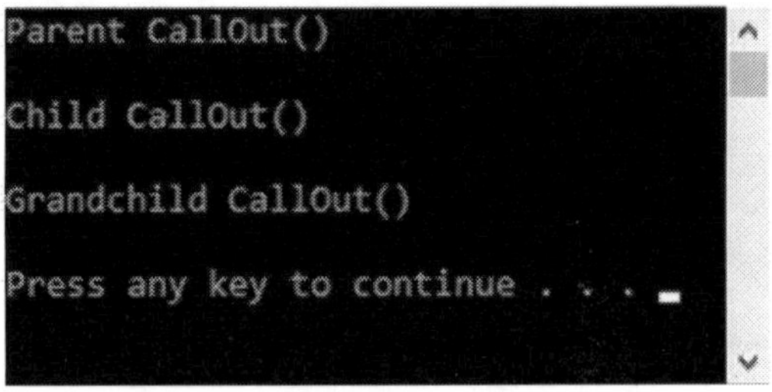

Figure 4.21: Polymorphism in Action

This shows that each time we access an element in `ObjectArray`, when calling `CallOut`, the type of the actual object, not the pointer, is used to determine which override of the `CallOut` function is called.

We have now seen how casting works using `dynamic_cast`. Casting is used in Unreal Engine quite frequently, as classes in Unreal Engine often belong to an inheritance hierarchy. We have seen that we can initialize a variable of type `Parent*` with a `Child` object. Casting to a type with which an object has an **is-a** relationship will succeed and the object will be returned in the form of the casted type, otherwise the cast will fail and return a null pointer.

We will next take a look at templates, which allow us to make our functions and classes more versatile.

Working with Templates

Templates allow programmers to treat types as if they were parameters. This means functions and classes can be created which don't restrict the type of the input parameters passed in upon their use. We will first observe template functions and see how they work.

Template Functions

Sometimes multiple versions of a function are needed in which the only thing that changes is the type of the input parameter. For example, observe the following function:

```
int Max(int A, int B)
{
        return A >= B ? A : B;

}
```

The above function takes two integer inputs and compares them, returning the larger of the two. It makes use of the **ternary operator** which takes three inputs: the first is a condition to check, in this case A >= B, the second is what gets returned if the condition is true, in this case A, and the third is what gets returned if the condition is false, in this case B. The above function results in the same exact result as the following:

```
int Max(int A, int B)
{
        if (A >= B)
        {
                return A;
        }
        else
        {
                return B;
        }

}
```

If we wanted a `float` version of the above function, we would need to create an override which takes two `float` arguments and returns a `float`:

```
float Max(float A, float B)
{
        return A >= B ? A : B;

}
```

And if we wanted a version that takes two `double` values, we would need to create yet another override, and so on. C++ has a handy method of allowing you to create a single function which will observe the type passed in and automatically construct the correct overload. Functions that do this are known as **template functions**. The following achieves the result we are after:

```cpp
template <typename T>
T Max(T A, T B)
{
      return A >= B ? A : B;

}
```

This function takes two input parameters and returns an output of the same type. We must mark it with the `template` keyword and pointy brackets containing `typename` `T`. This denotes `T` to be a **type parameter**–it is the type itself that can vary. When calling the function, the type passed in will determine the version of the function created. If `int` is passed in for `T`, the integer version will be created, and so on.

Classes can be created in which member variables can have a varying type as well. We will now take a look at how to create these.

Template Classes

We can create a **template class** in the following manner:

```cpp
#include <iostream>

template <typename T>
class NumberContainer
{
public:
      T GetData() { return data; }
      void SetData(T _data) { data = _data; }
private:
      T data;
};


int main()
{
      NumberContainer<int> Num;
      Num.SetData(4);
      std::cout << Num.GetData() << std::endl;
```

```
    system("pause");
}
```

In the above program, we create a template class called `NumberContainer`. The template parameter `T` is used as the type for the getter `GetData`, the setter `SetData`, and the `private` member variable `data`. In order to create an object of the `NumberContainer` class, we must specify the type with which `T` is to be replaced. We do so in pointy brackets when creating an instance called `Num`, using `int` as the template parameter. Keep in mind that since we specified the template parameter type to be an integer, if we were to pass in a `float` or `double` value, it would be automatically converted to an `int`, dropping any digits to the right of the decimal.

We now have the power to create functions and classes in which the parameter type is variable. This allows us to only write a function or class once and be able to utilize it for any type we wish.

When we create a template function which uses a comparison operator, such as our `Max` function, we must make sure only to pass in objects that can be compared with that operator. If our objects don't have the ability to be compared, we can specify how to compare them by overloading the operator.

Using Operator Overloading to make Custom Operator Functionality

Keep in mind any operations performed on parameters or variables must be defined for that particular type. For example, the following:

```
    NumberContainer<int> A;
    NumberContainer<int> B;

    Max(A, B);
```

would result in a compiler error because the >= operator is not defined for comparing two objects of this type (the type being `NumberContainer<int>`). We can, however, overload the comparison operator > to define what happens when two objects of the `NumberContainer` type are compared. Observe the following example:

```cpp
#include <iostream>

template <typename T>
T Max(T A, T B)
{
      return A >= B ? A : B;
}

template <typename T>
class NumberContainer
{
public:
      T GetData() { return data; }
      void SetData(T _data) { data = _data; }
      bool operator>=(NumberContainer<T>& right)
      {
            return ( data >= right.GetData() ) ? true : false;
      }
private:
      T data;
};


int main()
{
      NumberContainer<int> A;
      A.SetData(3);
      NumberContainer<int> B;
      B.SetData(4);
      std::cout << Max(A, B).GetData() << std::endl;

      system("pause");

}
```

In the above example, we overload the >= operator by using the `operator` keyword. An operator can be thought of as a special type of function. The only difference between operators and functions is that functions take their input parameters in their parentheses in the form of a comma-separated list, whereas operators don't use parentheses. **Binary operators** (operators which take two inputs) perform some action on the item immediately to the left and immediately to the right of the operator, such as the comparison operator >=. Some operators only act on a single input, such as the pre-increment and post-increment operators.

We overload the >= operator, specifying the return type to be `bool`. The input parameter is the object to the right of the >= when the operator is used. It must be of type `NumberContainer<T>` because we are defining the operator overload for the `NumberContainer` class. In the function we use the ternary operator to compare `data` from the current class with the value returned by `GetData` from the object to the right of the operator. When two objects of type `NumberContainer` are compared with the >= operator, the object to the left calls the operator overload function, and the object to the right is passed into it. In the above program, we create two objects of type `NumberContainer<int>`. We call `SetData` to give their `data` members values. We then print to the screen the result of `Max(A, B).GetData()`. First, `Max` is called, passing in `A` and `B`. The flow of control jumps from the `main` function into the `Max` function. In `Max`, `A` is compared with `B` using the >= operator. This causes `A`'s operator overload function to be called, so the flow of control now jumps into `A`'s `operator>=` function, passing in `B` by reference as a parameter. In this function, `A`'s data member is compared with the result returned by `B`'s `GetData` function. If `A`'s `data` member is larger than or equal to the value returned by `B`'s `GetData` function, `true` is returned, otherwise `false` is returned. The boolean result is returned to the ternary operator in `Max`, resulting in either `A` or `B` being returned by `Max`. Keep in mind `Max` doesn't take its input parameters by reference so it is returning a copy of either `A` or `B`. The flow of control jumps back into the `main` function, where we take the result returned by `Max`, which is an object of type `NumberContainer<int>`, and call `GetData` on it, printing it to the screen. The result of the above program is:

Figure 4.22: Overloading the >= Operator

To make the `Max` function more efficient, we can change its signature to `T& Max(T& A, T& B)`, passing the variables in by reference and returning the result by reference. This will avoid the creation of a copy of the inputs `A` and `B`, as well as ensure that the same object is returned which was passed in.

We have learned how to create functions which can take any parameter type by marking them as template functions. We have also learned how to create template classes which can also take a variable type. We learned that the correct version of the function or class is created once the type is specified. We also learned that a template function which uses a comparison operator on its parameters must only be used on types for which that comparison is defined. We also learned that if a comparison is not defined for a particular class, we can overload that operator for the class, thus defining that comparison for the class type. We did this with our `NumberContainer` class, defining the `>=` operator for that class. Now that we understand templates, we are ready for the next section: header files!

Header Files

Up until now, we have only included header files that already exist, such as `<iostream>` and `<string>`. But we can create our own header files to keep code secluded into its own area which we can include when we need using the `#include` directive. This is a common practice and comes in handy with large programs (like video games). To create a new header file, in the **Solution Explorer**, right click on the project name and select *Add -> New Item*. Select *Header File (.h)* and name the file *Character.h*. Now *Character.h* will appear in the **Header Files** folder in the Solution Explorer. It will open in its own tab next to the *HelloWorldSource.cpp* tab.

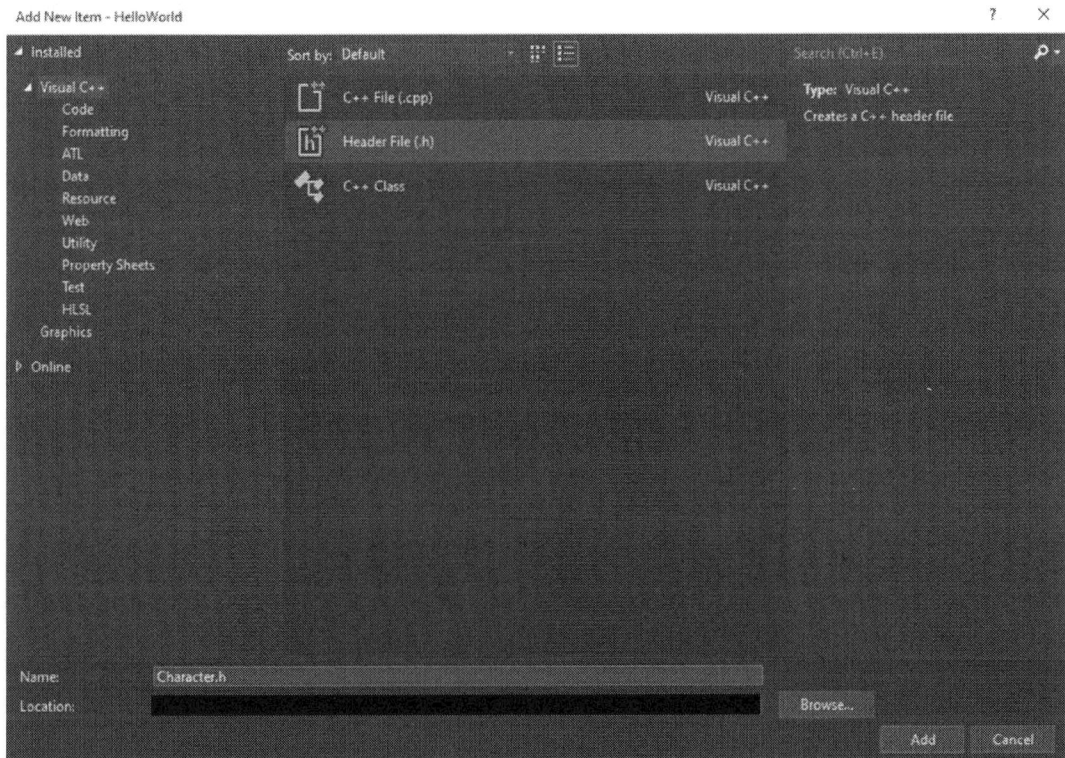

Figure 4.23: Creating a New Header File

We will be placing our `Character` class into the header file. We will be only be placing declarations into the header file, however. The definitions will go into their own source (*.cpp*) files. This will allow us to keep the header file neat and easy to read. To create a new source file, in the **Solution Explorer**, right click the project name and select *Add -> New Item*. Select *C++ file (.cpp)* and name the file *Character.cpp*.

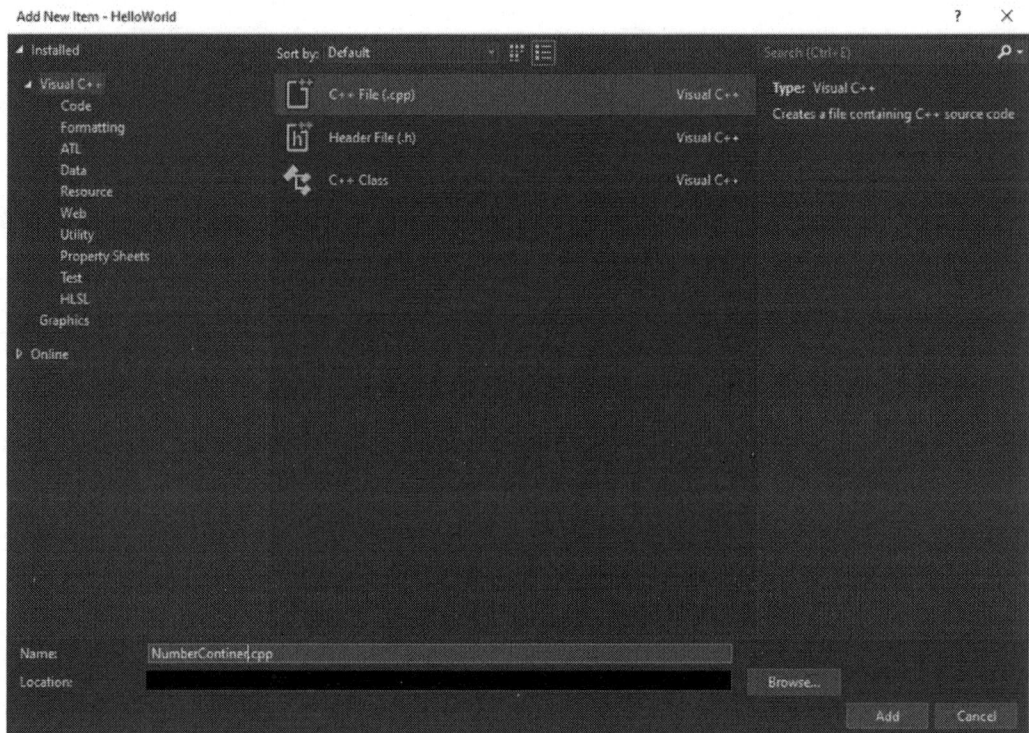

Figure 4.24: Creating a Source File

In the *.h* file, notice the `#pragma once` directive. This ensures that if this header file is accidentally included more than once, the compiler will not include more than a single copy of the code in the file in which it is included.

In the *Character.h* file, we will place the declaration of our class along with its member functions and variables.

```cpp
#pragma once
#include <string>

class Character
{
public:
    Character();
    Character(std::string name);
    Character(std::string name, int level, float power);
    ~Character();
```

```
      void SetName(std::string name);
      void SetLevel(int level);
      void SetPower(float power);
      std::string& GetName();
      int GetLevel();
      float GetPower();
      void SetAttributes(std::string name = "default name",
int level = 1, float power = 0.f);
      void PrintAttributes();

private:
      std::string Name;
      int Level;
      float Power;

};
```

In *Character.cpp*, we will define these functions:

```
#include <string>
#include <iostream>
#include "Character.h"

Character::Character()
{
      SetName("Unnamed");
      SetLevel(1);
      SetPower(10.f);
}

Character::Character(std::string name)
{
      SetName(name);
      SetLevel(1);
      SetPower(10.f);
}

Character::Character(std::string name, int level, float
power)
{
      SetAttributes(name, level, power);
```

```
}

Character::~Character()
{
      std::cout << "Destroying Character: " << Name <<
std::endl;
}

void Character::SetName(std::string name)
{
      Name = name;
}

void Character::SetLevel(int level)
{
      Level = level;
}

void Character::SetPower(float power)
{
      Power = power;
}

std::string& Character::GetName()
{
      return Name;
}

int Character::GetLevel()
{
      return Level;
}

float Character::GetPower()
{
      return Power;
}

void Character::SetAttributes(std::string name, int level,
float power)
{
```

```
    SetName(name);
    SetLevel(level);
    SetPower(power);
}

void Character::PrintAttributes()
{
    std::cout << "Name: " << Name << std::endl;
    std::cout << "Level: " << Level << std::endl;
    std::cout << "Power: " << Power << std::endl;

}
```

We have created three overloads of the constructor. The first takes no parameters and assigns default values to the `private` member variables. The second takes a string and assigns its value to `Name`. The third takes three input parameters and assigns them to the corresponding member variables. You may have noticed the strange line `~Character();`. This is known as a **destructor**. A destructor runs when an object is deleted, and is usually used to take care of any clean up that needs to be done, such as deleting dynamically allocated member variables (of which this class has none). We simply print a message to the screen to let the world know the current Character has been destroyed. We also have standard getters and setters for the three `private` variables. We then created a setter function `SetAttributes`, which sets all three member variables in one fell swoop. This is the function used in the constructor which takes three inputs. Notice that in the signature for `SetAttributes` we have set default values for the inputs. This can be done by using the assignment operator in the function declaration. If there is a default value for an input parameter, it becomes optional; if omitted when the function is called, that input parameter will be assigned the default value. It is important to know that if a function has at least one default parameter, all parameters that come after it in the comma-separated parameter list must have defaults. Finally, we created a `PrintAttributes` function which uses `std::cout` to print the attributes to the screen. Let's see how our `Character` class looks in action in our main source file, *HelloWorldSource.cpp*:

```
#include <iostream>
#include "Character.h"
```

```cpp
int main()
{
    std::cout << "Creating a new Character with the first
constructor:\n";
    Character* Default = new Character();
    Default->SetAttributes();
    std::cout << std::endl;
    std::cout << "Printing the character's attributes: "
<< std::endl;
    Default->PrintAttributes();
    std::cout << std::endl;

    std::cout << "Creating a new Character with the second
constructor:\n";
    Character* Susan = new Character("Susan");
    Susan->SetPower(99.9f);
    Susan->SetLevel(80);
    std::cout << std::endl;
    std::cout << "Printing Susan's attributes: " <<
std::endl;
    Susan->PrintAttributes();
    std::cout << std::endl;

    std::cout << "Creating a new Character with the third
constructor:\n";
    Character* Shandra = new Character("Shandra", 12,
35.f);
    std::cout << std::endl;
    std::cout << "Printing Shandra's attributes: " <<
std::endl;
    Shandra->PrintAttributes();
    std::cout << std::endl;

    delete Shandra;
    delete Susan;
    delete Default;

    system("pause");

}
```

We first create a `Character` called `Default` using the first constructor. We then call `SetAttributes` on it, passing in no parameters. Since the function has default values for the parameters, those are used and the results are printed to the screen when we call `PrintAttributes`. We next create a `Character` called `Susan` using the second constructor overload, passing in "`Susan`" as the argument value. We then call `SetPower` and `SetLevel` to give her some values for these members, then print her values to the screen. Finally, we create a `Character` called `Shandra` and use the third constructor, passing in values to assign to all three member variables, and print her values to the screen. Before the program is finished, we call the destructors of the three objects, in reverse order of their construction. The results of the above program are the following:

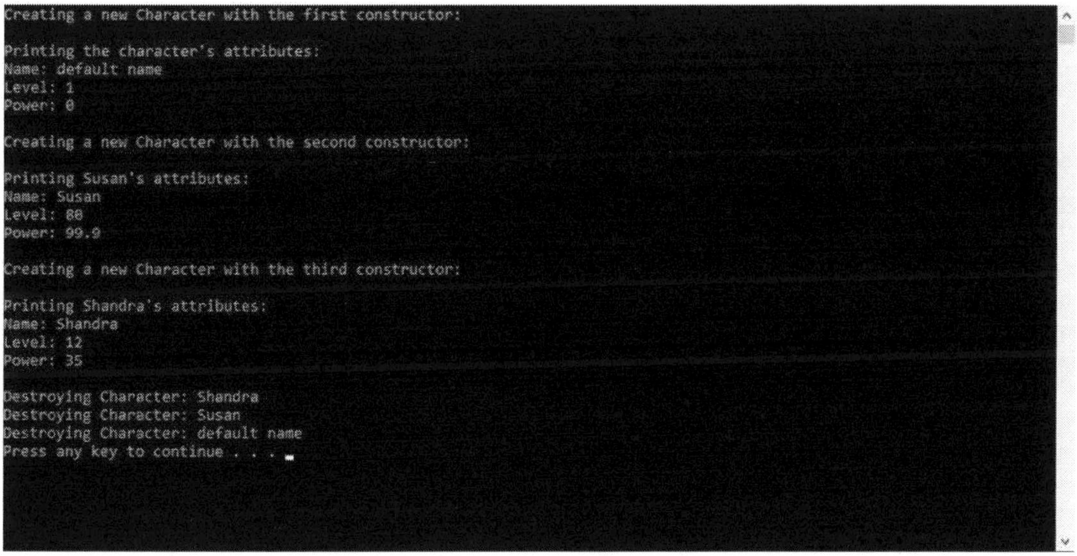

Figure 4.25: Use of the Character Class

We now have experience creating header files and using them to separate the code for classes. We have created a source file for our `Character` class to contain the definitions for the functions declared in the header file. We learned that the `#pragma once` directive ensures that a header file is only included once in any given file. We created a destructor to run when the class is deleted. We learned that we could give functions default values, which makes those parameters optional.

Congratulations! You now understand the basics of the C++ programming language. The language itself is vast and the full scope of its complexities cannot be covered in a single chapter. In fact, there are many books on the language and the reader is encouraged to read more on the language for additional information. For the purposes of this book, this chapter covers the essentials one must know to create video games in Unreal Engine.

Now that we have experience using C++, it's time to jump into Unreal Engine and begin creating some C++ classes that we can use in our games!

Summary

We dove straight into C++ by learning how to print text to the screen, choosing to print the traditional "Hello World!" We learned about variables, and how each variable has its own explicitly chosen data type, each of which determines the type of data for a given variable and the size it occupies in memory. We then learned that functions are routines consisting of one or more lines of code which execute when the function is called by name. We learned that functions can accept input parameters and use the values of those parameters when executing some functionality, such as performing computations. We saw that input parameters are given copies of the values passed in, unless they are passed in by reference, in which case, no copies are made, and any changes made to the input parameters are imparted on the actual variables fed into the function. We learned about macros and symbols, a relic from the C programming language, and we saw a use case where a macro can give unexpected and incorrect results. We learned about classes, and how they are a way to define a custom data type complete with its own variables and functions. We learned about inheritance, a phenomenon which allows classes to pass down inherited values to child classes, a feature of object-oriented programming, or OOP. We then learned that pointers are variables that hold addresses of variables, and are much more efficient than regular variables, because an address occupies a much smaller section in memory than an entire object in many cases. Next, we learned that `structs` are identical to classes, except for the fact that their bodies are `public` by default, whereas bodies of classes are `private` by default. We learned about the `enum` type, and how it can be used to store the state of a particular aspect of the program. We learned the various techniques of flow control, including if statements, else clauses, for and while loops, and we saw several examples of these techniques in action. We then learned how casting can be used to convert an object from one type into another, which can be especially useful when working with classes and inheritance. We then learned how to create template functions, allowing a single function definition for various versions of the function when the input parameter type varies. We also saw that template classes can take advantage of the same ability. Finally, we learned that header files can be created with the intention of including them in other files, and saw that this is an excellent way to organize code and keep programs efficient.

Phew! Now that we've covered the main features of the C++ programming language, it's now time to put them to use in Unreal Engine! All of the skills we've learned throughout this chapter comprise the foundations for your software development career, whether you decide to program games or program any other type of application. We'll now open Unreal Engine and create one of the most basic classes in the Unreal Engine hierarchy: The Actor.

Chapter 5 – The Actor Class

Now that we have a basic understanding of the C++ programming language, we are ready to open Unreal Engine and start making some classes in the engine. We will create a class based off of the `Actor` class, then learn how to make a Blueprint based off of our `Actor`. We'll discuss some of the automatically generated files built into the Unreal Engine code base, as well as Unreal Engine's reflection system–a program that observes the game code at runtime, making things like **garbage collection** (the automatic deletion of unused objects) and code exposure to Blueprints possible. We'll then use the `Tick` and `BeginPlay` functions in the C++ class for our `Actor`. Then we'll learn how special macros can be used to mark variables and functions to expose them to Blueprints. We'll conclude the chapter by adding a component to our `Actor`, a **Static Mesh** (a piece of geometry). This will give our `Actor` a visual representation that we can see in the world.

In this chapter, we'll cover the following topics:

- Creating a C++ Class – The Actor

- Generated Files, Garbage Collection, and the Unreal Header Tool

- `Tick` and `BeginPlay`

- `UPROPERTY` Macros

- `UFUNCTION` Macros

- Components – Adding a Static Mesh

- Getting and Setting an Actor's Rotation and Location

Creating a C++ Class – The Actor

We will start by creating a new class based off Actor.

5. In the **Content Browser**, right-click on the **Content** folder, select **New Folder** and name it *Chapter5*. Click on the folder to navigate to it.

6. Click the green **Add New** button and choose *New C++ Class*:

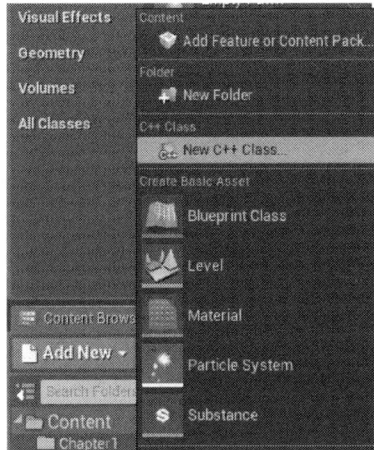

Figure 5.1: Adding a New C++ Class

7. The C++ Class Creation Wizard will pop up. Select *Actor* and hit **Next**:

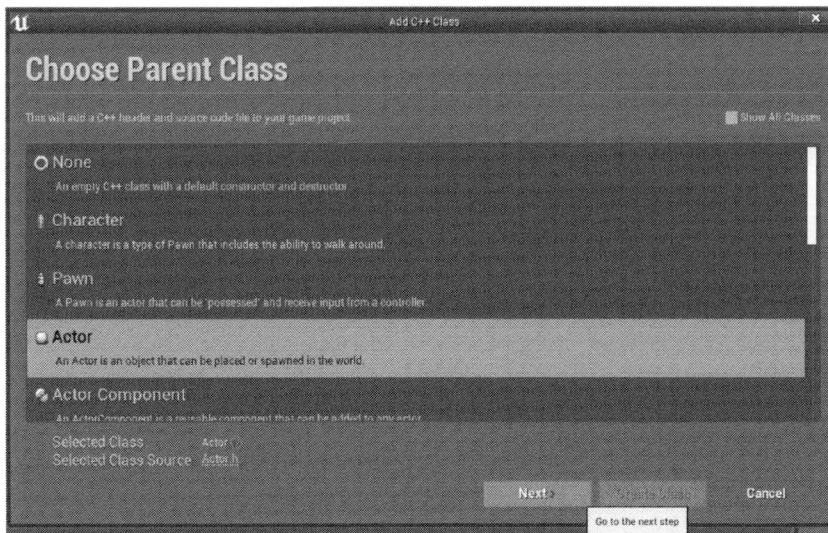

Figure 5.2: The C++ Class Creation Wizard

8. For the Name, enter *FirstActor* and click **Create Class**.

9. Allow the class creation process to occur. Visual Studio will automatically be opened. Do not close it. Allow it to generate all the necessary files for our class. A blue strip at the bottom of the Visual Studio editor will say *Ready*, as in the following image:

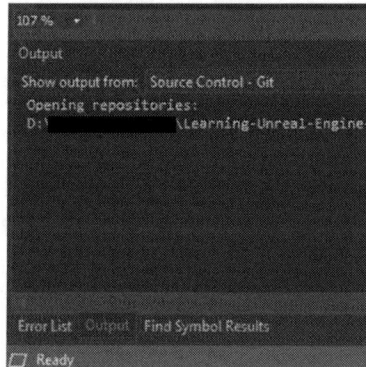

Figure 5.3: Visual Studio Finished Generating Files

Notice that our new class, FirstActor, has some code already in the header (.*h*) and source (.*cpp*) files. The header file includes some headers that are necessary for the Actor class to function:

- *CoreMinimal.h*: This header contains a bunch of other headers that will allow us to access utilities in the engine. You can search for *CoreMinimal.h* in the **Solution Explorer** to open it and see all the headers included in it.

- *GameFramework/Actor.h*: This is the class from which we are deriving our FirstActor class.

- *FirstActor.generated.h*: This is an auto-generated class. This .*generated* header include must be the bottommost include (you cannot place a #include below it in this file, or you'll get a compilation error). This is because the reflection system gives us code we will use throughout the file and other header files placed after the .*generated* file will interfere with it.

You will notice some macros (the purple items in all caps). These are associated with the reflection system. You also may have noticed that the name of our `Actor` has been prefixed with an A. This is because Unreal Engine's convention is to prefix any class derived from `Actor` with a capital A. This makes it easy to recognize an `Actor` in code, and this convention is used with other types of classes in Unreal Engine as well. Classes derived from the `Object` class are prefixed with a U. Structs in Unreal Engine are typically prefixed with an F (standing for `float`; this comes from the fact that `struct`s are used for mathematical utilities, and most math in Unreal Engine is performed using `float` values). You will also notice that these declared functions have definitions in the *.cpp* file.

Now that we've created our first `Actor` class, it's time to look at how Unreal Engine's auto-generated code works behind the scenes.

Generated Files, Garbage Collection, and the Unreal Header Tool

It's important to understand some of the stuff that goes on under the hood of the engine. Some important details are the automatic generation of special files, garbage collection, and how the Unreal Header Tool works. We'll discuss these now.

Generated Files

Unreal Engine automatically generated the *FirstActor.generated.h* file for us. It contains code specific to the reflection system. But what exactly does it do? What is reflection, and why do we care? **Reflection** is the ability of a program to observe itself at runtime. This is done for different reasons in different programs, but we can gain some understanding of how it behaves in Unreal Engine, starting with garbage collection.

Garbage Collection

As we saw in the previous chapter, dynamically creating an instance of a class at runtime places that object in heap memory. Dynamically allocated objects constructed using the new keyword, must be manually deleted using the delete keyword, otherwise they will continue to take up heap memory until the program terminates. Garbage collection is the automatic memory management of selected classes. In Unreal Engine, classes marked with the UCLASS() macro are designated to participate in the garbage collection system.

An object of any class that participates in Unreal Engine's garbage collection system is **reference counted**. This means that if the number of pointers that point to it drop down to zero, it will be marked for deletion, and thus deleted upon the next periodic garbage collection cycle. This means you can dynamically construct objects on the heap without ever worrying about deleting them yourself. Because programming games in Unreal Engine typically involves the use of garbage collected items, you will seldom, if at all, ever use the new and delete keywords in your programming.

The special macros we see in our class are what mark pieces of code for participation in the reflection system. But how does it all work? It works via the use of the Unreal Header Tool.

The Unreal Header Tool (UHT)

The Unreal Header Tool is a **parsing** and **code generation tool**. This means it goes over the lines of a header file (parses it) searching for special macros and uses those macros to generate custom code. This results in reflection system features. This includes recognizing the UCLASS() macro on a class and ensuring that it gets garbage collected (among other things). It also allows us to mark functions and variables with macros that tell the UHT to generate the necessary code to expose them to Blueprints. We'll get more experience using this feature in the UPROPERTY Macros and UFUNCTION Macros sections of this chapter, as well as throughout the course of this book.

So now that we have a basic understanding of how the Unreal Header Tool parses header files and automatically generates code, enabling the reflection system to work, we're ready to start coding. Let's start with two functions that belong to the Actor class by default: Tick and BeginPlay.

Tick and BeginPlay

We will now become familiar with the `Tick` and `BeginPlay` functions. These are two of the most important functions for an `Actor` and are used frequently in game programming.

Tick

The `Tick` function is called every frame during the game. Frames are updates which usually occur between 60 and 120 times per second. The frequency is constantly varying during the game, depending on the level of computations taking place and taking up resources. `Tick` takes a `float` parameter called `DeltaTime`. `DeltaTime` is the amount of time that has passed since the last frame.

You will notice that `Tick` has the following line in the function body:

```
Super::Tick(DeltaTime);
```

This is a call to the parent `Tick` function, that on the `Actor` class. `BeginPlay` has a similar call.

We will begin by logging information to the **Output Log**. The **Output Log** can be accessed by going to *Window -> Developer Tools -> Output Log*. A tab will appear next to the **Content Browser** called **Output Log**.

The **Output Log** shows information that is logged throughout the game process by the engine. Errors and warning show here, and we can even log to the **Output Log** ourselves. We will use a special macro that allows us to log a warning:

```
UE_LOG(LogTemp, Warning,
TEXT("DeltaTime: %f"), DeltaTime);
```

The first argument, `LogTemp`, is the category of the log. The second is the verbosity. Depending on the

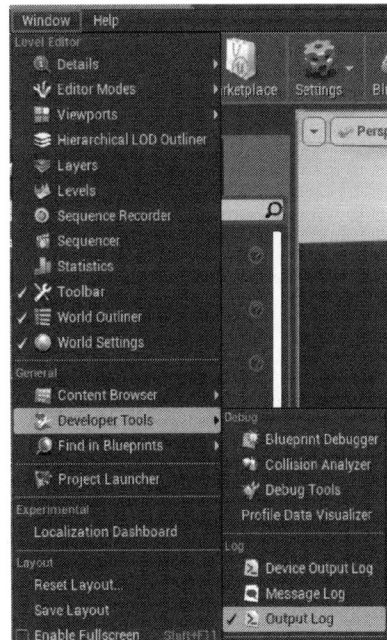

Figure 5.4: Enabling the Output Log

verbosity settings, a log may or may not log to the output. We will discuss the mechanics of logs in more detail in *Chapter 10 - Logging, Debug Tools and Tracing*. The third argument uses a `TEXT` macro to ensure that the string printed to the Output Log is a **UNICODE** string. UNICODE is a text encoding protocol which makes it convenient for systems to be able to accommodate for a large variety of characters. The text in this macro is what will be printed to the **Output Log**. The `%f` symbol in the string is an **escape sequence**, a symbol that tells the string to replace `%f` with the next `float` value passed in, which we provide for the next argument: `DeltaTime`. After the `TEXT()` supplied, we can supply any number of arguments, provided the corresponding escape sequences are provided in the text string. We will get more practice doing this throughout this book. As the text gets printed to the Output Log, the value of `DeltaTime` will be passed in and the `%f` will be replaced by that value.

Compile the Visual Studio solution by either going to *Build->| Build Solution* or using the keyboard shortcut *CTRL + SHIFT + B*. Once the build is completed, we can test out our new log functionality!

Once the Visual Studio project is compiled, in the Unreal Engine editor, in the **Content Browser**, click on *C++ Classes -> First Game*, and you will see the C++ classes we have created. Click on *FirstActor* and drag it out into the world. Since there is no geometry to give this `Actor` a visual representation, we will not be able to see it in the **Viewport**, but we will be able to see it in the **World Outliner**. It should show up as `FirstActor`. If we ever need to edit the properties on the `Actor` or even delete it, we can always do so from the **World Outliner**.

Click on the **Output Log** to see the **Output Log** and press **Play**. You should see the log message printed to the **Output Log** each frame. Functionality that is performed each frame, or very frequently, like this is known as **spamming**. Witness the log message as it spams the output log and prints the value of `DeltaTime` for each frame.

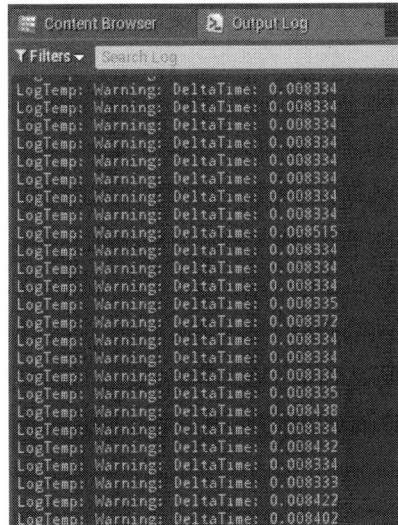

Figure 5.5: Spamming the Output Log by Printing DeltaTime

Logging functionality is useful for developers. It can be used to show if and when certain functions are called, as well as print values as we have done here.

You may have noticed in the `FirstActor` constructor the line:

```
PrimaryActorTick.bCanEverTick = true;
```

This is a boolean that will enable or disable ticking functionality for the `Actor` depending on the value of it. `Actor`s are set to allow ticking functionality by default; you can set this value to `false` to disable ticking for this particular `Actor`.

Another useful function is `BeginPlay`. We will explore it now.

BeginPlay

`BeginPlay` is an important function in Unreal Engine game programming. It is called at the start of an `Actor`'s lifetime. This means the start of the game for `Actor`s that are already in the level. For `Actor`s that are **spawned** (created in the world) dynamically, `BeginPlay` is called upon the creation of those `Actor`s.

Since we are spamming the log from `Tick`, we will want to comment out the `UE_LOG` macro there with two slashes, `//`. In `BeginPlay`, just under the `Super` call, we will place a new log:

```
UE_LOG(LogTemp, Warning, TEXT("Actor: %s was created!"),
*GetName());
```

This time, we use the escape sequence `%s` which is used for strings. We call the function `GetName`, which is inherited from `Actor` (which inherits it from `Object`, and so on). The function `GetName` returns an `FString`, which is a type in Unreal Engine like the `string` class from the C++ Standard Library. This object type is itself not a string literal (a series of character values) but the string literal can be accessed by prefixing the `FString` value with an asterisk (`*`). This is an operator overload that exists for the `FString` class, which returns the string literal value from the `FString` object.

`GetName` gets the name of the Actor on which we are calling it. When we print this value to the Output Log for our `FirstActor` Actor, we should get something like the following.

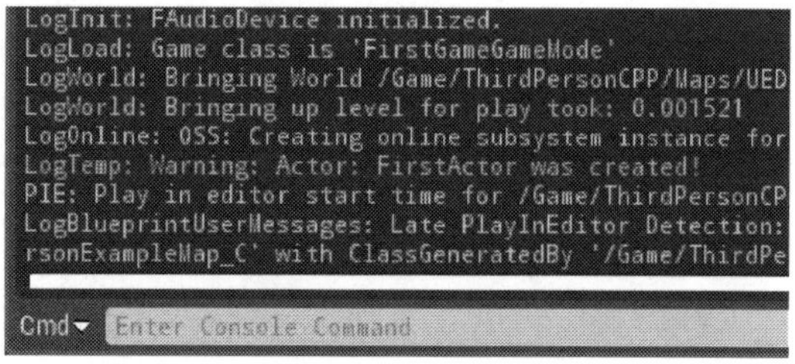

Figure 5.6: Logging the Result of GetName

This can be useful when trying to determine which `Actor` in the game is calling a particular function at a particular time.

Now that we have some practice working with `Tick` and `BeginPlay`, it's time to start using some of the features of the reflection system to enhance our game development skills. One of the most useful features of the reflection system is the ability to expose variables to Blueprints. We will now visit this capability.

Marking Variables with UPROPERTY Macros

We can mark variables in our `Actor` with the UPROPERTY macro. This designates them to participate in garbage collection. It also allows us to expose them to Blueprints. The UPROPERTY macros can take arguments, called **specifiers**, which determine the various qualities of that particular UPROPERTY.

We will start by creating a couple of variables and marking them with UPROPRTY macros.

1. In the *.h* file, in the `public` section, just under the `FirstActor` constructor, add:

```
UPROPERTY(VisibleAnywhere)
float ActorLifetime;

UPROPERTY(EditAnywhere)
int32 ActorLevel;
```

Notice that we don't place semicolons at the end of lines with UPROPERTY macros. Our first variable, `ActorLifetime`, we designate to be `VisibleAnywhere`, which means we can see the property on the Blueprint (once we create it) in the **Details** panel, as well as in the **Details** panel for an individual instance of the `Actor` in the game. The second variable, `ActorLevel`, we designate to be `EditAnywhere`, which means we can not only see the value in the **Details** panel for the Blueprint as well as in the **Details** panel for an instance in the game, but we can change it from the **Details** panel as well. Also notice that we don't use the `int` data type for our integer. We use `int32`, a special type which ensures that the integer will be 32 bits. This is because the `int` type may or may not be exactly 32 bits, depending on the system on which the game is deployed. Specifying the size makes the game more **portable** (capable of running on multiple platforms).

`ActorLifetime` is a `float`, and for it to represent the lifetime of the `Actor`, we'll need to update it. `Tick` is the perfect function in which to do this.

2. Add this line to the `Tick` function:

```
ActorLifetime += DeltaTime;
```

This will result in `ActorLifetime` being updated each frame, incremented by the length of time passed since the previous frame.

To see these variables exposed to Blueprints, we will need to create a new Blueprint based on the `FirstActor` C++ class.

3. In the **Content Browser**, find `FirstActor`, right-click on it, and select **Create Blueprint Class Based on FirstActor**. Call this *FirstActor_BP* and select the *Chapter5* folder. The **Blueprint Editor** for this `Actor` will automatically pop up. In the **Details** panel, under the **First Actor** section, notice the two variables we exposed to Blueprints as shown in the following screenshot:

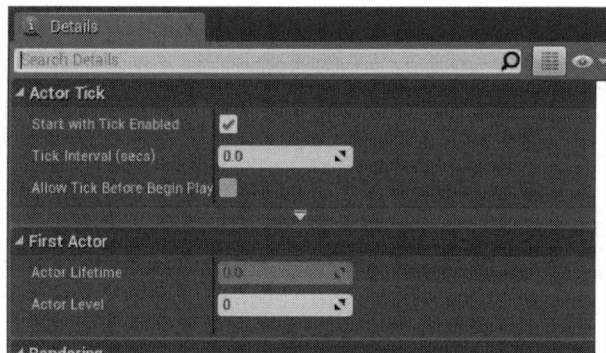

Figure 5.7: Exposing ActorLifetime and ActorLevel to Blueprints

Notice a couple things. First, spaces were provided between words in the variable names. When using **camel case** (capitalizing words in variable names, keeping the rest of the variable name lowercase), Unreal Engine discerns that the variable name consists of multiple words and automatically separates them when showing them in Blueprints. Also notice that *Actor Lifetime* is grayed out; you cannot change it. *Actor Level*, on the other hand, is not grayed out, and you can click in the text box and enter in any integer value you like. This is because we designated the `ActorLifetime` variable to be `VisibleAnywhere`, a specifier that prevents it from being altered either in the default Blueprint or on an instance in-game, and `ActorLevel` to be `EditAnywhere`, a specifier that allows it to be altered either in the default Blueprint or on an instance in-game.

We can see the values on an instance in the game by clicking on our `Actor` in the **World Outliner** to select it. The **Details** panel in the **Level Editor** will populate with context-sensitive data for the selected Actor, including the variables we exposed to Blueprints.

Hit play, then select the `FirstActor` in the **World Outliner**. You will see that the value for *Actor Lifetime* is updating very rapidly. Each frame, the `DeltaTime` value is added to it, showing in real-time the `Actor`'s lifetime in seconds.

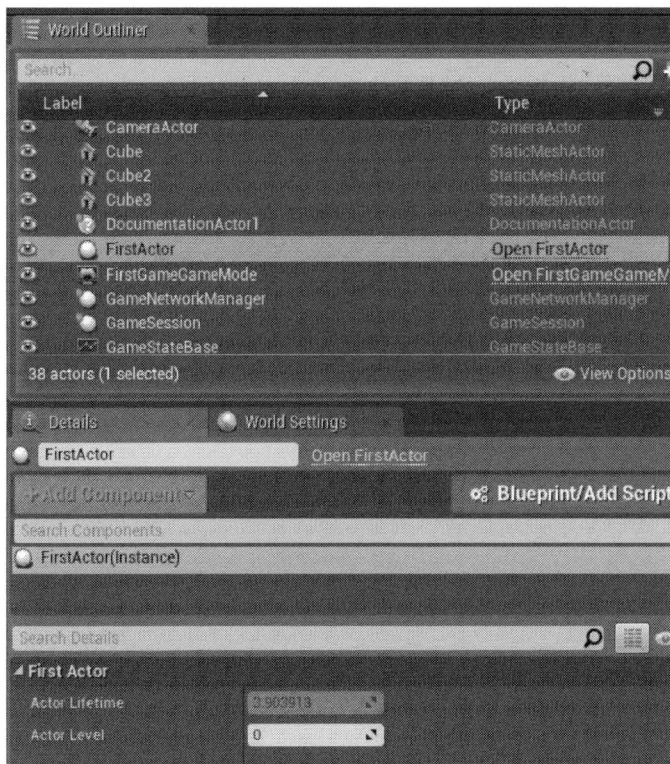

Figure 5.8: Actor Lifetime Updated in Real-Time

Now, we have two ways to check on the values of our variables in-game. One is to log them to the **Output Log** with a log message using UE_LOG, and the other is to expose the variable to Blueprints and observe the value by selecting the individual instance of the `Actor` from the **World Outliner** and finding the exposed variable.

Notes on Defaults vs. Instances

Remember, the **Blueprint Editor** for a given Actor shows the default values for that class in its **Details** panel. The **Details** panel for an individual instance of an Actor in the level shows the properties of the individual instance. Changing default properties affects all instances; changing the properties of an instance does not affect any other instances, nor does it affect the properties in the default Blueprint.

Now that we know how to expose variables to Blueprints, we need to understand a few important specifiers that can help us gain more control over the data in our game. The following is a list of important specifiers that will come in handy throughout this book:

- VisibleAnywhere: The property is visible in the **Details** panel for the default Blueprint as well as in the **Details** panel for instances of the Actor in the level. It is not editable in either case.

- VisibleDefaultsOnly: The property is visible in the **Details** panel for the default Blueprint, but not in the **Details** panel for instances of the Actor in the level. It is not editable.

- VisibleInstanceOnly: The property is only visible in the **Details** panel for an instance in the level. It cannot be edited.

- EditAnywhere: The property is visible and editable in the **Details** panel both in the default Blueprint and in the **Details** panel for instances in the level.

- EditInstanceOnly: The property is visible and editable in the **Details** panel for instances in the level, but it is not visible in the **Details** panel in the default Blueprint.

- EditDefaultsOnly: The property is visible and editable in the **Details** panel in the default Blueprint, but it is not visible or editable for instances in the level.

Whether or not a property is visible or editable in the defaults or on an instance has nothing to do with whether or not it can be used in the **Event Graph**. For a C++ variable to be useable in the **Event Graph** as a Blueprint node, you must designate it as such in the variable's UPROPERTY macro. A UPROPERTY macro can contain multiple specifiers, as in the following example.

4. Add these specifiers to the variables we created earlier:

```
UPROPERTY(VisibleAnywhere, BlueprintReadOnly, Category
= "Learning About Specifiers")
    float ActorLifetime;

UPROPERTY(EditAnywhere, BlueprintReadWrite, Category =
"Learning About Specifiers")
    int32 ActorLevel;
```

We added BlueprintReadOnly to ActorLifetime, thus enabling it to be accessed and used in the **Event Graph** in the default Blueprint. Notice also the Category specifier. This will result in the variables being placed in their own category, given the label we chose: *Learning About Specifiers*. We can see this category in the **Details** panel in the figure below.

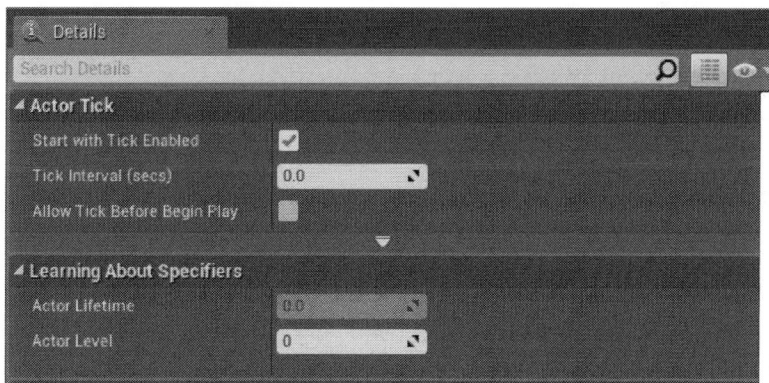

Figure 5.9: Variables in the Learning About Specifiers Category

5. Right-clicking in the **Event Graph** and typing Actor lifetime will result in the *Get Actor Lifetime* option showing up.

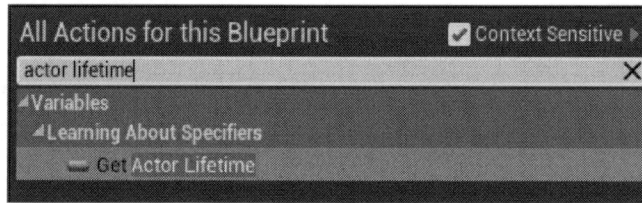

Figure 5.10: Searching for Actor Lifetime in the Event Graph

6. Clicking on *Get Actor Lifetime* results in access to an *Actor Lifetime* node, the return pin of which will return the value of *Actor Lifetime* in the **Event Graph** as shown in the following screenshot:

Figure 5.11: Accessing Actor Lifetime from the Event Graph

However, we cannot set the value for it, as it is *read only*. We did, however, add `BlueprintReadWrite` to `ActorLevel`, enabling it to be accessed and used, as well as set from the **Event Graph**.

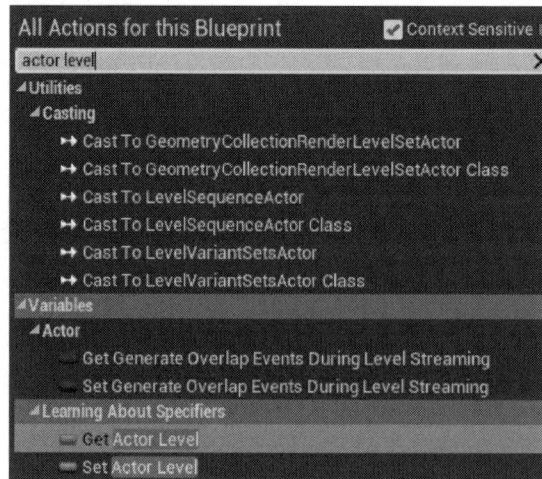

Figure 5.12: Accessing Get Actor Level and Set Actor Level in the Event Graph

7. Select *Set Actor Level.* This allows us to get a *Set Actor Level* node in the **Event Graph** and thus we can set its value from in the default Blueprint, using, for instance, *Event Begin Play* as follows.

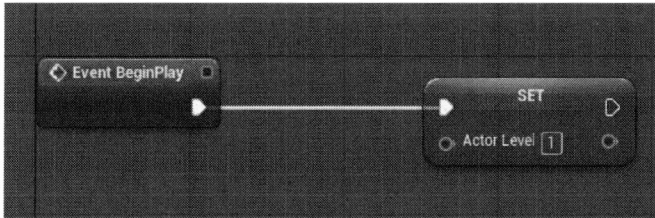

Figure 5.13: Setting Actor Level to a Value of 1 with Begin Play

This makes it possible not only to manipulate data in C++, but also in the Blueprint. To summarize:

- `BlueprintReadWrite`**:** The property can be accessed and set in the **Event Graph** of the default Blueprint.

- `BlueprintReadOnly`**:** The property can be accessed in the **Event Graph**, but it cannot be set from within the default Blueprint.

In order to see the results of our setter in the **Event Graph** for *Actor Level*, we must create an instance based on our Blueprint. Thus far, we have merely dragged in an instance of the C++ class called `FirstActor`. This instance contains only the C++ features of the class, but none of the features in the Blueprint itself.

8. Bring a *FirstActor_BP* into our level by simply clicking and dragging it in. Once we do so, we can see a white ball where we dragged our `Actor` into the world. This shows us where the `Actor` is (a benefit we don't get when we simply drag in an instance based on a C++ class directly). Notice `FirstActor_BP` in the **World Outliner** as well.

Press **Play**, then click on the **Output Log** to see the output log. You will see the log messages from `BeginPlay` printed to the screen:

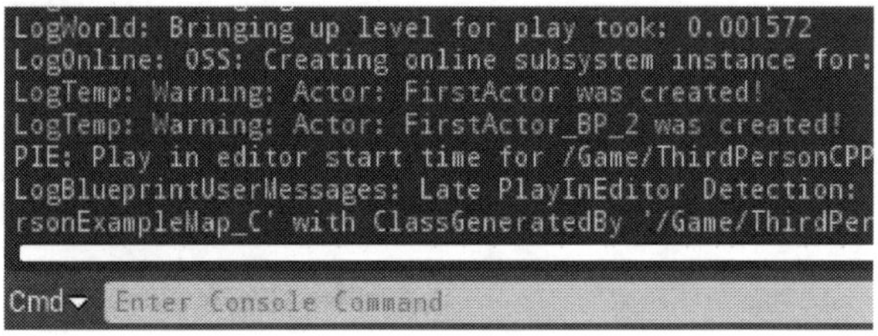

```
LogWorld: Bringing up level for play took: 0.001572
LogOnline: OSS: Creating online subsystem instance for:
LogTemp: Warning: Actor: FirstActor was created!
LogTemp: Warning: Actor: FirstActor_BP_2 was created!
PIE: Play in editor start time for /Game/ThirdPersonCPP
LogBlueprintUserMessages: Late PlayInEditor Detection:
rsonExampleMap_C' with ClassGeneratedBy '/Game/ThirdPer
```

```
Cmd ▾  Enter Console Command
```

Figure 5.14: Log Messages from Both Actors in the Level

You can also select *FirstActor_BP* in the **World Outliner** and see that the *Actor Level* property has a value of 1, whereas the *Actor Level* property of the `FirstActor` class (based on a C++ class directly) still has its default value of 0, because it does not have any Blueprint functionality.

It is now clear how much power the C++ programmer holds over the variables in each `Actor` class. With the `UPROPERTY` macro, specifiers can be used to designate whether a variable can be visible or editable in the **Details** panel in the default Blueprint or on an instance in the level. Specifiers can also be used to enable a variable in a C++ class to be used in the **Event Graph** in the Blueprint for that class and determines whether the variable can be accessed or editable in that Blueprint.

Functions can also be exposed to Blueprints via the use of `UFUNCTION` macros. We will now observe how to do this with an example.

UFUNCTION Macros

Functions can be exposed to Blueprints, in a similar manner to the way variables can be exposed to Blueprints. The `UFUNCTION` macro allows for this.

1. In the `FirstActor`'s *.h* file, just under the `class UStaticMeshComponent* FirstActorMesh;` line, add:

```
UFUNCTION(BlueprintCallable)
void CheckLifetime();

UFUNCTION(BlueprintImplementableEvent,
BlueprintCallable)

void PrintLevel();
```

We give the `CheckLifetime` function the `UFUNCTION` macro specifier `BlueprintCallable`, which allows the function to be callable from the **Event Graph** in the Blueprint. We give the `PrintLevel` function the specifier `BlueprintImplementableEvent`, which designates this function to be an event which will be implemented in Blueprints. This means that we will not define the function here in C++ but will define its implementation in the **Event Graph**.

2. We still, however, need to provide a definition for the `CheckLifetime` function, so we will add the following to the *.cpp* file:

```
void AFirstActor::CheckLifetime()
{
    ActorLevel = ActorLifetime;

}
```

This function takes the `ActorLifetime` variable, which is a `float`, and assigns it to the `ActorLevel` variable, an `int32`. Because the types are not the same, an implicit type conversion is carried out, converting the value of `ActorLifetime` to an `int32`, which results in the truncation of the decimal portion of the value. This will result in the value of `ActorLevel` being increased by a value of 1 each second. None of this will occur, however, if the function is never called, so we need to call it somewhere. Since we made this function `BlueprintCallable`, why not call it from Blueprints?

3. In the **Event Graph** for `FirstActor_BP`, add the following:

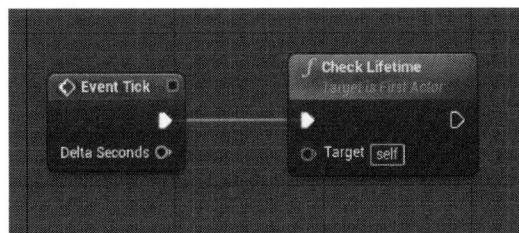

Figure 5.15: Calling CheckLifetime from the Event Graph

We are using the *Event Tick* event in the **Event Graph** to call *Check Lifetime* once per frame.

4. Now for the `PrintLevel` function. To implement this function in Blueprints, right-click in the **Event Graph** and type "printlevel" as shown in the following screenshot:

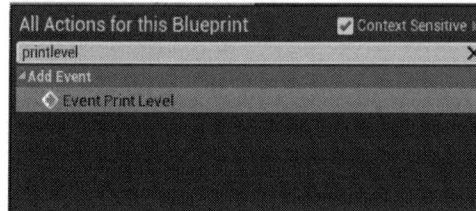

Figure 5.16: Searching for Event Print Level

5. Select this and you will see the *Event Print Level* node, which resembles the other event nodes in the **Event Graph**:

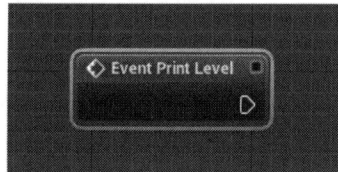

Figure 5.17: The Event Print Level Node

We can define the functionality for the *Print Level* function here in Blueprints.

6. Drag off of the output execution pin and release. Then type "print string" and select *Print String*.

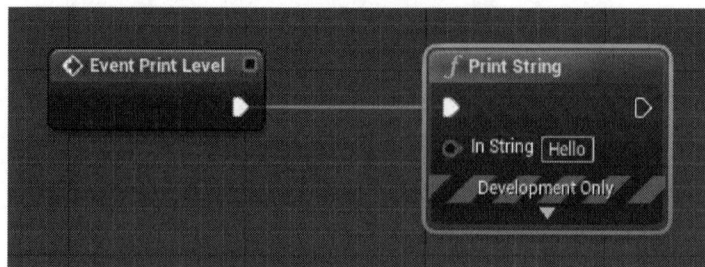

Figure 5.18: Calling Print String from Print Level

7. Right-click in the **Event Graph** and type "get Actor level" and select *Get Actor Level*. You will now see an *Actor Level* node.

8. Drag the output pin from *Actor Level* into the input *In String* pin in the *Print String* node. A conversion from integer to String node will automatically appear, performing the conversion for you.

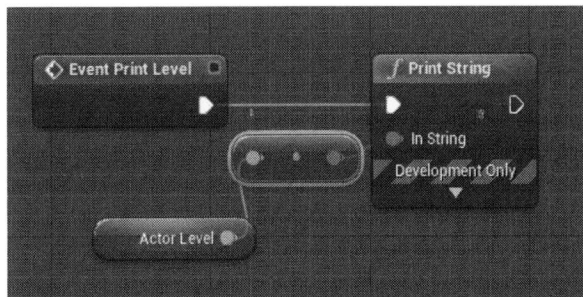

Figure 5.19: Implementing Event Print Actor Level

Now when *Print Level* gets called, the functionality defined in the **Event Graph** will be carried out. We simply need to call the function somewhere. We can call the function from the *Tick* event.

9. Drag off of the output execution pin on *Check Lifetime* and type "print level" and select *Print Level*.

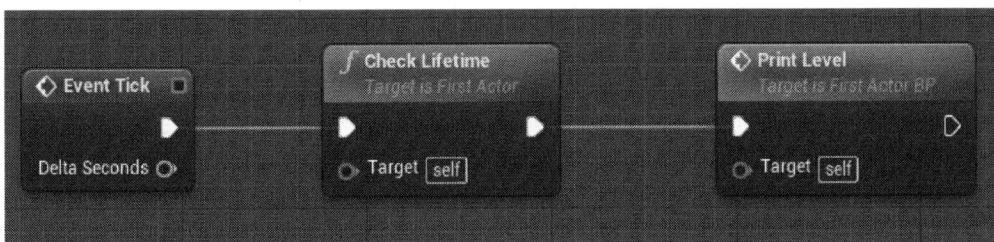

Figure 5.20: Calling Print Level in Begin Play

Now the *Print Level* function will be called each frame, printing the current value of *Actor Level* to the screen.

Test these functions out by pressing **Play** and noticing the spamming of the **Viewport** with the result of the **Print String** function. Then select *FirstActor_BP* in the **World Outliner** and see the *Actor Level* variable updating in real-time, increasing by 1 each frame.

We will gain much more experience using these capabilities throughout this book. Now that we have a taste of them, we are ready to move on to the next feature of the `Actor` class: components.

Components – Adding a Static Mesh

Components are objects that belong to other objects. An `Actor` often needs a visual representation in the world, and this is typically in the form of a mesh. Our project has several meshes already, thanks to the fact that we chose to include starter content when we created the project.

While we can easily add components from the **Blueprint Editor**, we may wish to create the component in C++ so we can have a variable that can give us access to the component in our game code. We will create a component of the type `StaticMeshComponent` and expose it to Blueprints.

1. Just under the `ActorLifetime` and `ActorLevel` variables, add:

```
    UPROPERTY (VisibleAnywhere, BlueprintReadWrite,
Category = "Learning About Components")
    class UStaticMeshComponent* FirstActorMesh;
```

We have created a pointer to `StaticMeshComponent`. While classes derived from the the `Actor` type have names prefixed with an `A`, the `StaticMeshComponent` type name is prefixed with a `U`, indicating that it is based on the `UObject` class, and that it is not an `Actor`. You will also notice the use of the `class` keyword. This is known as a **forward declaration**–a way of telling the compiler that the header for the class in question is not included in this immediate file, but that it will be included somewhere down the line. This satisfies the compiler when it stumbles upon the `UStaticMeshComponent` class type in a file that does not contain the header which defines it. The compiler will, however, expect to see that header file if the variable of that particular type ends up getting used. We will use the variable in the *.cpp* file, thus we will need to include a header file there. By forward declaring it in the *.h* file, we skirt around the requirement to include its header file there, thus only needing to include it where it's really needed: the *.cpp* file. By keeping the amount of header file inclusion to a minimum, we can reduce **code bloat** (the tendency for code to be unnecessarily large).

So how do we know which header file we will need to include for the `UStaticMeshComponent` type? One way is to check the Unreal Engine official documentation. By searching for "UE4 UStaticMeshComponent" in your favorite search Engine, or by visiting the official Unreal Engine documentation page directly at https://docs.unrealengine.com you can search the documentation for the class type in question. Searching for `UStaticMeshComponent` will bring you to the documentation for the class, showing the inheritance hierarchy for it, as well as other information including the header file you must include to use the class.

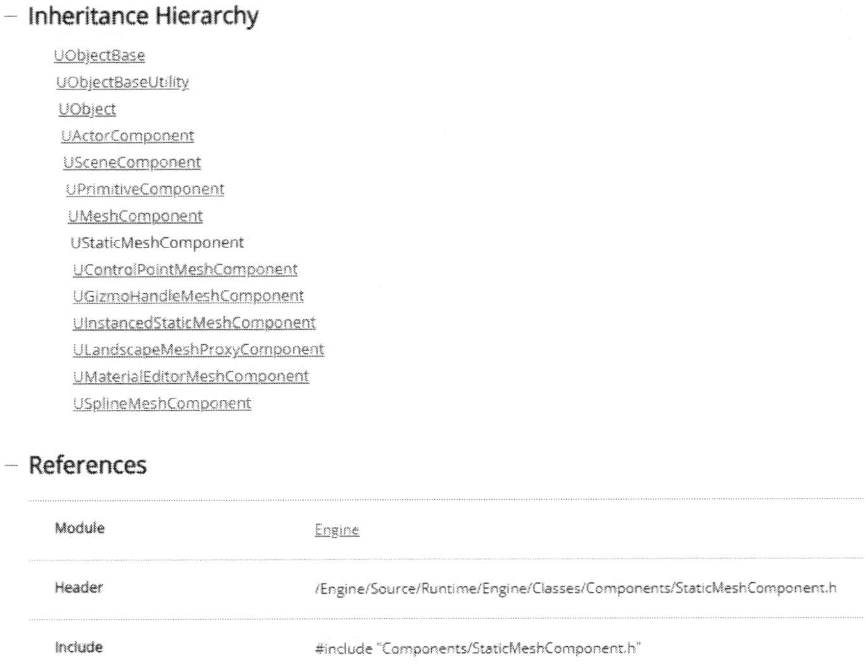

Inheritance Hierarchy

UObjectBase
UObjectBaseUtility
UObject
UActorComponent
USceneComponent
UPrimitiveComponent
UMeshComponent
UStaticMeshComponent
UControlPointMeshComponent
UGizmoHandleMeshComponent
UInstancedStaticMeshComponent
ULandscapeMeshProxyComponent
UMaterialEditorMeshComponent
USplineMeshComponent

References

Module	Engine
Header	/Engine/Source/Runtime/Engine/Classes/Components/StaticMeshComponent.h
Include	#include "Components/StaticMeshComponent.h"

Figure 5.21: The Documentation Page for UStaticMeshComponent

We will thus use the include given here in the .*cpp* file for `FirstActor`.

2. Add the following line to the *FirstActor.cpp* file, just under `#include "FirstActor.h"`:

```
#include "Components/StaticMeshComponent.h"
```

Now when we use the type in the .*cpp* file, it will be defined and the compiler will be happy.

So, we now have a variable called `FirstActorMesh`, of type `UStaticMeshComponent*`, which is a pointer. But we haven't actually created an instance of this type. We simply have a pointer, which is an address to a memory location, but we need to actually create a `StaticMeshComponent` to fill that memory location. We learned in *Chapter 4 – C++ Programming Basics* that we can use the `new` keyword to dynamically create a new object, but then we would need to keep track of it and delete it with the `delete` keyword when we are finished with it. But in Unreal Engine, we have garbage collection, so we typically don't use the `new` keyword. So how to we construct our component?

It turns out that there is a special **Factory function** (a function that creates a new object and returns that object) designed to create new **subobjects** (components belonging to a given object) in the constructor of an object. This function is called `CreateDefaultSubobject` and it is a template function (refer to *Chapter 4 – C++ Programming Basics* for more information on template functions).

3. We will create our new component by adding the following lines to the constructor, just below `PrimaryActorTick.bCanEverTick = true;`:

```
FirstActorMesh =
CreateDefaultSubobject<UStaticMeshComponent>(TEXT("FirstActorMeshComp"));

SetRootComponent(FirstActorMesh);
```

The function `CreateDefaultSubobject` takes a template type parameter, for which we supply `UStaticMeshComponent`. The argument in the parentheses is a `TEXT` macro in which we supply a text label for our component (used internally in the labeling of this object). This function call results in the construction of an object of type

`UStaticMeshComponent` and returns its address. We then are able to store that address in the pointer variable we created, called `FirstActorMesh`.

4.   Now that we have created our new component, maneuver back into the **Blueprint Editor** for *FirstActor_BP* and see `FirstActorMesh` in our **Components** panel:

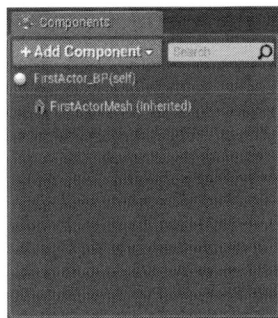

Figure 5.22: Our FirstActorMesh Component

5.   Click on this component to select it. Once selected, the **Details** panel will now show the properties of the new *Static Mesh Component*.

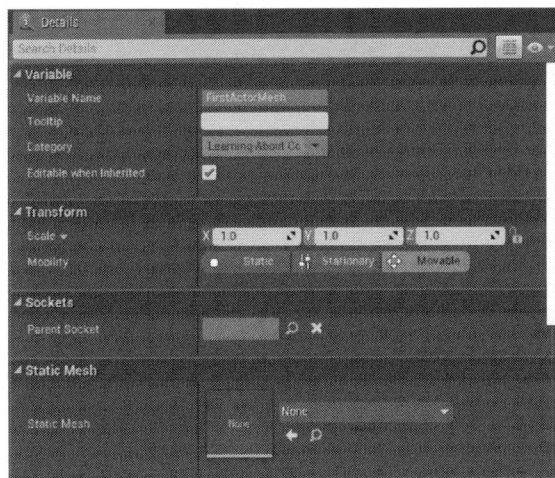

Figure 5.23: Details Panel for the Static Mesh Component

Among these properties is a *Static Mesh* property. This can be populated with a Static Mesh from the dropdown menu.

6. Select *Shape_QuadPyramid* from the dropdown list. The mesh will appear in the **Viewport** in the **Blueprint Editor**.

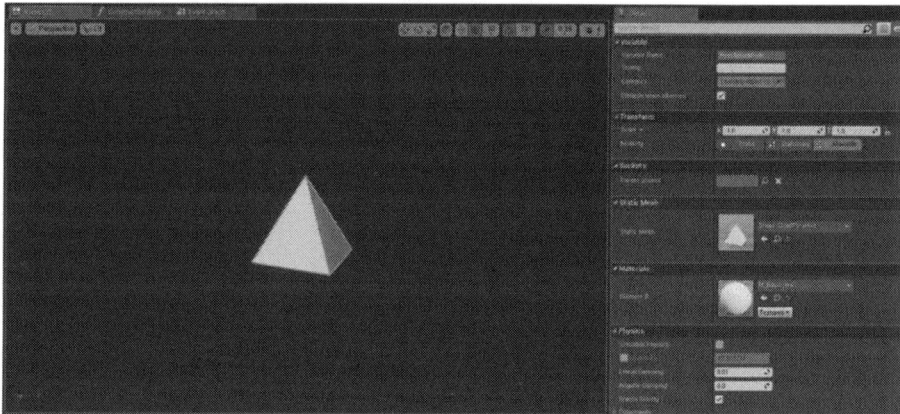

Figure 5.24: Selecting a Pyramid for the Static Mesh Property

Now we have chosen the Static Mesh for our Static Mesh Component. Maneuvering back to the **Level Editor**, we can see that by selecting *FirstActor_BP* in the **World Outliner** and pressing the *F* key to focus on the Actor in the level, our Actor now has a visual representation: a pyramid!

Notes on Static Mesh vs. Static Mesh Component

The Static Mesh Component is not a piece of geometry. The Static Mesh Component is based on the `UStaticMeshComponent` class. The `UStaticMeshComponent` class is a C++ class which contains a number of functions and variables, one of which is of type `UStaticMesh`, and it is called `StaticMesh`. This `UStaticMesh` variable is the actual mesh, and it is this variable that we are populating with data when we select a mesh from the dropdown menu for the *Static Mesh* property in the **Details** panel.

We have seen that we can create a new component by first declaring the component in the *.h* file. We learned that we can forward declare the class using the `class` keyword, which tells the compiler that the header file for the particular type is not present in the current file but that it will be included down the line where the variable will actually be used. We then saw how we could use the `CreateDefaultSubobject` template function to construct a new object and return its address, which we stored in the `FirstActorMesh` pointer variable. We then learned that the `UStaticMeshComponent` is a class containing variables and functions, one variable of which is called `StaticMesh`, of type `UStaticMesh`. We then set the value for that variable in the **Details** panel for the Static Mesh Component in the **Blueprint Editor**.

Now that we know how to add components to our class, we can take a look at a few more useful functions inherited by the `Actor` class designed to get and set an `Actor`'s location and rotation.

Getting and Setting an Actor's Rotation and Location

An Actor's location and rotation are accessible via the inherited getter functions, `GetActorLocation` and `GetActorRotation`, respectively. They can also be set with `SetActorLocation` and `SetActorRotation`, respectively.

1. In the `Tick` function, just below the line `ActorLifetime +=
   DeltaTime;`, add:

```
FVector Location = GetActorLocation();
FRotator Rotation = GetActorRotation();
UE_LOG(LogTemp, Warning, TEXT("%s Location: (%f, %f,
%f), Rotation: (%f, %f, %f)"), *GetName(), Location.X,
Location.Y, Location.Z, Rotation.Pitch, Rotation.Yaw,
Rotation.Roll );
Location.Z += 15.f * DeltaTime;
Rotation.Yaw += 45.f * DeltaTime;
SetActorLocation(Location);

SetActorRotation(Rotation);
```

Here, we are creating two **local variables** (variables that exist within the scope of the given block, in this case, the scope of the `Tick` function), `Location` and `Rotation`. `GetActorLocation` gets the location of the Actor in the form of an `FVector`. `FVector` is a `struct` that contains the `X`, `Y`, and `Z` components of the Actor's location in the form of `float` values. They can be accessed via the dot (`.`) operator, as is done in the `UE_LOG` call. `GetActorRotation` gets the rotation of the Actor and returns it in the form of an `FRotator`. `FRotator` is similar to `FVector`, only it contains the `Yaw`, `Pitch`, and `Roll` components of the Actor's rotation in the form of `float` values. We then use `UE_LOG`, printing a string of text with several escape sequences: `%s` for the Actor's name, three `%f` symbols for the `X`, `Y`, and `Z` components of the location, and three `%f` symbols for the `Yaw`, `Pitch`, and `Roll` of the Actor's rotation.

We then access the `Z` component of the `Location` variable and add a `float` value of `15.f * DeltaTime` to it. We access the `Yaw` component and add a `float` value of `45.f * DeltaTime` to it. We then use `SetActorLocation`, a function that takes an input parameter of type `FVector`, to set the location of the Actor. We also use `SetActorRotation`, a function that takes an input parameter of type `FRotator`, to set the rotation of the Actor.

Using Delta Time

We used `DeltaTime` as a scale factor for the amounts we added to the `Location` and `Rotation` variables each frame. This is because the frequency of the `Tick` function varies as the game's use of the computer's resources varies. To avoid the `Location` and `Rotation` change rates varying with the frequency of the frame rate, we compensate for the change by multiplying by `DeltaTime`. When the frame rate is higher, `DeltaTime` is lower. When the frame rate is lower, `DeltaTime` is higher. Adding a value of `45.f * DeltaTime` to the rotation of an `Actor` results in setting a constant rotation rate of 45 degrees per second.

2. Before we test this code, we should delete the `FirstActor` C++ class instance from our level. Do so.

The reason is because the C++ code for both the C++ `Actor` and the Blueprint Actor will run, and we will have two different `Actors` spamming the log at once, making it difficult to make any sense of the information. Locate *FirstActor* in the **World Outliner** and hit the *Delete* key on your keyboard. Now that we have just one *FirstActor* in the world, *FirstActor_BP*, we can test out our code. Drag the *FirstActor_BP* to a spot in front of the Third-Person Character so you can see it when you press **Play**.

Press **Play**, then click on the **Output Log**.

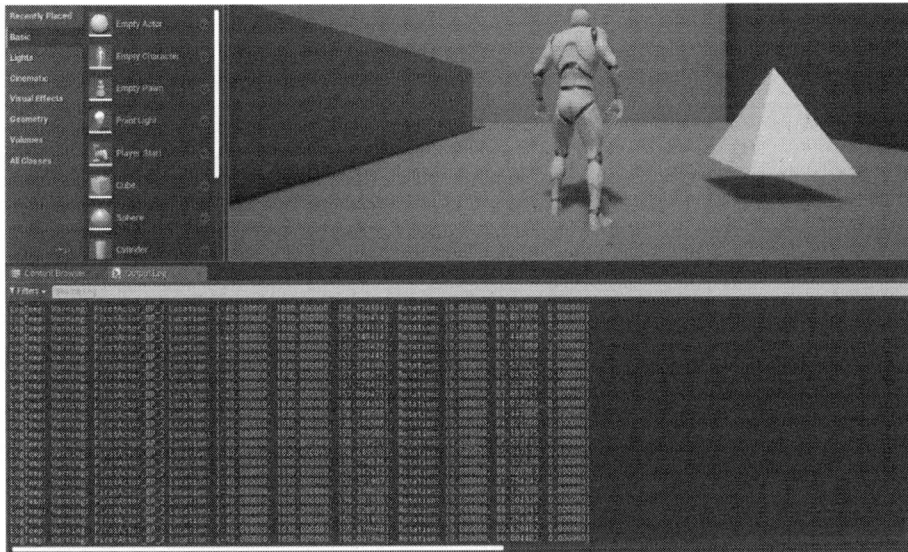

Figure 5.25: Changing Location and Rotation of the Pyramid and Printing it to the Output Log

Notice two things: the pyramid is raising and spinning, and the **Output Log** is spamming the Actor's location and rotation.

Now that we have the basics of the `Actor` class down, we are ready to venture into more complicated classes in Unreal Engine. We will continue our journey in the next chapter by diving into the `Pawn` class.

Summary

We learned that Unreal Engine has the capability to create classes from the Unreal Engine class hierarchy, and when doing so, the classes come with some automatically generated macros that enable the class to participate in the Unreal Engine reflection system. We learned that reflection is the ability of a program to observe itself at runtime and the Unreal Header Tool (UHT) scans the class for the automatically generated macros which tell it to generate reflection code. We learned that the reflection system includes garbage collection, which manages memory management for us, so we don't need to use the `new` and `delete` keywords when allocating memory with garbage-collected objects and variables. We then learned how to use `Tick` and `BeginPlay` in C++, and that these are virtual functions inherited and overridden in our `Actor` class. We then learned how to use UPROPERTY and UFUNCTION macros to expose variables and functions to Blueprints, as well as control whether exposed variables can be editable, either on the Blueprint or on instances in the level. We then learned how to add components to our `Actor` class, and added a Static Mesh to give our Actor a visual representation in the world. Finally, we visited some functions used to access the location and rotation of an Actor and used logging capabilities to record this information to the **Output Log**.

Now that we have some experience creating Unreal Engine classes and have a grip on the capabilities of an `Actor`, we are ready to look at a class derived from `Actor` which has more specialized capabilities: The `Pawn`.

Chapter 6 – The Pawn Class

We now understand the basics of Actor creation. It's time to start digging deeper into Unreal Engine's class hierarchy. Derived from `Actor` is the `Pawn` class, the `Pawn` inherits all of the characteristics of an `Actor` (including the ability to be placed in the level), but also has additional features. We will examine some of these features in this chapter, including mapping user input (mouse clicks, keyboard strokes, etc.), choosing the *Default Pawn* in the *Game Mode*, binding functions to our mouse and keyboard key mappings, and adding features that are common with Pawns, such as a *Camera Component*.

In this chapter, we're going to cover the following topics:

- Creating a Pawn

- Input – Action and Axis Mappings

- The *Game Mode* and the *Default Pawn*

- Binding Functions to Action and Axis Mappings

- Moving the Pawn

Let's get started with creating a Pawn.

Pawn Creation

We will begin by creating a Pawn. This process is as simple as creating an Actor.

1. In the **Content Browser**, right click the **Content** folder. Select **New Folder**. Name it *Chapter6*.

2. In the *C++ Classes* folder, open the *FirstGame* folder. Right-click and select **New C++ Class**.

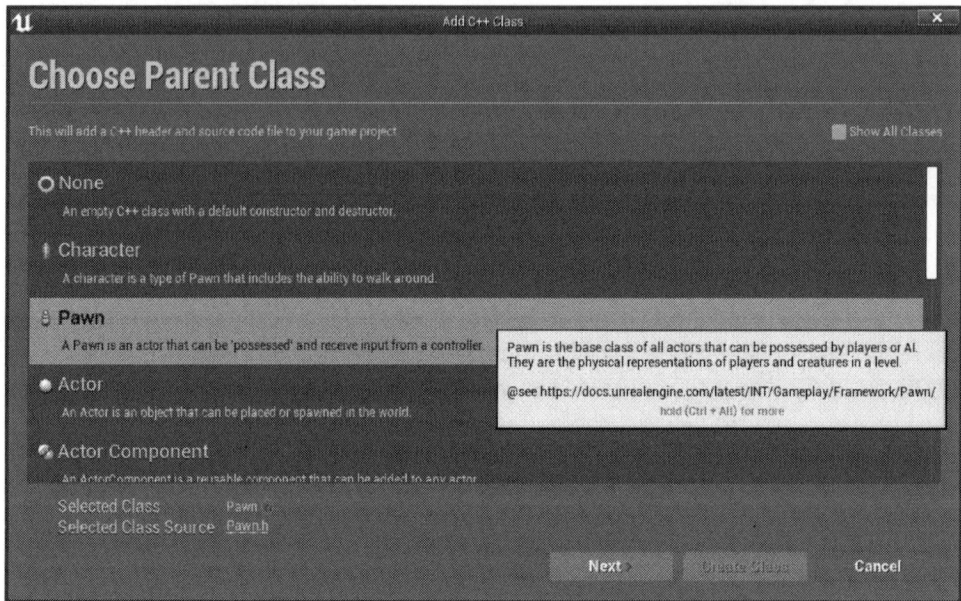

Figure 6.1: Choosing Pawn in the Class Creation Wizard

3. Name the Pawn *FirstPawn*.

4. Allow the class to be created. Visual Studio will open and generate the files.

You will notice that our new `Pawn` class contains some code, similar to the Actor we created in the previous chapter. In *FirstPawn.h*, notice that `BeginPlay`, `Tick`, and `SetupPlayerInputComponent` are marked with the `virtual` and `override` keywords. The `BeginPlay` and `Tick` functions are inherited from the `Actor` class. `SetupPlayerInputComponent` is inherited from the `Pawn` class. We have already seen what `BeginPlay` and `Tick` do. The `SetupPlayerInputComponent` function is used to designate which functions should be mapped to inputs such as keyboard strokes and mouse-clicks. Let's now find out how we can map inputs.

Input – Action and Axis Mappings

Every game requires input of some form. For most traditional video games, this input comes in the form of button presses, mouse clicks and drags, and thumb sticks. Unreal

Engine has the ability to map many different types of user input, meaning it can result in some sort of functionality occurring in response to it.

Setting Up Mappings in Project Settings

Perform the following steps to add inputs to our project.

1. Click *Edit -> Project Settings…* and scroll down to the **Engine** section. Click on **Input**. You will see the following:

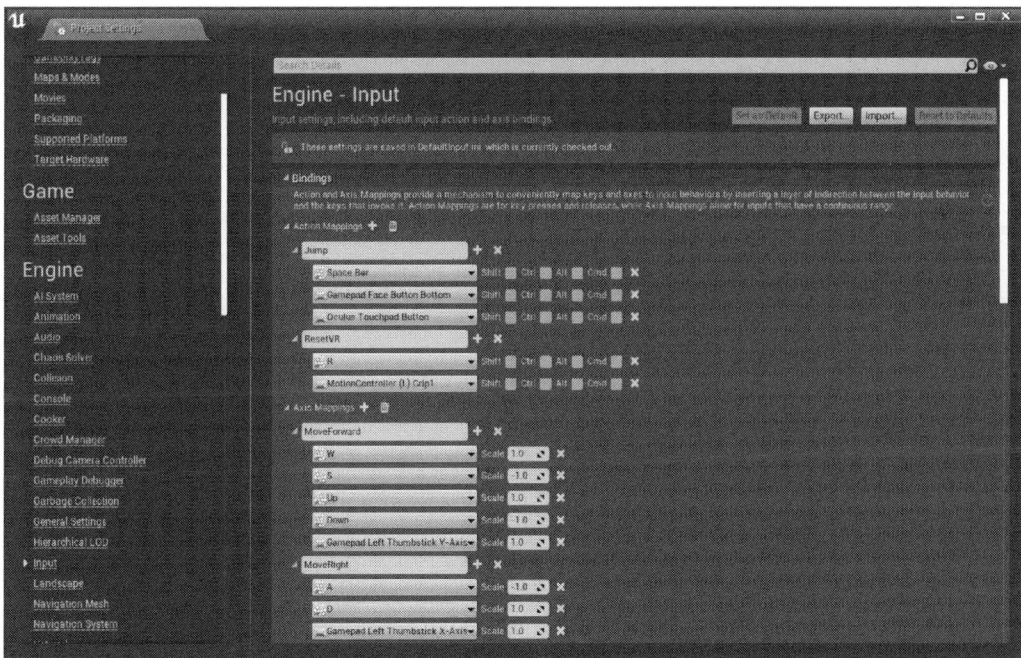

Figure 6.2: Inputs in Project Settings

2. Under **Bindings**, notice that there are already a great deal of bindings already here. We'll examine each of these in more detail shortly. In Unreal Engine, bindings are divided into two categories: *Axis Mappings* and *Action Mappings*. They are explained as follows:

- **Action Mappings**: These allow a response to occur in the event of a key press or a key release. They are "one-offs" in the sense that they fire off a function once each time the press or release occurs.

- **Action Mappings**: These allow a continuous response. Here we use the word continuous to mean each frame. Every frame, like the `Tick` function, the mapping is checked for its value (whether or not a key is currently pressed or not pressed, etc.).

3. Add an action mapping by clicking on the **+** symbol next to **Action Mappings**. A new action mapping will show up just under the *ResetVR* action mapping.

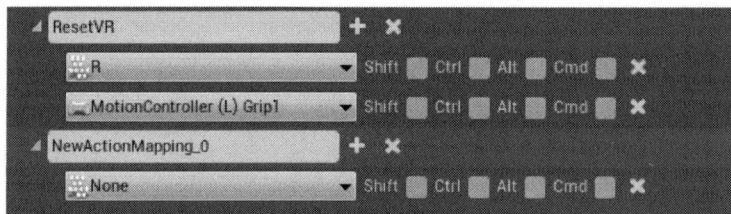

Figure 6.3: New Action Mapping

4. Rename the new action mapping *E_Key*.

5. Click the dropdown menu below the new action mapping and select **Keyboard**, then search for the *E* key.

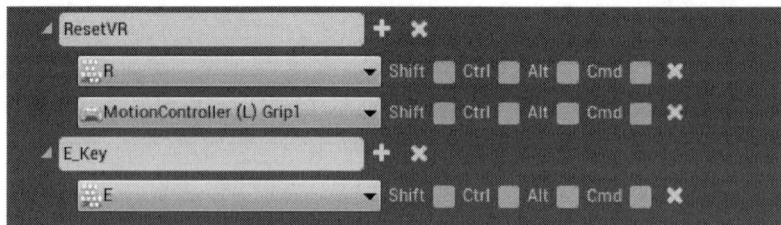

Figure 6.4: Mapping the E Key

6. Press the **+** symbol next to **Axis Mappings**. Scroll down to see that the new axis mapping has appeared below the *LookUp* axis mapping.

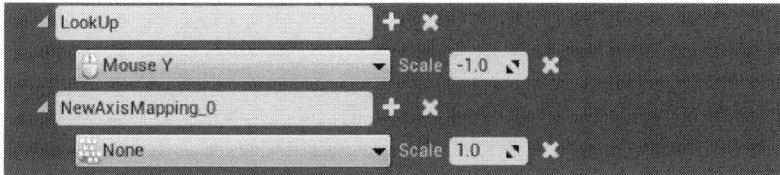

Figure 6.5: New Axis Mapping

7. Rename the new axis mapping *SHIFT_Key*.

8. Select the dropdown below the new axis mapping and find *Left Shift*.

9. Click the **+** symbol next to *SHIFT_Key*. A new dropdown will appear which says *None*. Click this dropdown and search for "right shift" and select *Right Shift*.

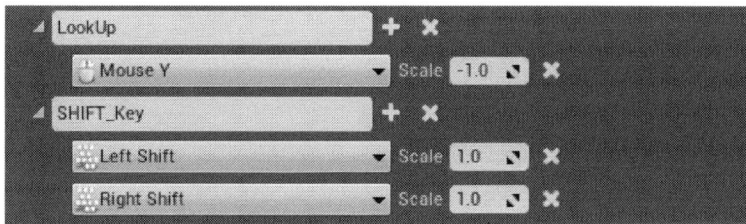

Figure 6.6: Mapping the SHIFT Keys

10. Dock the **Project Settings** tab to the top of the **Level Editor** by clicking the tab and dragging it up next to **ThirdPersonExampleMap**.

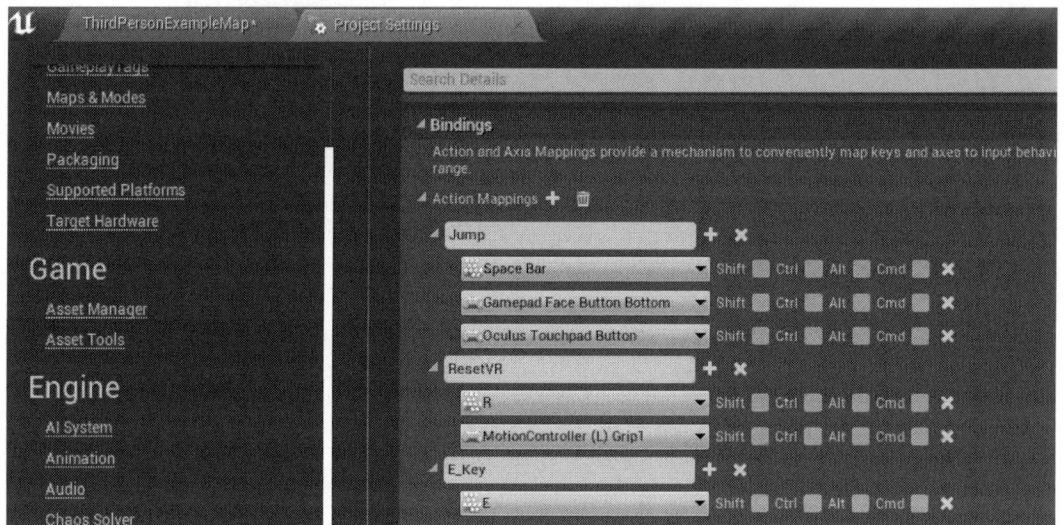

Figure 6.7: Docking the Project Settings Tab to the Top of the Level Editor

Now that we have added a new axis mapping and an action mapping, let's now discover how to use them. Maneuver back to Visual Studio.

The SetupPlayerInputComponent Function

Let's take a look at `SetupPlayerInputComponent`. This function is called at the beginning of the game, after the constructor, but before `BeginPlay`. It takes a pointer to an object of type `UInputComponent` as a parameter, which contains the capability to bind functions to input mappings.

Creating Functions for our Mappings

We'll need some functions that we wish to be called when the keys are pressed. Add the following function declarations to *FirstPawn.h*, just under `BeginPlay`:

```
// Called when the E Key is pressed
void E_KeyPressed();

// Called when the E Key is released
void E_KeyReleased();
```

```
    // Called each frame, with Value being 0.0 when SHIFT
is up, and 1.0 when SHIFT is down
    void ShiftKey(float Value);
```

We will need to define these functions in *FirstPawn.cpp*. Just under the body of BeginPlay, add:

```
void AFirstPawn::E_KeyPressed()
{
    UE_LOG(LogTemp, Warning, TEXT("E Key Pressed"));
}

void AFirstPawn::E_KeyReleased()
{
    UE_LOG(LogTemp, Warning, TEXT("E Key Released"));
}

void AFirstPawn::ShiftKey(float Value)
{
    //UE_LOG(LogTemp, Warning, TEXT("SHIFT Key Axis Value:
%f"), Value);
}
```

Notice we commented out the UE_LOG in ShiftKey. This is because ShiftKey, which will correspond to an axis mapping, will be called each frame, spamming the output log. This will make it difficult to see the messages logged by the E_KeyPressed and E_KeyReleased functions. We'll first test those functions. Then we'll uncomment the log in ShiftKey and test that one out.

Now that we have functions that we can bind to our action and axis mappings, let's do the actual mapping. Add the following code to SetupPlayerInputComponent, just under the call to Super::SetupPlayerInputComponent:

```
    // Set up gameplay key bindings
    check(PlayerInputComponent);

    // Action Mappings
    PlayerInputComponent->BindAction("E_Key", IE_Pressed,
this, &AFirstPawn::E_KeyPressed);
```

```
    PlayerInputComponent->BindAction("E_Key", IE_Released,
this, &AFirstPawn::E_KeyReleased);

    // Axis Mappings
    PlayerInputComponent->BindAxis("SHIFT_Key", this,
&AFirstPawn::ShiftKey);
```

Notice that as soon as we access a function on `PlayerInputComponent` we are met with a red underline indicating an error. Hovering over this underlined identifier, we can see an error that says "pointer to incomplete class type is not allowed." This is because Intellisense will not recognize this class type until we add the proper include. Add this to the includes at the top of *FirstPawn.cpp*:

```
#include "Components/InputComponent.h"
```

Now let's take a look at the code we added to `SetupPlayerInputComponent`.

The check Assertion

We used the `check` macro, passing in `PlayerInputComponent`. The `check` macro is an **assertion**, a routine that checks a particular condition and performs an action depending on the check. The `check` macro in particular will make sure that the argument passed in is valid (i.e. not null) and if the check fails, it will halt execution. This is useful because if the value of `PlayerInputComponent` were null, we would not have input binding functionality, and we would also attempt to access functions via a null pointer, which can result in a crash.

The BindAction Function

After this, we make a call to the `BindAction` function.

- The first argument, a string literal, is the name of the mapping which we chose in **step 4** above. This is case sensitive and must be an exact match to the name given to the mapping.

- The second argument is an `enum` constant belonging to the `EInputEvent` enum. `IE_Pressed` corresponds to the button being pressed down, whereas `IE_Released` corresponds to the button being released.

- The third argument is a pointer to the class on which the binding is occurring. The `this` keyword returns a pointer to the current class in which it is used. The argument passed in is almost always `this`.

- The fourth argument is a pointer to the function we wish to bind to this axis mapping. Just as with variables, functions themselves have their own addresses, which can be accessed with the address-of (`&`) operator. Thus we must prefix the function name with the address-of operator and fully qualify its name. Notice that we don't add the parentheses to the end of the function name. This isn't a function call. We are simply passing in the address to the function.

The result of the `BindAction` function call is that each time any key associated with the Action Mapping is *pressed*, the function bound to that mapping will be called. The next call to `BindAction` does the same thing with a difference: the `enum` constant passed in as the second argument is `IE_Released`. This results in the function bound to the mapping to be called when any key associated with the Action Mapping is *released*.

The BindAxis Function

Finally we call the `BindAxis` function. This behaves similarly to `BindAction`, except that it binds a function to an axis mapping instead of an action mapping.

- The first argument is a string literal, which must be the same as the name given to the axis mapping.

- The second argument corresponds to the third argument in `BindAction` – `this` is almost always passed in, because we are binding an axis on this particular Pawn.

- The third argument is a pointer to the function we wish to bind to this particular axis mapping. The result is that this function will be called each frame, and the value passed into that function (corresponding to the `float` input parameter we called `Value`) will be 0.0 if the key is not pressed, and 1.0 if the key is pressed. Recall that next to each Axis Mapping there was a *Scale* value, as shown in the figure below.

Figure 6.8: Changing the Scale Value on an Axis Mapping

This will scale the value passed into the function bound to this particular axis mapping. Change the *Scale* value for the *Left Shift* mapping to 2.0 as shown in the image above.

Now it's time to test out our axis and action mappings. In order for the mappings to be responsive, we must be possessing the Pawn in which the mappings have been bound.

Learning How Pawn Possession Works

In the *ThirdPersonExampleMap*, there is already a Pawn – the *ThirdPersonCharacter*. This is the Character that has come with this map by default, which we possess and control once the **Play** button is pressed.

Figure 6.9: The ThirdPersonCharacter in the Map

Select the *ThirdPersonCharacter* by left-clicking on it, and press *DELETE*. Hit **Play**, and notice that you are still controlling a *ThirdPersonCharacter*. This Character is being spawned at the location of the *Player Start*, an object that exists in the map that determines where the *Default Pawn* should be spawned. If you hit **Stop** and search in the **World Outliner** for *Player Start*, select it, then hit *F*, you will focus on the *Player Start*.

Select the *Player Start*, delete it, and once again, press **Play**. You will find that, once again, you are controlling the *ThirdPersonCharacter*. Why do we still have a Pawn when

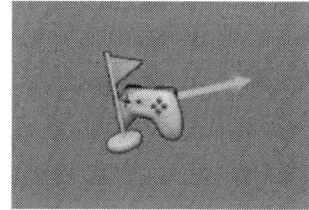

Figure 6.10: The Player Start

we've deleted it from the level? What's going on here? To answer this question, we must look at the *Game Mode*, where the *Default Pawn* is designated, which we will do in the following section.

We now understand that action and axis mappings are used to bind functionality to user input, and provide us with the convenience of allowing for multiple inputs to trigger the same mappings, as we saw when we mapped the left and the right *SHIFT* keys to the SHIFT_Key axis mapping. We saw that an action mapping has "one-off" functionality – a function call is made when an input is fired (a button is pressed or released) as opposed to axis mappings which result in continuous (per frame) behavior.

Now we will learn how to test our code from this section by setting the *Default Pawn* to the Pawn class we created, namely the FirstPawn.

The Game Mode and the Default Pawn

The explanation for why we still get a Pawn spawning in our world lies in the *Game Mode*.

Setting the Game Mode in Project Settings

If you go back to **Project Settings**, which you should still have open in its own tab (if you closed it, re-open it with *Edit -> Project Settings*), and in the left column, search for **Maps and Modes**, you will see the following:

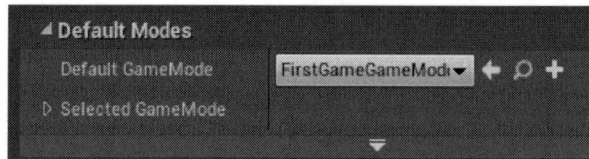

Figure 6.11: The Default Game Mode

This results in the `FirstGameGameMode` class being selected as the *Default Game Mode* for the game. Now maneuver back to Visual Studio, and in the Solution Explorer, go to *Games -> FirstGame -> Source -> FirstGame -> FirstGameGameMode.cpp*. Alternatively, you could simply search for *FirstGameGameMode.cpp* in the **Search Bar**. Double-click on *FirstGameGameMode.cpp*. You will see code in this file inside the constructor which has to do with setting the *Default Pawn* class for the game.

Setting the Default Pawn in the GameMode class

You will see a definition for the constructor of the `FirstGameGameMode` class, inside of which are the following lines of code:

```
// set default pawn class to our Blueprinted character
static ConstructorHelpers::FClassFinder<APawn>
PlayerPawnBPClass(TEXT("/Game/ThirdPersonCPP/Blueprints/Thi
rdPersonCharacter"));
if (PlayerPawnBPClass.Class != NULL)
{
    DefaultPawnClass = PlayerPawnBPClass.Class;

}
```

The code above results in setting the default Pawn class for this game mode. By creating a static variable of type `ConstructorHelpers::FclassFinder<APawn>` called `PlayerPawnBPClass`, we have instantiated an object that contains a member called `Class`. This member is of type `TSubclassOf<APawn>`. We will cover this type in more detail later in the book, but for now, it is enough to understand that this type is the equivalent of a C++ variable that points to a Blueprint or a class from the **Content Browser**. `ConstructorHelpers` is a static library (a class which contains static functions). Static functions do not require an instance of the class to which they belong to be instantiated. They can simply be called by fully qualifying the class name.

FClassFinder is a template struct. When created, the template type parameter must be passed in; in our case, we pass in APawn. The struct object we create as a result, PlayerPawnBPClass, can be used to create a variable that corresponds to a particular Blueprint from the editor. The Blueprint is determined with the file path passed in when creating the variable PlayerPawnBPClass. Finally, the FirstGameGameMode class inherits a variable called DefaultPawnClass, which we can set equal to the Blueprint corresponding to the PlayerPawnBPClass variable. As long as the FirstGameGameMode class is set as the default Game Mode for the game, this Pawn is used as the Default Pawn, and it will be spawned when the game starts, regardless of whether there is an actual Pawn in the level before the game starts.

Comment out the entire section of code as follows:

```
/*
static ConstructorHelpers::FClassFinder<APawn>
PlayerPawnBPClass(TEXT("/Game/ThirdPersonCPP/Blueprints/Thi
rdPersonCharacter"));
    if (PlayerPawnBPClass.Class != NULL)
    {
        DefaultPawnClass = PlayerPawnBPClass.Class;
    }
*/
```

Compile and maneuver back to the **Level Editor** and press **Play**. Now you will notice that there is no Unreal Engine mannequin. Click in the **Viewport**. Notice that you can move the mouse to look around, and that you can fly around in the level with the *WASD* keys as well as the arrow keys. Hit *SHIFT + F1* to show the mouse cursor and in the **World Outliner**, type "Pawn." Notice the *Default Pawn*. This is the Pawn that has been spawned. If there is no designated Default Pawn, Unreal Engine will spawn the Default Pawn, which has the built-in capability to fly around in the level.

Setting our own Default Pawn Class

Now we're going to designate our FirstPawn class to be the Default Pawn. In the **Content Browser**, go to *C++ Classes -> FirstGame* and right-click on *FirstPawn*. Select

Copy Reference. This copies the path to this class in the editor. Now go back to *FirstGameGameMode.cpp*, go into the constructor and uncomment the code. For the text in the TEXT macro in the PlayerPawnBPClass instantiation, highlight the string literal and delete it, and use *CTRL + V* or right-click and select paste to paste the text path we copied when we selected *Copy Reference*. The code should look as follows:

```
        static ConstructorHelpers::FClassFinder<APawn>
PlayerPawnBPClass(TEXT("Class'/Script/FirstGame.FirstPawn'"
));
        if (PlayerPawnBPClass.Class != NULL)
        {
                DefaultPawnClass = PlayerPawnBPClass.Class;

        }
```

Now compile and maneuver back to the **Level Editor**. Click on the **Output Log** panel to make sure you can see the **Output Log**. Then press **Play**. Click in the **Viewport** and press and release the *E* key. You should see the messages "E Key Pressed" and "E Key Released" printed to the **Output Log**.

Next, go back to *FirstPawn.cpp* and uncomment the UE_LOG call in the ShiftKey function. Compile and go back to the **Level Editor**, press **Play**, and search in the **World Outliner** for *FirstPawn*. Notice that a *FirstPawn* object has been spawned. Now, with the **Output Log** visible, click in the **Viewport** and press the left *SHIFT* key. Notice the warning message being spammed to the log showing a value of 2.0 corresponding to the axis value, scaled by 2.0 since we changed the *Scale* value next to the *Left Shift* mapping in **Project Settings**. Next, press the Right *SHIFT* key and notice the value of 1.0 in the message that is spamming the log. Thus we now see that, even though the two *SHIFT* keys are mapped to the same axis mapping, they send different values to the ShiftKey function.

We now understand that the GameMode class determines which Pawn is spawned in the world, and we have seen that even if we delete the Pawn from the level, an object of the class designated by the Default Pawn is spawned. We saw that if a Default Pawn is not set, the DefaultPawn class is used, which contains the ability to look around and fly throughout the level. We saw that we can create a variable for a Blueprint or class within the **Content Browser** by using the ConstructorHelpers static library and instantiating an object of the FObjectFinder struct, supplying a file path to the class in the **Content Browser**. We saw that using the `Class` member of this `struct` gives us the value which we can set on the `DefaultPawnClass` variable, which is inherited from the `AGameModeBase` class, from which `FirstGameGameMode` derives.

We noticed in **Project Settings** that there are a few axis and action mappings already set up for this game project, since this project is based on the Third Person project template. This is why the `ThirdPersonCharacter` Pawn is capable of movement. We will now use some of these action and axis mappings to map functionality to our Pawn class.

Binding Functions to Action and Axis Mappings

We will now add functionality for moving the Pawn. Before we do this, let's create a Blueprint based on our C++ class `FirstPawn` and learn how we can set the Default Pawn class from within the **Level Editor**.

Creating a Blueprint Based on the FirstPawn Class

First, comment out the code in the `FirstGameGameMode` constructor in *FirstGameGameMode.cpp*:

```
/*
static ConstructorHelpers::FClassFinder<APawn>
PlayerPawnBPClass(TEXT("Class'/Script/FirstGame.FirstPawn'"
));
if (PlayerPawnBPClass.Class != NULL)
{
     DefaultPawnClass = PlayerPawnBPClass.Class;
}
*/
```

Compile the code. Next, we will create Blueprints based on `FirstPawn` and `FirstGameGameMode`.

1. In the **Content Browser**, maneuver to *C++ Classes -> FirstGame*. Right-click on *FirstPawn* and select *Create Blueprint class based on FirstPawn*. Select the folder *Chapter6* and name the Blueprint *FirstPawn_BP*.

2. The *FirstPawn_BP* **Blueprint Editor** will open. Click the tab at the top and dock it to the top of the **Level Editor**.

3. In *C++ Classes -> FirstGame*, right-click on *FirstGameGameMode* and select *Create Blueprint Based on FirstGameGameMode*. Select the folder *Chapter6* and name the Blueprint *FirstGM_BP*.

4. In the **Details** panel in *FirstGM_BP*, under the **Classes** section, notice the *Default Pawn Class* item. Click on the dropdown and select *FirstPawn_BP*. **Compile**, **Save**, and close this Blueprint.

5. Back in *Project Settings ->* `Input`, for *Default Game Mode*, click the dropdown and select *FirstGM_BP*.

6. Maneuver back to the **Level Editor**. From the **Modes** panel, find a *Player Start* and drag one into the level.

Now press **Play**. In the **World Outliner**, search for "pawn" and notice that now we have *FirstPawn_BP* in the world. Notice also that the Pawn was spawned at the location of the *Player Start*. With the **Output Log** open, click in the **Viewport** and test out the *E* key, the Left *SHIFT* key, and the Right *SHIFT* key. The log messages should be functional.

Before we add code to move our Pawn, it would be nice to have a visual representation for it, such as a mesh. We would also like to have a camera, which we can add as a component to our Pawn class.

Adding Components to the FirstPawn Class

We first must declare the variables for the mesh, camera, and a Spring Arm Component.

Declaring the Variables for Components in FirstPawn

Add the following code to *FirstPawn.h*, just below the `GENERATED_BODY()` macro, just above the `public` section (this is a `private` section, as the body of a class is `private` by default).

```
      /** Mesh component to give the Pawn a visual
representation in the world */
      UPROPERTY(VisibleAnywhere, BlueprintReadOnly, Category
= Camera, meta = (AllowPrivateAccess = "true"))
      class UStaticMeshComponent* MeshComponent;

      /** Camera boom positioning the camera behind the Pawn
*/
      UPROPERTY(VisibleAnywhere, BlueprintReadOnly, Category
= Camera, meta = (AllowPrivateAccess = "true"))
      class USpringArmComponent* CameraBoom;

      /** Follow camera */
      UPROPERTY(VisibleAnywhere, BlueprintReadOnly, Category
= Camera, meta = (AllowPrivateAccess = "true"))

      class UCameraComponent* FollowCamera;
```

The first item is a forward declaration for a pointer to the class type `UStaticMeshComponent`, called `MeshComponent`. The `UPROPERTY` macro is marked with `VisibleAnywhere`, allowing us to see this item in the **Details** panel for the Blueprint as well as in the **Details** panel for instances in the level, but we cannot edit it. `BlueprintReadOnly` makes this item accessible in the **Event Graph** (via a Get node), but not changeable (via a Set node). We have also used a new keyword: meta. The syntax looks a bit weird, but adding:

```
meta = (AllowPrivateAccess = "true")
```

to the `UPROPERTY` macro results in a form of access modification in Blueprints. The `AllowPrivateAccess` property, when set to true, results in this property being exposed to Blueprint, but only to graphs internal to this class.

The next two variable declarations are for a `USpringArmComponent` and a `UCameraComponent`, respectively. A spring arm is a type of object that allows us to have something to which we can attach our camera, like a camera boom, hence the name, `CameraBoom`. The camera is what will allow us to have our view in the **Viewport** focus on the Pawn in the game, like the camera on the *ThirdPersonCharacter* did.

We now need to instantiate these items in the *FirstPawn.cpp* file.

Instantiating Objects for the Components

In the constructor, just under the `PrimaryActorTick.bCanEverTick = true;` line, add:

```
        MeshComponent =
CreateDefaultSubobject<UStaticMeshComponent>(TEXT("MeshComp
onent"));
        SetRootComponent(Cast<USceneComponent>(MeshComponent))
;

        CameraBoom =
CreateDefaultSubobject<USpringArmComponent>(TEXT("CameraBoo
m"));
        CameraBoom->SetupAttachment(RootComponent);

        FollowCamera =
CreateDefaultSubobject<UCameraComponent>(TEXT("FollowCamera
"));

        FollowCamera->SetupAttachment(CameraBoom,
USpringArmComponent::SocketName);
```

The use of the function `CreateDefaultSubobject` results in creating an instance of each of the three components. The function `SetRootComponent` is used to designate `MeshComponent` to be the root. This will prevent the default Root Component from being generated automatically. Because the inherited variable `RootComponent` is of type `USceneComponent`, we must cast the `MeshComponent` variable to a `USceneComponent`. Because `MeshComponent` is of type `UStaticMeshComponent`, which derives from `USceneComponent`, the cast will be successful. This results in the Static Mesh Component `MeshComponent` being set as the Pawn's Root Component. This means that any transformations performed on `MeshComponent`, such as setting its location, rotation or scale in the world, will be applied to all the other components in the object.

The `CameraBoom` component is instantiated in the same manner as `MeshComponent`, namely with `CreateDefaultSubobject`. Then the `SetupAttachment` function is used to attach the Spring Arm Component to the Root Component. This results in the spring arm being attached to `MeshComponent`, since it is the root.

`FollowCamera` is instantiated similarly to the previous two components, except a different overload of the `SetupAttachment` function is called, namely an overload that takes a second parameter. This parameter is of type `FName`, an Unreal Engine type that contains a string. The `USpringArmComponent` class has a property called `SocketName`, which is the name of a socket built into the `USpringArmComponent` class. Sockets are elements on objects that can have other items attached to them. By using `SetupAttachment` and passing in this socket name, we attach the Camera Component to this socket on the spring arm. This socket is at the end of the spring arm and is oriented toward the object to which the spring arm is attached; in this case, this is `MeshComponent`.

Intellisense will not recognize the `UCameraComponent` and `USpringArmComponent` types, so we will need to add the following includes to the top of the .*cpp* file:

```
#include "Camera/CameraComponent.h"
#include "GameFramework/SpringArmComponent.h"
```

Now compile and maneuver back to the *FirstPawn_BP* Blueprint. Our new components should be visible in the **Components** panel:

Figure 6.12: MeshComponent, CameraBoom, and FollowCamera

Now that we have our components in the Blueprint, we can select a mesh for our *MeshComponent*. Remember, the `UStaticMeshComponent` class contains a member called `StaticMesh`, and we can select the value for this member in the **Details** panel. With *MeshComponent* selected, in the **Details** panel, find *Static Mesh* and click the dropdown and select *Shape_Sphere*. You will see the sphere appear in the Blueprint **Viewport**.

Next, select the *CameraBoom* component in the **Components** panel. You will see the Spring Arm Component become visible in the Blueprint **Viewport**. If you hit the *E* key to enter Rotation Mode, you will find that rotating the spring arm results in the camera following, because it is attached to the socket at the end of the spring arm. Rotate the spring arm by 20 degrees as in the following image.

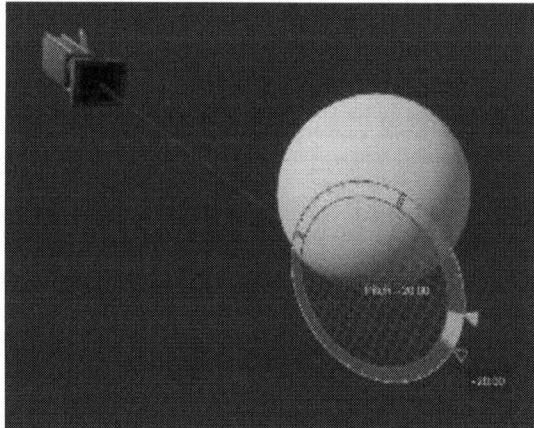

Figure 6.13: Spring Arm Component Rotated 20 Degrees

Now from the **Level Editor**, press **Play**. Notice that we can see the sphere, and we are looking from the point of view of the camera, angled downward at 20 degrees.

Creating Functions for the Action and Axis Mappings

Now we are ready to create functions and bind them to action and axis mappings in order to move our Pawn. Recall that there are already action and axis mappings set up from the template project. We will now be using some of these, so let's open **Project Settings** once more and take a look. We won't be needing the *ResetVR* action mapping, which is designed for virtual reality, so click the **x** next to this mapping to delete it. Likewise, we don't need the *Oculus Touchpad Button* mapped to the *Jump* mapping, so delete that one as well. Finally, since we are working with a Pawn class, there is no built-in jumping functionality, so we won't be using the *Jump Action* mapping either. Delete this as well. The action mappings should look as follows:

Figure 6.14: The Action Mappings

We have already created a function and bound it to this mapping, so all that is left are the axis mappings. For now, we will only concern ourselves with moving the Pawn. We will program turning capabilities once we create a Character class. Delete *TurnRate*, *Turn*, *LookUpRate*, and *LookUp*. Notice that the *Up* and *Down* keys are mapped to *MoveForward*, with the *Down* key scaled by -1.0. We also want the *Left* and *Right* keys mapped to *Move Right*, so click the **+** symbol next to *Move Right* twice, and from the new dropdowns that appear, select *Right* for the first, and *Left* for the second, and enter a value of -1.0 into the *Scale* field for the *Left* key. Scaling the *Down* and *Left* keys by -1.0 is a way to prevent us from needing an additional axis mapping for the *Down* and the *Left* keys. The values passed into the functions we bind to these mappings will handle the movement the same way, except that the movement direction will be scaled by -1.0. The axis mappings should look as follows:

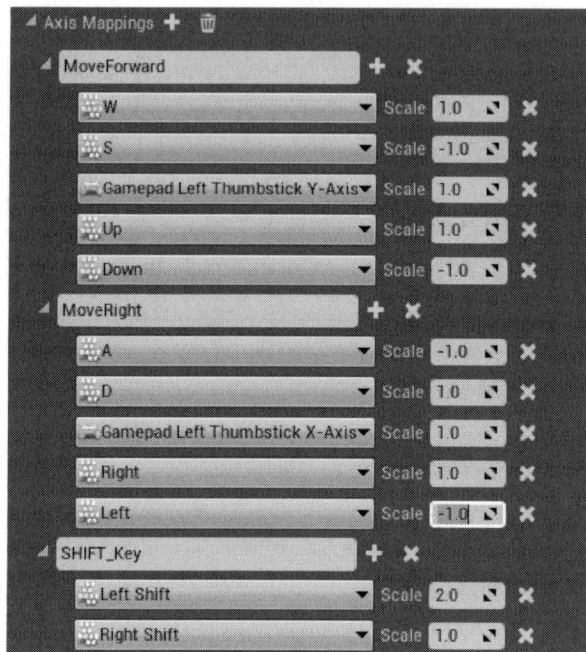

Figure 6.15: The Axis Mappings

The next step is to create the **callback functions** – functions passed as arguments to other code that is expected to call them at a given time – which we will bind to these mappings. The mappings we need functions for are MoveForward and MoveRight.

The MoveForward and MoveRight Functions

Let's create functions for these action mappings. For simplicity's sake, we'll name the functions MoveForward and MoveRight, respectively. In *FirstPawn.h*, just under the line void ShiftKey(float Value);, add:

```
/** Called for forwards/backward input */
void MoveForward(float Value);

/** Called for side to side input */

void MoveRight(float Value);
```

These functions need definitions, so in *FirstPawn.cpp*, just under the ShiftKey function, add:

```
void AFirstPawn::MoveForward(float Value)
{
    if (Value != 0.0f)
    {
        UE_LOG(LogTemp, Warning, TEXT("MoveForward: %f"),
Value);
    }
}

void AFirstPawn::MoveRight(float Value)
{
    if (Value != 0.0f)
    {
        UE_LOG(LogTemp, Warning, TEXT("MoveForward: %f"),
Value);
    }
}
```

Now we have functions that will send messages to the **Output Log** when called. This will inform us that the functions are working. We also check to see if `Value` is 0.0 first, that way, we don't spam the **Output Log** unless one of the keys mapped to these mappings are actually pressed. The last thing to do is to actually bind these functions to the axis mappings, as we have done in the Input – action and axis mappings section. In the `SetupPlayerInputComponent` function, just under `PlayerInputComponent->BindAxis("SHIFT_Key", this, &AFirstPawn::ShiftKey);`, add:

```
    PlayerInputComponent->BindAxis("MoveForward", this,
&AFirstPawn::MoveForward);

    PlayerInputComponent->BindAxis("MoveRight", this,
&AFirstPawn::MoveRight);
```

Now that we have functions bound to the *MoveForward* and *MoveRight* Axis Mappings, it's time to test them out! Before we compile, let's comment out the `UE_LOG` in the `ShiftKey` function, since it will be spamming the **Output Log** and making it difficult to read any other code. Compile the code, maneuver to the **Level Editor**, and press **Play**. Make sure the **Output Log** is open, and click in the **Viewport**. Press the *WASD* keys, and notice the printed values change.

We now have confirmation that our functions are reacting to our key presses. The last thing to do is to actually make the Pawn move in response to our input. We will now handle movement in the following section.

Moving the Pawn

We now have a way to know when our keys are being pressed, and now we'd like to actually move the Pawn in response to this input. If we were working with the `Character` class, rather than the `Pawn`, we would have lots of cool movement code at our disposal. But since this chapter is about the Pawn, we'll have to do without those features. Don't worry, we'll dive into them in *Chapter 7 – The Character Class*.

We need a way to store the current state of our input. When we hit the *W, A, S, D* or *Up*, *Left*, *Down* or *Right* keys, the values passed into the `MoveForward` and `MoveRight` functions will change. Pressing *W* or *Up* will result in the `MoveForward` function receiving a value of 1.0, whereas pressing *S* or *Down* will result in the `MoveForward` function receiving a value of -1.0. Pressing *W* and *S* at the same time, or *Up* and *Down* at the same time, has the effect of cancelling the two inputs out, and the value becomes 0.0. The *A, D, Left*, and *Right* keys will have similar effects on the value passed into the `MoveRight` function.

We would like a variable for the speed at which to move the pawn, as well as a variable for the direction. In *FirstPawn.h*, just under the `MoveRight` function, add:

```
/** Speed to scale movement by */
UPROPERTY(EditDefaultsOnly, BlueprintReadWrite,
Category = "Movement")
float Speed;

/** To store the X and Y components of the Pawn's
direction */
UPROPERTY(VisibleAnywhere, BlueprintReadOnly, Category
= "Movement")

FVector2D Direction;
```

`Speed` is marked `EditDefaultsOnly`, to prevent the `Speed` variable from being editable on the instance of the `Pawn`. It is marked `BlueprintReadWrite` so it can be accessed and set from within the **Event Graph**. `Direction` is marked

`VisibleAnywhere`, since we don't want to be able to set it on the **Details** panel anywhere, as this variable should be determined by key presses. We thus made it `BlueprintReadOnly`, so it can be accessed in the **Event Graph** but not settable, for the same reason. `Direction` is a variable of type `FVector2D`. `FVector2D` is similar to `FVector`, only it has two components, `X` and `Y`, instead of three. This is sufficient since we are planning on being able to move the `Pawn` in the X and Y directions, but not the Z direction.

Next we'll give `Speed` and `Direction` default values in the constructor:

```
Speed = 500.f;
Direction = FVector2D(0.f, 0.f);
```

And finally, we must store the values from `MoveForward` and `MoveRight` in the `Direction` vector. In `MoveForward`, outside the `if` statement, add:

`Direction.X = Value;`

And in `MoveRight`, outside the `if` statement, add:

`Direction.Y = Value;`

We don't want these lines inside the `if` statement because once they have nonzero values, the `if` check would prevent them from being updated.

Next, we must use this `Direction` value, coupled with `Speed`, to move the Pawn. An excellent place to do this is in the `Tick` function. In `Tick`, below the call to `Super::Tick(DeltaTime);`, add:

```
FVector Location = GetActorLocation();
FVector DeltaLocation = FVector(Direction.X,
Direction.Y, 0.f);
DeltaLocation.Normalize();
DeltaLocation *= Speed * DeltaTime;
Location += DeltaLocation;

SetActorLocation(Location);
```

The first thing we do is create a local `FVector` called `Location` and store the Pawn's current location in it, which was returned by `GetActorLocation`. Next we create an

FVector called DeltaLocation and initialize its X and Y components from those of Direction. We initialize its Z component with a value of 0.0. Next, we use a function that belongs to the FVector struct, called Normalize. What this function does is scales the vector so that it has a magnitude (length) of 1. We do this because in the event that we are pressing the *Up* and *Right* keys at the same time, or *Down* and *Left*, the X and Y components of the Direction vector will both be 1.0 (or -1.0) and the Direction vector would have a higher magnitude (longer length). If we used this vector to move the Pawn, we would get faster movement when moving diagonally than when moving left, right, up, or down.

After normalizing the vector, we multiply it by Speed and DeltaTime. The reason for multiplying it by DeltaTime is because Tick is called each frame, and frame rates vary throughout the game. This means that when the frame rate is high, the Tick function is called more often, resulting in faster movement. When the frame rate is low, the Tick function is called less often, resulting in slower movement. We want our movement to be scaled by DeltaTime, which is the time since the previous frame. This way, when the frame rate is high, DeltaTime is low, and thus DeltaLocation is scaled appropriately.

DeltaLocation, having been normalized to a magnitude of 1.0, then scaled by Speed and DeltaTime, will be added to the Location vector, and Location will move in the direction of movement just the right amount each frame to keep a smooth, constant movement rate. In fact, since Location is changing by 500 units multiplied by the time per frame, the Pawn's location will move at a speed of 500 units per second, which is the value of the Speed variable.

We finally call the SetActorLocation function, which Pawn inherits from Actor.

We can compile this and test it out by maneuvering to the **Level Editor**. Press **Play**, click in the **Viewport**, and move around using the arrow keys or the *WASD* keys!

Summary

We have learned how to create a Pawn class. We saw that Pawns can take input, and in order to do so, axis mappings and action mappings must be set up. We learned how to set these up in the **Project Settings**, and we created some axis and action mappings of our own. We learned how to create callback functions, binding them so that they would be called in response to the inputs associated with their mappings. We learned that the Game Mode determines the Default Pawn class, and that the Default Pawn could be set in the constructor of the Game Mode in C++ or from a dropdown menu in the Game Mode Blueprint. We then created Blueprints from the `FirstPawn` and `FirstGameGameMode` C++ classes. We set the Default Game Mode to our newly created Game Mode Blueprint in Project Settings, and set our Default Pawn in the Blueprint for this Game Mode. We finally set up axis mappings for moving the pawn, and used the `Tick` function to change the location of the Pawn in order to move it. We learned that there is built-in movement functionality in the `Character` class, which we could not access since we were working with the `Pawn` class. Now that we understand the `Pawn` class, we are ready to take our game development one step further, by diving into the `Character` class. The `Character` class is derived from the `Pawn` class, but it also contains additional features made especially for Characters in games.

In the next chapter, we will create our own `Character` class and become familiar with these features. This class contains much more functionality than the `Pawn` and `Actor` classes. It comes with a Capsule Component for handling collision, a mesh component for visual representation, and functions designed to help us create movement functionality appropriate for humanoid Characters. In the next chapter, we will become familiar with these features.

Chapter 7 – The Character Class

One of the most important classes in the Unreal Engine class hierarchy is the `Character` class. For beings in your game that need to be able to run, walk, jump, or do things a humanoid creature is designed to do, the `Character` class is the best choice. The `Character` comes with a **Capsule Component**, a pill-shaped volume that encompasses the general shape of the Character and is used to collide with the ground and other basic pieces of geometry in the world. The `Character` class already has a `Mesh` variable, and when we create a class derived from `Character`, our class will inherit this variable. The Character has a **Movement Component**, a class designed to handle movement for humanoid-type Characters. It has a **Player Controller**, which we will use when coding movement mechanics for our `Character` class. Throughout this chapter, we'll cover the following topics:

- **Adding Assets – Environments, Characters and Animations**: We will take a look at sources for assets, and download some of our own to use in our game development.

- **Character Movement**: We will create functionality for Character movement, including moving the Character around in the world, as well as moving the camera around the Character in order to look around.

- **AnimInstances and the Animation Blueprint**: We will create a class called the `AnimInstance`, which is the base class for the **Animation Blueprint**, a Blueprint that determines what pose the Character should be in at any given point in time in the game.

- **Creating Blendspaces**: We will create an asset called a **Blendspace** and use it to blend between idle, walking, and running animations for our Character based on movement speed.

Technical Requirements

For this section, we will be downloading more content to add to our game project. You must ensure that you have enough hard disk space for the assets you download in this chapter. The amount of hard disk space depends on how much content you choose to download. If you fill up your hard disk and you attempt to download an asset that requires more space than you have, you will be unable to download the content!

Adding Assets – Environments, Characters and Animations

We already have a Character mesh in our project: The Unreal Engine mannequin. This is a useful starting point, but eventually we will want our own mesh assets so our game looks less like an Unreal Engine starter project and more like a professional game. We will also want to use a more interesting environment than the Third Person Example Map as well, so we'll look at several sources for more interesting environments. Finally, we'll find some animations that we can use for our Character once we've got the mesh assets we need.

Adding an Environment to our Project

Unreal Engine provides a lot of starter content to its developers, so they don't need to just stick with the example maps that come with the basic project templates.

Environment assets exist in many different places. One of the easiest ways to get your hands on some of these assets is through the Unreal Engine Marketplace. There are assets in the Marketplace available for sale, as well as for free. Any given asset package may be free for a limited time, for promotional reasons. There are also asset packs that are permanently free.

To access the Unreal Engine Marketplace, open the **Epic Games Launcher**. Click on **Unreal Engine** at the left of the Launcher:

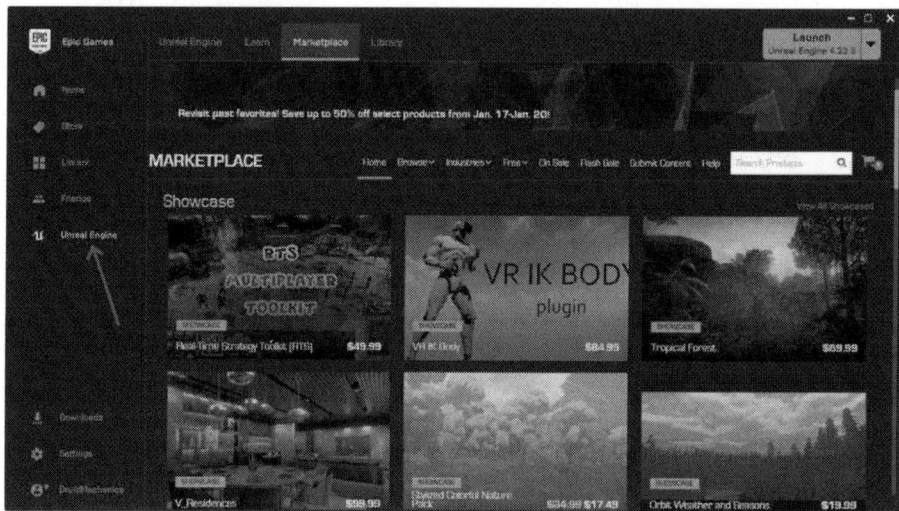

Figure 7.1: The Unreal Engine Tab in the Epic Games Launcher

From here, click the **Marketplace** icon at the top.

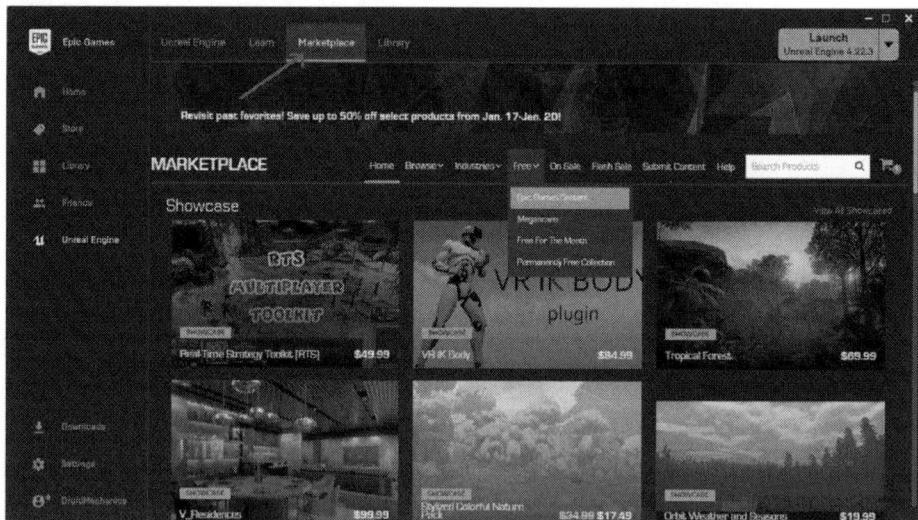

Figure 7.2: The Marketplace Tab in the Epic Games Launcher

From here, you can scroll down to browse items in the Marketplace, or you can select categories to browse in, or you can search for specific topics. If you click on **Free**, you can select **Epic Games Content** and **Permanently Free Collection**. Here you will see assets that will always be free on the Marketplace. You can also select **Epic Games Content**. This is content provided by Epic Games for developers to use in their projects. Click **Permanently Free Collection** or **Epic Games Content** and select an item on the marketplace that contains environment assets. To follow along with this chapter, select **Soul Cave**.

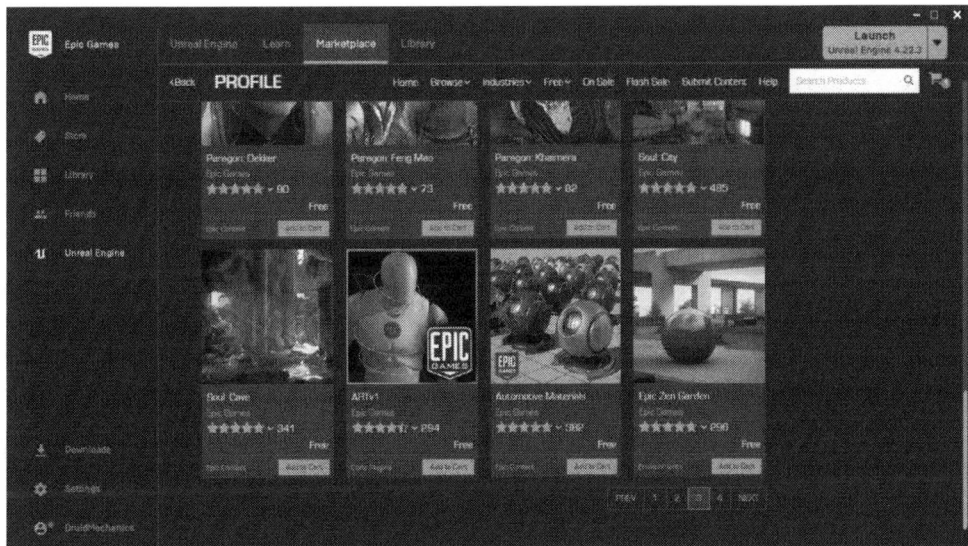

Figure 7.3: Selecting a Free Item on the Marketplace

This takes you to a landing page for the item, and you can click the **Free** button to get it. Once you do so, the button will say **Add to Project**. Click this and you will be prompted to select the project you would like to add the assets to. Choose the *FirstGame* project and click **Add to Project**. The **Add to Project** button will be replaced with a progress bar:

Figure 7.4: Progress Bar for Adding an Asset Package from the Marketplace

Once the progress bar completes, the assets will be in your project.

In the **Content Browser**, you will now see a folder called *Soul Cave*. Open this folder, and inside it, open *Maps*. There will be several maps in this folder. Double click *LV_Soul_Cave*.

While the level is loading, you will see a message at the bottom-right of the screen that says "Compiling Shaders" and until it's complete, the level will look mostly like gray geometry. Once the shaders have been compiled, however, the level will look like a full-fledged environment, as in the following figure:

Figure 7.5: The Soul Cave Level

Now that we have a level, we can set this level to be the default startup level in **Project Settings**. Go to **Project Settings**, select **Maps and Modes**, and in **Default Maps**, set *Editor Startup Map* and *Game Default Map* to *LV_Soul_Cave*.

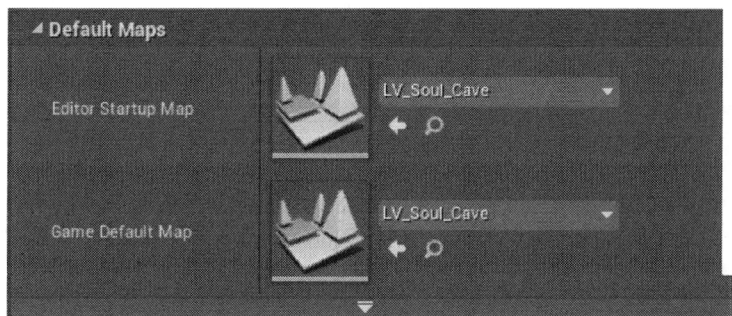

Figure 7.6: Editor Startup Map and Game Default Map

Editor Startup Map is the map that will be loaded by default when the editor loads. *Game Default Map* is the map that will load by default when no other level loads.

Now that we've got a level to work with, let's get our hands on some Character assets.

Adding a Character to our Project

Now we would like a Character asset with more originality than the Epic Games default Mannequin. In the **Marketplace**, select *Free -> Epic Games Content*, and take a look at the Paragon Characters. These are AAA-quality assets that Epic Games released for Unreal Engine developers for free when they decided to discontinue development on the game Paragon. This was a generous move on their part, because the high-quality assets released to Unreal Engine developers are collectively worth literally millions of dollars. For this project, we will choose a Character designed for melee combat. The Countess Character is perfect for this, so we will select it. Obtain the asset in the same manner that we obtained the Soul Cave pack, and add it to your project.

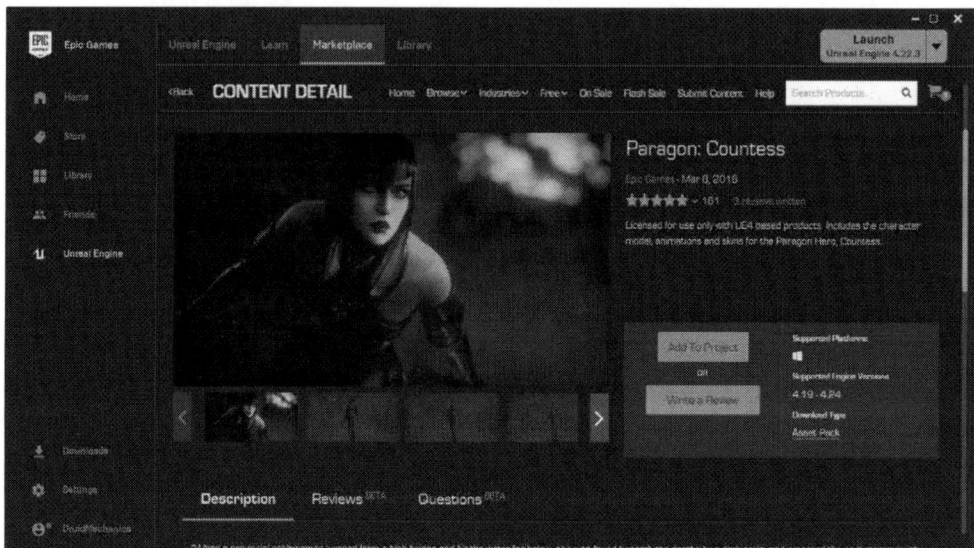

Figure 7.7: The Countess Character from Epic's Paragon Assets

Once the asset is done being loaded into your project, you will have a new folder in the **Content Browser** called *ParagonCountess*. In *ParagonCountess -> Characters -> Heroes -> Countess -> Meshes*, you can see the mesh asset for this Character. Just as we needed to wait for shaders to compile when loading the Soul Cave level, we must allow shaders to be compiled for the mesh. Notice that this asset is a skeletal mesh asset, as opposed to the Static Mesh asset of which we are already familiar. You can see this by hovering your mouse cursor over the asset and seeing a popup box which says "SM_Countess (Skeletal Mesh)." The SM portion of the name is a typical prefix that lets developers know that the asset is either a Static Mesh or a skeletal mesh.

The Difference Between a Static Mesh and a Skeletal Mesh

The **Static Mesh** asset is a simple piece of geometry. It has mesh information as well as one or more materials that can be applied to it. The yellow couches we used in *Chapter 2 – Actor Creation and Blueprints* are Static Meshes, for example.

A **skeletal mesh** is a mesh that has a **skeleton**—a hierarchical framework of **bones** (sometimes referred to as **joints**) which behave in many ways like real bones in biological creatures. The bones can be programmed to move in certain sequences (animations) and the mesh asset forms to conform to the skeleton's configuration.

Because game Characters often need to morph into various configurations during gameplay (when walking, running, or attacking, for example) the `Mesh` variable in the `Character` class is of type `USkeletalMeshComponent`.

Since the mesh for the Countess Character is a skeletal mesh, this means it is capable of being morphed and contorted if the skeleton is fed animation data. Luckily, the Countess asset package we added contains a wealth of animations! In the **Content Browser**, maneuver to *ParagonCountess -> Characters -> Heroes -> Countess -> Animations*. Find the asset called *Sprint_Fwd* either by searching for "sprint" in the **Search Bar** or scrolling down and finding it manually. Double-click it. This will open the **Animation Editor** and the Countess mesh will begin to move according to the information in the *Sprint_Fwd* animation asset:

Figure 7.8: The Countess Character in the Sprint_Fwd Animation

The **Animation Editor** provides you with a **Viewport** in which you can watch the animation as it's being played. Notice, however, in the upper-right of the screen, the following icons:

Figure 7.9: Icons in the Top-Right of the Animation Editor

215

These icons provide quick access to various editors associated with different aspects of the skeletal mesh component. This is because each of these aspects are related. Let's go through each of them. Start by clicking on the first icon in **Figure 7.9, Skeleton**.

Here in the **Skeleton Editor**, you can see the hierarchy of bones in the mesh's skeleton, as in the following figure:

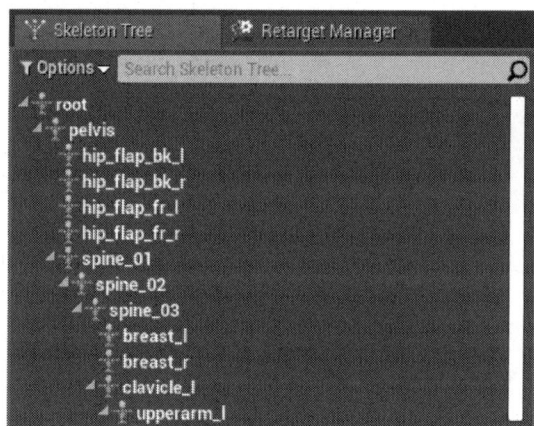

Figure 7.10: The Skeleton Tree Tab

You can select any of the bones by left-clicking on them, and the selected bone will highlight on the mesh, showing you its location. Select *upperarm_l* in the **Skeleton Tree** panel, and with Rotation Mode enabled, rotate the bone. The arm will rotate along with the bone, because the mesh is **rigged** (programmed to morph along with the bones of the skeleton). **Figure 7.11** shows the mesh after rotating the bone upward.

Figure 7.11: The Result of Rotating the upperarm_l Bone

Now press *CTRL + Z* to undo the change. Now in the top-right of the screen, select the **Mesh** icon.

Here, you can see the mesh in the **Viewport**, similarly to the **Skeleton Editor**, except here you can see all the different materials applied to the mesh in the **Asset Details** panel.

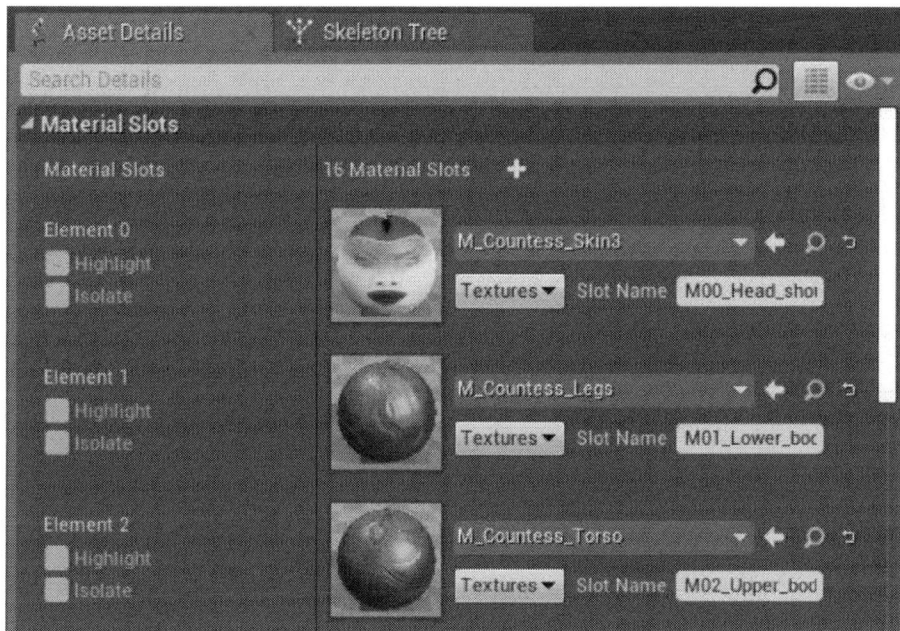

Figure 7.12: Materials Applied to the Countess Skeletal Mesh

Now click on the **Animation** Icon in the top-right once more. In the bottom-right of the screen, in the **Asset Browser**, you can see all animations in the project associated with the skeleton assigned to the Countess Character.

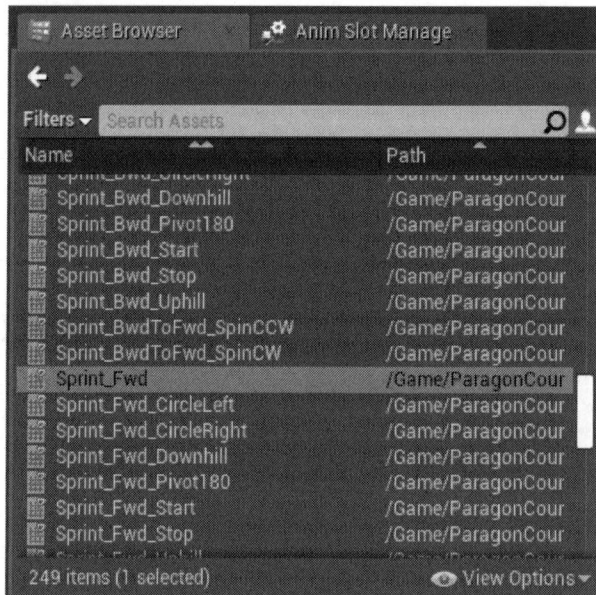

Figure 7.13: Animations Associated with the Countess Character Skeleton

To preview one of these animations, simply double-click on it. Double-click on
Sprint_Bwd to play the backward sprinting animation. At the bottom of the screen is a
gray strip as shown in **Figure 7.14**.

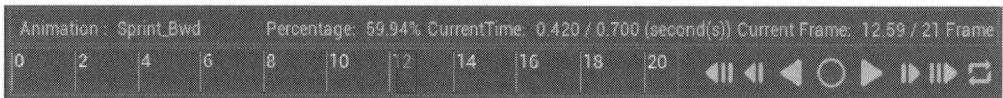

Figure 7.14: Scrubbing Through the Animation

Press the **Play** or `Pause` icon to play or pause the icon, respectively. Clicking on the red
rectangle (or anywhere in the strip) and dragging left and right allows you to scrub
through the animation and stop it at any point. We will visit more sections in the
Animation Editor as the need for them arises.

Click on the **Physics** icon on the top-right. Here, you can see some capsules associated
with various limbs on the Character. These belong to a **Physics Asset**, an asset similar
to a skeleton but more concerned with how the Character deals with physical reactions,
such as collision with objects in the event of a **ragdoll** (when the Character falls limp
and bounces off of the floor or walls in the level).

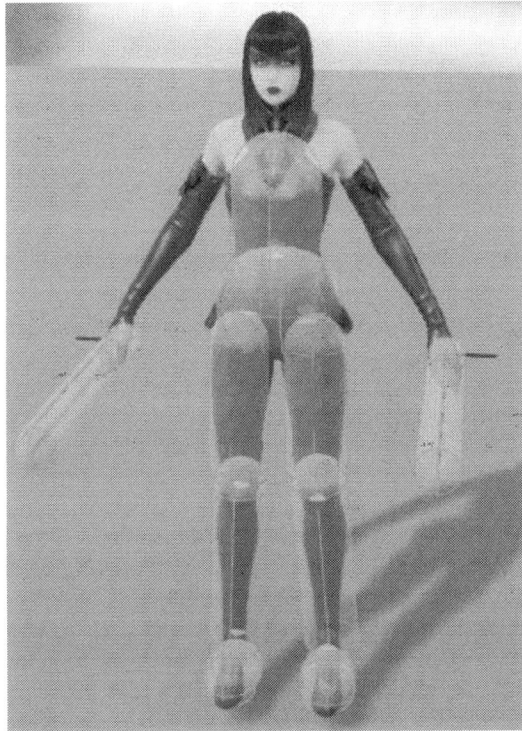

Figure 7.15: Capsules in the Physics Asset

We will visit the Blueprint section once we have created our own Animation Blueprint and learn how it works with Characters.

We now know where we can access new game assets for our games, including environments, Characters, and animations. We also saw the various editors linked together for skeletal mesh assets, and how each one works. We learned that skeletons are hierarchical sets of bones that are designed to morph the mesh associated with them, which allows for the mesh to become animated. We saw that the **Animation Editor** provides us with a way to preview animations. We saw that the Physics Asset is a system of Capsule Collision volumes designed to be used when a Character rag dolls, or falls limp to collide with the geometry of its surroundings.

Now what we are familiar with skeletal meshes and how they are associated with several different types of assets, we are now ready to begin developing our Character's functionality. This will involve Character movement, and with that, animation. First, we will create our class based on `Character` and give it the ability to move around.

Implementing Character Movement

Character movement involves taking user input, either from the mouse, keyboard, a console Controller, or some other means, and feeding that information into our Character. To do this, we will first need to create our new class based on `Character`.

Creating a Class Based on Character

We will now create a new class based on `Character`.

1. In the **Content Browser**, under *Content*, create a new folder called *Chapter7*. Now maneuver to C++ *Classes -> First Game* and create a new C++ class based on Character. Call it *MainCharacter*. Allow Visual Studio to generate the files for this new class.

2. Right-click on the newly created *MainCharacter* class in the **Content Browser** and create a new Blueprint based on it, called *MainCharacter_BP*. Place it in the *Chapter7* folder. The Blueprint editor should open for *MainCharacter_BP*. Notice that we already have some components in the **Components** panel:

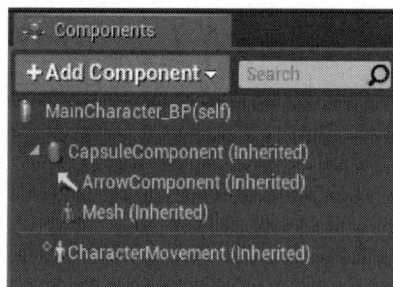

Figure 7.16: Components that come with the Character Class

In all classes derived from the `Character` class, the Capsule Component is the Root Component. You cannot assign another component to be the root. All other components are indirectly attached to the root. You will see an arrow component, which can be seen in the **Viewport**. This is useful for showing us which direction is forward for the Character. The forward direction is the Character's positive X-axis direction. Also attached to the Capsule Component is the Mesh Component, called *Mesh*. We will be assigning a mesh to the *Static Mesh* member of this component.

3. Click on *Mesh* in the **Components** panel, then in the **Details** panel, find the **Static Mesh** section and click the dropdown next to *Static Mesh*. Choose *SM_Countess*. You will notice that the Countess Character is facing the wrong direction and is elevated a bit too high.

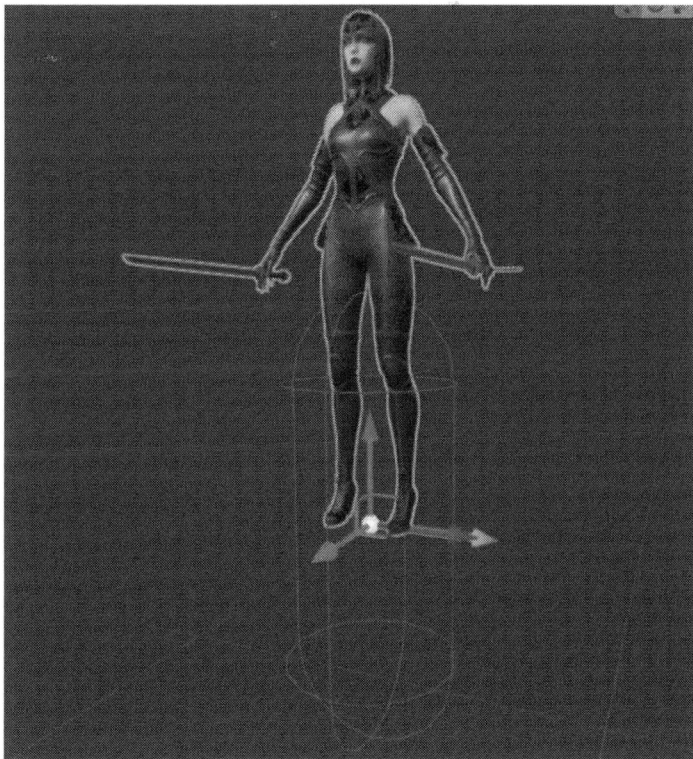

Figure 7.17: The Default Position of the Countess Mesh

4. Drag her down by about 90 units and rotate her counter-clockwise by 90 degrees. She should appear as in the following figure.

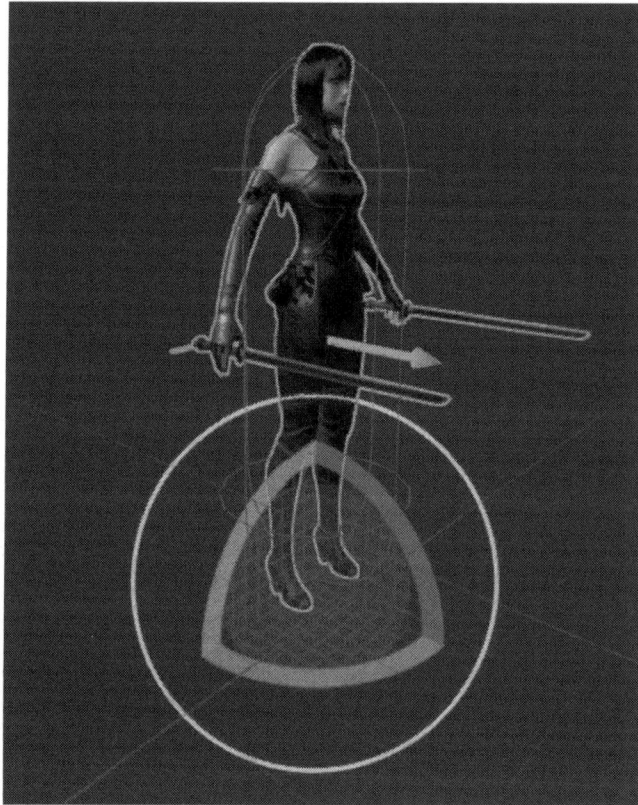

Figure 7.18: The Countess in the Correct Orientation

5. Preview how she looks in an animation by locating the **Animation** section in the **Details** panel with the *Mesh* selected, and from the dropdown for *Animation Mode*, selecting *Use Animation Asset*, then from the dropdown near *Anim to Play*, selecting *Idle_AO*.

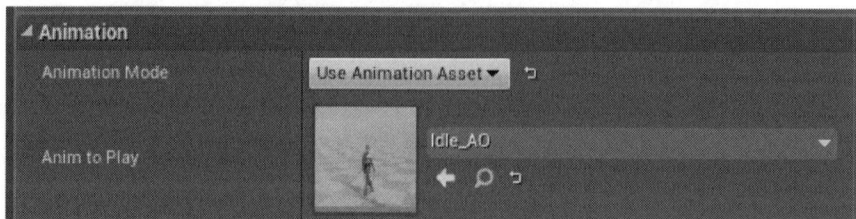

Figure 7.19: Selecting an Animation to Preview

Now that we have a mesh selected, we are ready to begin implementing functionality. We will start with basic movement and work our way up to the more complicated game mechanics.

Creating MoveForward and MoveRight Functions

Now let's implement some movement capabilities. First, we'll need to make sure we have the correct input mappings. Go to *Edit -> Project Settings -> Input*. Notice that we have *Move Forward* mapped to the *W, S, Up*, and *Down* keys and *Move Right* mapped to the *A, D, Left*, and *Right* keys. We'll need to create some callback functions that will respond to these inputs, so let's maneuver back into Visual Studio and look at *MainCharacter.h*.

The first thing you will likely notice is that our `Character`-derived class already has a constructor, as well as the `BeginPlay`, `Tick`, and `SetupPlayerInputComponent` functions. Refer to *Chapter 5 – The Actor Class* for more information on `Tick` and `BeginPlay`, and *Chapter 6 – The Pawn Class* for more information on `SetupPlayerInputComponent`.

We'll need `MoveForward` and `MoveRight` functions, similar to those created in *Chapter 6 – The Pawn Class*.

1. Add the following code, just under the declaration for `BeginPlay`:

    ```
    /** Called for forwards/backward input */
    void MoveForward(float Value);

    /** Called for side to side input */

    void MoveRight(float Value);
    ```

2. These functions will need definitions in the *MainCharacter.cpp* file, so open it and add these under the function body of `BeginPlay`:

```
void AMainCharacter::MoveForward(float Value)
{
    FVector Forward = GetActorForwardVector();
    AddMovementInput(Forward, Value);
```

```
}

void AMainCharacter::MoveRight(float Value)
{
    FVector Right = GetActorRightVector ();
    AddMovementInput(Right, Value);

}
```

And lastly, we must bind these functions to our *Move Forward* and *Move Right* axis mappings.

3. In the body of the `SetupPlayerInputComponent` function, just under `Super::SetupPlayerInputComponent(PlayerInputComponent)` `;`, add:

```
PlayerInputComponent->BindAxis("MoveForward", this,
&AMainCharacter::MoveForward);

PlayerInputComponent->BindAxis("MoveRight", this,
&AMainCharacter::MoveRight);
```

Now, since we are actually using the input component, we must include the proper header.

4. Add this to the top of the file, just under `#include "MainCharacter.h"`:

```
#include "Components/InputComponent.h"
```

Now, compile the code and maneuver back to the **Level Editor**. In the **Content Browser**, go to the folder in *Content* called *Chapter6* and open *FirstGM_BP*, the Blueprint for our Game Mode. For *Default Pawn Class*, click on the dropdown and select our newly-created Character Blueprint, *MainCharacter_BP*.

Now, from within the Soul Cave map, notice that the *Game Mode* is overridden in the **World Settings** panel. We must set the Game Mode to our *FirstGM_BP*, so click the dropdown next to *Game Mode* and do so.

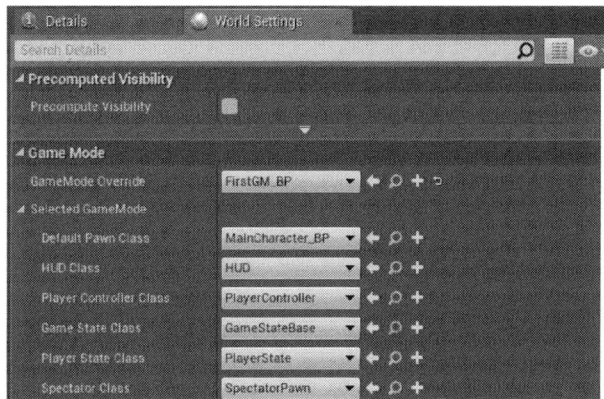

Figure 7.20: Overriding the Game Mode in World Settings

With our own Game Mode selected now, we are set up to possess the Pawn we chose, *MainCharacter_BP*. Press **Play** and click in the **Viewport**. Use the *WASD* and *Up*, *Right*, *Left*, and *Down* keys to move about. Notice, however, that we can't quite see our Character. Press *Shift + F1* while the game is still running to gain control over the mouse cursor. Press the **Eject** button.

Figure 7.21: The Eject Button

This allows us to disconnect from the Pawn and move around in the world. Use the mouse to move forward and turn around to see that our Character, the Countess, is indeed in the world.

We are now ready to add a Camera and Spring Arm, as well as the ability to look around with the use of the mouse. We will do so now.

Adding Camera and Spring Arm Components

The mouse can provide information we can use to move the Camera. First, we must add the Camera and Spring Arm Components to the Character.

225

1. Just above the first `public` section in *MainCharacter.h*, just under
   `GENERATED_BODY()`, add:

```
    /** Camera boom positioning the camera behind the
character */
    UPROPERTY(VisibleAnywhere, BlueprintReadOnly, Category
= Camera, meta = (AllowPrivateAccess = "true"))
    class USpringArmComponent* CameraBoom;

    /** Follow camera */
    UPROPERTY(VisibleAnywhere, BlueprintReadOnly, Category
= Camera, meta = (AllowPrivateAccess = "true"))

    class UCameraComponent* FollowCamera;
```

First, we forward declare a variable of type `USpringArmComponent` called
`CameraBoom`, and make it `VisibleAnywhere`, `BlueprintReadOnly`, give it the
category `Camera` (quotations are optional for the category) and mark it with a `meta`
specifier to allow private access in the Blueprint. We do the same for the Camera
Component, giving it the same `UPROPERTY` specifiers.

2. Next, we must construct these objects in the constructor. Just under
   `PrimaryActorTick.bCanEverTick = true;`, add:

```
    // Create a camera boom (pulls in towards the player
if there is a collision)
    CameraBoom =
CreateDefaultSubobject<USpringArmComponent>(TEXT("CameraBoo
m"));
    CameraBoom->SetupAttachment(RootComponent);
    CameraBoom->TargetArmLength = 300.0f; // The camera
follows at this distance behind the character
    CameraBoom->bUsePawnControlRotation = true; // Rotate
the arm based on the Controller

    // Create a follow camera
    FollowCamera =
CreateDefaultSubobject<UCameraComponent>(TEXT("FollowCamera
"));
    FollowCamera->SetupAttachment(CameraBoom,
USpringArmComponent::SocketName); // Attach the camera to
```

the end of the boom and let the boom adjust to match the
Controller orientation

```
        FollowCamera->bUsePawnControlRotation = false; //
Camera does not rotate relative to arm
```

We first create the spring arm with `CreateDefaultSubobject`. We then attach it to the Root Component using `SetupAttachment`, passing in the inherited variable `RootComponent`, which, as we know, is the Capsule Component by default. Through `CameraBoom` we access the variable `TargetArmLength` and set it to `300.f`, altering the variable directly. Next, we access the Boolean variable `bUsePawnControlRotation`. This variable sets the spring arm to follow along with the rotation of the Controller, which we will explain shortly.

The Camera Component is created in the same manner as the Spring Arm Component. We attach it to the Spring Arm Component, however. `SetupAttachment` has an overload that takes two arguments, as we saw in *Chapter 6 – The Pawn Class*. We attach it to the socket at the end of the Spring Arm called `SocketName`. Notice also that though the Spring Arm Component was set to use the Controller's rotation, the Camera was not, as we set `bUsePawnControlRotation` to `false` for the camera. This is because we do not wish for the camera to rotate along with the Controller; we only wish for the spring arm to do that, and the camera will move along with the spring arm.

3. And we must add the following includes to our list at the top:

```
#include "Camera/CameraComponent.h"
#include "GameFramework/SpringArmComponent.h"
```

Now our classes `USpringArmComponent` and `UCameraComponent` are no longer undefined.

So now that we have a Spring Arm Component and a Camera Component, and the Spring Arm is set to use the rotation of the Controller, you're probably wondering what this mysterious Controller is. We'll explain that now.

The Controller Class

Think of a Controller as an invisible component. It doesn't have a mesh, or any visual representation at all, for that matter. It's like a ghost, a part of the Pawn, following it around, but really, it doesn't have a location of its own.

It does, however, have a rotation. It can be oriented in any given direction, and it can receive input that can allow it to rotate. And if the Controller can rotate, other components can inherit the Controller's rotation and orient themselves in the same direction as the Controller. That's what our Spring Arm Component is going to do.

The `Character` class inherits a variable called `Controller`, of type `AController`. `AController` is the parent class of `APlayerController`. The `Character` class gets assigned a Player Controller, an object of type `APlayerController`, and its value is stored in the `Controller` variable. Remember, since `APlayerController` is the child class of `AController`, and a pointer to a parent type can hold the value of an object of a child type.

Since we have access to the Player Controller, and we have set up our Spring Arm to use the Controller's rotation, we can now program the capability to rotate the Controller with user input. We will use the mouse to direct this movement.

We will need to add axis mappings to take mouse input. We will do this now.

Programming Mouse Input to Rotate the Controller

In *Edit -> Project Settings -> Input*, we can now add two more axis mappings:

Figure 7.22: Adding Turn and LookUp Axis Mappings

Call these *Turn*, mapped to the *Mouse X* input, and *LookUp*, mapped to the *Mouse Y* input. We will to bind these to callback functions in `SetupPlayerInputComponent`. Add the following in the body of

`SetupPlayerInputComponent`, just under our bindings for `MoveForward` and `MoveRight`:

```
    PlayerInputComponent->BindAxis("Turn", this,
&APawn::AddControllerYawInput);

    PlayerInputComponent->BindAxis("LookUp", this,
&APawn::AddControllerPitchInput);
```

Notice that we didn't create our own custom callback functions, but instead opted to call `APawn::AddControllerYawInput` and `APawn::AddControllerPitchInput` directly. These functions are designed to check to see if there is a Player Controller, and if there is, add input to the `Yaw` and `Pitch` components of its rotation, respectively. The values passed into these functions come from the movement of the mouse. The mouse movement is measured each frame, and if the mouse is sitting still, the value passed in will be zero. But if the mouse is being moved, the value will be nonzero and the Controller will thus be moved.

Now, compile the code, and in the *MainCharacter_BP* Blueprint, notice that we now have a Spring Arm and a Camera Component. Select the Spring Arm to see it as a red line, connecting the Camera to the Mesh in the **Viewport**.

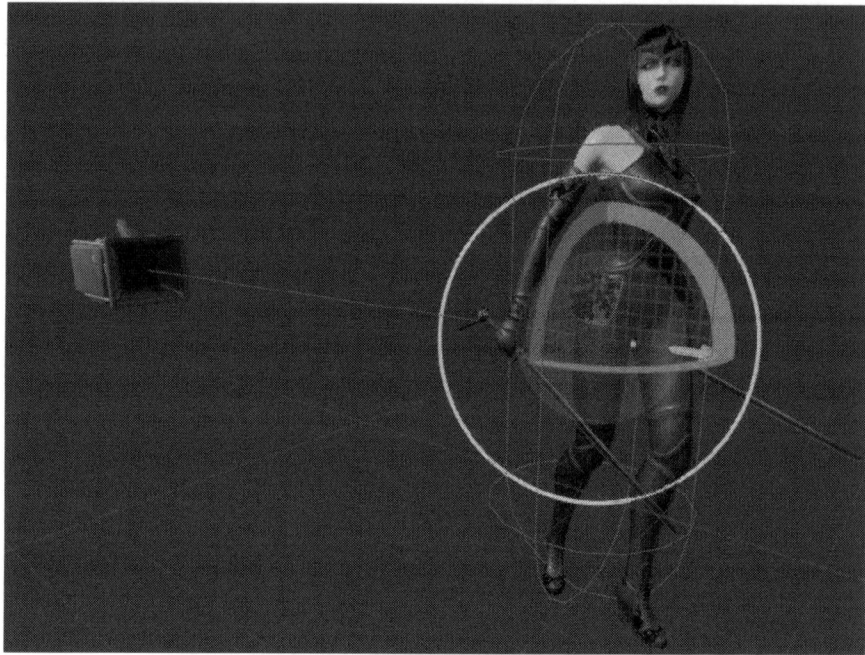

Figure 7.23: The Camera and the Spring Arm Components

Now we can maneuver back to the **Level Editor** and press **Play** and see that we now have control over the rotation of the Controller, and since the Spring Arm is set to inherit its rotation, and the Camera is connected to the Spring Arm, the Camera view will rotate along with the mouse movement. You may notice that dragging the mouse down will result in the camera looking up, which may be the opposite of what you desire. If so, in *Project Settings -> Input*, simply set the Scale value to -1.0 for *Mouse Y* in the *LookUp* axis mapping:

Figure 7.24: Setting the Scale Value to -1.0 for Mouse Y

Now dragging the mouse down will result in the camera looking down.

We have seen that the `Character` class inherits the `BeginPlay`, `Tick`, and `SetupPlayerInputComponent` functions, just as the `Pawn` class does. We saw that the `Character` class gets a Capsule Component as its root, and that no other components can be the root in the `Character` class. We also saw that the `Character` class inherits a `Mesh` variable of type `USkeletalMeshComponent`, designed to accommodate for the visual representation of the Character. We assigned the *SM_Countess* skeletal mesh asset to the *Skeletal Mesh* member of this component. We saw that we could select an animation for our Character mesh to use, and we chose an idle animation. We then programmed functionality for moving around using keyboard input, as well as rotating the camera by using mouse input to rotate the Controller. We saw that the Controller class is an invisible component assigned to the Character, and that it has its own rotation, which we use to rotate the Spring Arm Component. Because we attached the Camera Component to the end of the Spring Arm Component, the Camera rotates along with it when we move the mouse.

Now we can move around and rotate the Camera. But our Character looks silly, standing in her idle pose while gliding about in the cave. We'd like to play some running animations while she's moving, to give her a more realistic look. To do this, we must create an Animation Blueprint, a Blueprint based on the `AnimInstance` C++ class. We will do this now.

AnimInstances and the Animation Blueprint

We will now create a class based on the `AnimInstance` C++ class, which will receive information from our Character. This information will be used to determine which animations should be played at any given time during the game.

Creating a Class Based on AnimInstance

In the **Content Browser**, in *C++ Classes -> FirstGame*, right-click, and choose *New C++ Class*, and in the Class Creation Wizard, check the box at the top-right that says **Show All Classes**.

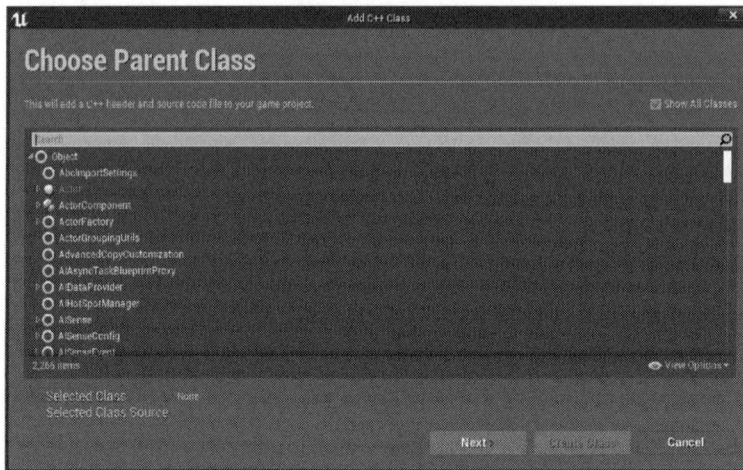

Figure 7.25: Showing all Classes in the Class Creation Wizard

Now you can see all of the classes on which we can base our new C++ class. In the search bar, type "AnimInstance," and choose *AnimInstance*.

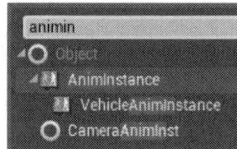

Figure 7.26: The AnimInstance Class

Click **Next**, and name the class *MainAnimInstance*. Click **Create Class** and allow Visual Studio to generate the class files. Next, maneuver to the *Chapter7* folder, right-click, and select *Animation -> Animation Blueprint*.

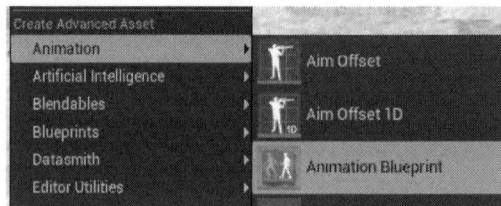

Figure 7.27: Creating an Animation Blueprint

You will be prompted to choose a parent class. Choose *MainAnimInstance*, the C++ class we just created. For Skeleton, choose *S_Countess_Skeleton*, the skeleton assigned to our Countess skeletal mesh. (If uncertain, you can verify that this is indeed the correct skeleton by opening the *SM_Countess* asset and scrolling down in the **Asset Details** to the **Mesh** section, and seeing the skeleton assigned to the *Skeleton* item).

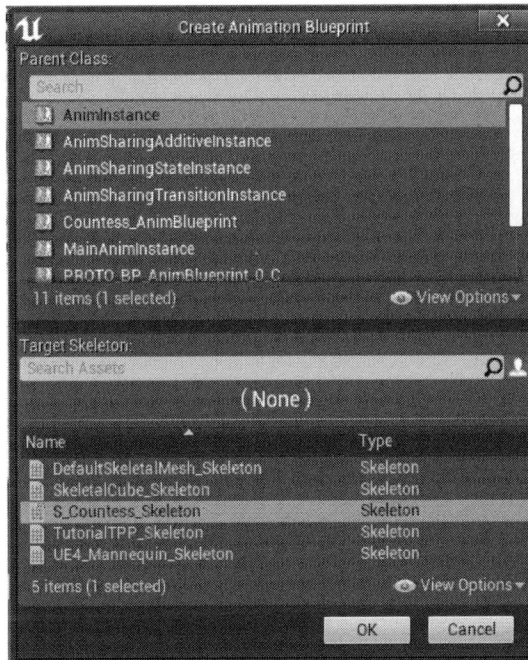

Figure 7.28: Creating the Animation Blueprint

Rename this new asset *MainAnim_BP*, and double-click on it to open it. You will see in the middle section two tabs: the **Event Graph** and the **Anim Graph**. We will first visit the **Anim Graph**, where we will create a State Machine – a system of States, each of which can be reached based on some logic. Each State will determine what animations should be played for our mesh.

Creating a State Machine

In the **Anim Graph**, you will see an *Output Pose* node. This node receives information for the pose that the Character should be in. We can provide this information by creating a State Machine. Right click in the graph, type in "State Machine" and select

Add New State Machine. A new node will be created. Click on its title, *New State Machine*, and rename it *Ground Locomotion.* Click and drag out from the humanoid output pin and connect it to the humanoid input in on *Output Pose.* The result should look like the following:

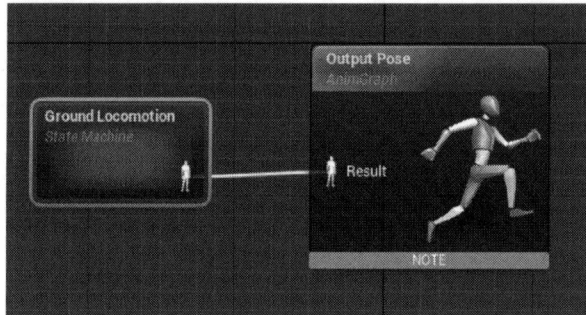

Figure 7.29: Adding a New State Machine

We will determine what States the State Machine can be in, and how it can transition among these States. Double-click on the *Ground Locomotion* node to open the State Machine. There will be a single *Entry* node, with an output pin. Click and drag off of this pin and release, then choose *Add State…* to create a new State. The State's name will be highlighted, and you can rename it. Rename it *Idle*. Double-click the *Idle* State to open it. Notice that the tab previously labeled *AnimGraph* now says *Idle (state)*. Below it is a strip that shows how deep into the layers of the Animation Blueprint you've ventured: First into the *AnimGraph*, then the *Ground Locomotion* State Machine, then the *Idle* State. You can click on *Ground Locomotion* or *AnimGraph* on this strip to come out to those respective layers.

Figure 7.30: Maneuvering through the Layers of the AnimGraph

In the *Idle* State, click on the **Asset Browser** tab at the bottom-right of the screen, and find the *Idle_Relaxed* animation. Drag it in and connect its output pin with the *Output Animation Pose* pin.

Figure 7.31: Adding an Idle Animation to the Idle State

Now click *Ground Animation* on the black strip at the top of the graph to exit this State and go back to the *Ground Locomotion* State Machine. Hover your mouse cursor over the gray border of the *Idle* State node, and notice that it highlights.

Figure 7.32: Hovering Over the Edge of the Idle State Node

Click and drag off of the border and select *Add State…* and create another State. Repeat this process until you have the following State Machine:

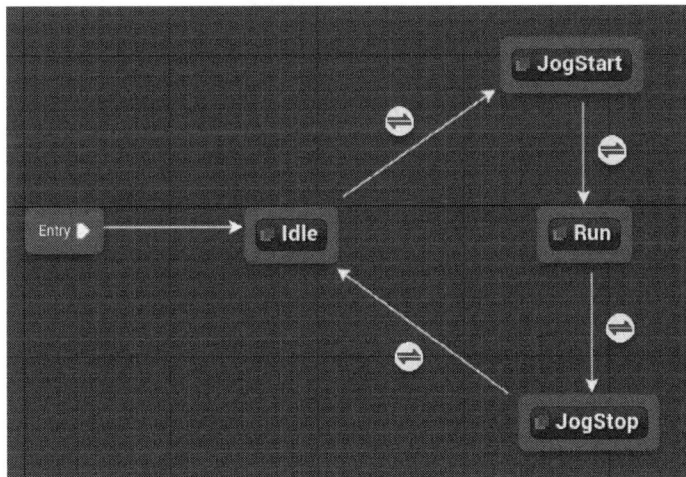

Figure 7.33: Adding More States to the State Machine

Make sure the arrows are all pointed in the correct directions. Each of these States will feed different animation information to the animation pose. The circle icons on the connecting arrows are called **transition rules**—they will contain logic within them that determines whether or not the State to which their arrow points should be entered or not. Repeat the process of double-clicking the States and dragging in animations for them. Use the animation *Jog_Fwd_Start* for the *JogStart* State, *Jog_Fwd* for the *Run* State, and *Jog_Fwd_Stop* for the *JogStop* State. Make sure to connect the output and input pins as was done for the *Idle* animation in **Figure 7.31**.

The animations that will be assigned to the mesh will be determined by which State the State Machine is in at any given point in time. By default, the *Idle* State will be entered, because this is connected to the *Entry* Node. Without entering any logic into the transition rules associated with each of the arrows connecting the States, the State Machine will simply stay in the *Idle* State, and thus the *Idle_Relaxed* animation will be the only animation played. So how do we determine when the State Machine should transition from the *Idle* State to the *Jog Start* State? The simplest way to determine whether the Character should be playing a running animation is by checking its movement speed. If the speed is zero, the Character should be playing the *Idle_Relaxed* animation. But if the Character's speed is not zero, it must be moving, and thus a running animation should be played. We will obtain this information from within the MainAnimInstance C++ class, and access it from within the *MainAnim_BP* Blueprint.

Obtaining Movement Information in the MainAnimInstance Class

Maneuver back to Visual Studio. We will now code the ability to get movement information for the Character.

1. Open *MainAnimInstance.h*. Just below GENERATED_BODY(), add:

```
public:
    virtual void NativeInitializeAnimation() override;

    UFUNCTION(BlueprintCallable, Category =
AnimationProperties)
    void UpdateAnimationProperties();

    UPROPERTY(VisibleAnywhere, BlueprintReadOnly, Category
= Movement)
    float MovementSpeed;
```

```
    UPROPERTY(VisibleAnywhere, BlueprintReadOnly, Category
= Movement)
    bool bIsInAir;

    UPROPERTY(VisibleAnywhere, BlueprintReadOnly, Category
= Movement)
    bool bIsAccelerating;

    UPROPERTY(VisibleAnywhere, BlueprintReadOnly, Category
= Movement)
    class APawn* Pawn;

    UPROPERTY(VisibleAnywhere, BlueprintReadOnly, Category
= Movement)

    class AMainCharacter* Main;
```

We create a `public` section so our UPROPERTY macro specifiers will be compatible. First, we declare an override for the virtual function `NativeInitializeAnimation`, which is similar to `BeginPlay` in Actor classes: it is called once at the beginning of the game. We do not give this function a UFUNCTION macro, as we only wish to call it from within C++. Next, we declare a function called `UpdateAnimationProperties`. We mark this with a UFUNCTION macro, passing in `BlueprintCallable`, thus making this function callable from within Blueprints (See *Chapter 5 – The Actor Class* for more information on the `BlueprintCallable` specifier). We will be calling this function from within the *MainAnim_BP* Animation Blueprint each frame. We then declare a `float` variable called `MovementSpeed`, Making it `VisibleAnywhere` and `BlueprintReadOnly`. We will not be able to edit the variable in the **Details** panel, and we will not be able to set it in Blueprints, because while the game is running, we only want C++ code to alter it, though we can see it in Blueprints. We created a `bool` variable called `bIsInAir`, which we will set to `true` when the Character is in the air, and to `false` when the Character is on the ground. We gave it the same UPROPERTY specifiers as `MovementSpeed`, for the same reasons. We also wish to know when our Character is accelerating, so we have created a `bool` called `bIsAccelerating`. Finally, we declare a variable of type `APawn`, to store a reference to the Pawn that is currently using this `AnimInstance`, and a variable of type `AMainCharacter`, so that we can store a reference to the

Pawn in the form of an `AMainCharacter`, which we can easily get with the use of casting, as we will see when we define the function `UpdateAnimationProperties`.

Now let's define the functions `NativeInitializeAnimation` and `UdateAnimationProperties`.

2. First, we will need add the following include, just under `#include` `"MainAnimInstance.h"`:

```
#include "MainCharacter.h"
#include "GameFramework/Pawn.h"
#include "GameFramework/CharacterMovementComponent.h"
```

These are necessary because we intend to use the classes `AMainCharacter`, `UCharacterMovementComponent`, and `APawn`. As a reminder, if you don't know which header files to include for a given class, revert to the Unreal Engine Documentation and search for `APawn` or `UCharacterMovementComponent`, and you will be presented with information about the class, including the correct header to include.

3. Beneath this, add:

```
void UMainAnimInstance::NativeInitializeAnimation()
{
    Super::NativeInitializeAnimation();
    if (Pawn == nullptr)
    {
        Pawn = TryGetPawnOwner();
        if (Pawn)
        {
            Main = Cast<AMainCharacter>(Pawn);
        }
    }
}
```

The first thing we do is call the parent version of this overridden function, as is usually done when overriding a virtual function inherited from a parent, in order to ensure that any code in the parent class gets called. Next, we check to see if the `Pawn` variable is null. If `Pawn` is null (the first time, it should be), we use the inherited function

`TryGetPawnOwner`. This function will return the Pawn that "owns" this `AnimInstance`. Since the `MainCharacter_BP` will be the Pawn to which this `AnimInstance` is assigned, it will be returned in the form of an `APawn` value. We then check to see if this function succeeded with the `if (Pawn)` check. If, for any reason, the function fails and returns a null value, this `if` body will not be entered, thus preventing us from attempting to access a null pointer, which could cause a crash. We then cast the Pawn to an `AMainCharacter` and store the result of this cast in the `Main` variable. If both `if` checks succeed, we will have a variable with access to the owning Pawn in the form of an `APawn`—`Pawn`—and we will have a variable with access to the owning Pawn in the form of an `AMainCharacter`—`Main`. Thus, if we need to access functions from the `APawn` class, we can do so via the `Pawn` variable, and if we need to access functions defined in the `AMainCharacter` class, we can do so via the `Main` variable.

4. Next, we will define `UpdateAnimationProperties` as follows:

```cpp
void UMainAnimInstance::UpdateAnimationProperties()
{
    if (Pawn == nullptr)
    {
        Pawn = TryGetPawnOwner();
    }

    if (Pawn)
    {
        FVector Speed = Pawn->GetVelocity();
        FVector LateralSpeed = FVector(Speed.X, Speed.Y,
0.f);

        MovementSpeed = LateralSpeed.Size();

        bIsInAir = Pawn->GetMovementComponent()-
>IsFalling();

        if (Main == nullptr)
        {
            Main = Cast<AMainCharacter>(Pawn);
        }
```

```
        if (Main)
        {
            if (Main->GetCharacterMovement()-
>GetCurrentAcceleration().Size() > 0)
            {
                bIsAccelerating = true;
            }
            else
            {
                bIsAccelerating = false;
            }
        }
    }

}
```

First, we check to see if Pawn is null. We do this just in case UpdateAnimationProperties gets called before NativeInitializeAnimation. If it does, Pawn will be null, and we will need to get it via TryGetPawnOwner, and assign the value returned by this function to the Pawn variable. If, on the other hand, NativeInitialization is called before UpdateAnimationProperties is called for the first time, Pawn will already have a valid value, and the check if(Pawn == null) will fail, and there will be no need to enter the if body to get the value returned by TryGetPawnOwner.

Next, we check to make sure TryGetPawnOwner was successful, by checking to see if Pawn is valid (not null). If it is, then the second if body will be entered, where we can access the Pawn's speed. The Pawn class has a function called GetVelocity, which returns an FVector. This quantity has a direction and a magnitude. The direction is the direction of the Character's movement, and the magnitude is the speed of that movement. Thus, we must get the magnitude of this vector. First, we zero out the Z-component of this vector, just in case the Character is moving upward or downward in the Z-direction, as we only want the horizontal component of the velocity. We store this new value into an FVector called LateralSpeed, then we call the FVector function Size in order to return the magnitude of this vector in the form of a float. We store this value in the MovementSpeed variable, which we declared in the *MainAnimInstance.h* file.

Next, we need to determine if the Character is in the air. This can be determined by accessing the Character's **Movement Component**. The Movement Component, much like the Controller, is an invisible component that contains functionality pertaining to the Character's movement, and is of type `UPawnMovementComponent`. Objects of the `Character` class get a Movement Component constructed for them by default, and this Movement Component can be accessed through a function inherited from the `APawn` class called `GetMovementComponent`. For Characters, the object is of type `UCharacterMovementComponent`, but when accessed from a variable of type `APawn`, it comes in the form of `UPawnMovementComponent`. We can access the function `GetMovementComponent`, thanks to our previous setup which has given us access to the owning Pawn in the form of an `APawn` variable, called `Pawn`. We then call a function on the `UPawnMovementComponent` returned by this, called `IsFalling`. `IsFalling` returns a `bool` value, which will be `true` if the Character is in the air, and `false` if the Character is on a surface. We store this value in the variable `bIsInAir`, which we declared in *MainAnimInstance.h*.

Since we plan on calling `UpdateAnimationProperties` each frame, the values of `MovementSpeed` and `bIsInAir` will be updated continuously, and we should always have access to the owning Pawn both in the form of an `APawn`, to access functions belonging to the `Pawn` class, and in the form of an `AMainCharacter`, to access functions that belong to the `MainCharacter` class.

Finally, we use the `Main` variable, which is of type `AMainCharacer`, to call a function inherited from the `Character` class called `GetCharacterMovement`. This would not be accessible from the `Pawn` variable because the `APawn` class does not inherit this function. This function returns the Movement Component in the form of an `UCharacterMovementComponent`. The `UCharacterMovementComponent` class contains a function called `GetCurrentAcceleration`, a function not accessible from a variable of type `UPawnMovementComponent`. This function returns the Character's acceleration in the form of an `FVector`, from which we call the `Size` function to get its magnitude. We check to see if this value is greater than zero, and if it is, we set `bIsAccelerating` to true. We have an `else` statement for when the acceleration is zero, in which we set `bIsAccelerating` to `false`. All of this is inside an if(Main) check, so we don't attempt to call a function on the Main variable in the event that it may be null.

5. Compile this code, and return to *MainAnim_BP*. We will now be calling our UpdateAnimationProperties function, which we made BlueprintCallable, from the Animation Blueprint's **Event Graph**. Click on the *EventGraph* tab, and you should see the following:

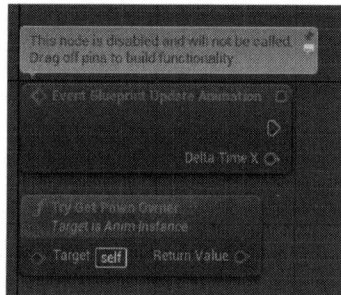

Figure 7.34: Default Nodes in the Animation Blueprint Event Graph

These nodes are grayed out because they aren't being used, but they are presented here because they are commonly used in Animation Blueprints. The first node, *Event Blueprint Update Animation*, works much like the *Tick* event in Actor Blueprints (and Blueprints of classes derived from Actor). It is fired each frame, and the green output node, *Delta Time X*, returns the float value of *Delta Time*, or the amount of time in seconds that has passed since the previous frame. Beneath this node, we have *Try Get Pawn Owner*, which returns the owning Pawn of this Animation Blueprint, just like its C++ counterpart, which we used in *MainAnimInstance.cpp* to get the owning Pawn.

6. Drag off of the white output execution pin on *Event Blueprint Update Animation* and search for "UpdateAnimationProperties." Select our BlueprintCallable function.

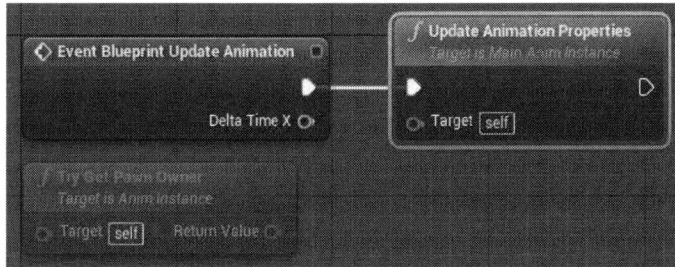

Figure 7.35: Calling Update Animation Properties in the Event Graph

Now, *Update Animation Properties* will be called each frame, and the C++ code we added to this function in *MainAnimInstance.cpp* will run, updating the `MovementSpeed` and `bIsInAir` variables.

Now we can access the information we need in order to provide logic to our State Machine so it knows when to transition between States. We will fill in this logic now.

Providing Logic for the Transition Rules in the State Machine

Return to the *AnimGraph* in the Animation Blueprint, enter the *Ground Locomotion* State Machine, and hover your mouse cursor over the transition rule between the *Idle* and *JogStart* States. A window will popup that says *Idle to JogStart* and will show *False*, indicating that this transition rule will never succeed.

1. Double-click on the circle icon to enter the transition rule.

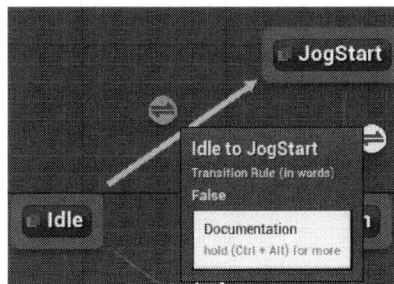

Figure 7.36: The Transition Rule Between the Idle and JogStart States

2. From within the transition rule, right-click and search for "movement speed," and select *Get Movement Speed* to get a node for the *Movement Speed* variable.

3. Do the same for "is in air." These values are accessible because we provided these variables with the `BlueprintReadOnly` specifier in their UPROPERTY macros in *MainAnimInstance.h*.

4. Drag off of the *Movement Speed*'s green output pin and search for the greater-than sign (>) and select *float > float*. This will create a node that takes two `float` inputs and returns a value of `true` if the first is greater than the second.

The green wire connected from *Movement Speed* to the first node will result in the value for *Movement Speed* being passed in as the first input. Leaving the second input blank will result in a default value of zero passed in, thus the node checks to see if *Movement Speed* is greater than zero, and returns `true` if it is, and `false` if it is not.

5. Drag off of the red output pin from *Is In Air* (remember, Boolean variables exposed to Blueprints will not show the prefixed "b" at the beginning of the name) and search for the logical NOT sign (!). Choose *NOT Boolean*.

This will create a *NOT* node, which takes a Boolean value as input and returns the opposite of that value as output. Thus if the Character is in the air, the value of *Is In Air* will be `true` and the *NOT* node will return false. Likewise, if the Character is not in the air (i.e. on the ground), the value of *Is In Air* will be `false` and the *NOT* node will return true. We only want to enter the transition from *Idle* to *JogStart* if both of these are true, i.e., *Movement Speed* is greater than zero and the Character is not in the air. We can achieve this with an *AND Boolean* node. Drag off of the red output from the *float > float* node, search for "and" and choose *AND Boolean*. This node will take two Boolean inputs and return `true` only if they are both true. If one or the other or both is false, the node will return false. Make sure both Boolean outputs from the *float > float* and *NOT* nodes are connected to the *AND Boolean* node, and the output from the *AND Boolean* is connected to the *Can Enter Transition* node, as shown in the following figure.

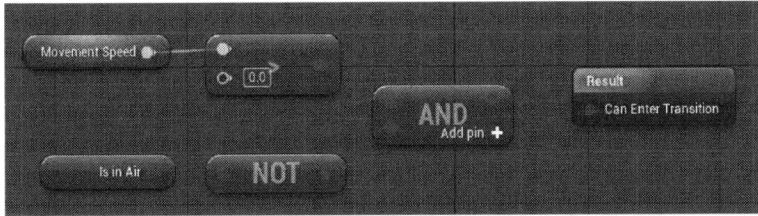

Figure 7.37: Transition Rule from the Idle State to the JogStart State

Now for the transition from the *JogStart* to the *Run* State, we want the transition to occur immediately, as soon as a certain fraction of the *JogStart* animation is complete.

6. We can configure this by clicking on the transition rule (single-click) and in the **Details** panel, under transition, checking the checkbox next to *Automatic Rule Based on Sequence Player in State*. In **Blend Settings**, set *Duration* to 0.8. Now at approximately 80% through the *Jog_Fwd_Start* animation, the animation will begin to fade into the *Jog_Fwd* animation, which we assigned in the *Run* State.

7. Now, for the transition rule between the *Run* and *JogStop* States, we wish to transition if we are no longer accelerating. Double-click on this transition rule, right-click and search for "is accelerating," select *Get Is Accelerating*. Drag off of this node, type "not" and select *NOT Boolean*, then connect the *NOT* node's output pin to *Can Enter Transition*.

Figure 7.38: Transition Rule from the Run State to the JogStop State

8. Now select the transition rule between *JogStop* and *Idle* (single-click), and in the **Details** panel under **Transition**, check the checkbox next to *Automatic Rule Based on Sequence Player in State*, and set the *Duration* under **Blend Settings** to 0.4. This will transition between States when the animation for

Jog_Fwd_Stop is 40% complete. In addition, we want to make sure we are not accelerating, so hover your mouse over the border of the *JogStop* State, drag out and connect another arrow to the *Idle* State.

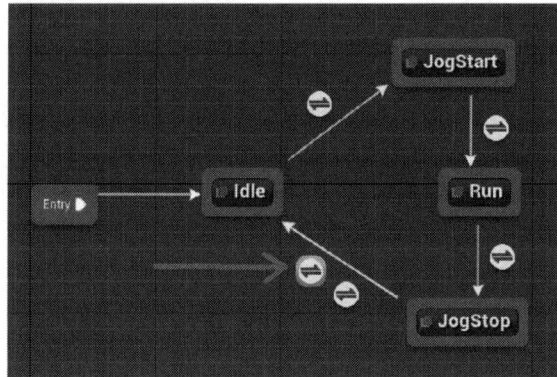

Figure 7.39: A Second Transition Rule

Make sure you select the new transition rule icon you can be certain if the *Automatic Rule Based on Sequence Player in State* checkbox is unchecked in the **Details** panel.

9. For this second transition rule, double-click its circle icon, right-click and search for "is accelerating," and select *Get Is Accelerating*, and connect it to *Can Enter Transition*, as in the following figure.

Figure 7.40: Transition Rule between the JogStop State and the Idle State

You may be wondering why we would want to ensure that we are accelerating when transitioning from the *JogStop* to the *Idle* State. The truth is that the acceleration vector for an object will be non-zero if the object's velocity is changing. That's the definition of **acceleration**: the change in an object's velocity. So if an object is sitting still, or the object is traveling at constant speed, its acceleration is zero. But if the object is either speeding up or slowing down, its acceleration is non-zero. Thus, we want to make sure the Character is indeed slowing down while deciding whether or not to transition back into the *Idle* State.

Finally, we can tweak some parameters to make these animations look a bit more agile. Double-click the *JogStart* State to enter it and click on *Jog_Fwd_Start*. In the **Details** panel, under **Settings**, set the *Start Position* value to 0.32. This will result in starting the animation 32% of the way into it, to shave off a small bit of time from the beginning of the animation. Enter the *JogStop* State and do the same for *Jog_Fwd_Stop*, except use a value of 0.6. These are things a developer can do if the animations don't look quite right as-is.

Now, with our code compiled, we can assign the *MainAnim_BP* Animation Blueprint to the Character. Open the *MainCharacter_BP* Blueprint, select *Mesh* and in the **Details** panel, in the **Animation** section, set *Animation Mode* to *Use Animation Blueprint* and set *Anim Class* to *MainAnim_BP*.

Enter the **Level Editor** and press **Play** and run around with the Character! The Character will play the correct animations for running and stopping.

Now, this would behave just fine if we didn't have the ability to move sideways with the *A*, *D*, *Left*, and *Right* keys. Notice while using these keys, the Character moves sideways, but the mesh continues to face the direction of the Camera. This is not ideal, so we will need a more sophisticated way to handle the `MoveForward` and `MoveRight` functions. Let's fix this now.

Creating More Sophisticated MoveForward and MoveRight Functions

We have seen that we can use the mouse to control the rotation of the Controller. We would, however, like for the Character to be able to move in the direction of its own movement, regardless of the direction of the Controller, so we will make the following changes to our code.

1. In *MainCharacter.cpp*, in the constructor, just under

   ```
   PrimaryActorTick.bCanEverTick = true;
   ```
   , add:

   ```
   // Don't rotate when the Controller rotates. Let that
   just affect the camera.
   bUseControllerRotationPitch = false;
   bUseControllerRotationYaw = false;
   ```

```
    bUseControllerRotationRoll = false;

    // Configure character movement
    GetCharacterMovement()->bOrientRotationToMovement =
true; // Character moves in the direction of input...
    GetCharacterMovement()->RotationRate = FRotator(0.0f,
540.0f, 0.0f); // ...at this rotation rate
```

2. And, since we are using the UCharacterMovementComponent class, we
    must add the include:

```
#include "GameFramework/CharacterMovementComponent.h"
```

The first three Boolean variables we set to false ensure that the Character itself does
not inherit the pitch, yaw, or roll from the Controller. This way, the Controller can have
its own rotation, independent and uncoupled from that of the Character itself. The
Camera and Spring Arm can still follow the Controller's rotation, but the rest of the
Character will not.

Next, we use the GetCharacterMovement function to access the Character
Movement Component, setting its bOrientRotationToMovement Boolean
variable to true. This is a handy built-in function that will smoothly rotate the
Character for us according to the direction it is moving. RotationRate, which we
access from the Character Movement Component as well, determines the rate at which
the Character will rotate toward its movement. The Pitch and Roll components are
zeroed out, because we only want the Character to rotate toward the movement in the
yaw rotational direction. The value of 540.0 is hardcoded here, and the higher the value,
the more quickly the Character will rotate toward the direction of its movement.

3. Next, we will change the implementation of the MoveForward and
    MoveRight functions to the following:

```
void AMainCharacter::MoveForward(float Value)
{
    if ((Controller != NULL) && (Value != 0.0f))
    {
        // find out which way is forward
        const FRotator Rotation = Controller-
>GetControlRotation();
        const FRotator YawRotation(0, Rotation.Yaw, 0);
```

```
        // get forward vector
        const FVector Direction =
FRotationMatrix(YawRotation).GetUnitAxis(EAxis::X);
        AddMovementInput(Direction, Value);
    }
}

void AMainCharacter::MoveRight(float Value)
{
    if ((Controller != NULL) && (Value != 0.0f))
    {
        // find out which way is right
        const FRotator Rotation = Controller-
>GetControlRotation();
        const FRotator YawRotation(0, Rotation.Yaw, 0);

        // get right vector
        const FVector Direction =
FRotationMatrix(YawRotation).GetUnitAxis(EAxis::Y);
        // add movement in that direction
        AddMovementInput(Direction, Value);
    }

}
```

4. And we will need the following include:

```
#include "GameFramework/Controller.h"
```

First, in `MoveForward`, we check to make sure the `Controller` is not null (the `NULL` macro is a symbol for 0, a special memory address that is equivalent to null). We also make sure that `Value` is not 0.0, because if it is, we don't need to move. We then create a local `FRotator` variable called `Rotation`, set to the value returned from the function `GetControlRotation`, called from the `Controller` variable. This function returns the current rotation of the Controller. We then zero out the pitch and roll components to this vector and store the result in a new local variable, `YawRotation`. Next, we create a `const FVector Direction`, and assign it the value returned by the statement

`FRotationMatrix(YawRotation).GetUnitAxis(EAxis::X)`. This statement does the following: first, we are creating an `FRotationMatrix`. This is a `struct`, like the `FVector`, only it is a different type of mathematical quantity. Whereas the `FVector` has three components, the `FRotationMatrix` has more than three. It is not necessary to understand the mathematics behind the operation, but in simple terms, passing in the `YawRotation` `FRotator` results in an `FRotationMatrix` that is characteristic of the rotation value passed in. The function belonging to the `FRotationMatrix` `struct` called `GetUnitAxis` returns a unit vector (a vector with a magnitude of 1) in the direction of the axis specified by the `enum` constant passed into it. The value `EAxis ::X` is passed in, resulting in the `FVector` value whose direction is in the X direction of the rotation corresponding to `YawRotation`. In short, **the Rotation Matrix allows us to obtain a vector pointing in the forward direction corresponding to the rotation passed into the matrix**.

We then use the function `AddMovementInput`, passing in the value of `Direction` and `Value`, moving the Character in the direction of `Direction`. This will always be in the direction that the Controller is pointed in, with the `Pitch` and `Roll` components zeroed out.

The same technique is used for `MoveRight`, only instead of `EAxis::X`, we pass in `EAxis::Y` into the `GetUnitAxis` function instead. This is essentially the right vector corresponding to the Controller's rotation, thus pressing *A, D, Left,* or *Right* will result in moving the Character in the direction either right or left to the Controller's orientation.

Compile and now test out movement in the level. Notice that the Character moves in the direction of the movement, regardless of which direction the Camera is facing.

Now we would like to add jumping functionality for our Character. This is as simple as adding an action mapping in **Project Settings** and binding it to a function in `SetupPlayerInputComponent`.

5. Add an action mapping called *Jump*, mapped to the *Spacebar* key. Then add the following line to `SetupPlayerInputComponent`:

```
PlayerInputComponent->BindAction("Jump", IE_Pressed,
this, &ACharacter::Jump);

PlayerInputComponent->BindAction("Jump", IE_Released,
this, &ACharacter::StopJumping);
```

The `Character` class has a built-in function called `Jump`, which launches the Character into the air. You will notice that the Character is launched, however it doesn't play any jumping animations, because we haven't set that up yet. In order to do so, we will set up another State Machine for handling jumping animations, and learn how to use both State Machines in unison.

Setting Up Jumping Animations

To set up jumping animations, we will make use of **State Machine Caching**—storing a State Machine's pose data for use in the **Anim Graph**.

1. In *MainAnim_BP*, in the **Anim Graph**, disconnect the output wire from the *Ground Locomotion* State Machine by holding *ALT* and clicking on the humanoid figure to which the output wire is connected. Drag a wire out from this output pin and type "cache" into the search bar, and select *Save New Cached Pose*. Click on the name text on the new node and rename it *Ground Loco*. Next, right-click on the graph and type "State Machine" and select *Add New State Machine* to create a new State Machine. Rename it *Locomotion*. Double-click this new State Machine to enter it.

2. Create new States according to the following figure:

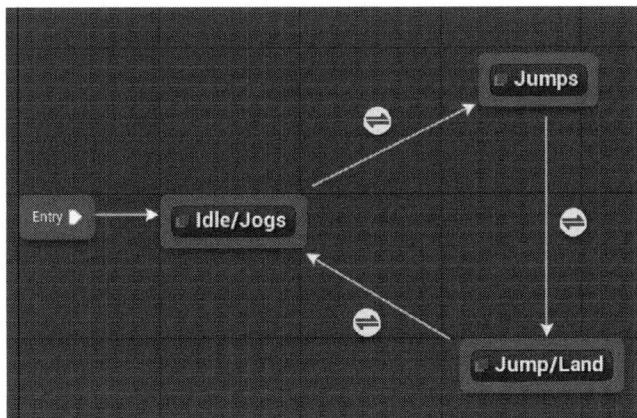

Figure 7.41: New States in the Locomotion State Machine

3. We will use this State Machine to determine when the Character should play jumping animations. For the transition rule between the *Idle/Jogs* State and the *Jumps* State, we will simply need to check the *IsInAir* Boolean variable. Double-click this transition rule, right-click in the graph and search for "IsInAir" and select *Get Is In Air*. Connect the pin to *Can Enter Transition*.

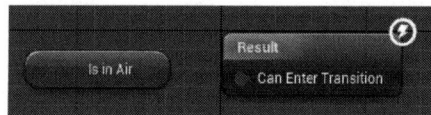

Figure 7.42: Transition Rule Between the Idle/Jogs State and the Jump State

4. For the transition rule between *Jumps* and *Jump/Land*, we will simply check if the *Is In Air* variable is false, using the *NOT Boolean* node. Double-click this transition rule to enter it, and get the *Is In Air Variable*. Create a *NOT Boolean* node and plug *Is In Air* into it, then connect it to *Can Enter Transition*.

Figure 7.43: Transition Rule Between the Jumps State and the Jump/Land State

5. Now for the transition rule between *Jump/Land* and *Idle/Jogs*, we will use *Automatic Rule Based on Sequence Player in State* by left-clicking the transition rule and checking the checkbox for this option in the **Details** panel under **Transition**. Under **Blend** Settings, leave *Duration* at 0.2. In addition, hover your mouse cursor over the border of the *Jump/Land* State and click and drag off to get another arrow, and connect it to the border of the *Idle/Jogs* State to get a second transition rule. Double-click this second transition rule to enter it and get *Is In Air* and plug it into *Can Enter Transition*. It should look exactly like the transition rule in **Figure 7.42**. We do this so we will still transition to the *Idle/Jogs* State when *Jump/Land* completes, even if the Character is in the air, indicating that another jump has occurred. If the Character is in the air, this would result in transitioning to the *Jumps* State again.

6. Now we must add animation data to each of the States. We will start with the *Idle/Jogs* State. Double-click it to enter it. We will use the *Ground Locomotion* State Machine data. We can do this because we have cached the animation data from that State Machine and stored it in the cached pose called *Ground Loco*. Right-click and type "ground loco" and select *Use Cached Pose 'Ground Loco*. Plug this into *Output Animation Pose*. Now when the *Idle/Jogs* State is reached, information from the *Ground Locomotion* State Machine will be used.

Figure 7.44: Using the Cached Ground Loco Pose Data

7. Now we must take care of the *Jumps* State. In the animations for the Countess Character, we have different animations for the various stages of a jump. We will be using four animations total to take care of jumping: *Jump_Start*, *Jump_Apex*, *Jump_Land*, and *Jump_Recovery_Additive*. The first three will be used in the *Jumps* State. The fourth, *Jump_Recovery_Additive*, will be used in the *Jump/Land* State. The reason for this is because we want to blend the *Jump_Recovery_Additive* State with the *Idle* State to make the landing transition smooth. Search for these four animations in the **Asset Browser** and double-click them to play them and see what each of these animations look like. Then enter the *Jumps* State.

8. To handle the *Jump_Start*, *Jump_Apex*, and *Jump_Land* animations, we will create another State Machine here. From within the *Jumps* State, right-click and type "State Machine" and select *Add New State Machine...* and rename it *Jumps*. Connect it to *Output Animation Pose*.

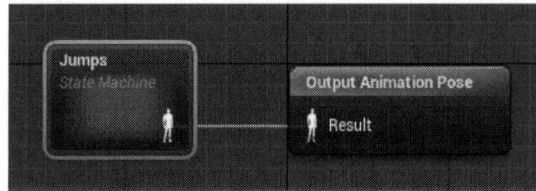

Figure 7.45: Adding a Jumps State Machine

9. Double-click the *Jumps* State Machine to enter it and add the following States: *JumpStart, JumpApex, and Jump_PreLand*, as in the following figure.

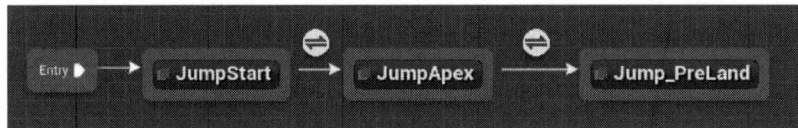

Figure 7.46: The Jumps State Machine

10. Click on the transition rule between *JumpStart* and *JumpApex* and select *Automatic Rule Based on Sequence Player in State* and do the same for the transition rule between *JumpApex* and *Jump_PreLand*. Double-click *JumpStart* and drag in *Jump_Start* from the **Asset Browser**. Do the same for *JumpApex* and *Jump_PreLand* States, except use the *Jump_Apex* and *Jump_Land* animations, respectively.

11. Now enter the *Jump/Land* State. Here, we will blend the *Ground Loco* cached pose with *Jump_Recovery_Additive* with the use of a *Play Additive* node. Right-click, type "ground loco" and select *Use Cached Pose 'Ground Loco*. Next, drag in the *Jump_Recovery_Additive* animation from the **Asset Browser**. Now we will blend the two. Right-click and type "apply additive" and select *Apply Additive*. Plug in the *Ground Loco* cached State Machine into *Base* and *Play_Jump_Recovery_Additive (additive)* into *Additive*. Connect the output pin from the *Apply Additive* node to *Output Animation Pose*. The *Alpha* value determines how much the Additive will be blended with the Base pose. Set this to 0.4.

Now we have created a State Machine for handling jumping called *Jumps*, and used it inside the *Jumps* State which exists in the *Locomotion* State Machine. Using State Machines inside of State Machines like this can help keep State Machines orderly and prevent them from getting too complicated, which introduces the possibility of errors.

12. Return back to the **Anim Graph**, where we created our new *Locomotion* State Machine. We can cache this new State Machine for future use. Drag off of its output pin, type "cache," and select *New Save cached pose...* and call the new cached pose *Loco Pose*. Finally, right-click on the graph and type "loco pose" and select *Use cached pose 'Loco Pose*. Connect this node to the *Output Pose* node, as shown in the following figure.

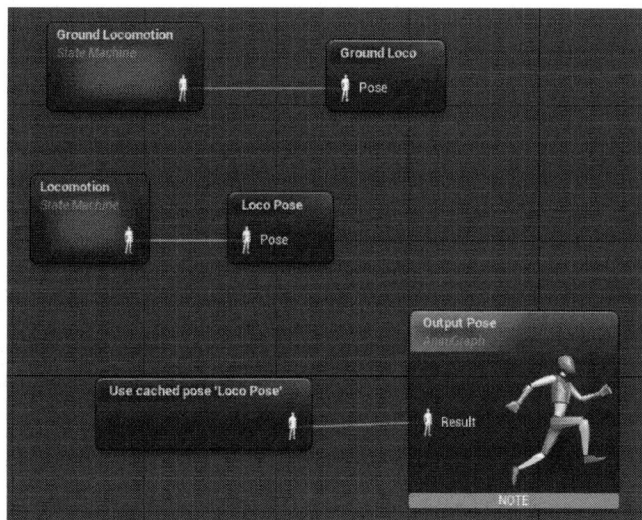

Figure 7.47: Using the Cached Pose Loco Pose for the Output Pose

Now if we return to the **Level Editor** and press **Play**, we will see that the Character will play jumping animations when the Character jumps. Because the animation is split into sections, we can tweak the parameters of each one to make the jumping look as smoothly as possible. One parameter that is useful to adjust is the *Play Rate*. When landing, the animation *Jump_Land* might be too quick. Enter the *Jump_PreLand* State in the *Jumps* State Machine, select the *Play Jump_Land* node, and in the **Details** panel, under **Settings**, Adjust the *Play Rate*. A value of 0.1 or 0.2 may suffice. If you wish for the *Jump_Start* animation to be quicker, simply enter the *JumpStart* State, select the *Play Jump_Start* node, and set the *Play Rate* to a value of about 2.

We have learned how to implement basic movement for our Character, including how to create an `AnimInstance`, the base class for the Animation Blueprint, and we created variables for this class to determine the speed of the Character, whether or not it is in the air, and whether or not it is accelerating. We used these variables to determine when to change States in an animation State Machine in our Animation Blueprint, resulting in our Character playing the correct animation based on how it is moving. We refined our `MoveForward` and `MoveRight` functions so that the Character moves in the direction relative to the current Controller rotation, and we set the Character to turn toward the direction of its movement. We have learned that State Machines can be created inside other State Machines to keep logic orderly and reduce the likelihood of bugs. We did this by creating a *Locomotion* State Machine in which we use a cached version of the *Ground Locomotion* State Machine, combined with a new *Jump* State Machine, allowing our Character to transition into jumping animations.

Now, we are ready to create a **Blendspace**—an animation asset designed to blend between Character animations based on data passed into it. We will use a Blendspace to make the Character blend between leaning versions of the running animation based on whether or not the Character is currently changing directions mid-run.

Creating Blendspaces

Blendspaces are a special tool in Unreal Engine designed to blend animations together. This is useful, for example, when you would like your Character to lean to one side or another based on whether or not they are turning while running. This is the functionality we will be creating with our Blendspace.

Creating a Blendspace 1D

In the *Chapter7* folder, right-click and select *Animation -> Blendspace 1D*. You will be prompted to select a skeleton for this Blendspace. Select *S_Countess_Skeleton*, and name the Blendspace *LeaningRun*. Open this asset.

The gray strip in the middle under the **Viewport** is a horizontal axis on which you can drag animations. By default, there are four grid divisions, but you can change that in the **Asset Details** panel under **Axis Settings**, where an item called *Horizontal Axis* exists. Click the dropdown for this item. By adjusting *Number of Grid Divisions*, the horizontal axis will adjust. Here, you can also see *Name*, *Minimum Axis Value*, and *Maximum Axis Value*. *Name* is a name that will be assigned to the **axis variable**, a variable that will be given a value in the **Animation Blueprint** which will determine a location on the axis. This location will thus determine how to blend the animation pose once animations are dragged onto the axis. Rename the *Name* value *Lean*, *Minimum Axis Value* to -90, and *Maximum Axis Value* to 90.

In the **Asset Browser**, find the *Jog_Fwd_CircleLeft* animation and drag it onto the leftmost grid line on the axis. Drag *Jog_Fwd_CircleRight* onto the rightmost grid line, and drag *Jog_Fwd* onto the central grid line. Now you can hold the *SHIFT* key and move the mouse cursor left and right to see how the Character pose blends between the animations in the **Viewport**.

Figure 7.48: The Horizontal Axis on the Blendspace

Now open the **Animation Blueprint** and go to the *AnimGraph*, enter the *Ground Locomotion* State Machine, and double-click on the *Run* State. Select the *Play Jog_Fwd* node and delete it. Drag in *LeaningRun* from the **Asset Browser** and connect its output pin to the input pin in the *Output Animation Pose* node.

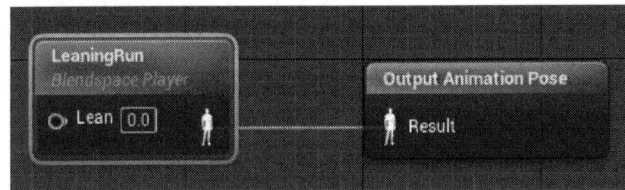

Figure 7.49: Using the LeaningRun Blendspace in the Animation Blueprint

Notice the green input pin on the *LeaningRun* node. The Blendspace expects `float` value to assign to the *Lean* variable, which is the axis variable we renamed in the *LeaningRun* Blendspace. Each frame, the value passed in for *Lean* will determine where on the horizontal axis of the Blendspace we will be. This determines the pose of the Character.

We will need to calculate just how much lean we would like based on the turning motions of the Character.

Calculating the Character's Lean Value

We will need to know how much the Character has rotated between the current frame and the previous frame. In *MainAnimInstance.h*, add, just under `bool bIsAccelerating;`,

```
    UPROPERTY(EditAnywhere, BlueprintReadOnly, Category =
Movement)
    float YawDelta;

    UPROPERTY(EditAnywhere, BlueprintReadOnly, Category =
Movement)
    FRotator RotationLastFrame;
```

First, we create a `float` called `YawDelta`, to quantify the amount the Character has rotated since the previous frame. Next, we create an `FRotator` called `RotationLastFrame` to store the actual rotation of the Character the previous frame. This will aid us in our calculations. Next, we will add an input parameter to `UpdateAnimationProperties`, for `DeltaTime`. Change the function declaration in *MainAnimInstance.h* to:

```
void UpdateAnimationProperties(float DeltaTime);
```

And in *MainAnimInstance.cpp*, add this change to the function signature as well.

Then, in `UpdateAnimationProperties`, just under `bIsInAir = Pawn->GetMovementComponent()->IsFalling();`, add:

```
FRotator Rotation = Pawn->GetActorRotation();
FRotator Delta =
UKismetMathLibrary::NormalizedDeltaRotator(RotationLastFrame, Rotation);
float Target = Delta.Yaw / DeltaTime;
float Interp = FMath::FInterpTo(YawDelta, Target, DeltaTime, 6.0f);

YawDelta = FMath::Clamp(Interp, -90.f, 90.f);

RotationLastFrame = Rotation;
```

And include the following:

```
#include "Kismet/KismetMathLibrary.h"
```

Here, we create a local `FRotator` called `Rotation` to store the current location this frame, which we get from the Pawn by calling `GetActorRotation`. Next we calculate a **delta**, a change between to values, by using a function from the function library called `UKismetMathLibrary`. This library contains many useful mathematical functions which will come in handy throughout this book. We use `NormalizedDeltaRotator`, which takes the difference between two `FRotator`s, and returns a normalized `FRotator`. We take the difference between the value of the rotation last frame and this frame, and store this normalized value in the local `FRotator` variable `Delta`.

Now we take the `Yaw` component of `Delta` and divide it by `DeltaTime`. `DeltaTime` is a small number, so dividing it will make the result a larger number. It will also be scaled by the amount of time passed since last frame, resulting in a rate that doesn't get affected by the variations in frame rate. We then crate a `float` called `Interp`, which we populate from the result of the following calculation. First, we use a math function from the `FMath` class—a class that contains many useful mathematical functions—called `FInterpTo`. F stands for `float`, and `Interp` is short for **interpolation**. An interpolation function is designed to be used each frame. It takes a current value and a target value and returns a result that is somewhere between the current and the target values. The next frame, the altered value is passed is as the current value, and the overall outcome is that the value changes smoothly from the initial to the target value over time. The speed at which this transition occurs can be adjusted, and this value is called the **interpolation speed**.

- The first argument in the `FInterpTo` function is the value being interpolated.

- The second argument in the target value.

- The third argument is `DeltaTime`, which is required for the interpolation calculation.

- The fourth parameter is the interpolation speed.

Finally, we take our variable `YawDelta`, which we declared in *MainAnimInstance.h*, and **clamp** it—restrict it so that it never goes over or under certain specified limits. We choose -90 for the lower limit and 90 for the upper limit. `FMath` contains a handy function for this called `Clamp`. If the value passed in for the first argument is higher than 90, the result returned will be 90. Similarly, if the value passed in is lower than -90, then -90 will be returned. The second and third parameters are the lower and higher clamp limits, respectively. We perform this clamp because our axis values in the Blendspace do not go lower than -90 or higher than 90.

The final step is to make sure our Blendspace is receiving the value for the *Lean* axis variable. In *MainAnim_BP*, in the *Run* State, right-click and type "yaw delta" and select *Get Yaw Delta*. You might have noticed that she leans the wrong way unless we negate the value of the Lean as follows:

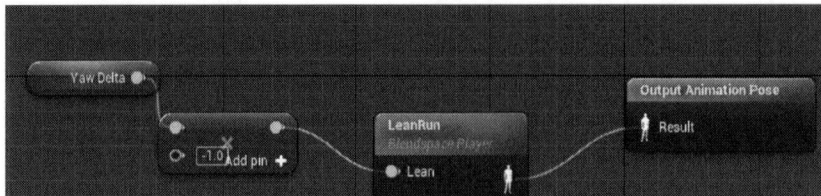

Figure 7.50: Passing the Lean Value into LeanRun

We also need to make sure `UpdateAnimationProperties` is being passed in `DeltaTime`. In *MainAnim_BP*, in the **Event Graph**, make sure the *Delta Time X* output from *Event Blueprint Update Animation* is connected to the *Delta Time* input on the Update Animation Properties node.

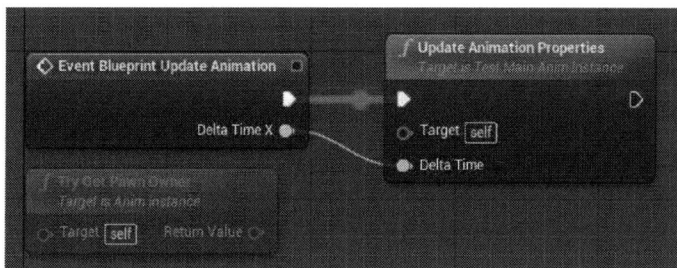

Figure 7.51: Passing in Delta Time to Update Animation Properties

Compile and return to the **Level Editor** and press **Play**. The Character should now lean based on the severity of turning while running.

Summary

We have now introduced one of the most versatile classes in the Unreal Engine hierarchy—the `Character` class. We saw that the `Character` class comes with Character-specific features built in: it automatically has a Capsule Component, which is the Root Component. We learned that the Root Component cannot be reassigned to another component. We learned that the Character class has its own inherited skeletal mesh variable called `Mesh`. We created a class based on `Character` called `MainCharacter` and used free assets provided by Epic Games on the Marketplace, a source where developers can purchase and download assets such as meshes, animations, and more. We saw that there are many free assets, some of which are provided by Epic Games. We then programmed movement functionality for our Character by setting up axis and action mappings in the **Project Settings** menu. We then created callback functions for these inputs, allowing for us to implement movement functionality. We then learned that Characters can use Animation Blueprints, a Blueprint based off of the `AnimInstance` class, and we created our own class based on `AnimInstance` called `MainAnimInstance`. We created variables and functions in this class and exposed them to Blueprints so we could use them in the Animation Blueprint to determine when to enter specific animations. We finally used the **Anim**

Graph in the Animation Blueprint, where we created State Machines to determine which animations should be played. We used transition rules to provide the logic for entering the various transitions. We saw that we could create multiple State Machines, and even use State Machines inside other State Machines, and we did this with the *Ground Locomotion*, *Locomotion*, and *Jump* State Machines. We created a Blendspace in order to blend between animations, allowing our Character to lean to the side based on a parameter which we calculated in the `MainAnimInstance` with the help of functions from the `FMath` and `UKismetMathLibrary` classes. By the end of the chapter, we had a functional Character class that can run, jump, and lean.

We now have the basis for a fully functional third-person action game! We are now ready to dive deeper into engine features, starting with collision. In the next chapter, we will learn about Overlap Events, Hit Events, Collision Presets, Collision Hulls, and Physics Settings, and how each of these affects a different aspect of gameplay.

Chapter 8 – Collision

In all video games, collision comes into play in some way. Whether you are bashing through walls, toppling towers, or hitting a baseball, objects will be colliding or overlapping with other objects, and when this happens, we will almost always want some sort of functionality to be triggered. In this chapter, we will cover how to detect when collision and overlap occurs in the game, and how to fire off our own code in response to it. Specifically, we will cover:

- **Overlap Events:** When objects are set to overlap with one another, we can create functions that will be called at the beginning of the overlap as well as at the end of the overlap.

- **Hit Events:** Some objects are not allowed to overlap. Instead, they will collide upon contact, and the physics engine will impart forces on these objects. This results in the objects bouncing off one another. When this happens, we can detect the collision and fire off code in response.

- **Collision Presets:** We have the option to determine exactly how certain objects behave in relation to one another. An object may be set to collide, overlap, or ignore others. Whether we wish for the object to behave the same toward all other objects or differently depending on properties of those objects, we must decide and configure it to do so.

- **Collision Hulls:** Objects that are intended to collide with others have **collision hulls**, or geometry designed to handle collision. We will learn how to see the collision hulls for meshes, and if they have none, we will learn how to add them.

Working with Overlap Events

Overlap Events are used for many things in games. In a racing game, the first person to cross the finish line wins. An overlap volume is the perfect way to determine who gets there first. As soon as the leading racer overlaps with the overlap volume, a function can be triggered, resulting in all the things that happen when that player wins the game – their name is displayed on the screen, along with their score, etc. Another common use of Overlap Events involves pickups. **Pickups** are items in the world of a game which can be "picked up" by the Character. Once the Character overlaps with it, it disappears and often emits a sound or special effect, and affects gameplay in one way or another. We can easily create Overlap Events in Unreal Engine using C++. We will do so now.

In the **Content Browser**, maneuver to *ThirdPersonCPP -> Maps* and double-click on *ThirdPersonExampleMap*. We will do some experimenting here. Since we set our Default Game Mode in *Project Settings*, we can press play here and our Countess Character will show up, and we can control her.

In order to learn how Overlap Events work, we will wish to create an Actor for handling these events.

Creating an Overlap Actor

We will wish to create an Actor for handling overlap functionality. In the **Content Browser**, in the *FirstGame* folder, right-click and select *New C++ Class…* and choose *Actor*. Name the Actor *OverlapActor*. Click *Create Class*.

Adding an Overlap Volume

Overlap volumes can take on different shapes. These are typically in the form of components that we can add to our Actor. Some examples of overlap volume shapes are boxes, spheres, and capsules. We will add a Box Component to our Overlap Actor, as well as a Static Mesh Component, so we can have a visual representation of our overlap item. In *OverlapActor.h*, just under AOverlapActor(); add:

```
UPROPERTY(VisibleAnywhere, Category = "Pickup")
class UStaticMeshComponent* PickupMesh;

UPROPERTY(VisibleAnywhere, Category = "Pickup")
class UBoxComponent* OverlapBox;
```

We are forward declaring the UStaticMeshComponent and UBoxComponent classes, and marking these variables as VisibleAnywhere as well as putting them into the *Pickup* category. We will also need to construct these objects. In *OverlapActor.cpp*, the constructor, just under, add:

```
    PickupMesh =
CreateDefaultSubobject<UStaticMeshComponent>(TEXT("PickupMe
sh"));
    SetRootComponent(PickupMesh);

    OverlapBox =
CreateDefaultSubobject<UBoxComponent>(TEXT("OverlapBox"));
    OverlapBox->SetupAttachment(GetRootComponent());
```

Now we must add the following at the top, just under `#include`
`"OverlapActor.h"`:

```
#include "Components/StaticMeshComponent.h"

#include "Components/BoxComponent.h"
```

Now we have the basic class for an item we can overlap with. Compile, then return to the **Level Editor**. We are now ready to create a Blueprint based on the `OverlapActor` class.

Creating a Blueprint for our OverlapActor Class

Create a new folder in the **Content Browser** called *Chapter8*. Then in *C++ Classes* -> *FirstGame*, right-click on *OverlapActor* and choose Create Blueprint class based on *OverlapActor*, and place it in the *Chapter8* folder. Name this Actor *OverlapActorBP*.

Open the **Blueprint Editor** for *OverlapActorBP*. You will see the pink outline of a box. This is the *OverlapBox Component*, which we created in C++ based on `UBoxComponent`.

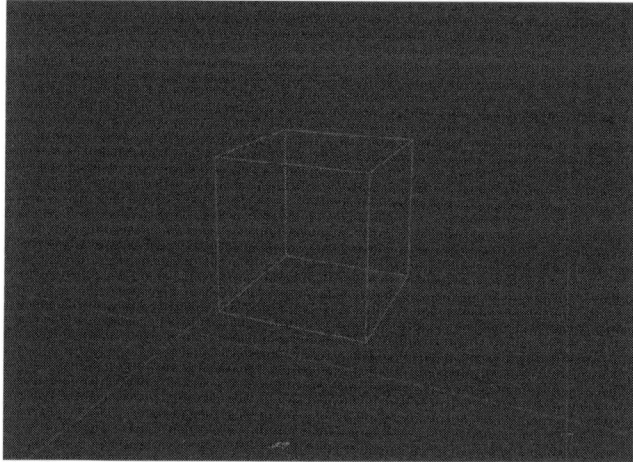

Figure 8.1: The Box Component

In the **Components** panel, you will see the *PickupMesh* component, which is the Root Component, and *OverlapBox*, which is attached to it.

Figure 8.2: The Components in the Components Panel

Now select *PickupMesh* in the **Components** panel and then find the *Static Mesh* property in the **Details** panel. Choose *Shape_NarrowCapsule*. You will see the following in the **Viewport** for *OverlapActorBP*:

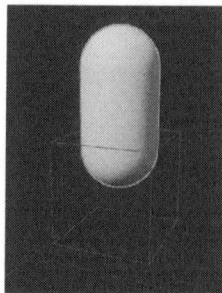

Figure 8.3: Adding a Capsule Component

Now we have a mesh for our overlap Actor. We can resize the capsule, but we must keep in mind that the Static Mesh is the Root Component, and any other components attached to it will scale along with it. If you wish to resize the mesh without affecting the other components, you cannot scale the Root Component. An easy way to avoid needing to worry about this is to simply use a `USceneComponent` for the Root Component. The `RootComponent` variable inherited by the `Actor` class is actually derived from `USceneComponent`, as can be seen in the Unreal Engine documentation for the `UStaticMeshComponent` class, as seen in the following image:

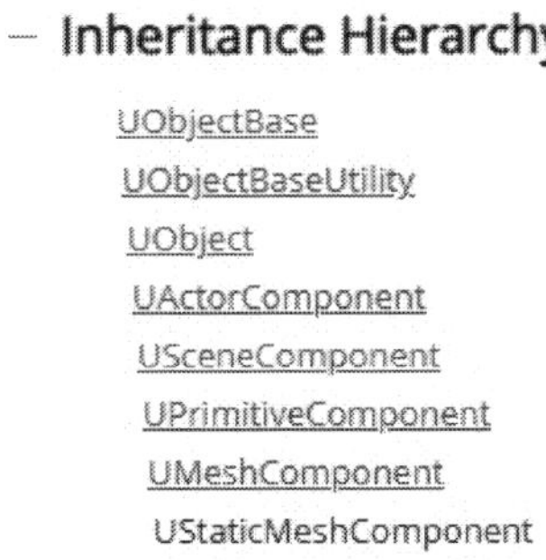

— Inheritance Hierarchy

UObjectBase
UObjectBaseUtility
UObject
UActorComponent
USceneComponent
UPrimitiveComponent
UMeshComponent
UStaticMeshComponent

Figure 8.4: Inheritance Hierarchy Shown in the Unreal Engine Documentation

Since `UStaticMeshComponent` inherits from `USceneComponent`, a pointer variable that points to an object of type `USceneComponent` can point to an object of type `UStaticMeshComponent`, thanks to the **is-a** relationship between `UStaticMeshComponent` and `USceneComponent`. This is the reason why we can set a Static Mesh to be the Root Component.

A Scene Component has its own transform, including location and rotation information, and supports attachment (components can be attached to it) so it is perfectly acceptable as a Root Component, but it is not capable of having a Static Mesh, like the `UStaticMeshComponent` is. Thus for our purposes, we will simply use a `UStaticMeshComponent`.

Click on *OverlapBox* in the **Components** panel. With *OverlapBox* selected, you can move the component relative to the Root Component. Use Translation Mode to move it up to the center of the Capsule Component. Then in the **Details** panel, notice in the **Shape** section, we have *Box Extent*.

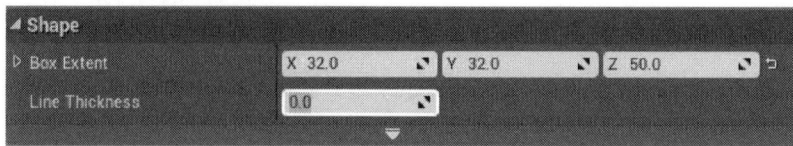

Figure 8.5: The Shape Category in the Details Panel for the Box Component

For the **Box Component**, you can change the *X*, *Y* and *Z* components of the *Box Extent* without actually scaling it (the *Transform* property is unaffected). Thus if a component were attached to the Box Component, changing the *Box Extent* would not change the size of any attached components. Change the *Z* component to 50. The *Line Thickness* property allows you to have thicker lines for the box. Change *Line Thickness* from 0.0 to 3.0.

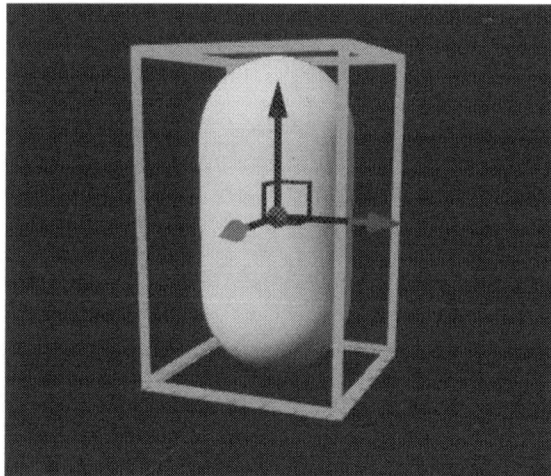

Figure 8.6: Changing the Box Extent and the Line Thickness

The lines of the box are visible in the Blueprint **Viewport**, but they will not be visible in the game by default. In the **Details** panel, under **Rendering**, you will see two properties: *Visible*, and *Hidden in Game*.

Figure 8.7: Visible and Hidden in Game for the Box Component

These allow you to toggle whether or not you wish to see the Box Component at all (*Visible*) and whether or not you wish for the Box Component to be seen in the game (*Hidden in Game*). Uncheck *Hidden in Game*. Now in the **Content Browser**, in *Chapter8*, drag out an *OverlapActorBP* into the level.

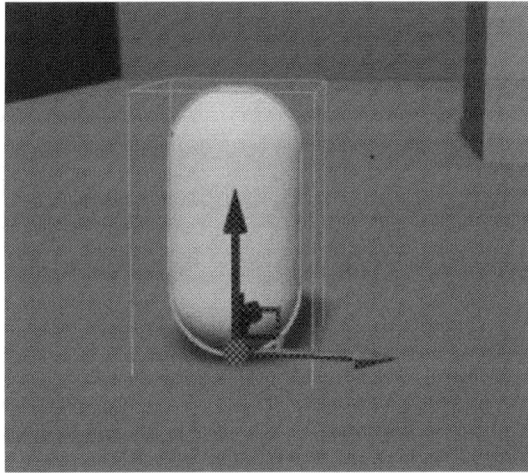

Figure 8.8: An OverlapActorBP in the Level

Now we have created an Actor for our Character to overlap with. But how do we actually fire off some logic when the Character overlaps with it? We will learn how to do so now.

Creating BeginOverlap and EndOverlap Functions

In order to add overlap functionality, we must take advantage of some built-in code in the engine. Unreal Engine has built-in **Delegates**, a type of class that can have functions bound to it. We will wish to create a function that will be called when our Box Component is overlapped by something. We will also create a function to be called when an object stops overlapping with the Box Component as well.

Before we create these functions, it is important to know that a function bound to a Delegate must have the appropriate function signature. In order to know what that function signature needs to be, we must understand a little more about the Delegate classes themselves. In Visual Studio, in the *Solution Explorer*, search for

PrimitiveComponent.h. If you refer back to **Figure 8.4** above, you will see that `UPrimitiveComponent` exists in the Unreal Engine hierarchy just above `UMeshComponent`. Because `UPrimitiveComponent` is a parent of `UBoxComponent`, the `UBoxComponent` class inherits the code in `UPrimitiveComponent`. In *PrimitiveComponent.h*, search for `OnComponentBeginOverlap`, and you will see the following:

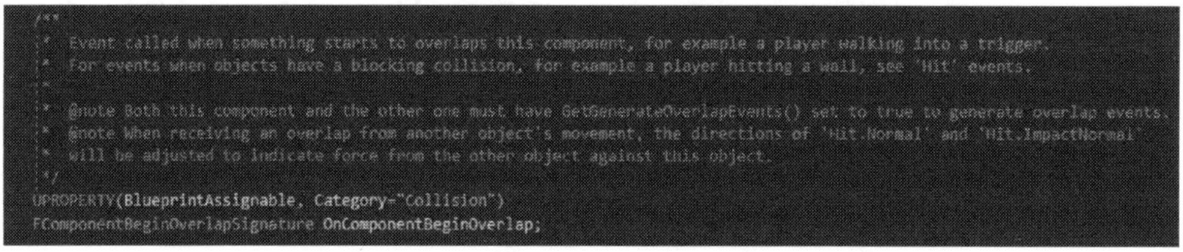

```
/**
 * Event called when something starts to overlaps this component, for example a player walking into a trigger.
 * For events when objects have a blocking collision, for example a player hitting a wall, see 'Hit' events.
 *
 * @note Both this component and the other one must have GetGenerateOverlapEvents() set to true to generate overlap events.
 * @note When receiving an overlap from another object's movement, the directions of 'Hit.Normal' and 'Hit.ImpactNormal'
 * will be adjusted to indicate force from the other object against this object.
 */
UPROPERTY(BlueprintAssignable, Category="Collision")
FComponentBeginOverlapSignature OnComponentBeginOverlap;
```

Figure 8.9: The Declaration of the FcomponentOverlapSignature Struct

This variable, `OnComponentBeginOverlap`, type, `FComponentBeginOverlapSignature`, exists here and is used in the creation of the Delegate for Overlap Events. If you search *PrimitiveComponent.h* for `FCcomponentBeginOverlapSignature`, you will come across the following line:

```
/** Delegate for notification of start of overlap with a
specific component */
```

```
DECLARE_DYNAMIC_MULTICAST_SPARSE_DELEGATE_SixParams(
FComponentBeginOverlapSignature, UPrimitiveComponent,
OnComponentBeginOverlap, UPrimitiveComponent*,
OverlappedComponent, AActor*, OtherActor,
UPrimitiveComponent*, OtherComp, int32, OtherBodyIndex,
bool, bFromSweep, const FHitResult &, SweepResult);
```

This macro takes the `FComponentBeginOverlapSignature` type, next `UPrimitiveComponent`, `OnComponentHit`, followed by a list of other parameters. This macro takes this list, and uses the types specified, along with the names which follow after each type. This macro will take these items and result in the formation of a Delegate which will have the ability to bind a function of our creation, granted its input parameters are proper for the Delegate. This macro tells us the types of the parameter inputs, in order, for the function signature for this Delegate. They begin after the `OnComponentHit` input in the macro. You will notice just below this code in *PrimitiveComponent.h* that there are similar macros including the following:

```
/** Delegate for notification of end of overlap with a
specific component */
```

```
DECLARE_DYNAMIC_MULTICAST_SPARSE_DELEGATE_FourParams(
FComponentEndOverlapSignature, UPrimitiveComponent,
OnComponentEndOverlap, UPrimitiveComponent*,
OverlappedComponent, AActor*, OtherActor,
UPrimitiveComponent*, OtherComp, int32, OtherBodyIndex);
```

This macro likewise shows us the input parameter types needed for a function that can be bound to an End Overlap Delegate. We will use this information for the following functions which we will declare in *OverlapActor.h*, just under `virtual void Tick(float DeltaTime) override;`:

```
    UFUNCTION()
    void BeginOverlap(UPrimitiveComponent*
OverlappedComponent, AActor* OtherActor,
UPrimitiveComponent* OtherComp, int32 OtherBodyIndex, bool
bFromSweep, const FHitResult & SweepResult);
```

```
    UFUNCTION()

    void EndOverlap(UPrimitiveComponent*
OverlappedComponent, AActor* OtherActor,
UPrimitiveComponent* OtherComp, int32 OtherBodyIndex);
```

We have created two functions: `BeginOverlap` and `EndOverlap`, which we will intend on binding to the `OnComponentBeginOverlap` and `OnComponentEndOverlap` variables inherited by the `UBoxComponent` class. Again, the function signatures use the types in order from the macro declarations above. If you copy them from the macro and paste them into your function definition, you will need to remove the commas that exist between the type and the name of each parameter. Make sure to ignore the first three parameters, as these are used to create the binding between the Delegate signature `struct` and the function. The functions also need to be marked as `UFUNCTION` to participate in the Delegate system. We will need to create function bodies in *OverlapActor.cpp*:

```
void AOverlapActor::BeginOverlap(UPrimitiveComponent
OnComponentBeginOverlap, UPrimitiveComponent*
```

```
OverlappedComponent, AActor* OtherActor,
UPrimitiveComponent* OtherComp, int32 OtherBodyIndex, bool
bFromSweep, const FHitResult & SweepResult)
{
     UE_LOG(LogTemp, Warning, TEXT("BeginOverlap"));
}


void AOverlapActor::EndOverlap(UPrimitiveComponent
OnComponentEndOverlap, UPrimitiveComponent*
OverlappedComponent, AActor* OtherActor,
UPrimitiveComponent* OtherComp, int32 OtherBodyIndex)
{
     UE_LOG(LogTemp, Warning, TEXT("EndOverlap"));

}
```

Now we have functions with the correct signatures for these Delegates. We have also added UE_LOG functionality to send a message to the **Output Log** when these functions get called, so we can see them in action. We are ready to bind these functions to the Delegates in our OverlapBox Component.

Binding our OverlapBegin and OverlapEnd Functions

The OnComponentBeginOverlap variable inherited by OverlapBox has a macro called AddDynamic, which we will use to bind out OverlapBegin function. Likewise the OnComponentEndOverlap variable uses a macro with the same name. Add the following in BeginPlay, just under Super::BeginPlay();:

```
     OverlapBox->OnComponentBeginOverlap.AddDynamic(this,
&AOverlapActor::BeginOverlap);

     OverlapBox->OnComponentEndOverlap.AddDynamic(this,
&AOverlapActor::EndOverlap);
```

The AddDynamic macro takes a UserObject input, and we will be simply passing in the this keyword, which is a pointer to the object in which it is used. The second parameter is the address to function we wish to bind to the Delegate. Functions have addresses, just like variables do. To pass a function into another function or a macro, you must use the address-of (&) operator, which we do here.

Now we have bound functions to `OnComponentBeginOverlap` and `OnComponentEndOverlap` Delegates. Compile this code, and test it out in the editor! You should see the log messages print to the screen when you begin and end overlapping with the box.

We now have the ability to fire off any code we wish when an object overlaps with one of our components in `OverlapActor`. This will come in handy throughout the course of this book as we create objects that have overlap functionality.

Some objects are not made to overlap each other. For example, the walls and the floor collide with our Character, and do not let her pass through them. But what if we wish to create functionality for when such a collision occurs? This is exactly what Hit Events are for. We will visit how to create Hit Events now.

Hit Events

We saw that in `PrimitiveComponent`, there exist macros for creating Delegates, and these macros contain a list of parameters which we can use to deduce the function signatures for the functions we wish to bind to these Delegates. We will use this same method to determine the function signature for a function we will use to take care of Hit Events as well. In *PrimitiveComponent.h*, locate the following lines of code:

```
DECLARE_DYNAMIC_MULTICAST_SPARSE_DELEGATE_FiveParams(
FComponentHitSignature, UPrimitiveComponent,
OnComponentHit, UPrimitiveComponent*, HitComponent,
AActor*, OtherActor, UPrimitiveComponent*, OtherComp,
FVector, NormalImpulse, const FHitResult&, Hit );

/** Delegate for notification of start of overlap with a
specific component */
```

These show us the parameter list for a function suitable for binding to the `OnComponentHit` Delegate. Using this information, we will declare the following function in *OverlapActor.h*, just under the `BeginOverlap` and `EndOverlap` function declarations:

```
UFUNCTION()
```

```
        void ComponentHit(UPrimitiveComponent* HitComponent,
AActor* OtherActor, UPrimitiveComponent* OtherComp, FVector
NormalImpulse, const FHitResult& Hit);
```

And we can give our function a definition in *OverlapActor.cpp*:

```
void AOverlapActor::ComponentHit(UPrimitiveComponent*
HitComponent, AActor* OtherActor, UPrimitiveComponent*
OtherComp, FVector NormalImpulse, const FHitResult& Hit)
{
        UE_LOG(LogTemp, Warning, TEXT("ComponentHit"));
}
```

Now we simply need to bind the function to the Delegate. We will use the `PickupMesh` for this. In `BeginPlay`, just under the calls to `AddDynamic` for the `OverlapBox`, add:

```
PickupMesh->OnComponentHit.AddDynamic(this,
&AOverlapActor::ComponentHit);
```

Now compile the code and test it out! You can use the Character to run into the capsule mesh and see the message print in the **Output Log**. As long as an object is colliding with the capsule, the message will spam the **Output Log**.

Why did we create functions with all these parameters in their signatures, yet we didn't use any of them? The answer is that we don't have to use them. They simply need to be in the function signature if we wish to bind these functions to the associated events, because the Delegates set up the functionality to work correctly if we do choose to use them. We will use these parameters in *Chapter 8 – Gameplay Events*.

Now that we understand overlap and Hit Events, we must learn some important details regarding overlapping and colliding objects in Unreal Engine. In the examples above, our Character just happened to pass through the Box Component, and collide with the capsule mesh component. Why didn't the Character collide with the Box Component, rather than pass through it? Why didn't she pass straight through the capsule? The answer involves collision presets, which we will now dive into.

Collision Presets

We can configure **collision presets** (configurations which determine how collisions work on an Actor's components) in C++, but first we will do so in Blueprints, so we can become familiar with how they work. In the next chapter, we will learn the functions that we can use to do it on the C++ side.

Using Custom Collision Presets

In our *OverlapActorBP* Blueprint, select the *OverlapBox* in the **Components** panel. Then in the **Details** panel, find the *Collision* section.

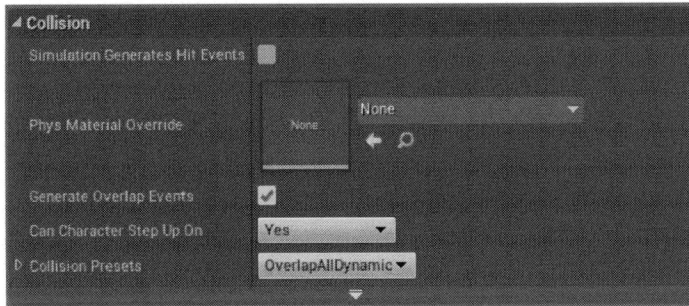

Figure 8.10: The Collision Section in the Details Panel for OverlapBox

The dropdown next to *Collision Presets* allows us to select various presets which are configured already for certain types of objects. The Box Collision component is set to *OverlapAllDynamic* by default. To see what this means, click the triangle next to *Collision Presets* to expand it.

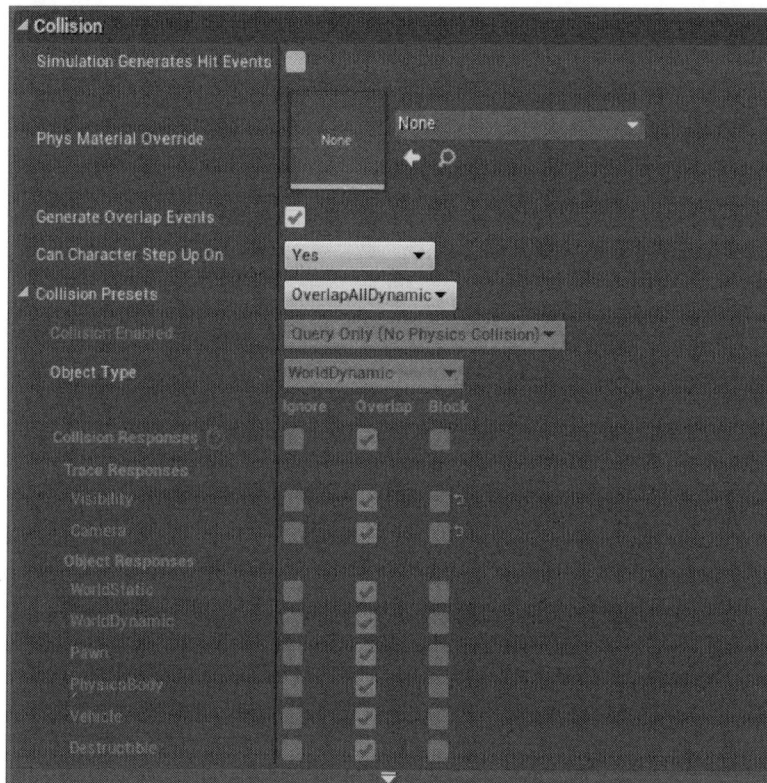

Notice that several items are now visible: *Collision Enabled*, *Object Type*, and a list of *Collision Responses* with checkboxes. You will find that they are set to values and they cannot be changed. This is because the *Collision Presets* dropdown has a particular preset configuration selected (*OverlapAllDynamic*). Click the dropdown and select *BlockAllDynamic*.

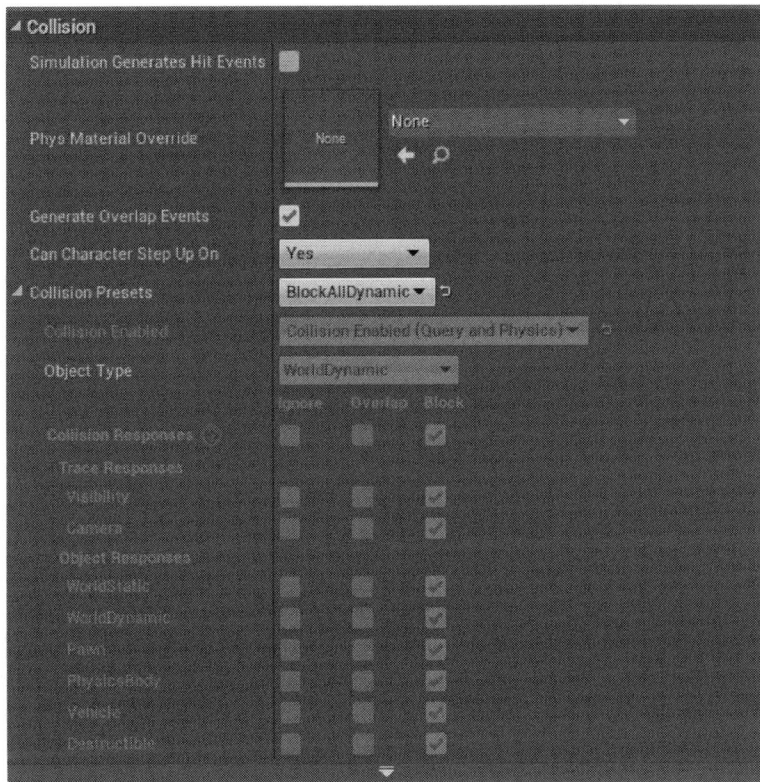

Figure 8.12: The BlockAllDynamic Collision Preset

Now notice that the values set in the items below *Collision Presets* are different. Whereas in **Figure 8.11** the *Collision Enabled* property was set to *Query Only (No Physics Collision)*, it is now set to *Collision Enabled (Query and Physics)*. In both the *OverlapAllDynamic* and *BlockAllDynamic* Collision Presets, the *Object Type* is the same: *WorldDynamic*. But the checkboxes are different in the *Collision Responses*; in *OverlapAllDynamic*, all of the responses are set to *Overlap*, whereas in *BlockAllDynamic*, they are all set to *Block*.

With the collision box *Collision Presets* set to *BlockAllDynamic*, scroll up in the **Details** panel to the **Shape** section and set the *Box Extent X* and *Y* parameters to 100 each.

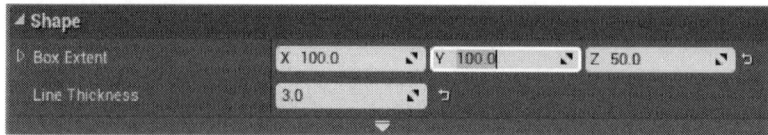

Figure 8.13: Increasing the X and Y of the Box Extent

Now press **Play** and try to run into the capsule mesh. You can't do it! This is because the *Collision Presets* for the Box Component have been set such that it blocks all objects. You will find that the Character can even jump up onto the box.

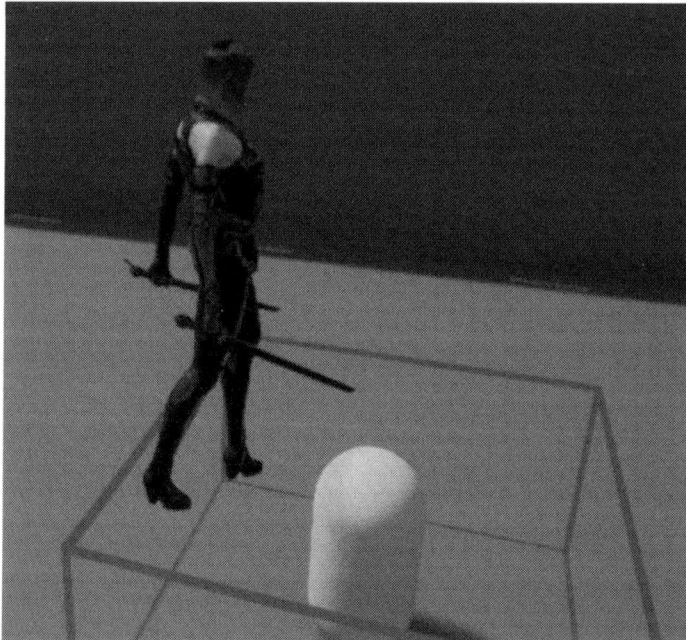

Figure 8.14: Standing on the Box Component set to BlackAllDynamic

Now we see that depending on the *Collision Presets* dropdown option selected, the object will behave differently. But what do each of these presets mean? We will visit each one in detail.

Open the *Collision Presets* dropdown and select *Custom…* and you will see that the options below it are now changeable. Whatever the *Collision Presets* was set to before setting it to *Custom…* will determine the settings its starts in. For example, since we had it in *BlockAllDynamic*, once we changed it to *Custom...*, all of the presets remained in the configuration set in *BlockAllDynamic*, except they are no longer grayed out.

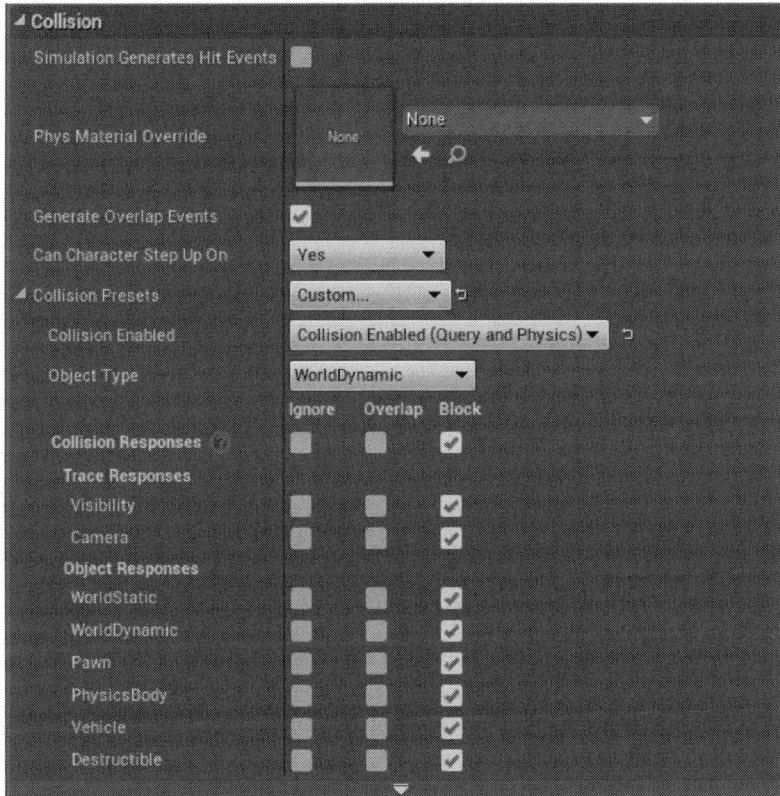

8.15: Selecting Custom... for the Collision Presets

We will now be able to see exactly what each of these presets does. We start with the *Collision Enabled* option.

Collision Enabled

There are four options for the *Collision Enabled* preset. They determine whether two types of collision are activated or not. These types of collision are **Physics Collision** and **Query Collision**. Physics Collision involves detecting collisions between objects. The physics engine detects whether an object would overlap another object, and using physical properties such as velocity and position, forces are imparted on the two objects in order to push them away from each other. When something bounces off another, this is what the physics engine is doing. When our Character stood on the Box Collision in **Figure 8.14**, the physics engine took the downward force of the Character due to gravity and imparted an equal force in the opposite direction (up) in order to counter that force. As a result, the Character does not pass through the box. Query collision involves detecting overlaps. This allows for Overlap Events such as those we learned earlier in this chapter. With query collision enabled, **sweeps** can occur. Sweeping is a method of determining whether or not two objects would have passed through one another in any given frame. The *Collision Enabled* preset has four options:

- **No Collision:** This is the simplest option. No objects will collide with this component, and no Overlap Events will occur. Even if you have a function bound to an overlap or Hit Event as we have done in this chapter, if *No Collision* is selected, that code will be ignored. This is the least computationally expensive option and most performant.

- **Query Only (No Physics Collision):** This option enables overlap detection. However, no physical collision will occur.

- **Physics Only (No Query Collision):** This option enables physics collisions, but overlap detection will not occur.

- **Collision Enabled (Query and Physics):** Both physics collision and overlap detection will occur. This is the most computationally expensive option.

We will now see how these options work by dropping an object onto our *OverlapActor* in the world. In the **Content Browser**, in *StarterContent -> Shapes*, drag a *Shape_Cube* into the world, just above our *OverlapActor*.

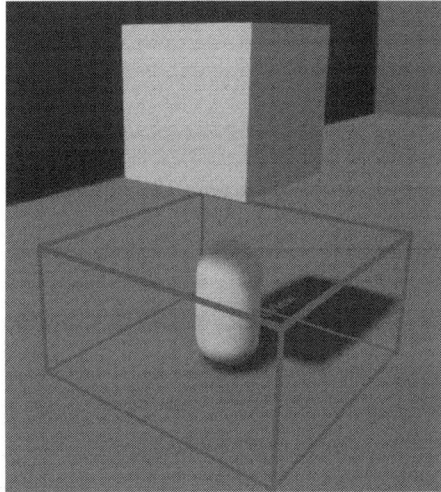

Figure 8.16: Placing a Shape_Cube Above the OverlapActor

Now, with the *Shape_Cube* in the world selected, in the **Details** panel, scroll down to the **Physics** section. Check the checkbox next to *Enable Gravity*. Make sure the checkbox next to *Simulate Physics* is checked.

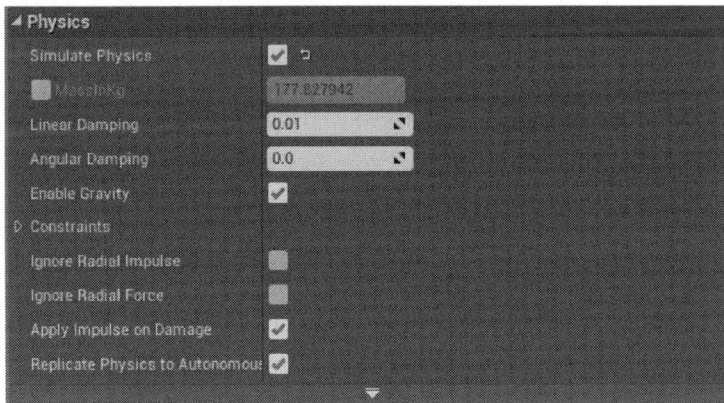

Figure 8.17: Physics Settings for the Shape_Cube

Now return to the *OverlapActorBP* Blueprint. Select the *PickupMesh* component, and make sure its *Collision Presets* value is set to *Block All*.

Select the *OverlapBox Component*. It should still have its *Collision Presets* set to *Custom...*

No Collision

In *Collision Enabled*, Select *No Collision*. Press **Play** and and make sure the **Output Log** is open. Watch the cube bounce off the capsule, but pass through the Box Collision. Our overlap message was not printed to the **Output Log**.

Query Only (No Physics Collision)

Now change the Box Component's *Collision Enabled* to *Query Only (No Physics Collision)*. Press **Play** and watch the cube behave in the same manner. We don't get our message. Why not? The reason is because we must enable Overlap Events on the cube. With the *Shape_Cube* selected in the world, in the **Details** panel, under *Collision*, check the box by *Generate Overlap Events*. Now press **Play**. You will see the log message in the **Output Log** from our BeginOverlap function. So this option must be checked on any object that you wish to trigger Overlap Events. If you go back into the *OverlapActorBP* Blueprint, select the *OverlapBox* and uncheck the *Generate Overlap Events* box there, you will disable Overlap Events for the box itself, thus preventing BeginOverlap from ever being fired, no matter what objects overlap with it.

Physics Only (No Query Collision)

Now change the Box Component's *Collision Enabled* to *Physics Only (No Query Collision)*. Press **Play** and watch the cube land on the Box Collision.

Collision Enabled (Query and Physics)

We will now see how *Collision Enabled (Query and Physics)* works. We will be using it on the Capsule Component, however, since we have already set up a Hit Event for it. Set the *Box Component* to *No Collision*. Then set the *PickupMesh Collision Presets* to *Custom...* and set Collision Enabled to *Collision Enabled (Query and Physics)*.

Now before we test this out, we must make sure the Capsule Component is set to generate Hit Events. With the *PickupMesh* selected, in the **Details** panel, under *Collision*, check *Simulation Generates Hit Events*.

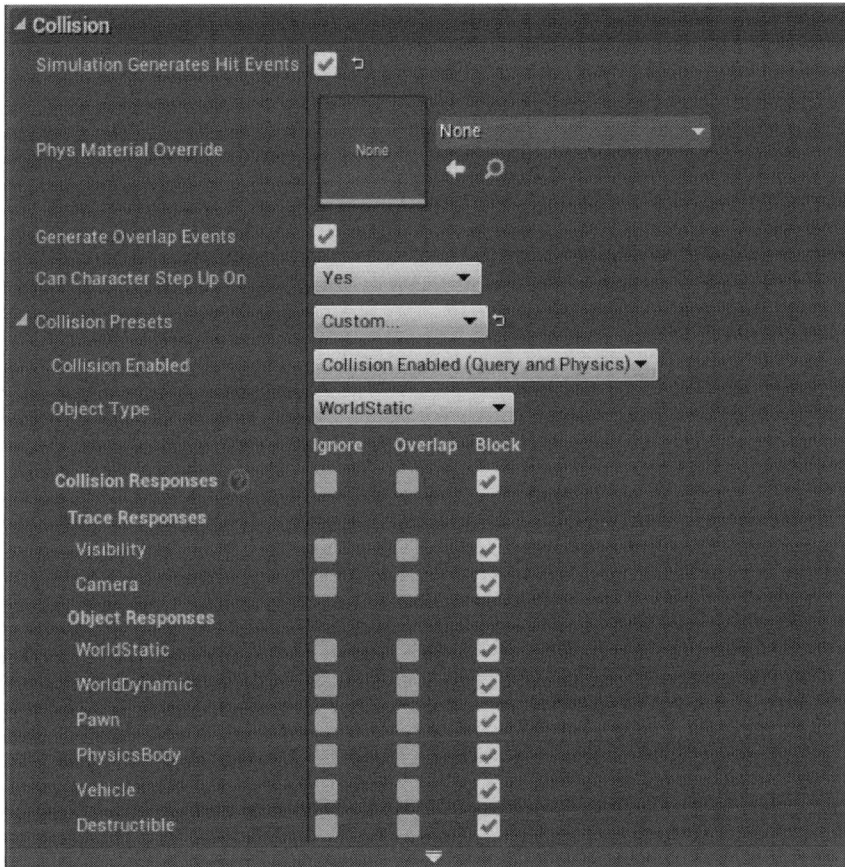

Figure 8.18: Collision Presets for PickupMesh

Now press **Play** and watch the cube hit the capsule and our `ComponentHit` log message print to the screen.

These events work as long as the objects are configured to react properly to each other's **Collision Object Type**. The Collision Object Type, as far as collision is concerned, is a category for the object which allows you to determine how it responds to other objects, depending on their Collision Object Type. We will now see how changing an object's *Collision Responses* to various Object Types affects collision.

Object Types

With *Shape_Cube* selected in the world, notice its *Collision Presets*. It should be automatically set to *Physics Actor*. If not, set it to this. Notice that for this preset, all of the boxes for its collision responses are set to *Block*. Also make sure *Generate Overlap Events* is checked.

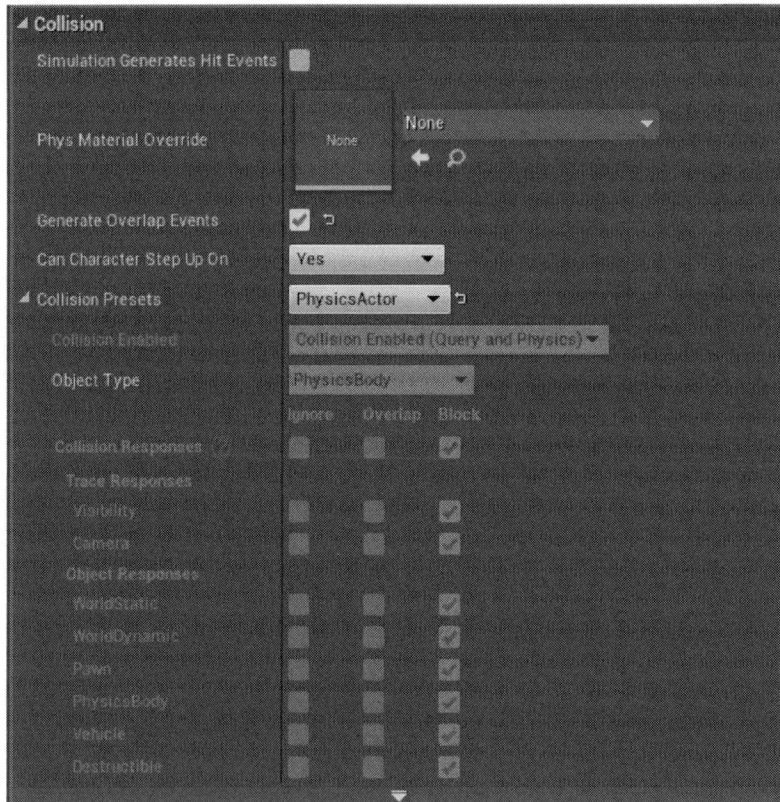

Figure 8.19: Collision Responses for all Object Types set to Block on the Shape_Cube

Since the *Shape_Cube* has a *Collision Object Type* of *PhysicsBody*, we can determine how to react to this Object Type from the perspective of the *Box Collision* in *OverlapActorBP*.

In the *OverlapActorBP* Blueprint, with the *OverlapBox* selected, set *Collision Enabled* to *Collision Enabled (Query and Physics)* and set the *Collision Response* to *Physics Body* to *Overlap*. Make sure *Generate Overlap Events* is checked.

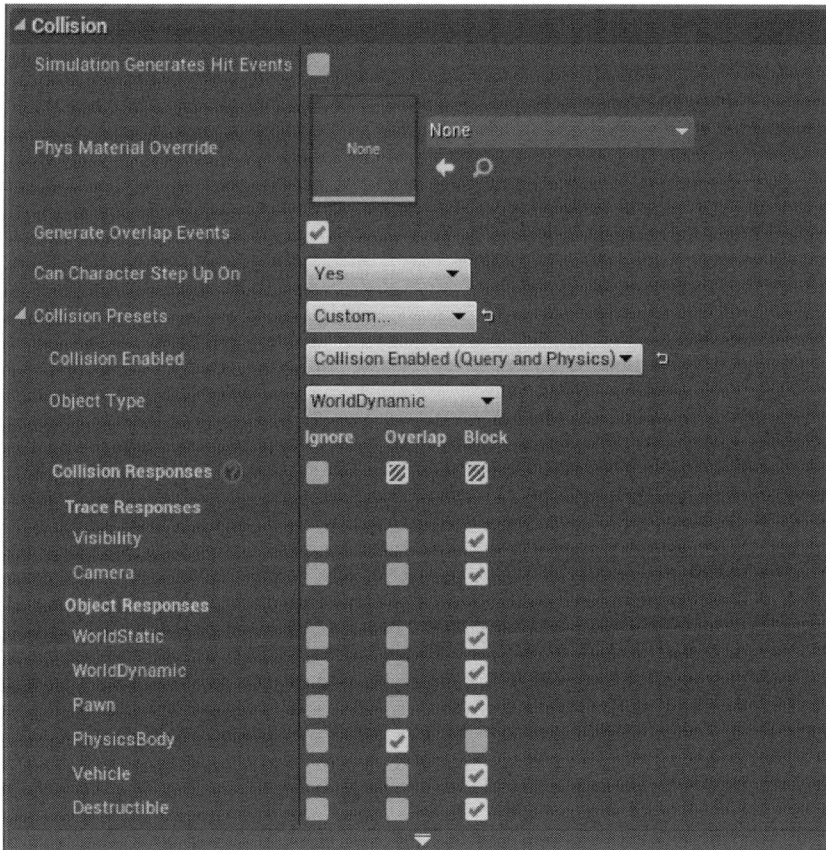

Figure 8.20: Collision settings for OverlapBox

Press **Play** and watch the cube fall through the box. We get "BeginOverlap" printed to the **Output Log** because the following were set:

- *Generate Overlap Events* is checked on both *Shape_Cube* and *OverlapBox*

- The *OverlapBox* has its *Collision Enabled* set to *Collision Enabled (Query and Physics)*

- *OverlapBox* has its *Collision Response* to *PhysicsBody* set to *Overlap*.

Notice that for Overlap Events, both objects need to have *Simulation Generates Overlap Events* checked. For Hit Events, only the object that triggers the Hit Event needs to have *Simulation Generates Hit Events* checked.

We now have seen how *Collision Presets* work and how we can customize how objects interact with one another. We saw that there are *Collision Presets* that have default configurations which are not changeable, and there is a *Custom...* option, which allows us to configure the presets to our liking. We saw the four types of *Collision Enabled* options, and how they behave concerning Overlap and Hit Events. We also saw that each object has its own *Collision Object Type*, which allows us to decide how objects choose to interact with other objects based on their *Object Types*. We saw that for Overlap Events to work, both objects overlapping need *Simulation Generates Overlap Events* checked. But when Hit Events are concerned, only the object set up for Hit Events must have *Simulation Generates Hit Events* checked.

Setting the *Collision Response* to *Ignore* for any type will result in no collision for Overlap Events for that type.

We now know how to configure collision presets for an object in Blueprints. In the next chapter, we will set these options in C++ with built-in functions that allow us to do this dynamically in code!

Now that we understand the control we have over Collision and Overlap Events, it's time to see the **collision hulls** of the meshes we are using in our game. The collision hull for a mesh is the geometry used by the physics engine when performing calculations necessary to simulate physics.

We will now learn how to see and even create collision hulls.

Collision Hulls

For a mesh to interact with the world, it must have a collision hull. You can see the collision hull for a Static Mesh, if it has one, in the **Mesh Editor**. In the **Content Browser**, in **StarterContent** -> **Shapes**, find the *Shape_QuadPyramid*. Drag it into the world, and in Rotation Mode, rotate it so that one of its corners is pointing roughly downward.

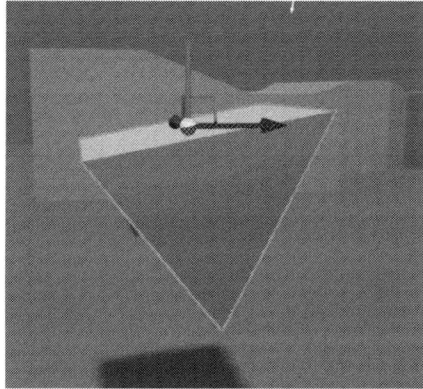

Figure 8.21: A Shape_QuadPyramid Pointing Downward

Now with the pyramid selected, in the **Details** panel under *Physics*, check *Simulate Physics* and make sure *Enable Gravity* is checked as well. Press **Play** and watch how the pyramid topples to the ground.

Now, in the **Content Browser**, double-click on the *Shape_QuadPyramid* to open the **Mesh Editor**.

Click on the **Collision** icon from the top panel and check *Show Collision -> Simple Collision*.

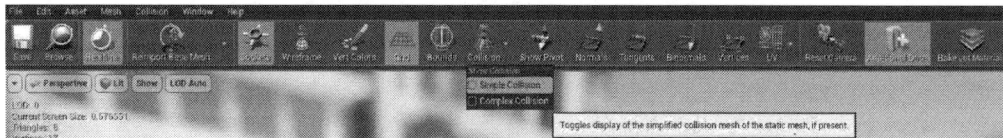

Figure 8.22: Showing Simple Collision in the Mesh Editor

Now a fine green outline will be visible on the mesh. This is its collision hull.

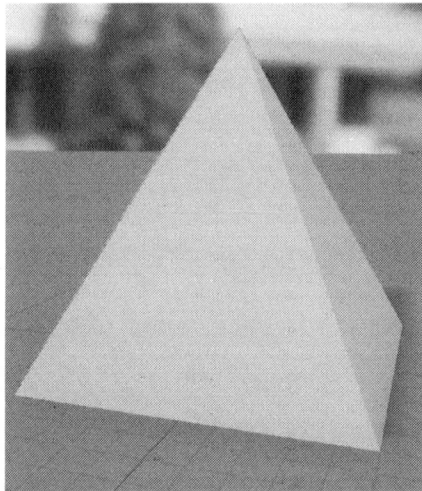

Figure 8.23: The Pyramid's Collision Hull

Now from the Menu Bar select *Collision -> Remove Collision*.

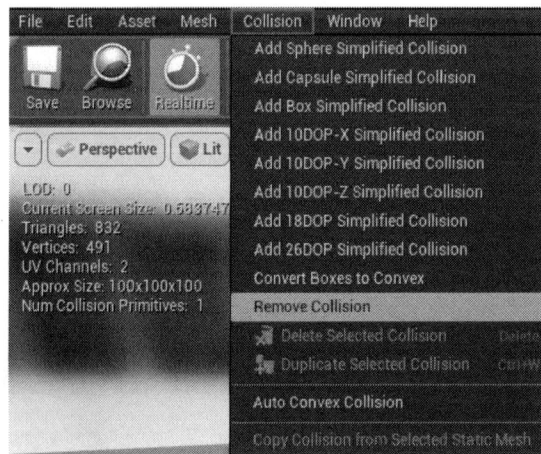

Figure 8.24: Removing the Collision Hull

The thin green outline will disappear. Return to the **Level Editor** and press **Play**. You will see the pyramid fall through the floor!

Return to the **Mesh Editor** and press *CTRL + Z* to undo the collision removal.

Now click the **Collision** icon again and this time select *Complex Collision*. You will see a turquoise outline on the mesh now. Notice that the *Complex Collision* isn't very different from the *Simple Collision*. In the case of the pyramid in fact, they are the same. Let's take a look at a mesh for which this is not the case.

In the **Content Browser**, double-click on *Shape_WideCapsule*. Enable *Show Collision* just as we did for the pyramid. Notice that the collision hull is much different than the shape of the mesh itself.

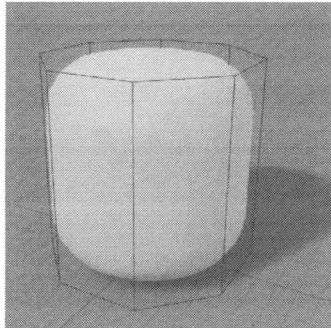

Figure 8.25: The Collision Hull for Shape_WideCapsule

Now drag one of these into the world and raise it from the ground a bit. Enable *Simulate Physics* and make sure *Enable Gravity* is checked.

Figure 8.26: A Shape_WideCapsule in the World

Now press **Play** and see how the capsule falls flat. Tilt the capsule a bit and you can see it hit the corner of its collision hull before turning over. We can choose to see collision hulls in the world while the game is running via a **console command**. Console commands are commands that can be issued at runtime to enable certain features. They are enabled by hitting the tilde (~) key on the keyboard while the game is running. With the game running, press this key and type "show col" and several options will be visible. These are console commands.

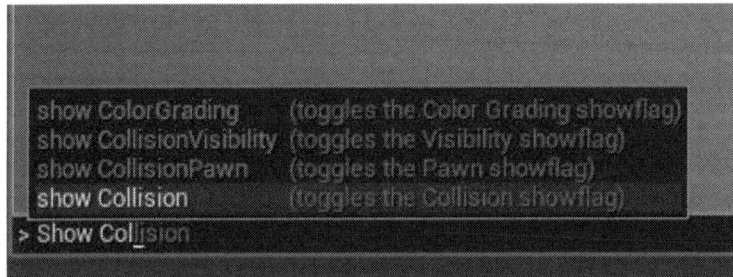

Figure 8.27: The Show Collision Console Command

Finish typing "show collision" and hit enter. Not only do we see the collision hull for the wide capsule, but for all objects, including our Character.

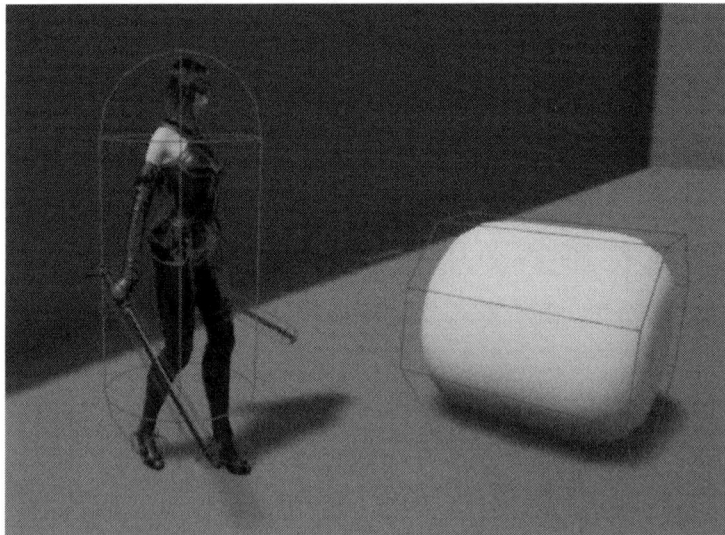

Figure 8.28: Showing Collision at Runtime

Now we see the collision hull for the wide capsule, as well as the Collision Capsule for our Character and even the collision components in her Physics Asset. The Collision Capsule is used for handling the Character's collision because its actual mesh consists of literally thousands of polygons. For the engine to calculate potential collisions for that many polygons, it would require so much computational power that it would slow the game down.

Now let's return to the **Mesh Editor**. *Enable Collision -> Show Collision -> Complex Collision.*

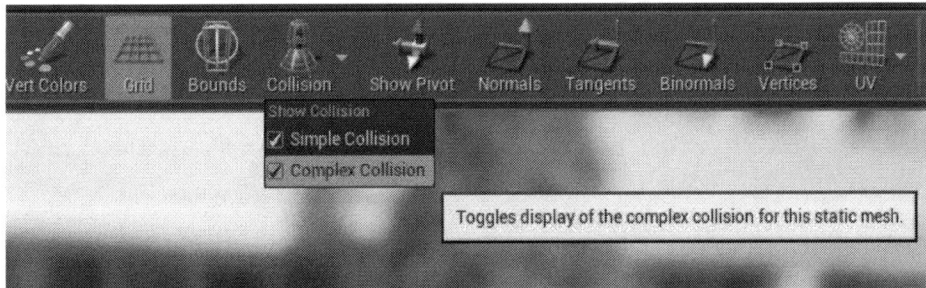

Figure 8.29: Enabling Show Complex Collision for the Wide Capsule

Now we see the turquoise outline for the wide capsule, and it consists of a great deal more polygons.

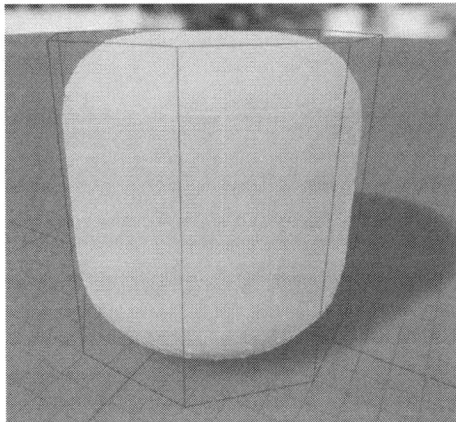

Figure 8.30: The Complex Collision for the Wide Capsule

At the top left, you can see statistics for the current mesh.

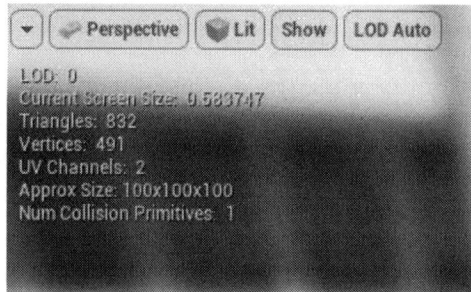

Figure 8.31: Statistics for the Current Mesh

We can see that this mesh consists of 832 triangles. That's quite a bit for such a simple piece of geometry! The number of polygons on a mesh quickly adds up. This is why it's so important to have collision hulls.

But what if your mesh doesn't have a collision hull? We can add one to our mesh. We will do so now.

Adding a Collision Hull to a Mesh

Adding a Collision Hull to a mesh is relatively simple. We will add a Collision Hull to our wide capsule, but first we will remove the hull it already has. From the menu bar, select *Collision -> Remove Collision* as we did in **Figure 8.24**.

We can add our own collision according to the options in the following figure.

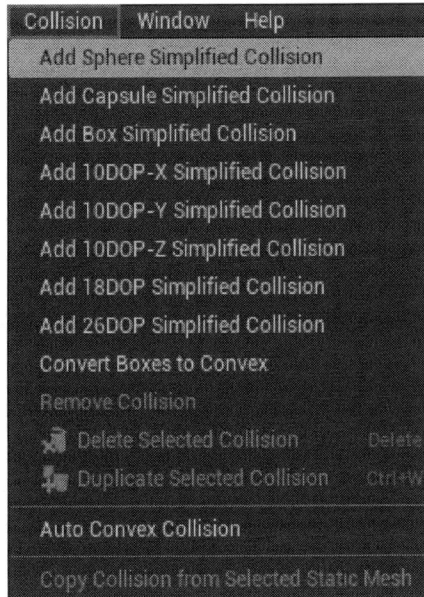

Figure 8.32: Options for Adding Collision

Some collision shapes are more appropriate than others for a given mesh. You can add and remove collision from this list to experiment, and watch how the mesh falls when you press **Play**.

The collision hulls can be adjusted in the **Mesh Editor** once added. Simply left-click on the green collision hull outline in the **Mesh Editor Viewport** and translate, rotate, or scale it as you would an object in the world.

Among the options in **Figure 8.32**, three deserve special attention:

- **Add 10DOP-X Simplified Collision**

- **Add 10DOP-Y Simplified Collision**

- **Add 10DOP-Z Simplified Collision**

- **Add 18DOP Simplified Collision**

- **Add 26DOP Simplified Collision**

These are generalized and referred to by **K-DOP**. DOP stands for discrete oriented polytope, and K is the number of axis-aligned planes.

These are algorithms for creating collision hulls based on the complex geometry of the mesh. The way they work is first a box is made around the mesh, then the edges and/or corners get beveled in until they hit the mesh. How many corners get beveled depends on the value of K, as follows:

- **10:** four edges of the box are beveled. You can choose X-, Y-, or Z-aligned axes.

- **18:** all edges of the box are beveled.

- **26:** all edges and all corners of the box are beveled.

Now remove the collision hull for the wide capsule. Add a *10DOP-Z* simplified collision hull. Notice that it is identical to the default collision hull that it had before.

Remove this collision and instead add a *10DOP-Y* simplified collision hull.

Figure 8.33: Adding a 10DOP-Y Collision Hull

Notice how this collision hull doesn't fit the mesh as well as the *10DOP-Z* simplified collision. This is because the four beveled edges are aligned with the Y-axis instead of the Z-axis. Thus we can clearly see that not all collision hull generating algorithms are appropriate for a given mesh.

Figures 8.34 and **8.35** show the *18DOP* and *26DOP* simplified collision on the wide capsule, respectively.

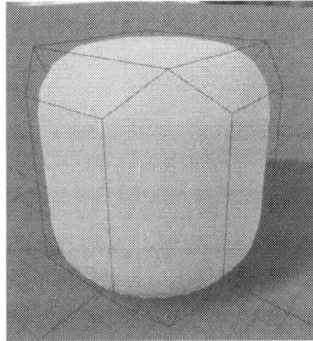

Figure 8.34: The 18DOP Simplified Collision Algorithm

Figure 8.35: The 26DOP Simplified Collision Algorithm

Notice that each time we increase the number of bevels, the collision hull gets more complex and it fits the mesh of the wide capsule better. Be aware that the more complex the collision hull, the more computationally expensive it is for the physics engine to perform calculations regarding physics collisions. As a general rule, if you can get away with less, you should.

We now understand how Collision Hulls work with meshes, and we now know how to add our own if our meshes don't have one. We can also remove and replace the collision hull on a mesh if we aren't satisfied with it.

Summary

In this chapter, we learned about Overlap Events and how they can be used to perform functionality in response to objects overlapping one another in the game. We saw that we needed to create our own callback functions which we desire to be called in the event of an overlap with a given component. We created the `OverlapActor` class and gave it a Static Mesh Component as well as a Box Component, and we created functions for beginning and ending overlap with the box, as well as a function for hitting the capsule. We then used the inherited variables `OnComponentBeginOverlap`, `OnComponentEndOverlap`, and `OnComponentHit` in order to bind functions to Delegates, or objects that can store references to functions and call them when appropriate. We printed log messages to the screen in our callback functions for these events in order to prove that they worked. We then learned about collision presets and how important it is to make sure they are configured correctly for a given object. We saw that there are a number of default collision presets to choose from, as well as a custom option that allows us to configure the presets ourselves. The learned that the *Collision Enabled* property determines whether the object uses *Physics Collision*, *Query Collision*, both, or neither. We learned that *Physics Collision* is collision involving collision hulls and the physics engine handles when objects block each other by imparting forces according to physical properties such as object velocity. We learned that *Query Collision* involves detecting overlaps and allows for sweeps, a technique used for overlap detection. We also saw that each object has its own *Collision Object Type*, and that objects can configure how they react to other objects based on their *Collision Object* type, opting to either *Ignore*, *Overlap*, or *Block* them. We saw that for Hit Events, the objects must be set to block each other's type, and for Overlap Events, they must be set to overlap each other's type. Setting either to ignore will prevent these events from occurring. We also saw that we must enable *Simulation Generates Hit Events* for an object that is set up to generate Hit Events in order for those events to work. We also saw that both objects must enable *Simulation Generates Overlap Events* in order for Overlap Events to work between them. Finally, we learned about collision hulls and how to see them in the mesh editor, as well as remove them and add our own.

Now that we have an understanding of how collision works in Unreal Engine, we are ready to put our knowledge to use! In the next chapter, we will use the concepts we learned in this chapter to create **gameplay mechanics** – elements in our game world that the player can interact with in some way. These are what give games life. Whether it is a hazard that can harm the Character or a health pickup that can heal it, Gameplay Mechanics are essential for all game developers who wish for their games to engage the player and keep them coming back.

Chapter 9 – Gameplay Mechanics

Gameplay mechanics are what make a game interactive. Moving the Character, picking up items, and defeating monsters are all gameplay mechanics. In this chapter, we will add more functionality to our Character and make the game more interactive, so that it resembles a real game. The topics we will cover include:

- **Combat Mechanics:** The Character will be able to attack and blend attack animations with running animations.

- **Health Pickups and Hazards:** Pickups to increase or decrease health provide help or hindrances to the Character's progress.

- **Floor Switches and Doors:** Interactive items that move on contact provide obstacles or helping platforms.

- **Pause Menu and Quit Game:** Pausing and quitting are essential mechanics for most games.

- **SaveGame:** The save game object allows for information to be saved per game session.

Now we will begin with one of the most essential aspects of action games: combat.

Combat Mechanics

The Countess Paragon assets pack includes attack animations that we will be using for our *MainCharacter*. We will create an asset called an **Animation Montage**. This type of asset uses animations and can assign them to certain **slots**. A Slot can then be used in an Animation Blueprint to blend animations together based on their slot.

Creating an Animation Montage

First, select *Content* in the **Content Browser** and create a new folder called *Chapter9*. In this folder, right-click and select *Animation -> Animation Montage*. You will see the following:

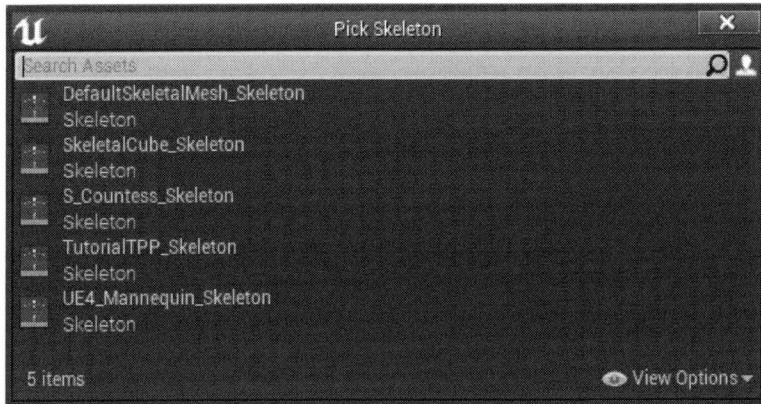

Figure 9.1: Pick Skeleton Menu for Animation Montage

Select *S_Countess_Skeleton* to ensure the montage is paired to the correct skeleton asset. Name this Animation Montage *CountessAttack*. Double-click it to open it, and below the **Viewport** you will see the following:

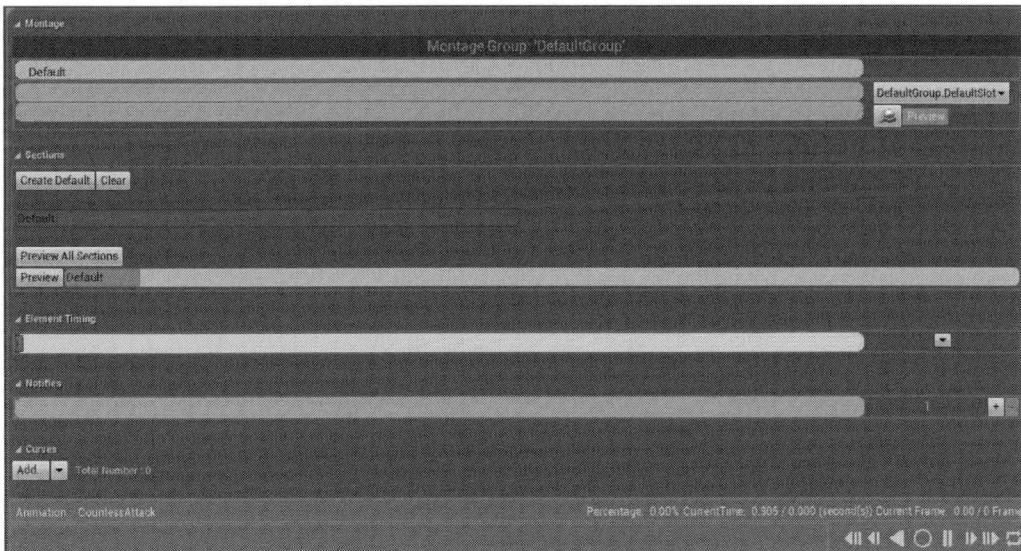

Figure 9.2: Montage Properties

Onto the gray ribbons in the *Montage* section under *Default*, we can drag animation assets from the *Asset Browser* section. Search for *Primary_Attack_A_Normal* and drag this onto the gray ribbon:

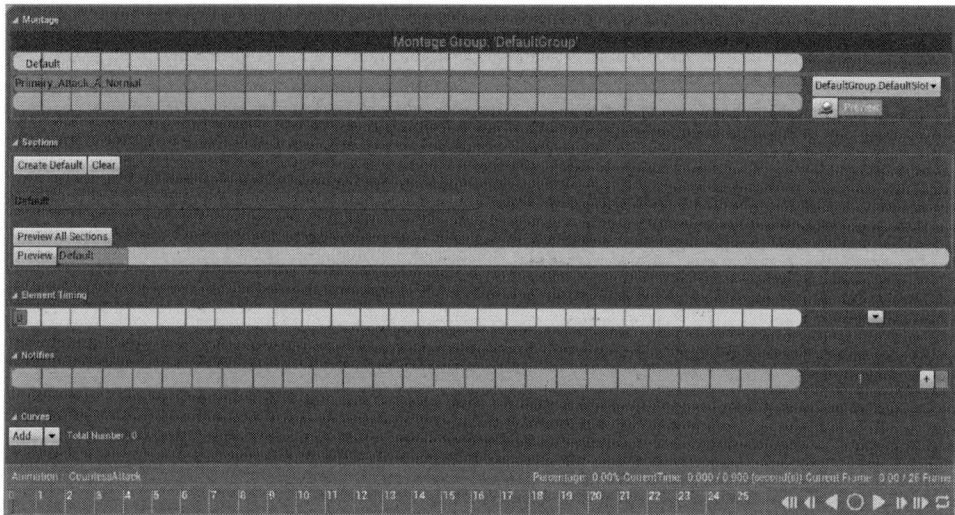

Figure 9.3: Adding an Animation to the Montage

Now one of the gray ribbons is green and is labeled with the name of the animation we dragged in. Notice the Timeline at the bottom. You can press the right-pointing triangle to play the animation and the Countess Character will animate in the **Viewport** window.

We will choose to play this animation whenever our Character is attacking. We can do this by assigning the montage to a particular slot, a group which this montage will belong to and will be blended in a certain way depending on how we set it up in the Animation Blueprint. Notice the dropdown next to the green ribbon where we dragged in our animation asset. You can select from any number of slots that are already created thanks to our Paragon assets. However, we will be creating our own slot.

Creating a Slot and Using our Animation Montage

Next we will create our own slot. In the Animation Blueprint, in the **Anim Graph**, right-click and type "use cached pose LocoPose" and select *Use cached pose 'Loco Pose'*. Drag off of its output pin and type "slot" and select *Slot "DefaultSlot"*.

We will need to change the slot to our new slot, but we must create it first. At the menu bar, select *Window -> Slot Manager*, as shown in the following figure:

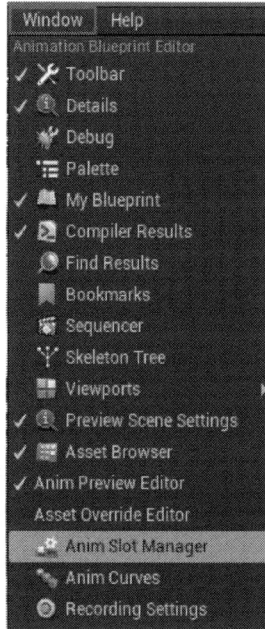

Figure 9.4: Enabling the Slot Manager

Now you will see the following where the **Asset Manager** was:

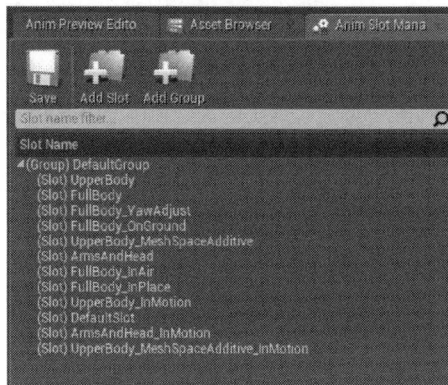

Figure 9.5: Anim Slot Manager

Here, we can create a new slot by clicking *Add Slot*. Add a new slot and name it *AttackSlot*. With our new slot node selected, in the **Details** panel, select our new *AttackSlot*. Drag off of its ouput pin and cache it by typing "cache" and selecting *New Save cached pose...* and calling this node *UpperBody*.

Now go back to the *CountessAttack* Animation Montage and select *AttackSlot* for its slot, as shown in the following figure:

Figure 9.6: Setting the Slot in the Animation Montage

Now our *CountessAttack* Montage uses the *AttackSlot*.

Playing an Animation Montage

We will program our attack functionality in C++, but while we are setting up our animation blending, we would like a quick way to play the Animation Montage while developing. We will use Blueprints to play the Animation Montage for testing purposes. In the *MainCharacter_BP* Blueprint, open the **Event Graph** and right-click, and type "R key" and find the *R* key input.

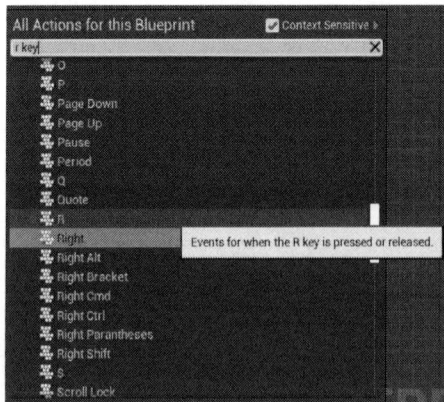

Figure 9.7: Adding a Key Press Input in Blueprints

Now, selecting *R*, create a *Play Anim Montage* node and select *CountessAttack* from the dropdown for Anim Montage, as in the following figure.

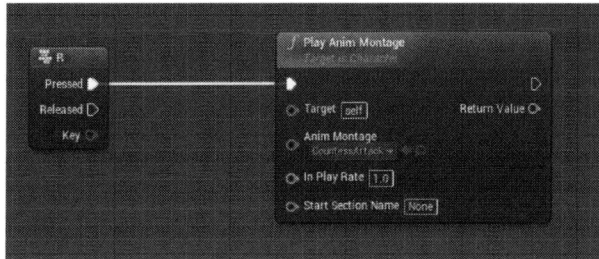

Figure 9.8: Playing an Anim Montage with the R Key

Now when we set up our **Anim Graph** to handle our montage, we will be able to test it by pressing the *R* key in-game.

Blending Animations

We now wish to be able to play our *CountessAttack* Montage. If we are standing still, playing the animation as-is will be fine. However, if we are running, we wish to blend animations together – we would like the legs to continue running, while the upper body plays the attack animation.

In our Animation Blueprint, in the **Anim Graph**, right-click and type "layered blend per bone" and select *Layered blend per bone*. This is the node we must use to blend between animations in the Animation Blueprint. We will create a *Use cached pose 'Loco Pose'* for the *Base Pose* input pin and *Use cached pose 'Upper Body'* for the *Blend Poses 0* input, as in the following figure:

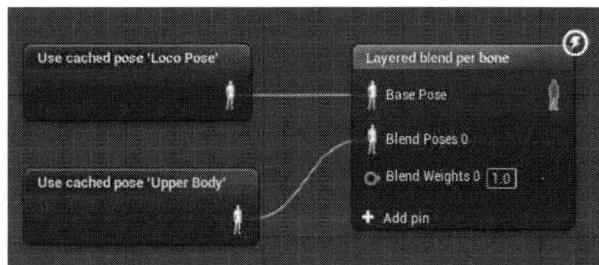

Figure 9.9: Layered Blend Per Bone Node

Now left-click on the *Layered blend per bone* node. In the **Details** panel, check the *Mesh Space Rotation Blend* checkbox. We wish for our blending to happen in mesh space, or the space relative to the mesh itself:

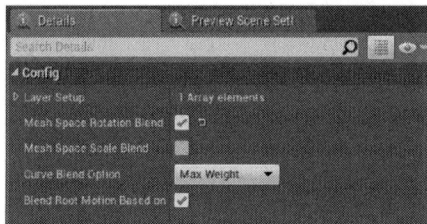

Figure 9.10: Mesh Space Rotation Blend Set to True

Next we need to specify where we wish for our animation to blend on the Character. This is done by specifying certain bones on the skeleton asset. Since we wish for our attacking animations to play above the waist while the legs still play the running animation, we will choose the pelvis bone. To see more clearly why we chose this bone, click on the **Skeleton** icon above the **Details** panel to enter the **Skeleton Editor** menu.

Figure 9.11: The Skeleton Icon Above the Details Panel

Now in the **Skeleton Tree** panel, search for "pelvis" and select the *pelvis* bone. You will see the bone highlight in the **Viewport** as shown in the following figure:

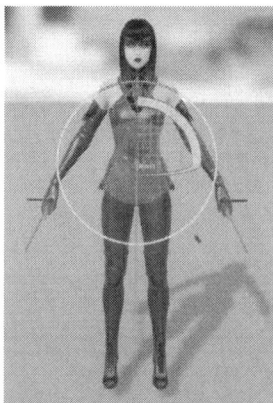

Figure 9.12: The Pelvis Bone

Now in the same manner, look at *thigh_l* and *thigh_r* to see where they are on the skeleton. These will come in handy shortly as well.

Click on the **Blueprint** icon above the **Details** panel to get back in the **Anim Graph**. With the *Layered blend per bone* node selected, look in the **Details** panel and expand the *Layer Setup* dropdown. Expand the *0* dropdown and notice the *Branch Filters* array.

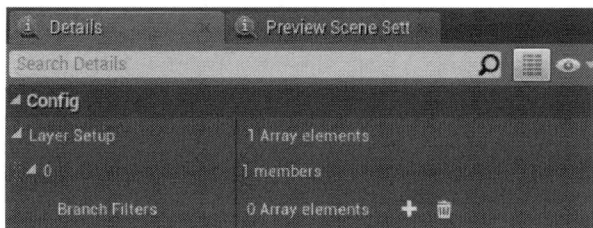

Figure 9.13: The Branch Filters Array

Branch Filters should say *0 Array Elements*. We will add one with the + icon. This will add an array element with an index of 0 which says *2 members*. Click the dropdown next to the 0 and you will see the following:

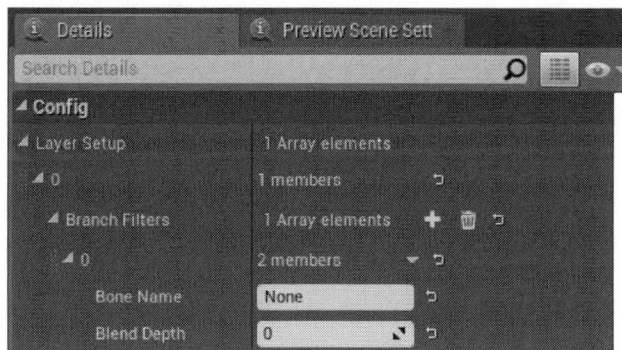

Figure 9.14: Adding an Element to Branch Filters

Notice each element in *Branch Filters* has two members: *Bone Name* and *Bone Depth*. For *Bone Name*, we will enter "pelvis". Be careful. This is case sensitive and the name of the bone is lowercase. *Blend Depth* is a measure of how much the blending will occur. We will try 1 and see how it works. Enter 1 for *Blend Depth*.

Now we will need to cache our pose after the *Layered blend per bone* node. Before we do this, we will be adding a node that will determine whether we should blend our poses or not. Luckily, we have a Boolean that we created called *IsAccelerating*. This will be `true` when we are running, so it is the perfect variable to use to check whether or not we should be blending the running and attacking animations. Drag off of the *Layered blend per bone* output pin and create a *Blend Poses by bool* node. For the Boolean input *Active Value*, get *IsAccelerating*, and connect it. Make sure the output from *Layered blend per bone* is connected to the *True Pose* input. Create a new *Use cached pose 'Upper Body'* node and connect it to the *False Pose* input. Leave *True Blend Time* and *False Blend Time* to their default values. These are for changing the blend time for the `true` and `false` cases, respectively:

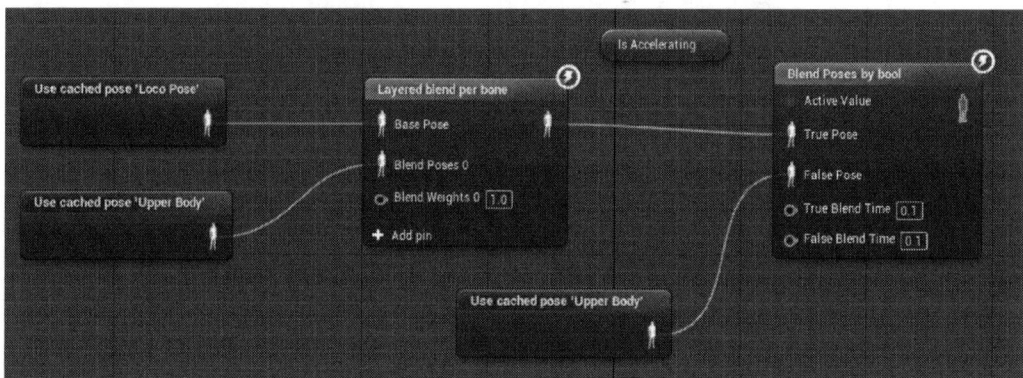

Figure 9.15: Layered Blend Per Bone and Blend Poses by Bool Nodes

The result of the above figure is that when *IsAccelerating* is true, *Blend Poses by bool* will choose the pose connected to the *True Pose* input, and when *IsAccelerating* is false, it will choose the pose connected to the *False Pose* input. We chose the blended pose returned by *Layered blend per bone*, since we know we will be running when *IsAccelerating* is true, therefore we will want the blended animation. We chose the *Upper Body* cached pose for *False Pose*, which will simply play the Animation Montage for attacking, and we don't care that it plays for the entire body, since the Character will be standing still.

Finally, we will cache the output of *Blend poses by bool* and call this cached pose *Full Body*. Also, we will need to use *Full Body* for the final *Output Pose* node, so that all our work will actually be used for the final pose of the Character. The results are as follows:

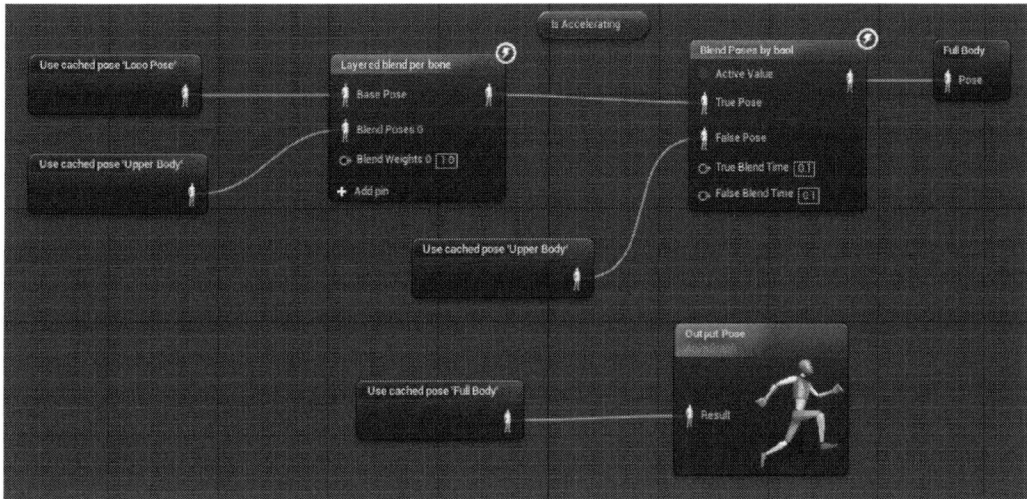

Figure 9.16: Nodes for Blending Animations

Next we can test this out and see if we need to make any adjustments. Press **Play** and run around while pressing the *R* key. You should see the Character swiping with her sword. However, the blending isn't quite right, as the Character's legs seem a bit stiff. We can adjust the *Blend Depth* for our *Branch Filter*. Change it from 1 to 4 and see how our Character behaves.

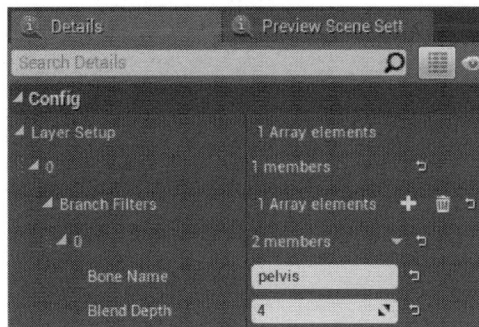

Figure 9.17: Setting Blend Depth to 4

This is better, but the legs are still a bit stiff. In order to exclude them from the attack animation, we can add new elements to the *Branch Filters*, one for each leg. Click the + icon twice next to *1 Array Elements for Branch Filters*. For one of them, enter *thigh_l* for

Bone Name and *-1* for *Bone Depth*. This will cause the bone (and all bones under it in the hierarchy) to be ignored. For the other, enter *thigh_r* for *Bone Name* and *-1* for *Bone Depth*. Now Brach Filters has three elements, as seen in the following figure:

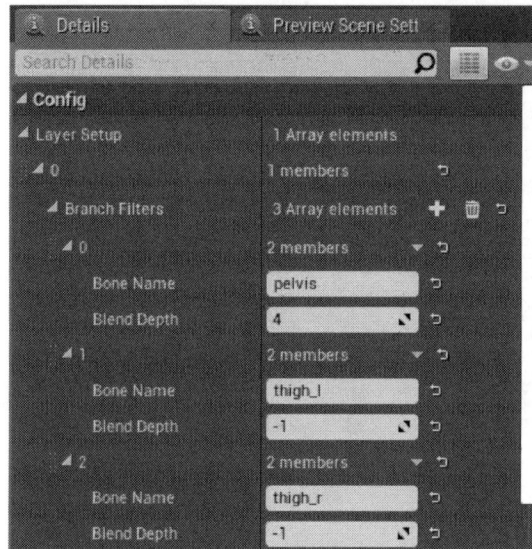

Figure 9.18: Three Array Elements for Branch Filters

Now, the Character runs around just fine, attacking with the upper half of the body while the legs continue to run. We now have attacking functionality! We are ready to implement attacking in C++.

Adding Attack Code

We will need to create a function for attacking. For a PC game, a typical user input for attacking is the left mouse button. We will use that for this game.

Adding the LMBDown Action Mapping

Since we only wish to know the moment the left mouse button is pressed, we can use an *Action Mapping*, rather than an *Axis Mapping*. Remember, an *Action Mapping* fires off once, whereas an *Axis Mapping* fires each frame, passing a `float` value based on the state of the button being pressed. Go to *Edit -> Project Settings -> Input* and add a new

Action Mapping. Call this one *LMBDown*, for "left mouse button down." Set the input to the *Left Mouse Button*.

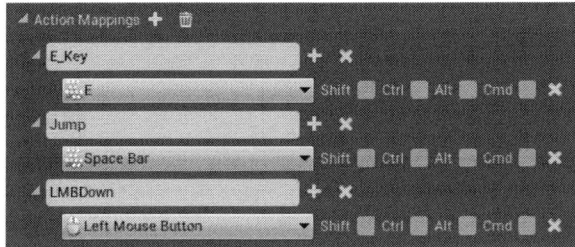

Figure 9.19: LMBDown Action Mapping set to Left Mouse Button

Now we can create a function for this action mapping in the `MainCharacter` class.

Adding the LMBDown Function

We will now create the `LMBDown` function.

1. Now in *MainCharacter.h*, just beneath the declaration for the `MoveRight` function, add:

   ```
   /** Called when the right mouse button is pressed */
   void LMBDown();

   /** Boolean for when the character is attacking */
   UPROPERTY(VisibleAnywhere, BlueprintReadWrite,
   Category = "Combat")
   bool bAttacking;
   ```

Thus, we have functions for when the left mouse button is pressed and released, as well as a Boolean for when we are attacking. We exposed this Boolean to Blueprints in case we need it in the future. Set the default value for `bAttacking` to `false` in the constructor (it's set to `false` by default, but this shows that we intend for it to start false).

2. And define the `LMBDown` function as follows:

```
void AMainCharacter::LMBDown()
```

```
{
      bAttacking = true;
}
```

Now we must bind the function to the action mapping.

3. Add the following to `SetupPlayerInputComponent`:

```
PlayerInputComponent->BindAction("LMBDown",
IE_Pressed, this, &AMainCharacter::LMBDown);
```

Now we need to be able to play the Animation Montage. We will create a variable on the `MainCharacter` class of type `UAnimMontage`. This is the base class for the Animation Montage, and we will be able to select our *CountessAttack* montage for this in the Blueprint.

4. Add the following to *MainCharacter.h*, just under the declaration for `bAttacking`:

```
UPROPERTY(EditDefaultsOnly, BlueprintReadOnly,
Category = "Anims")
      class UAnimMontage* CountessAttackMontage;
```

5. Now in *MainCharacter.cpp*, we will play the animation in `LMBDown`, just under `bAttacking = true;`, as follows:

```
UAnimInstance* AnimInstance = GetMesh()-
>GetAnimInstance();
      if (AnimInstance && CountessAttackMontage)
      {
            AnimInstance-
>Montage_Play(CountessAttackMontage);
      }
```

6. And we must add the `include` for the `UAnimInstance` class:

```
#include "Animation/AnimInstance.h"
```

Notice we called `GetAnimInstance` from the `Mesh`. Remember, `Mesh` is inherited by the `Character` class and is the Skeletal Mesh asset that we chose for our Countess. This variable has the function `GetAnimInstance` which returns the Anim Instance in the form of a `UAnimInstance` object. The Anim Instance has a function called `Montage_Play`, and it takes the Montage as the argument. There are additional arguments which have default values and are thus optional, such as a `Play Rate`. Notice that before we call this function, we first check to make sure the `AnimInstance` local variable we created as well as the `CountessAttackMontage` are both not null. Compile this code and return to the Unreal Engine editor.

7. Open the *MainCharacter_BP* Blueprint and notice that our new Boolean, along with our variable for the Animation Montage are there. Select the *CountessAttack* Montage from the dropdown for *Countess Attack Montage*:

Figure 9.20: Selecting CountessAttack for the variable CountessAttackMontage

Notice also that *Attacking* cannot be set, because we made it `VisibleAnywhere`.

Now we can delete the nodes in *MainCharacter_BP*'s **Event Graph** for playing the Animation Montage with the *R* key. We won't need them anymore. Nowp **Play** and test out our attacking capabilities!

You may have noticed something odd, however. You can press the left mouse button rapidly, and the Character will attack as many times as you press it, as quickly as you press it. We need to limit this. Since we already have a Boolean value telling us when we are attacking, we can simply check to see if this variable is set to `true` when attacking. If it is, we don't want to attack.

8. Add the following to the top of `LMBDown`:

```
if (bAttacking) return;
```

Now if `bAttacking` is true, the function will simply exit early without playing the montage. However, we need to be able to set this variable to false. We can do this with Anim Notifies.

Setting the bAttacking Boolean to False with an Anim Notify

An **Anim Notify** allows us to trigger an event at a certain point in an animation. These can be added to Animation Montages. Open the *CountessAttack* Animation Montage, and in the *Notifies* section under the **Viewport**, notice this ribbon:

Figure 9.21: The Notifies Ribbon

Right-click in this ribbon and select *Add Notify -> New Notify* and name this notify *AttackEnd*. Make sure the notify is placed near the end of the ribbon, as shown in the following figure:

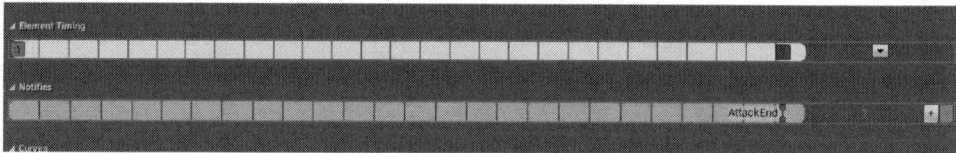

Figure 9.22: Adding the AttackEnd Notify

Now we will use this notify in the Animation Blueprint's **Event Graph**. Go there now. Right-click and type "attack end" and create an *AnimNotify_AttackEnd* node.

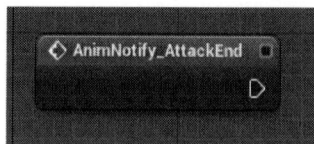

Figure 9.23: AnimNotify_AttackEnd Node

Using this event, we can access the *Main* variable, which stores a reference to the Character, and we can set the `bAttacking` variable since we made it `BlueprintReadWrite`. Remember, a Boolean exposed to Blueprints will not have the b on the front. Add the following functionality to the Animation Blueprint's **Event Graph**:

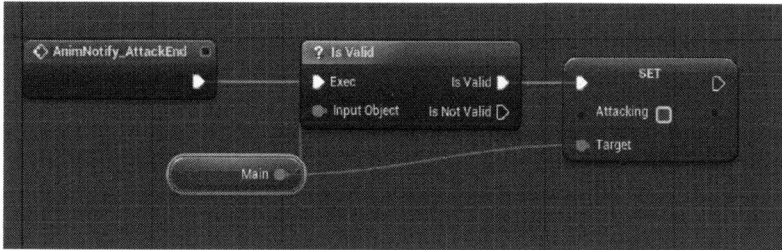

Figure 9.24: Changing the bAttacking Variable to False

Now when the attack animation finishes, this Anim Notify will trigger the *AnimNotify_AttackEnd* event and we will set the `bAttacking` variable to false. Once it is false, the `LMBDown` function will not exit early and will call the `Montage_Play` function, causing the Character to attack.

Test this out by pressing **Play** and spamming the left mouse button. Notice the Character only attacks once the previous attack has finished, as we desired.

Next, we are ready to create some more gameplay mechanics! Health pickups and hazards are common gameplay mechanics and are relatively easy to make. We will do so now.

Health Pickups and Hazards

The basic form of a pickup is an object that hovers in the air waiting for the Character to walk over it. As soon as the Character does so, it disappears, often with a sound or special effect and the Character gains some form of benefit such as a health boost. We will create a basic `Pickup` class based on the `Actor` class, and this class will contain functionality necessary for Overlap Events.

Creating the Pickup Class

We will now create the `Pickup` class.

1. In the **Content Browser**, in *C++ Classes -> FirstGame*, create a new C++ class based on *Actor*. Call this class *Item*.

2. In *Item.h*, just under `AItem();`, add:

```
/** Overlapping sphere   */
UPROPERTY(VisibleAnywhere, BlueprintReadWrite,
Category = "Item | Collision")
    class USphereComponent* CollisionVolume;

/** Base Mesh Component */
UPROPERTY(VisibleAnywhere, BlueprintReadWrite,
Category = "Item | Mesh")
    class UStaticMeshComponent* Mesh;

/** Toggles on/off rotating */
 UPROPERTY(EditAnywhere, BlueprintReadWrite, Category =
"Item | ItemProperties")
    bool bRotate;

/** Rate at which the mesh should rotate */
UPROPERTY(EditAnywhere, BlueprintReadWrite, Category =
"Item | ItemProperties")

    float RotationRate;
```

We are forward declaring a `USphereComponent` for the overlap volume for our pickup. This will be the sphere that will trigger the pickup functionality when the Character overlaps with it. We placed it in a category called *Item* with a subcategory of *Collision*, so there will be a dropdown in the **Details** panel in the *Item* section called *Collision* where this item will be placed. We forward declared `UStaticMeshComponent` for the actual mesh of the item and we placed it in the *Item* category in its own *Mesh* subcategory. We then declare a `bool bRotate` to toggle rotating and a `float RotationRate` for the rate at which our item will rotate in the air.

3. Next, we will set these variables up in the constructor. Just under
   `PrimaryActorTick.bCanEverTick = true;`, add:

```
CollisionVolume =
CreateDefaultSubobject<USphereComponent>(TEXT("CollisionVol
ume"));
    RootComponent = CollisionVolume;
```

```
    Mesh =
CreateDefaultSubobject<UStaticMeshComponent>(TEXT("Mesh"));
    Mesh->SetupAttachment(GetRootComponent());

    bRotate = false;

    RotationRate = 45.f;
```

4. And we must add includes at the top of the file for the `SphereComponent` and the `StaticMeshComponent`:

```
#include "Components/SphereComponent.h"

#include "Components/StaticMeshComponent.h"
```

Now we can declare a function for overlapping the Sphere Component.

5. Add the following to *Item.h* just under the declaration of the `Tick` function:

```
UFUNCTION()
    virtual void OnOverlapBegin(UPrimitiveComponent*
OverlappedComponent, AActor* OtherActor,
UPrimitiveComponent* OtherComp, int32 OtherBodyIndex, bool
bFromSweep, const FHitResult & SweepResult);
```

Now we can define it in *Item.cpp*, just under the `Tick` function body:

```
void AItem::OnOverlapBegin(UPrimitiveComponent*
OverlappedComponent, AActor* OtherActor,
UPrimitiveComponent* OtherComp, int32 OtherBodyIndex, bool
bFromSweep, const FHitResult & SweepResult)
{
    UE_LOG(LogTemp, Warning, TEXT("OnOverlapBegin"));

}
```

We have placed a UE_LOG so that we can see proof of the function being called in the **Output Log**. Now we must bind this function to a Delegate for the Sphere Component.

6. Add the following in the `BeginPlay` function, just under

```
Super::BeginPlay();:
```

```
        CollisionVolume-
>OnComponentBeginOverlap.AddDynamic(this,
&AItem::OnOverlapBegin);
```

Now when the Character overlaps with the sphere, `OnOverlapBegin` will be called and we should see a message in the **Output Log**.

Now we wish to make the mesh rotate at the rate of `RotationRate`.

7. Add the following to the `Tick` function, just under

```
Super::Tick(DeltaTime);:
```

```
if (bRotate)
{
        FRotator Rotation = GetActorRotation();
        Rotation.Yaw += DeltaTime * RotationRate;
        SetActorRotation(Rotation);
}
```

Now if `bRotate` is true, we get the current rotation of the Actor and store it in a local variable, `Rotation`. We then simply add to its `Yaw` component the value `DeltaTime * RotationRate` which will result in the rotation's yaw increasing by a constant rate of `RotationRate` per second. Compile this code and maneuver back to the Unreal Engine editor.

Creating the Item Blueprint

In the **Content Browser**, in *C++ Classes -> FirstGame*, right-click on Item and create a Blueprint based on it called *BaseItem*. Place this Blueprint in the *Chapter9* folder.

You will only see the Sphere Component in the **Viewport**, as seen in the following figure:

Select *Mesh* from the **Components** panel and click the dropdown on the *Static Mesh* property. Select *Shape_TriPyramid*:

Figure 9.25: The Sphere Component

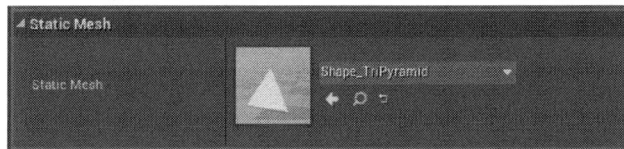

Figure 9.26: Selecting Shape_TriPyramid for the Static Mesh

Now we will scale it down a bit. In the *Transform* section in the **Details** panel, set the *X*, *Y*, and *Z* components of the scale each to 0.25:

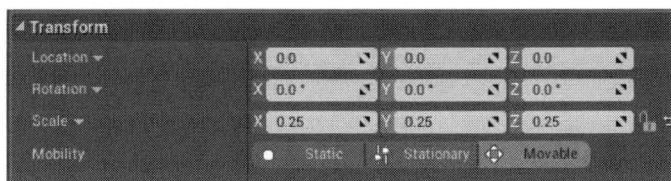

Figure 9.27: Scaling the Pyramid Shape down

Now before we place one of these *BaseItems* in the world, select *BaseItem(self)* in the **Components** panel. Now, in the **Details** panel, notice the following section:

Figure 9.28: The Item Category

This exists because of the subcategories we gave to our variables in the UPROPERTY macros. Properties can be edited for the respective variables here, and in particular, let's take a look at the *ItemProperties* subcategory. Click its dropdown:

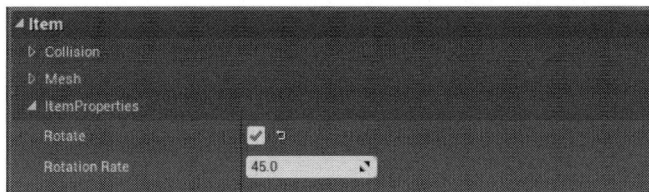

Figure 9.29: The ItemProperties Subcategory

We can change the values of *Rotate* and *RotationRate* because they were exposed to Blueprints using `EditAnywhere`. Check the *Rotate* checkbox.

Drag a *BaseItem* into the world and press **Play**. Notice that the pyramid rotates and with the **Output Log** open, we get the log message when the Character overlaps with it.

We typically see that items disappear once they are picked up or consumed. We can easily make this happen by deleting the Actor.

Deleting an Actor

Actors inherit a function called `Destroy`. This will mark the Actor for deletion on the next round of garbage collection and as far as the game is concerned, it is gone. In *Item.cpp*, add the following to the `OnOverlapBegin` function.

```
Destroy();
```

Now press **Play** and walk over to the pickup. It will disappear as soon as it is reached!

Increasing and Decreasing Health

Health pickups should increase the Character's health, and Hazards should decrease it. This can be achieved by giving the Character a base Health amount and incrementing/decrementing it accordingly. Add the following to *MainCharacter.h*, in the `protected` section under the declaration for `CountessAttackMontage`:

```
UPROPERTY(EditAnywhere, BlueprintReadWrite, Category =
"PlayerStats")
float Health;

UPROPERTY(EditDefaultsOnly, BlueprintReadOnly,
Category = "PlayerStats")
float MaxHealth;
```

Now we have a value to measure the Character's health. We have a maximum health value beyond which we need not consider increases in health. This way the Character cannot gain too much and become too powerful. In the constructor in *MainCharacter.cpp*, add the following lines:

```
Health = 85.f;

MaxHealth = 100.f;
```

Now `Health` and `MaxHealth` have initial values. We can now create health pickups and Hazards, using the base functionality in the `Item` class.

Creating the Health Pickup Class

We will create a new C++ class, this time not based on one of the basic classes in the Class Creation Wizard, but based on one of our own classes!

1. In the **Content Browser**, in *C++ Classes -> FirstGame*, right-click on *Item* and select *Create C++ class derived from item*. Call this item *HealthPickup*.

We will be overriding the `OnOverlapBegin` function here, providing custom functionality that will be unique to the `HealthPickup` class.

2. Add the following to *HealthPickup.h* just under `GENERATED_BODY()`:

```
public:
      AHealthPickup();

      /** Amount this pickup will heal the player by */
      UPROPERTY(EditAnywhere, BlueprintReadWrite, Category =
"Healing")
      float HealingAmount;


      virtual void OnOverlapBegin(UPrimitiveComponent*
OverlappedComponent, AActor* OtherActor,
UPrimitiveComponent* OtherComp, int32 OtherBodyIndex, bool
bFromSweep, const FHitResult & SweepResult) override;
```

First, we needed to declare a `public` section. We declare the `AHealthPickup` constructor so that we can initialize our variables. Next, we declare a `float` `HealingAmount` that will determine how much this health pickup will heal the Character by. Then we override the `OnOverlapBegin` function. Notice that we do not mark this function `UFUNCTION`, because it inherits that property from the parent version of the function, along with any macro specifiers, if any were passed into the macro in the parent version.

3. Now we can define our functions. Add the following to *HealthPickup.cpp*:

```
AHealthPickup::AHealthPickup()
{
     HealingAmount = 20.f;
}

void AHealthPickup::OnOverlapBegin(UPrimitiveComponent*
OverlappedComponent, AActor* OtherActor,
UPrimitiveComponent* OtherComp, int32 OtherBodyIndex, bool
bFromSweep, const FHitResult & SweepResult)
{
     UE_LOG(LogTemp, Warning,
TEXT("AHealthPickup::OnOverlapBegin"));
     Super::OnOverlapBegin(OverlappedComponent, OtherActor,
OtherComp, OtherBodyIndex, bFromSweep, SweepResult);

}
```

We initialize `HealingAmount` with a default value of `20.f`. This can, of course, be changed in Blueprints because we marked it `EditAnywhere`. We then define the `OnOverlapBegin` function, adding a `UE_LOG` so we can see a log message to prove that it is being called. We then add the `Super` call to the parent version of the function. This will result in the code in the parent version being called, which involves printing a log message to the screen, as well as calling `Destroy`, which will destroy the Actor. Without this call, the parent version will not be called and the pickup will not be destroyed.

Next, we will need to add getters and setters for the `Health` and `MaxHealth` variables in the *MainCharacter.h* file.

4. Just below `AMainCharacter();`, add:

```
     FORCEINLINE float GetHealth() { return Health; }
     FORCEINLINE void SetHealth(float Amount) { Amount >
MaxHealth ? Health = MaxHealth : Health = Amount; }
     FORCEINLINE float GetMaxHealth() { return MaxHealth; }

     FORCEINLINE void SetMaxHealth(float Amount) {
MaxHealth = Amount; }
```

These are simple functions and can be marked with FORCEINLINE so they are **inlined**, which means the compiler will replace any call to these functions with the code in the function bodies themselves at compile time, to minimize flow control from jumping into the functions during runtime. SetHealth makes use of the ternary operator which provides a check to make sure we aren't setting the Health value above the value for MaxHealth. If the value passed in is greater than MaxHealth, we set Health to the value of MaxHealth instead. Otherwise, Health is set to the value passed in.

5. Next, change the Health value in HealthPickup's OnOverlapBegin function, as follows:

```cpp
void AHealthPickup::OnOverlapBegin(UPrimitiveComponent*
OverlappedComponent, AActor* OtherActor,
UPrimitiveComponent* OtherComp, int32 OtherBodyIndex, bool
bFromSweep, const FHitResult & SweepResult)
{
    UE_LOG(LogTemp, Warning,
TEXT("AHealthPickup::OnOverlapBegin"));

    AMainCharacter* MainCharacter =
Cast<AMainCharacter>(OtherActor);
    if (MainCharacter)
    {
        MainCharacter->SetHealth(MainCharacter-
>GetHealth() + HealingAmount);
    }

    Super::OnOverlapBegin(OverlappedComponent, OtherActor,
OtherComp, OtherBodyIndex, bFromSweep, SweepResult);

}
```

Compile this code, and in the Unreal Engine editor, create a Blueprint based on this class. Call it *HealthPickup_BP* and put it in the *Chapter9* folder. Open this Blueprint and for the *Mesh* variable, set its *Static Mesh* property to *Shape_Torus*. In the **Transform** section, set the *X, Y,* and *Z* components for its *Scale* to 0.25, and set the *X* component for its *Rotation* to 90, as shown in the following figure:

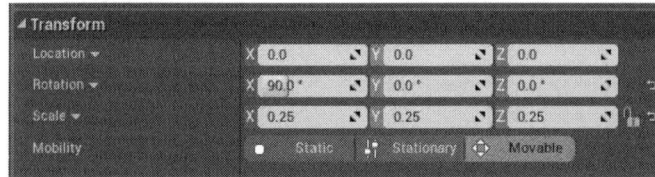

Figure 9.30: Scaling and Rotating the Mesh for HealthPickup_BP

For the *Material* property, click the dropdown and select *M_Metal_Gold*:

Figure 9.31: Changing the Material to Gold

Now the pickup looks a bit more valuable.

Next, check the checkbox for *Rotate* in the *Item -> ItemProperties* section. Now place one of these *HealthPickup_BP* Actors into the world and press **Play**!

In order to make sure this item actually changes our Health variable, we must be able to see its value at runtime. After pressing **Play** but before clicking in the **Viewport**, search in the **World Outliner** for "MainCharacter" and select *MainCharacter_BP*.

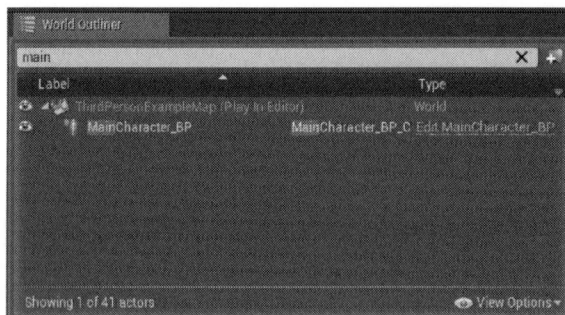

Figure 9.32: Searching for MainCharacter_BP in the World Outliner at Runtime

In the **Details** panel, search for "Health" and you will be able to see the value of the *Health* variable, because it is marked as EditAnywhere in C++.

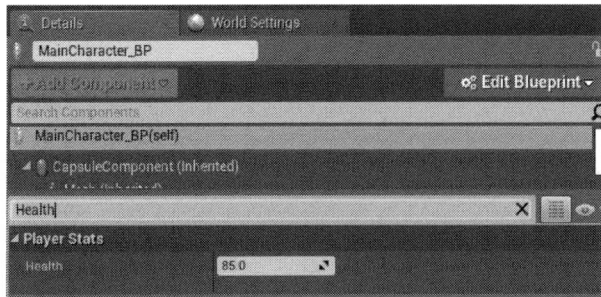

Figure 9.33: Viewing the Health Variable at Runtime

Next, click in the **Viewport** and run into the *HealthPickup_BP* Actor. The value of *Health* will change from 85.0 to 100.0.

Creating Hazards

We have created a Pickup that can alter the Character's health by adding a value to it. However, changing the value of `HealingAmount` to a negative value in the `HealthPickup` class will have the opposite effect – a negative value will be added, which results in decreasing the Character's Health. This is precisely the behavior we expect from Hazards. Before we use the same code, we must make sure the `SetHealth` function in the `MainCharacter` class doesn't allow for the Health variable to become negative. We can change the `SetHealth` function so that it checks for this condition, and if the value passed in results in a negative `Health`, we can set the `Health` to 0. Since this function is growing larger than a simple setter, we will remove the `FORCEINLINE` keyword and define the function in *MainCharacter.cpp*. Change the declaration in *MainCharacter.h* to:

```
void SetHealth(float Amount);
```

And add the following to *MainCharacter.cpp*, just under the body for the constructor:

```
void AMainCharacter::SetHealth(float Amount)
{
    if (Amount > MaxHealth)
    {
        Health = MaxHealth;
    }
```

```
else if (Amount < 0)
{
        Health = 0;
}
else
{
        Health = Amount;
}

}
```

Now if the value passed in would result in a `Health` value less than 0, `Health` is simply set to 0. Now we can use a negative value for the `HealingAmount` to create a Hazard. Compile the code, then in the **Content Browser**, in *C++ Classes* -> *FirstGame*, right-click on *HealthPickup* and create a Blueprint class based on it, called *HazardPickup_BP* and put it in the *Chapter9* folder.

For the *Mesh*, select *Shape_QuadPyramid* and scale it to the following dimensions:

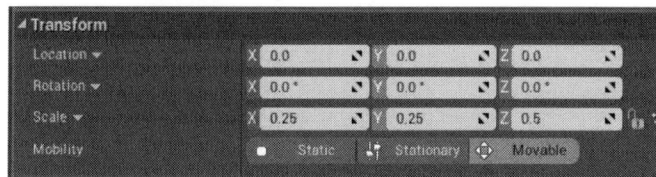

Figure 9.34: Scaling the Shape_QuadPyramid to a Spike

Now it looks a bit more dangerous. Change the *Material* to *M_Metal_Chrome*:

Figure 9.35: Changing the Material to Chrome

Now select *CollisionVolume(Inherited)* in the **Components** panel. In the **Details** panel, in the *Shape* section, set the *Sphere Radius* to 40.0. This will make the overlap sphere larger without affecting attached components, such as the pyramid. Now in the **Components** panel, select *HazardPickup_BP(self)* to select the overall Actor, and in the **Details** panel set the `HealingAmount` to -45.0.

Place a few of these Hazards in the world and press **Play**. With "MainCharacter" in the search bar in the **World Outliner**, select *MainCharacter_BP* and find the *Health* variable in the **Details** panel. Then click in the **Viewport** and run over some of the Hazards and see the *Health* variable decrease. Then run over the health pickup and watch it increase.

We have now created Hazards and health pickups! They are fully functional in that they disappear when picked up and they affect the Health of the Character. However, thus far we don't have an appealing way to show the player the effects of these gameplay mechanics. Typically in games, the Character's Health value is displayed with a **progress bar** – a bar that fills up or shrinks according to a particular value of **gameplay statistics**, or number that affects gameplay (also known as **gameplay stats**).

We will now learn how to create *Progress Bars* and we will use one to display the Character's Health.

Health and Progress Bars

We already have all the functionality for affecting the Character's Health. We simply need a way to show the player the results of these gameplay mechanics. This is where health bars come in. We will be creating **HUD (Heads Up Display)** – 2D images drawn to the screen to show information about the game. Once created, we will need to store variables on a class to keep track of them and handle code for showing and changing them. A typical class used to handle *HUD* elements is the `PlayerController` class. We will create a class based on this one, and use it with our Character.

Notes on HUD Elements

HUD code can be placed nearly anywhere. You can place it on the Character, its own HUD class dedicated to HUD elements, or in the Player Controller. The Player Controller is a common place for it in Unreal Engine for several reasons. For one, it helps to avoid cluttering the Character class with too much code. For another, in multiplayer games in which Characters can die and respawn, Character objects are frequently deleted. Information on that class such as Health and Experience points are deleted. However, the Player Controller is not deleted. A new Character is simply spawned and the same Controller possesses that new object. Thus HUD information can be stored on the Player Controller to avoid the need to save that information in some other way.

Creating a Custom Player Controller Class

We will now create a custom `PlayerController` class.

1. Create a new C++ class. Choose *Player Controller* from the Class Creation Wizard:

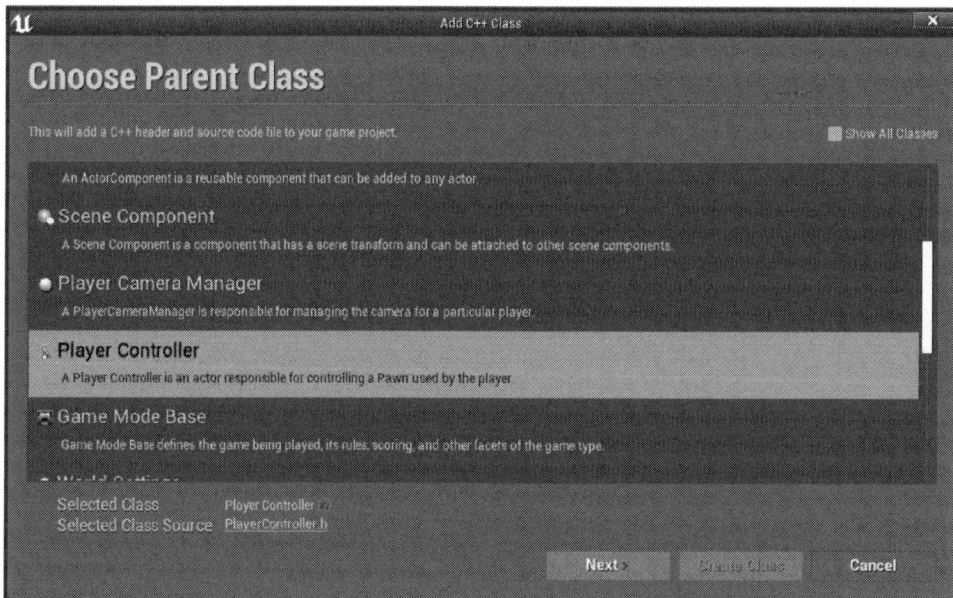

Figure 9.36: Choosing Player Controller as the Parent Class

Call this new class `MainPlayerController`.

2. In *MainPlayerController.h*, add the following:

```
public:

    /** Reference to the UMG asset in the editor */
    UPROPERTY(EditAnywhere, BlueprintReadWrite, Category =
"Widgets")
```

```
TSubclassOf<class UUserWidget> HUDOverlayAsset;

/** Variable to hold the widget after creating it */
UPROPERTY(EditAnywhere, BlueprintReadWrite, Category =
"Widgets")

UUserWidget* HUDOverlay;
```

`TSubclassOf` is a way to have a C++ variable that holds a Blueprint.

We first create a `public` section. Then we use `TSubclassOf`, a template class which takes a type as its template parameter. We forward declare `UUserWidget` class here. This is the class for a **HUD Widget** – a type of HUD element that can be drawn to the screen. We will create a HUD Widget Blueprint in the Unreal Engine UMG (Unreal Motion Graphics) system in the Unreal Engine editor shortly. Once we do, we will be able to select it from a dropdown to populate the *HUDOverlayAsset* variable in the Blueprint for our Player Controller once we create it. This is because `TSubclassOf` creates a variable whose value can be a Blueprint chosen from a dropdown, since it is exposed via `EditAnywhere`. `TSubclassOf` has the property that its value can only be of the type specified as its template parameter type (in the pointy brackets), or a class derived from it. Thus, when we select the value for this variable in the Blueprint we create based on `MainPlayerController`, we can select a Blueprint of any type derived from `UUsertWidget`.

Since the `TSubclassOf` variable `HUDOverlayAsset` will hold a Blueprint for a Widget, we can use it to create a new `UUserWidget`. We will store this widget in the `HUDOverlay` variable.

We create this Widget and store its variable in the `BeginPlay` function. Let's declare it now.

3. In *MainPlayerController.h*, under the declaration for the `HUDOverlay` variable, add:

```
protected:
    virtual void BeginPlay() override;
```

And in *MainPlayerController.cpp* add the following:

```
void AMainPlayerController::BeginPlay()
{
     Super::BeginPlay();

     if (HUDOverlayAsset)
     {
          HUDOverlay = CreateWidget<UUserWidget>(this,
HUDOverlayAsset);
          HUDOverlay->AddToViewport();
          HUDOverlay-
>SetVisibility(ESlateVisibility::Visible);
     }

}
```

First, we call `Super::BeginPlay`. Next, we check to make sure `HUDOverlayAsset` has been set in Blueprints. If it has not been set, it will be null here, so the if statement will not be entered. If it has been set, a new `UUserWidget` is created using `CreateWidget`. This function takes it as its first argument, to designate the `MainPlayerController` object to be the Widget's owning class. The second parameter is the Blueprint class to create. This is where we use the `TSubclassOf` variable that we will set in the `MainPlayerController` Blueprint. We then use `AddToViewport` to draw the Widget to the screen. Widgets also have a *Visibility* property that can be set, and we are setting it to `Visible` here, using the `enum` constant `Visible`, belonging in the scope of the `ESlateVisibility` enum.

4. Finally, we need to add the following `include`:

```
#include "Blueprint/UserWidget.h"
```

Now the `UserWidget` class will be defined here.

Adding the UMG, Slate and SlateCore Modules

We will need to set up our project to include the code for the UMG-related classes. We can do this by opening our *FirstGame.Build.cs* file. Find it in Visual Studio in the *Solution Explorer*, in *Games -> FirstGame -> Source -> FirstGame -> FirstGame.Build.cs*.

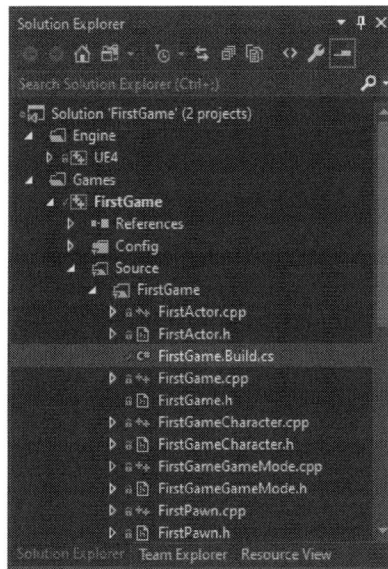

Figure 9.37: Finding FirstGame.Build.cs in the Solution Explorer

Notice the `PublicDependencyModuleNames` call to `AddRange`. This file is a C# file, but the language is similar to C++. We don't need to do any C# coding. We simply need to add "UMG" to the list in this function call. We will also create a similar line to this one, using `PrivateDependencyModuleNames`, and add "Slate" and "SlateCore" to this one. The code should look like the following:

```
        PublicDependencyModuleNames.AddRange(new string[]
{ "Core", "CoreUObject", "Engine", "InputCore",
"HeadMountedDisplay", "UMG" });


        PrivateDependencyModuleNames.AddRange(new string[]
{ "Slate", "SlateCore" });
```

Now that we have created the code for adding a Widget to the **Viewport**, we need to actually create a *MainPlayerController* Blueprint based on `MainPlayerController`. We also need to create the Widget Blueprint for the Health Bar so we can set the value of `HUDOverlayAsset`.

Creating the Health Bar Widget Blueprint

Now we must create a Widget Blueprint. In the **Content Browser** in the *Chapter9* folder, right-click and select *User Interface -> Widget Blueprint*. Call it *HUDOverlayWidget*. Double-click it to open it. You will be taken to the **UMG Editor**.

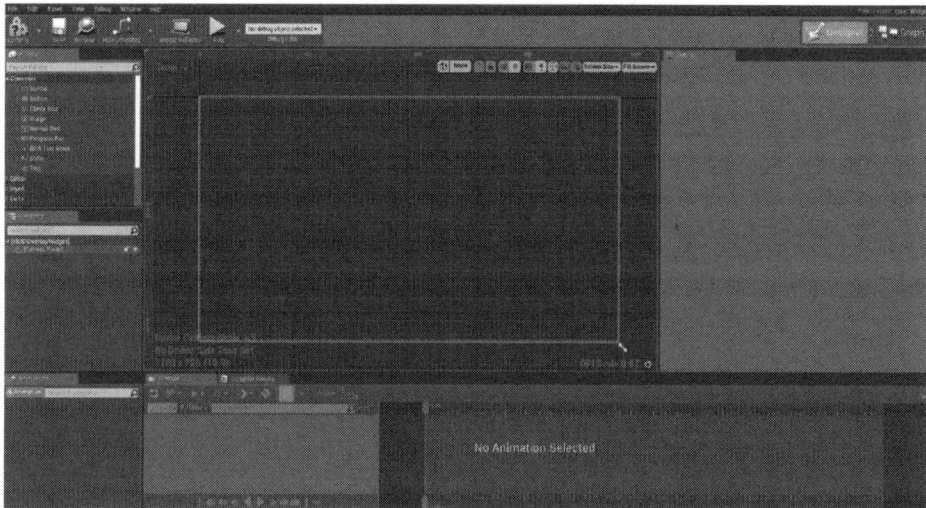

Figure 9.38: The UMG Editor

For now, we will simply add something to the HUD so we can verify that it is being created and added to the screen. In the **Palette** panel, click and drag *Progress Bar* into the graph area:

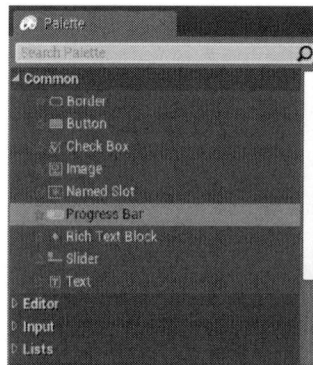

Figure 9.39: The Progress Bar in the Palette Panel

Now there should be a small gray rectangle in the graph area. This is a progress bar.

Next, create a Blueprint based on the *MainPlayerController* class. Put it in the *Chapter9* folder and call it *MainPlayerController_BP*. Open it and notice in the **Details** panel, there are the following properties:

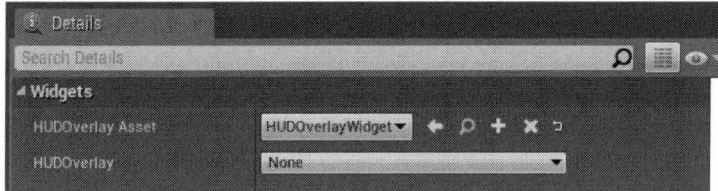

Figure 9.40: The HUDOverlayAsset and HUDOverlay Variables

Here we can click the dropdown for *HUDOverlayAsset* and choose our *HUDOverlayWidget* Blueprint we just created. *HUDOverlay Asset* is the `TSubclassOf` variable we created in *MainPlayerController.h*. `HUDOverlay` will remain with a value of *None* until `BeginPlay` gets called and the Widget gets created and its value is stored in `HUDOverlay`.

Setting the Default Player Controller

Go to *Edit -> Project Settings -> Maps and Modes* and under *Default Modes*, find *Player Controller Class* and set it to *MainPlayerController_BP*.

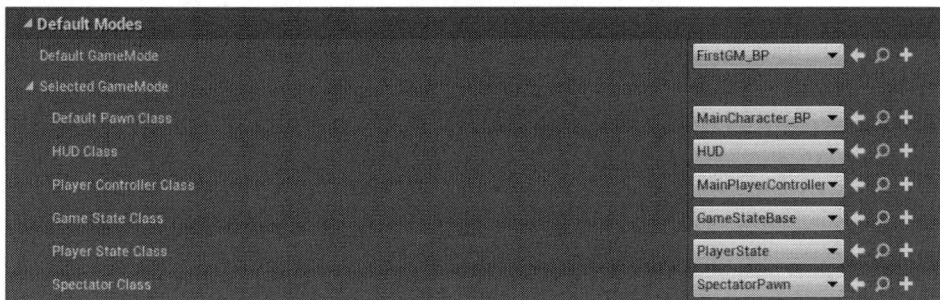

Figure 9.41: Setting the default Player Controller Class to MainPlayerController_BP

Now the default *Player Controller Class* will be set to the Blueprint we created. Press **Play** and notice the gray progress bar we dragged into the graph area in the **UMG Editor** on the screen.

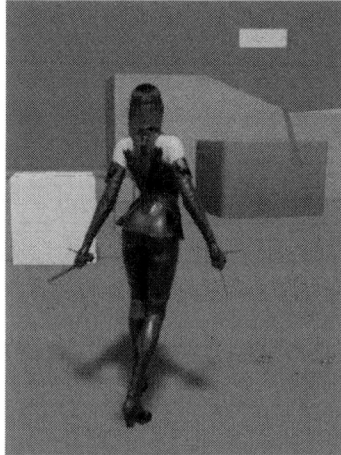

Figure 9.42: The Widget Blueprint Drawn to the Screen

Now that we know our HUD Widget is being drawn to the screen, we can actually make our progress bar reflect the Character's Health.

Binding the Progress Bar to the Character's Health

We will use the following steps to bind the progress bar to the Character's Health.

1. We can adjust the size of the progress bar in the **UMG Editor** graph. Click on the edge of the gray rectangle and drag it out to an elongated bar. Position it at the top-right of the graph area. In the **Details** panel, in the **Slot** section, notice the *Anchors* property. Select the dropdown and choose the symbol with a gray square at the top right:

Figure 9.43: Selecting the Top Right Anchor Mode

Notice that the medallion symbol (indicating where the Widget Element is anchored to) now shifts to the top-right of the graph area.

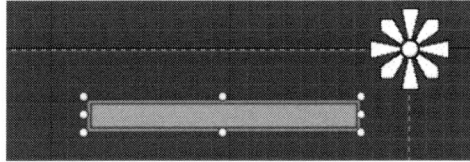

Figure 9.44: The Medallion in the Top Right of the Graph Area

Now, regardless of the screen size, the **Progress Bar** will always be a constant distance from the top-right corner.

2. We are now ready to **bind** the progress bar's *Percent*. This means the amount the progress bar will be filled will depend on a value we designate. To bind the *Percent*, in the **Details** panel, in the *Progress* section, find *Percent*. Click **Bind** and select *Create Binding*.

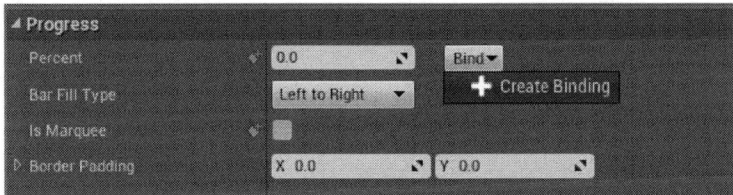

Figure 9.45: Binding the Percent

Now a new Blueprint function will be created and you will see the following in the graph:

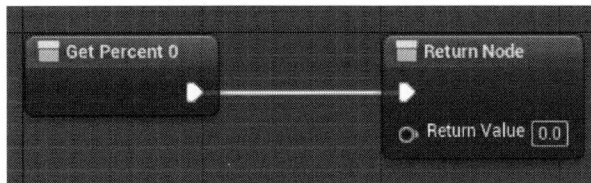

Figure 9.46: Function for Binding the Percent

Notice the *Return Node* has a `float` input, indicated by its green color. The `float` value fed into this node will determine the amount of the progress bar that will be filled, as a fraction between 0 and 1.

3. We will need to access our Character, which can be done with the *Get Owning Player Pawn* node. Right-click and search for this node and select it. We will need to cast its return value to *MainCharacter_BP* in order to access `Health` and `MaxHealth` from it. Create the following Blueprint nodes:

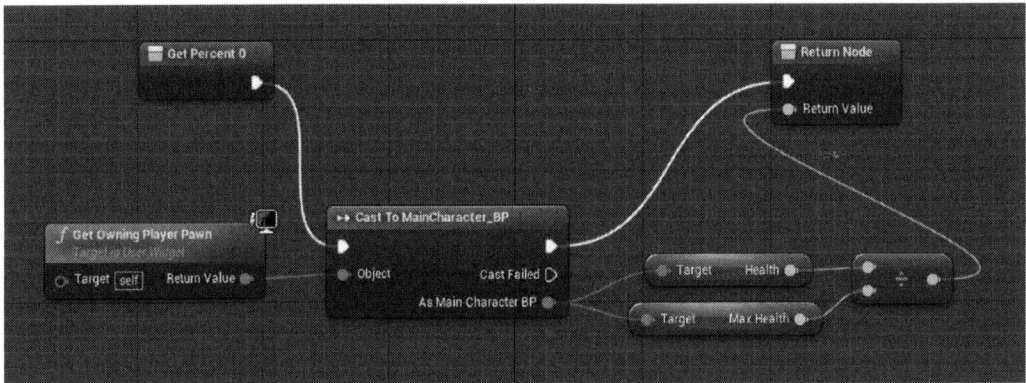

Figure 9.47: Getting Health and MaxHealth from the Owning Player Pawn

Now the health bar will reflect the correct percentage of the Character's *Health*. However, this function is called each frame and casting every frame gets expensive. We can, however, own a variable of type *MainCharacter_BP* and store the reference to the Character in it after our first successful cast.

4. In the **My Blueprint** panel, click + *Add New* and select *Variable*. Call it *Main*. Select *Main* in the **Variables** section in the **My Blueprint** panel. Now the **Details** panel shows pertinent information. Select *Variable Type* and search for "MainCharacter" and choose *MainCharacter BP -> Object Reference*.

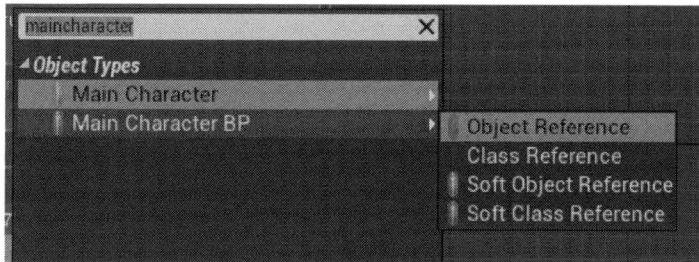

Figure 9.48: Changing Variable Type to MainCharacter_BP

5. Create a new `float` variable called *PercentOutput*. This will be fed into the *Return* Node. Now create the following Blueprint logic:

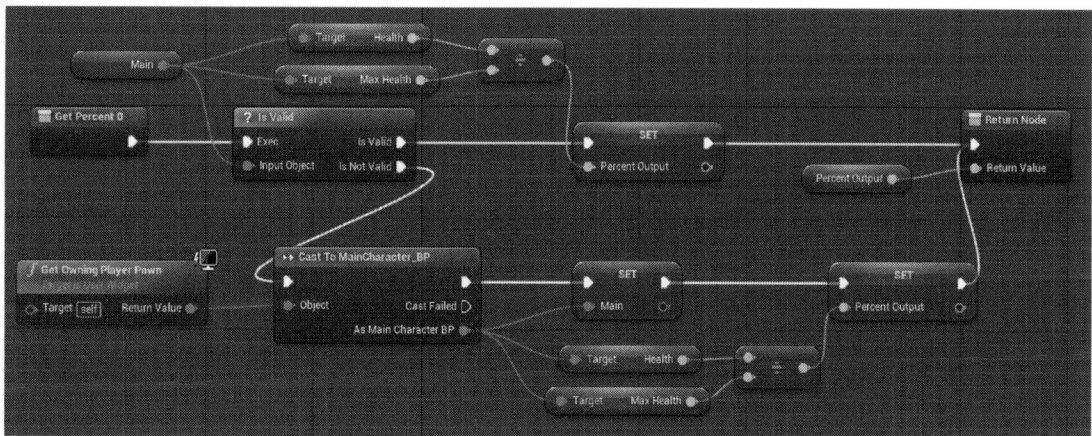

Figure 9.49: Storing a Reference to MainCharacter_BP

First, we check our *Main* variable to see if it is valid. At first, it should fail, at which point we use *Get Owning Player Pawn* and cast its return value to *MainCharacter_BP*. Then we use the results of this cast to set the reference *Main*. We then get *Health* and *MaxHealth* and divide them to get the amount as a fraction between 0 and 1. We set the value of *Percent Output* to this value. Finally the output wire is connected to *Return Node*. If the initial *Is Valid* check succeeds, which it should after the first successful cast, then *Health* and *MaxHealth* are accessed from the *Main* variable, divided, and *Percent Output* is set. The resulting line of execution is hooked up to *Return Node*. In both cases, *Percent Output* is plugged into *Return Node*.

6. Press **Play** and now run over the Hazards and health pickup and watch the health bar update!

In the top right of the **UMG Editor**, there are two icons labeled **Designer** and **Graph**.

Figure 9.50: The Designer and Graph Icons

These allow you to switch between the **Graph Editor** and the **Designer**, where we dragged the progress bar onto the graph area. Click **Designer**.

There are many properties you can mess with in the **Details** panel. In the *Appearance* section, for example, you can change the fill color and opacity. Fiddling with these features is left as a practice exercise to the reader. Also notice in the **Hierarchy** panel:

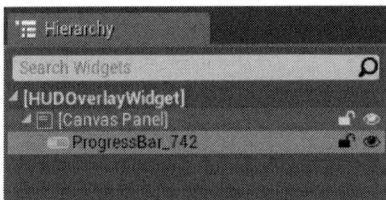

Figure 9.51: The Hierarchy Panel

The **Canvas** panel can be thought of as the default Scene Component in Actor Blueprints. It acts as the parent to which other elements are attached. The progress bar we added was given a default name here, and it can be selected and renamed. The more HUD elements you add, the more you will be able to arrange them here, and attach them to one another similarly to how Components are attached to one another in Actor Blueprints.

Now that we have created Character Health and show it on the screen with a progress bar, we are ready to move on to other gameplay mechanics. Floor switches and doors are present in many action games and make the world more interactive. We will dive into these next.

Floor Switches and Doors

A floor switch is a block that the Character can step up onto and trigger the opening of a door, the raising of a platform, or some other action in the game. These are common in action games, and we can easily implement this functionality using the overlap capabilities we have learned. We will also learn how to raise a door in a smooth manner according to a **Timeline** – a special tool for determining how a value changes over time.

Creating the FloorSwitch Class

We must create a new class for the floor switch. We will do so now.

1. Create a new C++ class based on `Actor` called `FloorSwitch`.

In Visual Studio, we will be adding some components. First, we will need a Box Component for overlapping, a Static Mesh for the floor switch, and a Static Mesh for the door itself. We will also make use of the constructor.

2. Add these to the *FloorSwitch.h* file, in the `public` section just under

    `AFloorSwitch();:`

    ```
    /** Box to trigger Overlap Events */
    UPROPERTY(VisibleAnywhere, BlueprintReadWrite,
    Category = "Floor Switch")
    class UBoxComponent* TriggerBox;

    /** Block for the character to step on */
    UPROPERTY(VisibleAnywhere, BlueprintReadWrite,
    Category = "Floor Switch")
    class UStaticMeshComponent* FloorSwitch;

    /** Door to raise when the floor switch is stepped on
    */
    UPROPERTY(VisibleAnywhere, BlueprintReadWrite,
    Category = "Floor Switch")

    UStaticMeshComponent* Door;
    ```

We will need functions for when the Character overlaps with the Box Component, so beneath the declaration for the `Tick` function, add:

```
UFUNCTION()
void OnOverlapBegin(UPrimitiveComponent*
OverlappedComponent, AActor* OtherActor,
UPrimitiveComponent* OtherComp, int32 OtherBodyIndex, bool
bFromSweep, const FHitResult & SweepResult);

UFUNCTION()

void OnOverlapEnd(UPrimitiveComponent*
OverlappedComponent, AActor* OtherActor,
UPrimitiveComponent* OtherComp, int32 OtherBodyIndex);
```

Now we can initialize our variables in the constructor and define our overlap functions, as well as bind them to the Overlap Events.

3. In *FloorSwitch.cpp* in the constructor, just under

```
PrimaryActorTick.bCanEverTick = true; add:

TriggerBox =
CreateDefaultSubobject<UBoxComponent>(TEXT("TriggerBox"));
RootComponent = TriggerBox;

TriggerBox-
>SetCollisionEnabled(ECollisionEnabled::QueryOnly);
TriggerBox-
>SetCollisionObjectType(ECollisionChannel::ECC_WorldStatic)
;
TriggerBox-
>SetCollisionResponseToAllChannels(ECollisionResponse::ECR_
Ignore);
TriggerBox-
>SetCollisionResponseToChannel(ECollisionChannel::ECC_Pawn,
ECollisionResponse::ECR_Overlap);

TriggerBox->SetBoxExtent(FVector(62.f, 62.f, 32.f));

FloorSwitch =
CreateDefaultSubobject<UStaticMeshComponent>(TEXT("FloorSwi
tch"));
```

```
FloorSwitch->SetupAttachment(GetRootComponent());

Door =
CreateDefaultSubobject<UStaticMeshComponent>(TEXT("Door"));

Door->SetupAttachment(GetRootComponent());
```

We create our `TriggerBox` and set it to be the `RootComponent`. Then we use `SetCollisionEnabled` in order to set the *Collision Enabled* property to `QueryOnly`. This is the same *Collision Enabled* property we learned about in *Chapter 8 – Collision*. This is the property shown in the following figure:

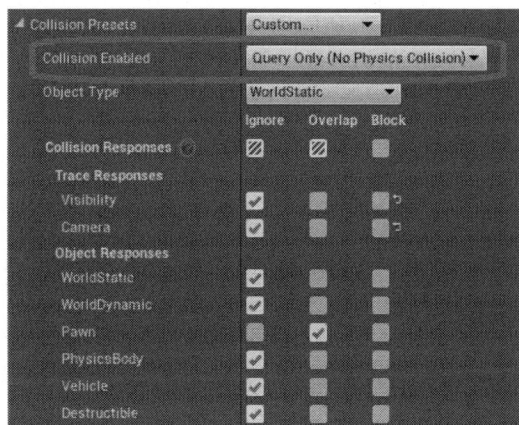

Figure 9.52: Showing the Collision Enabled Property

There exists an `enum` called `ECollisionEnabled` which contains the *Collision Enabled* options that we can choose from to set this property in C++. Since we chose `ECollisionEnabled::QueryOnly`, we will get *Query Only* for the *Collision Enabled* property and once we create a Blueprint from `FloorSwitch`, our Box Component will show the correct property as can be seen in the figure above.

We also make use of the function `SetCollisionObjectType` to set its type. There exists an `enum` called `ECollisionChannel` which contains options for different *Object Types*. This is the same *Object Type* that we learned about in *Chapter 8 – Collision*. We pass in `ECollisionChannel::ECC_WorldStatic` to `SetCollisionObject` type to change its *Object Type* to *World Static*, as can be seen in the following figure:

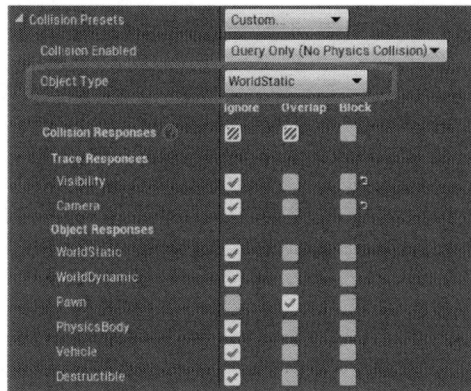

Figure 9.53: Showing the Object Type Property

We then use `SetCollisionResponseToAllChannels`, allowing us to set all of the collision responses to a specific collision response. There exists an `enum` called `ECollisionResponse` which contains these responses. We chose `ECollisionResponse::ECR_Ignore` and as a result, the responses were set to *ignore* for all channels. We also used the function `SetCollisionResponseToChannel` which allows us to select a channel and set its response directly. We chose the *Pawn* channel by passing in `ECollisionChannel::ECC_Pawn` for the first argument and set it to *Overlap* by passing in `ECollisionResponse::ECR_Overlap` for the second argument. The results can be seen in the following figure:

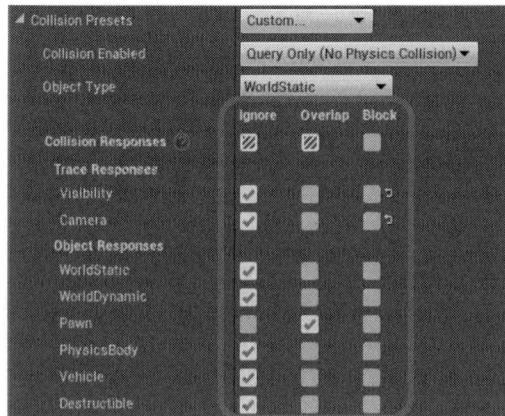

Figure 9.54: Showing the Collision Responses

We then call `SetBoxExtent` to set the dimensions of the Box Component without needing to affect its *Scale* property. This way, the Box Component will take on the dimensions we desire without the other components being affected, since the Box Component is the Root Component and the other components are attached to it and would be affected if we changed the *Transform* properties of the Box Component.

Next, we create our `FloorSwitch` and our `Door` Static Mesh Components and attach them to the `RootComponent`.

4. In order for these types to be useable, add the following `includes` to the top of *FloorSwitch.cpp*:

```
#include "Components/BoxComponent.h"
#include "Components/StaticMeshComponent.h"
```

Now we can set up our overlap functions.

5. Beneath the definition for the `Tick` function, add:

```
void AFloorSwitch::OnOverlapBegin(UPrimitiveComponent*
OverlappedComponent, AActor* OtherActor,
UPrimitiveComponent* OtherComp, int32 OtherBodyIndex, bool
bFromSweep, const FHitResult & SweepResult)
{

}

void AFloorSwitch::OnOverlapEnd(UPrimitiveComponent*
OverlappedComponent, AActor* OtherActor,
UPrimitiveComponent* OtherComp, int32 OtherBodyIndex)
{

}
```

And in `BeginPlay`, beneath `Super::BeginPlay();`, add:

```
    TriggerBox->OnComponentBeginOverlap.AddDynamic(this,
&AFloorSwitch::OnOverlapBegin);
```

```
TriggerBox->OnComponentEndOverlap.AddDynamic(this,
&AFloorSwitch::OnOverlapEnd);
```

Now we must decide what to do when the Character overlaps with the Box Component. Maneuver back to the Unreal Engine editor. Create a Blueprint based on FloorSwitch and place it in the *Chapter9* folder. Call it *FloorSwitch_BP*.

Thus far, there is only the Box Component in the **Viewport**.

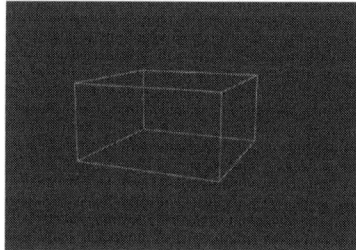

Figure 9.55: The Box Component in the Viewport for FloorSwitch_BP

We are ready to choose the *Static Mesh* for both the *FloorSwitch* and the *Door* Static Mesh Components.

6. For *FloorSwitch*, choose *Shape_Cube* and in the **Details** panel, in *Transform*, set the *Z* component of its *Location* to -80.0.

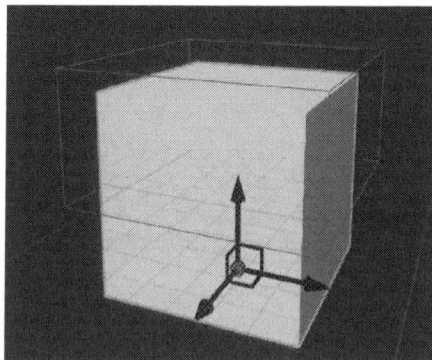

Figure 9.56: Choosing Shape_Cube and Setting its Z Location to -80.0

7. Now for *Door*, for the *Static Mesh* select *Shape_Cube* and change its **Transform** properties to those shown in the figure below.

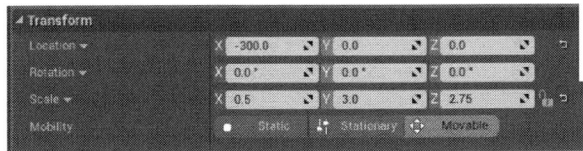

Figure 9.57: Transform Settings for the Door Static Mesh

Now we have a floor switch and a door. We now want to raise the door when the Box Component is overlapped by the Character, and we also want to lower the floor switch slightly. We can make use of a Timeline to do this, a particular Blueprint node that allows us to change a value with respect to time.

Creating a Timeline

We are ready to create a Timeline.

In the **Event Graph** for *FloorSwitch_BP*, right-click and search for "timeline" and select *Add Timeline* and name it *FloorSwitch Timeline*. Double-click the *FloorSwitch Timeline* node, and you will see the following:

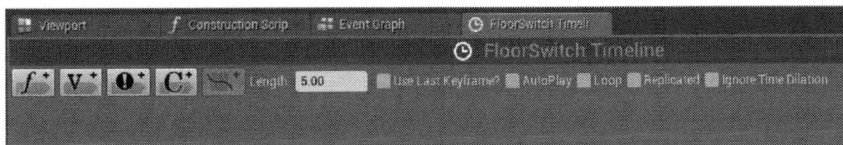

Figure 9.58: The FloorSwitch Timeline

From the icons on the left, just underneath the **Viewport**, **Construction Script**, **Event Graph** and **FloorSwitch Timeline** tabs, select the *f+* icon. This adds a **Float Track** – a track that can change a `float` with respect to time. Name this track *DoorTrack*. In the track, hold *SHIFT* and *left-click* on the graph area, to create a point. Click again to create a second point and you will see a line connecting them.

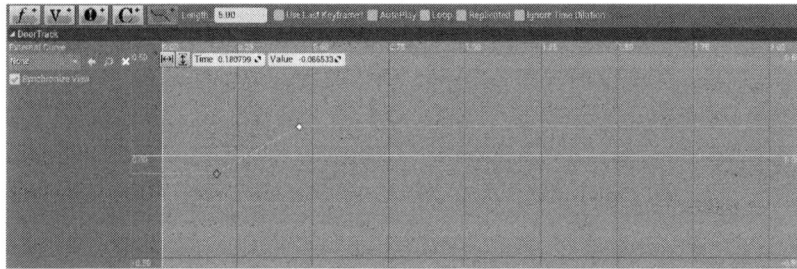

Figure 9.59: The DoorTrack with two Points

Each point has two associated values: *Time* and *Value*. If you click on one point, it will highlight orange and the *Time* and *Value* will be shown at the top of the graph. With the leftmost point selected, set the *Time* to 0.0 and the *Value* to 0.0. With the rightmost point selected, set the *Time* to 1.5 and the *Value* to 300.0. To the left of these text boxes are two icons: **Zoom to Fit Horizontal** and **Zoom to Fit Vertical**. Click both of these. They consist of horizontal and vertical double-arrows, shown in **Figure 9.60**:

Figure 9.60: Zoom to Fit Horizontal and Vertical

Now the graph area is scaled to accommodate the points at their locations. The line connecting these points represents what the track value will be at for the given time. Rather than changing linearly, though, it would be nice for the value to change in a smoother manner. We can achieve this by right-clicking each point and selecting *Auto*.

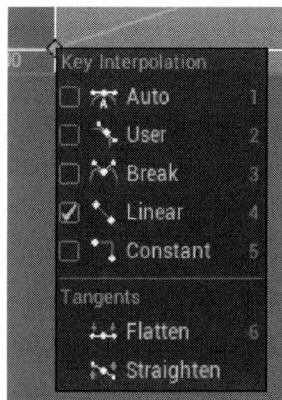

Figure 9.61: Using Auto to smooth the Curve

Now the graph is smooth and curved. You can alter the curve with the other options seen when you right-click each point. Experimenting with these is left as an exercise for the reader. The curved graph can be seen in the following figure:

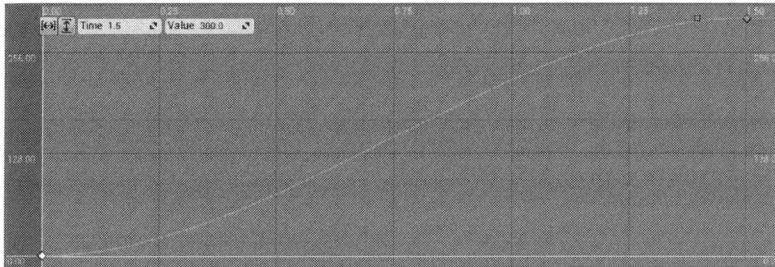

Figure 9.62: The Graph with a Smooth Curve

Now we have a track that will determine the value of an output `float` with respect to the time that has passed since the track started. We will learn how to use this information shortly. But first, we will add another track in this Timeline for the floor switch itself. Click the *f+* icon once again to create a new *Float Track*. Name this track *FloorSwitchTrack*. Add two points the same way we did with *DoorTrack* and for the first point, set *Time* to 0.0 and *Value* to 0.0. For the second point, set *Time* to 1.0 and *Value* to -15.0. Zoom to fit horizontal and vertical using the icons in **Figure 9.60**. Right-click each point and choose *Auto* to smooth the curve. Now click on the **Event Graph** tab and notice that the *FloorSwitch Timeline* node looks like the following:

Figure 9.63: New Float Outputs for the FloorSwitch Timeline

Notice that the node has two `float` outputs: *Door Track* and *Floor Switch Track*. These are outputs from the node while it is playing, and each frame, these track values will vary according to the graph on their tracks.

We now need to be able to start this Timeline, and we need a way to handle the information returned from it. In order to start the Timeline, an execution wire must be connected to the *Play* input pin. Thus we need an event that can fire at the proper time. We also need a Blueprint node that can be fired after the node, hooked up to its *Update* pin.

Since we wish for the Timeline to start once the Character has overlapped with the Box Component, we will create a Blueprint Implementable Event that we can call from C++ and implement in Blueprints. To handle the data, we will create a Blueprint Callable function that we can call from Blueprints which can take the `float` information from the Timeline tracks.

Starting the Timeline and Handling the Output Data

We will need a function to call that will start the Timeline, and we also need a function that will handle the data output from the Timeline. To start the Timeline, we will create a Blueprint Implementable Event. To handle the data, we will create a Blueprint Callable Function.

Creating the Functions to Activate the Floor Switch

We will now create functions to activate the Floor Switch.

1. In *FloorSwitch.h*, add the following function declarations, under the declaration for `OnOverlapEnd`:

```
/** Called when Box Component is overlapped, used in
Blueprints to start the timeline */
    UFUNCTION(BlueprintImplementableEvent, Category =
"Floor Switch")
    void ActivateFloorSwitch();

    /** When no longer overlapping, used in Blueprints to
reverse the timeline */
```

```
    UFUNCTION(BlueprintImplementableEvent, Category =
"Floor Switch")
    void DeactivateFloorSwitch();
```

We not only created `ActivateFloorSwitch` so that we can start the Timeline once the Character steps on the switch, but also `DeactivateFloorSwitch` so we can reverse the Timeline and lower the door and raise the switch back up when the Character is no longer on the switch.

Now, to handle data from the Timeline, we will create a Blueprint Callable Function.

2. Declare this beneath the declaration for `DeactivateFloorSwitch`:

```
    /** Called in Blueprints to pass in data from the
Timeline */
    UFUNCTION(BlueprintCallable, Category = "Floor
Switch")
    void UpdateFloorSwitchLocations(float DoorLocation,
float SwitchLocation);
```

Since `UpdateFloorSwitchLocations` will alter the locations of the `Door` and the `FloorSwitch`, we will need to know the initial locations of the `Door` and the `FloorSwitch` Components.

3. Thus we will add the following, just under the declaration for `Door`:

```
    /** Initial location for the door */
    UPROPERTY(BlueprintReadWrite, Category = "Floor
Switch")
    FVector InitialDoorLocation;

    /** Initial location for the floor switch */
    UPROPERTY(BlueprintReadWrite, Category = "Floor
Switch")
    FVector InitialSwitchLocation;
```

4. And we will store these locations in `BeginPlay`:

```
    InitialDoorLocation = Door->GetComponentLocation();
```

```
        InitialSwitchLocation = FloorSwitch-
>GetComponentLocation();
```

5. Now we can define `UpdateFloorSwitchLocations`:

```
void AFloorSwitch::UpdateFloorSwitchLocations(float
DoorLocation, float SwitchLocation)
{
      FVector NewDoorLocation = InitialDoorLocation;
      NewDoorLocation.Z += DoorLocation;
      Door->SetWorldLocation(NewDoorLocation);

      FVector NewSwitchLocation = InitialSwitchLocation;
      NewSwitchLocation.Z += SwitchLocation;
      FloorSwitch->SetWorldLocation(NewSwitchLocation);

}
```

This function takes the value for `InitialDoorLocation` and stores it in a local `FVector` variable `NewDoorLocation`. It then adds to the `Z` component of that `FVector` the amount passed in as `DoorLocation`. This will be the `float` amount output from the Timeline node while the Timeline is playing. Then the `Door` Static Mesh Component gets `SetWorldLocation` called passing in this new altered location. The same is done for the `FloorSwitch` component, only the value passed in as `SwitchLocation` is used.

Finally, we need to call `ActivateFloorSwitch` and `DeactivateFloorSwitch` when the Character overlaps with the Box Component.

6. We thus will call these functions in `OnOverlapBegin` and `OnOverlapEnd`, respectively:

```
void AFloorSwitch::OnOverlapBegin(UPrimitiveComponent*
OverlappedComponent, AActor* OtherActor,
UPrimitiveComponent* OtherComp, int32 OtherBodyIndex, bool
bFromSweep, const FHitResult & SweepResult)
{
      AMainCharacter* MainCharacter =
Cast<AMainCharacter>(OtherActor);
      if (MainCharacter)
      {
```

```
            ActivateFloorSwitch();;
        }
}


void AFloorSwitch::OnOverlapEnd(UPrimitiveComponent*
OverlappedComponent, AActor* OtherActor,
UPrimitiveComponent* OtherComp, int32 OtherBodyIndex)
{
        AMainCharacter* MainCharacter =
Cast<AMainCharacter>(OtherActor);
        if (MainCharacter)
        {
            DeactivateFloorSwitch();;
        }

}
```

We are casting `OtherActor` to `AMainCharacter`, so if something else in the world overlaps with the Box Component, this cast will fail and the body of the `if` statement will not run.

7. Since we are using the `AMainCharacter` type, include the proper header at the top of the file:

```
#include "MainCharacter.h"
```

We do not need to define the function bodies of `ActivateFloorSwitch` and `DeactivateFloorSwitch` as these are marked `BlueprintImplementableEvent` and can be implemented in Blueprints. Compile this code and go back into the **Event Graph** for *FloorSwitch_BP*.

Using the Functions to Activate the Floor Switch

Now we can use these functions in Blueprints. First we will implement our Blueprint Implementable Events. In the **Event Graph** of *FloorSwitch_BP*, right-click and search for "activate floor switch" and select *Event Activate Floor Switch* to create a node. Likewise do the same for "deactivate floor switch" and create a node for this event as well. Hook up *Event Activate Floor Switch* to the *Play* input to the Timeline and hook up *Event Deactivate Floor Switch* to the *Reverse* input to the Timeline, as in the following figure:

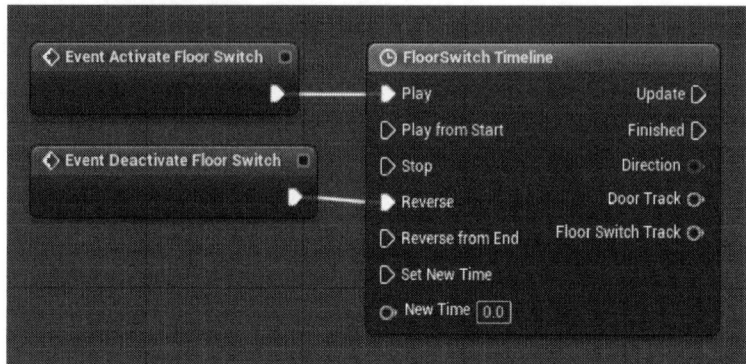

Figure 9.64: Using the Blueprint Implementable Events

Now when `ActivateFloorSwitch` gets called in C++, *Event Activate Floor Switch* will fire, resulting in starting the Timeline. When `DeactivateFloorSwitch` gets called in C++, *Event Deactivate Floor Switch* will fire, resulting in the Timeline reversing.

Now right-click in the graph area and search for "update floor switch locations" and select *Update Floor Switch Locations*. Connect the *Door Track* output from the Timeline to the *Door Location* input for *Update Floor Switch Locations*. Likewise, connect the Timeline's *Floor Switch Track* output to the *Switch Location* input, as in the following figure:

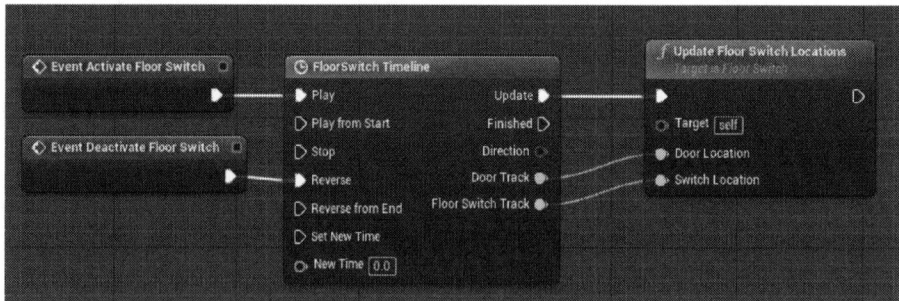

Figure 9.65: Calling Update Floor Switch Location from the Blueprint

Now, when the Timeline is running, it will output values for the *Door Track* and the *Floor Switch Track* according to the graph curves in the Timeline. These values will be fed into *Update Floor Switch Locations*, and the C++ body of this function will use this data to alter the `Door` and `FloorSwitch` locations.

You can move the walls around so that you can use this door as a barrier to a new location, as in the following figure:

Figure 9.66: Placing a FloorSwitch_BP as a Door

Now drag a *FloorSwitch_BP* into the world and press **Play**. Use the Character to run over the floor switch and watch the switch sink into the floor and the door raise into the air!

Figure 9.67: Activating the Floor Switch with the Character

Now we have a working floor switch and a raising door!

We are finally ready to move to the next important feature of video games: the pause menu. We must provide a way to pause the game, as well as to quit once the player wishes to do so. We will learn how to create this menu now.

Pause Menu and Quit Game

Menus are present in nearly all video games. We will create a basic pause menu that will allow us to not only pause the game, but also to quit if we so desire. This is a basic menu, but the concepts used to create it can be expanded into menus as complex as you wish.

Setting up Keyboard Input for the Menu

We will want our menu to pop up in response to a keyboard press. We can use the *Escape* key, but since that already ends our PIE session when playing in-editor, we will also add another input mapping for the Q key. In *Edit -> Project Settings -> Input*, add an *Action Mapping* called *ESC*. Add both the *Escape* and the *Q* key to this mapping.

Figure 9.68: Action Mappings for the Escape and Q Keys

Now we will create a function to bind to this action mapping in *MainCharacter.h*:

```
void ESCDown();
```

And define them in *MainCharacter.cpp*:

```
void AMainCharacter::ESCDown()
{

}
```

And we will bind this function in `SetupPlayerInputComponent`:

```
PlayerInputComponent->BindAction("ESC", IE_Pressed,
this, &AMainCharacter::ESCDown);
```

In this function, we will want to access the Player Controller class so we can display the Widget there. Thus we will need a reference to the Main Player Controller. We can add a variable to store this reference. In *MainCharacter.h*, add the following, just under the declaration for `FollowCamera`:

```
    /** Reference to the Player Controller */
    UPROPERTY(VisibleAnywhere, BlueprintReadOnly, Category
= "Controller")
    class AMainPlayerController* MainPlayerController;
```

And we can get this value in `BeginPlay`, just under the call to `Super::BeginPlay`:

```
MainPlayerController =
Cast<AMainPlayerController>(GetController());
```

Now we have a reference to the Player Controller. We will need to add the following `include` to *MainPlayerController.cpp* just under the declaration for `MaxHealth`:

```
#include "MainPlayerController.h"
```

We need to add variables for the pause menu in the `MainPlayerController` class.

Adding Widget Variables in the MainPlayerController Class

In *MainPlayerController.h*, add the following:

```
    UPROPERTY(EditAnywhere, BlueprintReadWrite, Category =
"Widgets")
    TSubclassOf<UUserWidget> WPauseMenu;

    UPROPERTY(VisibleAnywhere, BlueprintReadWrite,
Category = "Widgets")
    UUserWidget* PauseMenu;


    bool bPauseMenuVisible;
```

Similar to how we set up the health bar, we have created a `UUserWidget` called `PauseMenu`, and a `TSubclassOf` that we will be able to fill in inside the Blueprint. We have also created a Boolean for storing whether or not the pause menu is visible.

Now in `BeginPlay`, just under the `if` statement where we set up the health bar, add:

```
    if (WPauseMenu)
    {
        PauseMenu = CreateWidget<UUserWidget>(this,
WPauseMenu);
```

```
        if (PauseMenu)
        {
                PauseMenu->AddToViewport();
                PauseMenu-
>SetVisibility(ESlateVisibility::Hidden);
        }

    }
```

We check to make sure the WPauseMenu has been set in Blueprints. If so, we create the widget and store its value in PauseMenu. If that variable is valid, we then add it to the **Viewport** and set its visibility to Hidden. We will now create functions that can be called to display this menu.

Adding Functions to Display or Hide the Pause Menu

We will declare the following functions in *MainPlayerController.h*: just under the declaration for BeginPlay, in its own public section:

```
public:

    UFUNCTION(BlueprintNativeEvent, BlueprintCallable,
Category = "HUD")
    void DisplayPauseMenu();

    UFUNCTION(BlueprintNativeEvent, BlueprintCallable,
Category = "HUD")

    void RemovePauseMenu();
```

Compile the code first, then define them in *MainPlayerController.cpp*:

```
void
AMainPlayerController::DisplayPauseMenu_Implementation()
{
    if (PauseMenu)
    {
        bPauseMenuVisible = true;
        PauseMenu-
>SetVisibility(ESlateVisibility::Visible);

        FInputModeGameAndUI InputModeGameAndUI;
        SetInputMode(InputModeGameAndUI);
```

```
            bShowMouseCursor = true;
    }
}

void
AMainPlayerController::RemovePauseMenu_Implementation()
{
    if (PauseMenu)
    {
        PauseMenu-
    >SetVisibility(ESlateVisibility::Hidden);
        bShowMouseCursor = false;
        bPauseMenuVisible = false;

        FInputModeGameOnly InputModeGameOnly;
        SetInputMode(InputModeGameOnly);
    }

}
```

Notice that we made these functions and marked them with
`BlueprintNativeEvent`. This means we can implement part of their functionality
in C++ and part in Blueprints. For Blueprint Native Events, the function definition gets
`_Implementation` added to its name. When calling the function in C++ however,
you simply use the function name without this extra appendage. We will learn shortly
how to implement additional functionality for these functions in Blueprints. This will
come in handy when we want to define some of the functionality in Blueprints for
showing and hiding the menu.

The first thing we do in `DisplayPauseMenu_Implementation` is check to see if
`PauseMenu` is valid. Then we set `bPauseMenuVisible` to `true`. We set the pause
menu widget's `Visibility` to true. Then, we wish to prevent the player from
controlling the Character, since the game will be paused. To do this, we use the function
`SetInputMode` and feed in a `struct` of the type `FInputModeGameAndUI`. This
`struct`, when passed into the `SetInputMode` function, will result in the input for
the game responding first to the UI elements, giving the game functionality second
priority. We then access the inherited Boolean variable `bShowMouseCursor` and set

it to true. This results in the mouse cursor being visible, which we will want when the pause menu is visible.

Next, in `RemovePauseMenu_Implementation`, we make sure `PauseMenu` is valid, then we set `bShowMouseCursor` to `false`, as well as `bPauseMenuVisible`. Then we call `SetInputMode`, this time passing in a `struct` of type `FInputModeGameOnly`, which allows inputs to only control game elements. This should return the normal control over the Character to the player.

Now, in order to easily open or close the pause menu based on its current state, we will create a **toggle function** – a function that will alternate between two different functionalities each time it is called. Declare this function in *MainPlayerController.h*:

```
void TogglePauseMenu();
```

And define it in *MainPlayerController.cpp*:

```
void AMainPlayerController::TogglePauseMenu()
{
        if (bPauseMenuVisible)
        {
                RemovePauseMenu();
        }
        else
        {
                DisplayPauseMenu();
        }

}
```

Now if the menu is closed, `TogglePauseMenu` will open it, and if it is open, `TogglePauseMenu` will close it.

We now have our code set up for adding a pause menu and toggling its visibility. It's now time to actually create the Widget Blueprint for the menu.

Creating the Pause Menu Widget Blueprint

In the *Chapter9* folder, create a Widget Blueprint and call it *PauseMenu*. Double-click it to open it. In **Designer** mode, in the **Palette** panel, search for "vertical box" and drag in a Vertical Box. Scale it up and position it to the left of the **Canvas** panel as in the following figure.

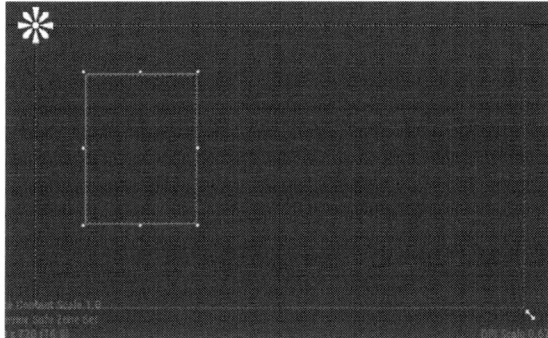

Figure 9.69: Dragging in a Vertical Box

The Vertical Box will arrange items vertically inside it. Drag four *Button* items from the **Palette** panel into the Vertical Box and notice that the **Hierarchy** panel shows them as children of the Vertical Box. Rename them here to *ResumeButton*, *SaveGameButton*, *LoadGameButton*, and *QuitButton* as shown below:

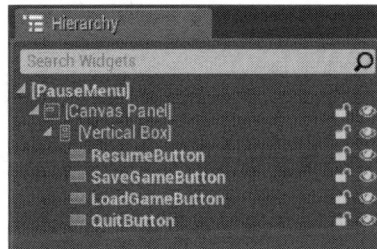

Figure 9.70: Renaming the Buttons in the Hierarchy Panel

One by one, select each button and in the **Details** panel, set its *Padding* to 10.0 and click *Fill* for its *Size* property.

Figure 9.71: Setting Padding and Size Properties

Now the buttons fill up the space in the Vertical Box and have some padding around them. From the **Palette** panel, drag in a Text onto each button. Change the text for the buttons to *Resume*, *Save Game*, *Load Game*, and *Quit*, respectively. The HUD element should appear as follows:

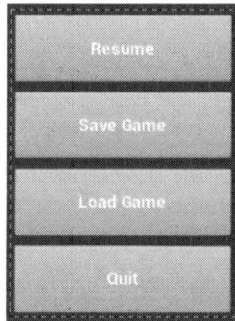

Figure 9.72: Adding Text to the HUD Buttons

We now have a menu HUD element. We can now go into the *MainPlayerController_BP* Blueprint and see the `TSubclassOf` variable *WPause Menu*. We will set it to the *PauseMenu* Widget we created.

Figure 9.73: Selecting the WPause Menu Variable

Now when we press the *Q* or *Escape* key, we wish for our `TogglePauseMenu` function to be called. We simply need to add the following to our `ESCDown` function in *MainCharacter.cpp*.

```
if (MainPlayerController)
{
        MainPlayerController->TogglePauseMenu();
}
```

Now press **Play** and hit the *Q* key (since the *Escape* key will end the PIE session). Notice that the menu shows up and the mouse cursor appears, and you can hover over the buttons and click them. We are now ready to give our buttons functionality.

Adding Resume and Quit Functionality

Adding resume and quit functionality are relatively simple steps. We will cover saving and loading in the next section, *Save Game*.

Binding to the Resume Button

Select the *Resume* button. In the **Details** panel, scroll all the way down to the bottom and in the **Events** section click the + button next to *On Clicked*.

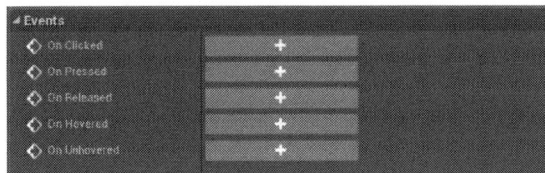

Figure 9.74: Binding Options for the Buttons

You will be taken to **Graph** mode and shown a new event called *On Clicked (ResumeButton)*. Add the following Blueprint Logic:

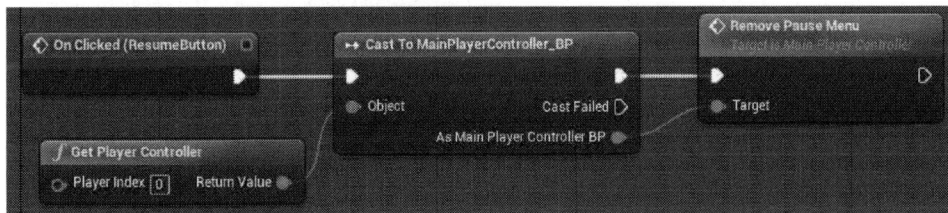

Figure 9.75: Logic for Clicking the Resume Button

We first use the *Get Player Controller* node, then cast its return value to *MainPlayerController_BP*. We get the Controller and call the Blueprint Callable function *RemovePauseMenu*.

Create a binding for the *Quit* button, and for the bound event, add the following logic:

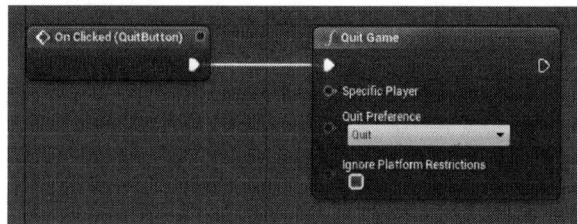

Figure 9.76: Using the Quit Game Node

We use the *Quit Game* node, which does what it sounds like – it causes the game to quit.

Recall that we made our `DisplayPauseMenu` and *RemovePauseMenu* functions Blueprint Native Events. This means that part of our functionality can be in C++ and part of it can be in Blueprints. Let's add some Blueprint functionality to make our menu a bit more fun.

Open *MainPlayerController_BP* and right-click in the **Event Graph** and search for "display pause menu" and select *Event Display Pause Menu*. Do the same for *Event Remove Pause Menu*. These are events that exist because we marked our functions as `BlueprintNativeEvent`. When we call the functions, such as when we called *Remove Pause Menu* in the *Pause Menu* Widget Blueprint, the Blueprint version gets called. The C++ code version doesn't get called unless we make a call to the parent here in the Blueprint. Do so now by right-clicking on *Event Display Pause Menu* and selecting *Add call to parent function*. Do the same for *Event Remove Pause Menu*. Next, add a call to *Play Sound 2D* for each event. For the *Sound* input, select from the dropdown *Camera_Shutter*. *Play Sound 2D* will play a sound when the node function gets called. The Blueprint logic looks as follows:

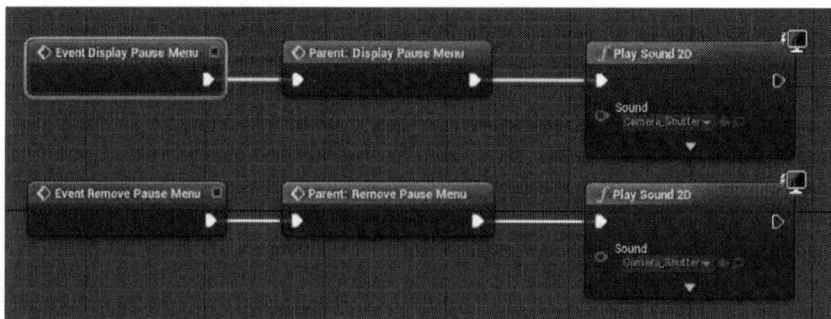

Figure 9.77: Adding Call to Parent and Playing Sound

Now a camera shutter sound will play when calling these functions. Press **Play** and test out the menu!

Next, we are ready to implement saving and loading functionality and binding this to the *Save Game* and *Load Game* buttons in our pause menu.

Save Game

Saving the game is an essential feature of just about every video game. In Unreal Engine, there is an object type called `USaveGame`. We will be creating a class derived from `USaveGame` so that we can store data that will persist between game sessions.

Creating the SaveGame Object

In the **Content Browser**, in *FirstGame*, right-click and select *New C++ Class…* and click the checkbox next to *Show All Classes* (you don't need to be in this folder to create a new C++ class, but we are maneuvering to it to show that once created, new C++ classes appear here). Search for "SaveGame" and select `SaveGame`. Call this class `CountessSaveGame`.

When saving a game, we can specify a player name, as well as a slot. We will create two variables, one of the type `FString` for the player's name, and one of type `uint32` for the player's slot. Add the following to *CountessSaveGame.h*, just under `GENERATED_BODY()`:

```
public:
    UCountessSaveGame();

    UPROPERTY(VisibleAnywhere, Category = Basic)
    FString PlayerName;

    UPROPERTY(VisibleAnywhere, Category = Basic)
    uint32 UserSlot;

    UPROPERTY(VisibleAnywhere, Category = Basic)
    float Health;
```

```
UPROPERTY(VisibleAnywhere, Category = Basic)
float MaxHealth;

UPROPERTY(VisibleAnywhere, Category = Basic)
FVector WorldLocation;

UPROPERTY(VisibleAnywhere, Category = Basic)

FRotator WorldRotation;
```

We created a `public` section and declared the constructor so we can initialize our variables. We created `PlayerName` and `UserSlot` and made them `VisibleAnywhere`. Notice that we gave these variables the Category of `Basic`. **This is not optional!** We must give our variables the Category of `Basic` if we want them to be savable. We also created `float` variables for `Health` and `MaxHealth` so we can save them, as well as an `FVector` for the Character's world location and an `FRotator` for the Character's world rotation. In *CountessSaveGame.cpp*, we will define the constructor:

```
UCountessSaveGame::UCountessSaveGame()
{
    PlayerName = TEXT("Default");
    UserSlot = 0;

}
```

The `USaveGame` class contains functionality for saving and loading the game. We are now ready to use this code in order to save our game and load it.

Creating Functions for Saving and Loading

Now we can create a function to save the game. We will create this function in the `MainCharacter` class. Add the following functions to *MainCharacter.h*, just beneath the declaration for `SetupPlayerInputComponent`:

```
UFUNCTION(BlueprintCallable)
void SaveGame();

UFUNCTION(BlueprintCallable)

void LoadGame();
```

Now we are ready to learn how to actually use the `SaveGame` object. Define the `SaveGame` function in *MainCharacter.cpp* as follows:

```cpp
void AMainCharacter::SaveGame()
{
    UCountessSaveGame* SaveGameInstance =
Cast<UCountessSaveGame>(UGameplayStatics::CreateSaveGameObj
ect(UCountessSaveGame::StaticClass()));

    SaveGameInstance->Health = Health;
    SaveGameInstance->MaxHealth = MaxHealth;

    SaveGameInstance->WorldLocation = GetActorLocation();
    SaveGameInstance->WorldRotation = GetActorRotation();

    UGameplayStatics::SaveGameToSlot(SaveGameInstance,
SaveGameInstance->PlayerName, SaveGameInstance->UserSlot);

}
```

First, we create a new variable of type `UCountessSaveGame*`. Next, we use a `UGameplayStatics` function called `CreateSaveGameObject`. We pass into this function `UCountessSaveGame::StaticClass()`. The `StaticClass()` function is a static function that returns a value of type `UClass`, which is equivalent to a Blueprint type, similar to `TSubclassOf`. We could have created a `TSubclassOf<UCountessSaveGame>` and set it in a Blueprint based on `UCountessSaveGame`. However, we don't need to do that if we simply use `StaticClass`. After creating the new `SaveGame` object, we pass this value into the Cast to `UCountessSaveGame`. We do this because `UGameplayStatics::CreateSaveGameObject` returns a value of type `USaveGame`. Once we cast it to `UCountessSaveGame`, we store it in the variable `SaveGameInstance`.

Important Notes on StaticClass

The `StaticClass` function returns a basic `UClass` value. If you have a C++ class based on `Actor`, for example, `StaticClass` will return a `UClass` based on that C++

class. If you have created a Blueprint based on your class, however, StaticClass will not contain any additional additions you have on that Blueprint. If you wish for a `UClass` variable that contains all of the modifications on a Blueprint, `TSubclassOf` is recommended, so you can select the Blueprint for the class in the `TSubclassOf` dropdown in Blueprints.

Once we have created this `SaveGame` object, we can set its variables. We set its `Health` variable to the Character's `Health`. We do the same for `MaxHealth`. We also use `GetActorLocation` and `GetActorRotation` to set the values of `WorldLocation` and `WorldRotation`, respectively.

Finally, we save the game using the `UGameplayStatics` function `SaveGameToSlot`. This function takes a `USaveGame` object, an `FString` for the player's name, and a `uint32` for the slot. We will simply use the values in the `PlayerName` and `UserSlot` variables, which will have their default values that we set in the `CountessSaveGame` constructor.

And we must `include` the following at the top of *MainCharacter.cpp*:

```
#include "CountessSaveGame.h"
```

```
#include "Kismet/GameplayStatics.h"
```

Now we have a function for saving. For loading, define `LoadGame` as follows:

```
void AMainCharacter::LoadGame()
{
    UCountessSaveGame* LoadGameInstance =
Cast<UCountessSaveGame>(UGameplayStatics::CreateSaveGameObj
ect(UCountessSaveGame::StaticClass()));

    LoadGameInstance =
Cast<UCountessSaveGame>(UGameplayStatics::LoadGameFromSlot(
LoadGameInstance->PlayerName, LoadGameInstance->UserSlot));

    Health = LoadGameInstance->Health;
    MaxHealth = LoadGameInstance->MaxHealth;

    SetActorLocation(LoadGameInstance->WorldLocation);
    SetActorRotation(LoadGameInstance->WorldRotation);
```

```
}
```

We create a `UCountessSaveGame` object using `CreateSaveGameObject`, and again we pass in the value returned by `UCountessSaveGame::StaticClass`. We cast it to `UCountessSaveGame` and store it in the local variable `LoadGameInstance`.

Next, we use `UGameplayStatics::LoadGameFromSlot` to load the game. This function takes an `FString` for the name and a `uint32` for the slot. Since we will be saving the game using the defaults for these variables in the `UCountessSaveGame` class, these are what we will pass in. This function returns the type `USaveGame`, so we cast it to `UCountessSaveGame` and store it back in the `LoadGameInstance` variable, overwriting the value it previously had. Now we can access the variables on this object, which will contain the saved values that were written to it when we saved the game. If we haven't saved the game, they will simply contain their default values. We access `Health` and `MaxHealth` and set these on the Character. We also access `WorldLocation` and `WorldRotation` and use `SetWorldLocation` and `SetWorldRotation` to set these for the Character as well.

Now, all that is left is to actually call these functions. Since we made these `BlueprintCallable`, we can call them from our *PauseMenu* Widget Blueprint. We will do this now.

Calling the Save and Load Functions from the Pause Menu

Now in the *PauseMenu* Widget Blueprint, click on the *SaveGame* button and in the **Details** panel, scroll down to the bottom and in the **Events** section, click the + button next to *On Clicked*. This will create an event for the *SaveGame* button. Do the same for the *LoadGame* button. In the **Event Graph**, you will have events *On Clicked (SaveGameButton)* and *OnClicked (LoadGameButton)*. Add the following Blueprint logic:

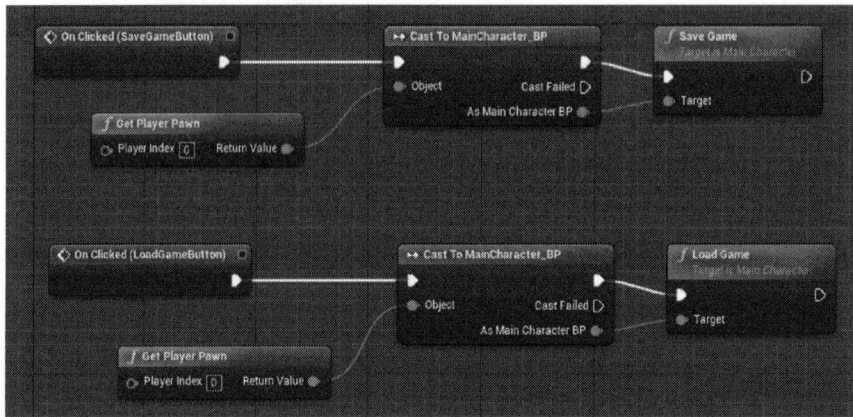

Figure 9.78: Blueprint Logic for Saving and Loading

We use *Get Player Pawn* to get the player pawn, then cast to *MainCharacter_BP*. From there we call our Blueprint Callable Functions `SaveGame` and `LoadGame`. Now when we click the *SaveGame* and *LoadGame* buttons, the `Health`, `MaxHealth`, `WorldLocation`, and `WorldRotation` values should be saved and loaded, respectively.

Now press **Play** and test this out! Run to a location in the world, take note of the health bar value, and press *Q* to bring up the pause menu. Click *Save Game*. Now run to another location, hit a Hazard or health pickup to change the *Health* value, then press *Q* to bring up the pause menu, and press *Load Game*. The Character should go back to the saved location and rotation, and the health bar should go back to its saved value!

Summary

We covered quite a lot in this chapter. First, we learned how to create `Anim Montages` and call the `Montage_Play` function to play animations outside of the *Animation Blueprint*. We learned how to blend animations so that the Character can continue running from the waist down and play the attack animation from the waist up.

We learned about *Anim Notifies*, which create events that will be fired when certain points in an animation are hit. We also learned how to create health pickups and hazards – gameplay mechanics that affect the Character's health in a positive or negative way. This also gives us as developers the ability to create any type of pickup we wish, since we know how to use Overlap Events and can use the `Destroy` function to delete the objects once they are picked up.

We then learned how to create floor switches and doors. We made a `FloorSwitch` class which has both a block switch and a raising door, and we made use of the *Timeline* node to change the values of their elevation with respect to time, according to a smooth curve on the *Timeline Track*.

We also created a Blueprint Native Event, which had partial implementation in C++ and partial implementation in Blueprints. We learned how to add a call to the parent version of it in Blueprints to make sure the C++ portion of the function would run.

We created a pause menu and learned how to pause the game and freeze the controls so that the player could only affect HUD elements while the game was paused. We created buttons on the Widget Blueprint for the pause menu and bound these to events. We learned how to quit and resume the game.

Finally, we learned how to create a `SaveGame` object in order to save information and load it back up, and we did this in Blueprint Callable functions that we bound to the *SaveGame* and *LoadGame* buttons in the pause menu, respectively.

We now have a working game with many of the necessary features common in most video games! We are now ready to continue learning tools for game developers.

In the next chapter, we will learn more about logging, debugging, and an interesting and important topic: **Tracing** – the ability to shoot an invisible line out in a direction and detect if something is hit, causing a Hit Event, then optionally using the results of that Hit Event in some way. We're making great progress!

Chapter 10 – Logging, Debug Tools and Tracing

Logging, debug tools, and tracing are tools a game developer can use while developing a game in order to make sure their code is functioning as it should. Being able to print messages to the **Output Log** or to the screen at certain times or when certain functions are executed can be invaluable. Drawing debug shapes to the screen can provide additional information as well. Tracing is a technique involving shooting out a ray or a shape and detecting whether an object was hit, often providing information regarding the collision such as location, the hit object, the normal vector of the hit surface, and so on. The topics we will cover in this chapter include:

- **UE_LOG and Levels of Verbosity**: We already know how to log warning messages, but there are other types of messages and verbosity levels that allow you to enable or turn off certain types of log messages.

- **Printing Debug Messages and Creating Debug Macros**: Logging messages to the screen at runtime can be extremely useful. Creating macros as shorthand for these functions can speed up development time when needing to use these capabilities.

- **Drawing Debug Shapes**: To be able to draw a shape to the screen in a certain location can be extremely useful to visualize when and where certain actions occur in the world.

- **Performing Ray Traces**: The ability to shoot a laser beam and extract information regarding whether an object was hit can be a very useful tool for developers. We will learn how to do this.

- **Traces of Various Shapes**: Straight line traces aren't the only kind we can do. Other shapes can be traced, and there are different scenarios for using different shapes. We will visit them in this section.

We will now dive into the UE_LOG capabilities and explain verbosity.

Using UE_LOG and Levels of Verbosity

As we have seen, sending messages to the **Output Log** are useful for making sure functions are being called. We have seen that we can also log information to the **Output Log**, showing us data that our code is working with. What we haven't seen yet is that information logged to the **Output Log** is also output into a log file, found in your game folder in *Saved -> Logs*. If you don't know where your game folder is located on your computer, simply open the *Epic Games Launcher*, in *Unreal Engine -> Library*, find your game project's icon, right-click, and select *Show in Folder*.

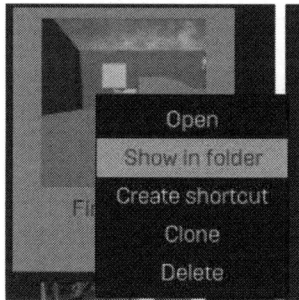

Figure 10.1: Finding the Project's File Location

Depending on the stage of development of your game, and the nature of the information being logged, you may or may not care about certain logs. For this reason, we have **verbosity levels** – levels that control what logs are printed based on their verbosity setting.

Log Type

Take a look at the log we've been using:

```
UE_LOG(LogTemp, Warning, TEXT("BeginOverlap"));
```

The UE_LOG macro takes the Log Type as its first argument. This log has the Log Type called *LogTemp*. You can see it in the **Output Log**:

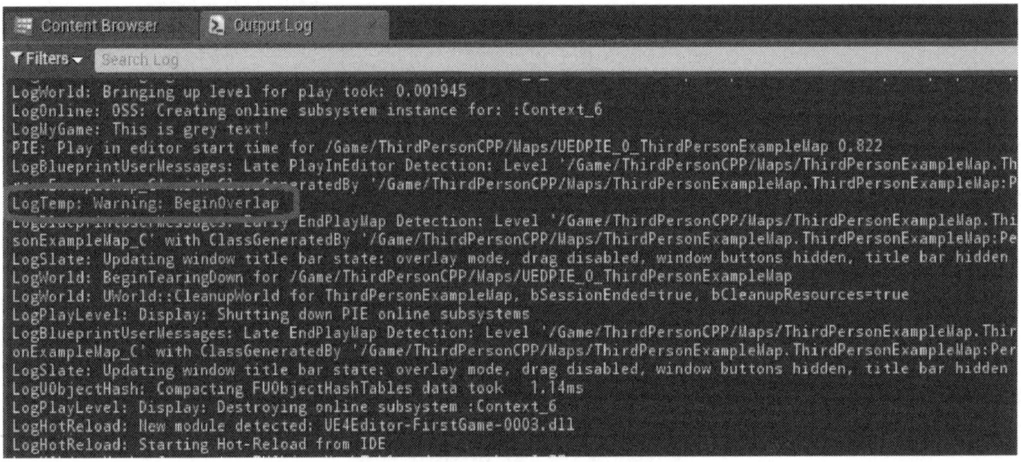

Figure 10.2: Using the LogTemp Logging Type

The first part of this message reads "LogTemp," indicating the Log Type. Notice that this log is surrounded by other logs as well, with their own Log Types: *LogBlueprintUserMessages, LogSlate, LogWorld*, etc.

LogTemp is a temporary logging category. It's used when developing and typically removed when the developer is done using it.

Verbosity

The second argument for the UE_LOG macro is the verbosity. The verbosity of a given log determines whether that log will show up in the **Output Log** or the Log File. verbosity levels include the following:

- **Display**: Logs with Display verbosity are printed to console and log files (activate the console with the tilde (~) key).

- **Log**: Logs with Log verbosity are printed to log files but not the console. You will still see these in the **Output Log**.

- **Warning**: Logs with Warning verbosity are printed to the console and to log files. By default, they appear yellow in the **Output Log**.

- **Error**: Logs with Error verbosity are printed to the console and to log files. By default, they appear red in the **Output Log**.

- **Fatal**: Logs with Error verbosity are printed to the console and to log files. These logs actually crash the game!

- **Verbose**: Logs with Verbose verbosity are printed to log files, but not the console. You will still see these in the **Output Log**.

- **VeryVerbose**: Logs with VeryVerbose verbosity are printed to log files, but not the console. You will still see these in the **Output Log**. These are used for logging more detailed information and typically they spam the output.

Thus far, we have only used the *Warning* verbosity level with the *LogTemp* Log Type. With yellow output text, the log messages are easy to spot among the gray text of the majority of the logging done in the **Output Log**. We can, however, choose any of the above verbosity levels for our Logs. The LogTemp Log Type will not print while using the Verbose or VeryVerbose Verbosity Levels, because these are higher Verbosity Levels than what the LogTemp type is set to. Keep in mind that using Fatal will cause a crash!

We can experiment with the Verbosity Levels by creating our own custom Log Type. We will do this now.

Creating a Custom Log Type

Open *FirstGame.h*. Here, we will define a new Log Type. This way, it will be defined in our other classes, such as `MainCharacter`. In *FirstGame.h*, just under `#include "CoreMinimal.h"`, add:

```
//Countess Log Type

DECLARE_LOG_CATEGORY_EXTERN(CountessLog, Log, All);
```

Now, in *FirstGame.cpp*, add:

```
//Countess Log

DEFINE_LOG_CATEGORY(CountessLog);
```

We have defined our own custom Log Type, called `CountessLog`. In *FirstGame.h*, we used `DECLARE_LOG_CATEGORY_EXTERN` to declare it. This macro takes three arguments. The first is the name of the custom Log Type. The second is the Default

Verbosity. This argument will determine what level of Verbosity will be printed to the log in game. The third argument is Compile Time Verbosity. Logs that do not fit within this Verbosity will not even compile into the code!

Let's see how these settings work. In *MainCharacter.cpp*, in `BeginPlay`, add the following:

```
    UE_LOG(CountessLog, VeryVerbose, TEXT("CountessLog
VeryVerbose"));
    UE_LOG(CountessLog, Verbose, TEXT("CountessLog
Verbose"));
    UE_LOG(CountessLog, Warning, TEXT("CountessLog
Warning"));
    UE_LOG(CountessLog, Display, TEXT("CountessLog
Display"));
    UE_LOG(CountessLog, Log, TEXT("CountessLog Log"));
    UE_LOG(CountessLog, Error, TEXT("CountessLog Error"));

    //UE_LOG(CountessLog, Fatal, TEXT("CountessLog Fatal -
This will crash the game!"));
```

We have used UE_LOG, specifying CountessLog as the Log Type. We use each of the above listed verbosities (commenting out the Fatal one, since we don't want our game to crash). Compiling and pressing **Play** results in the following printed to the **Output Log**:

CountessLog: Warning: CountessLog Warning
CountessLog: Display: CountessLog Display
CountessLog: CountessLog Log
CountessLog: Error: CountessLog Error

Figure 10.3: Printing Warning, Display, Log, and Error Log Types

In our declaration for CountessLog in *FirstGame.h*, we set our Compile Time Verbosity to All, meaning Logs of all Verbosities will compile into the code. However, we set the Default Verbosity to Log, which is lower than Verbose. VeryVerbose, of course, is even higher than Verbose. So all logs of higher Verbosity than Log will not be printed. This is why we do not see the "Verbose" and "VeryVerbose" log messages in **Figure 10.3**.

Now, go back into *FirstGame.h* and change the CountessLog declaration to:

```
DECLARE_LOG_CATEGORY_EXTERN(CountessLog, Verbose, All);
```

Compile and run the game again. The **Output Log** will now contain:

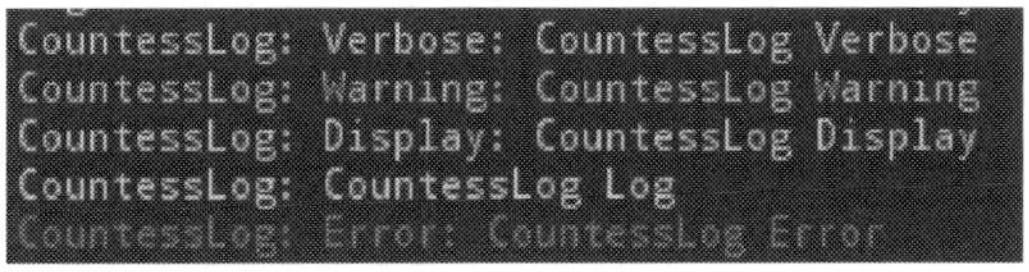

Figure 10.4: Adding Verbose to the Countess Log

If you don't see the above results, you might need to close the Unreal Engine editor and reopen it after a fresh compile. Notice that we get the Verbose Log, but not the VeryVerbose Log. This is of course because VeryVerbose is more verbose than Verbose. Now, change the `CountessLog` declaration to:

```
DECLARE_LOG_CATEGORY_EXTERN(CountessLog, VeryVerbose, All);
```

And now we get the following printed to the Output Log:

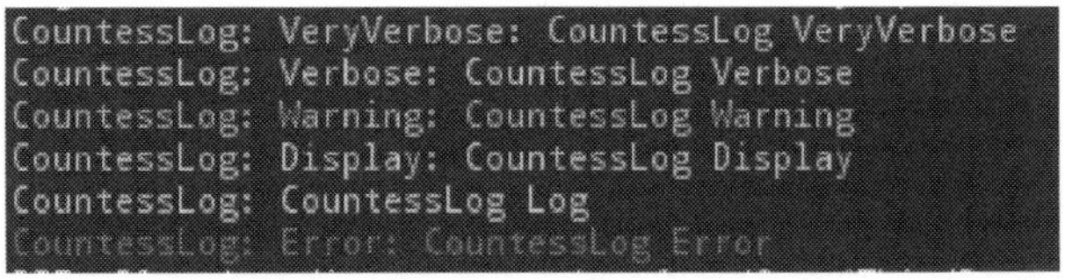

Figure 10.5: Adding VeryVerbose to the Countess Log

This is because we have raised the Verbosity for `CountessLog` to VeryVerbose, allowing for Logs declared with the verbosity level of VeryVerbose to be printed.

Now we can see the results of changing the Compile Time Verbosity. Change the declaration of `CountessLog` to:

```
DECLARE_LOG_CATEGORY_EXTERN(CountessLog, VeryVerbose, Log);
```

And now we see that in the Output Log we get:

Figure 10.6: Output Log with Log Level Compile Time Verbosity

This is because with the Compile Time Verbosity set to Log, Verbose and VeryVerbose logs don't even get compiled into the code. Setting the Compile Time Verbosity to Verbose will allow Verbose log messages, and setting it to VeryVerbose will allow VeryVerbose log messages.

We now understand the different Log Types and verbosities. We saw that warnings print yellow to the **Output Log** and errors print red. We saw how we could create our own custom Log Type and set its Default Verbosity and Compile Time Verbosity in order to control which logs of that type get printed based on their individual verbosities.

Logging to the **Output Log and** the game's Log File is useful. However, sometimes it's desired to print text to the game screen while playing. For this, we can print debug messages. We will dive into these now.

Printing Debug Messages and Creating Debug Macros

The class UEngine contains a function for adding debug messages to the screen. Actors inherit the variable GEngine, which can be used to call this function. It is used as follows. Place the following in *MainCharacter.cpp*, in BeginPlay:

```
if (GEngine)
{
        GEngine->AddOnScreenDebugMessage(-1, 1.5f,
FColor::Blue, TEXT("Printing a message to the screen!"),
false);

}
```

Depending on your version of Unreal Engine, you may need the following includes (Intellisense will happily remind you that the UEngine class is undefined if you need them):

```
#include "EngineGlobals.h"
```

```
#include "Engine/Engine.h"
```

The function AddOnScreenDebugMessage takes several arguments. The first is the Key. If the integer passed in is a positive number, only one message using that particular key will show on the screen at a time. This is useful for avoiding spamming the screen with messages. If -1 is passed in, the message will print to the screen regardless of whether or not messages using the -1 key are already displayed. Each new message pushes the previous message down by a line when it is printed. The second `float` parameter is the Time to Display and is in seconds. The third parameter is of type `FColor`, a `struct` representing a color. The `FColor struct` contains several variables corresponding to basic colors and you can see them all in *Color.h*. The next parameter of `FString` type is the Debug Message. You can simply pass in a `TEXT` macro as we did, or you can create an `FString` and pass it in. We will do this shortly. The final argument we passed in is a Boolean for whether the newer messages should show up on top, pushing older messages below it, or show up under older messages. This argument has the default value of `true`, so it can be omitted if `false` is not the desired value.

Pressing **Play** with the above code results in the following:

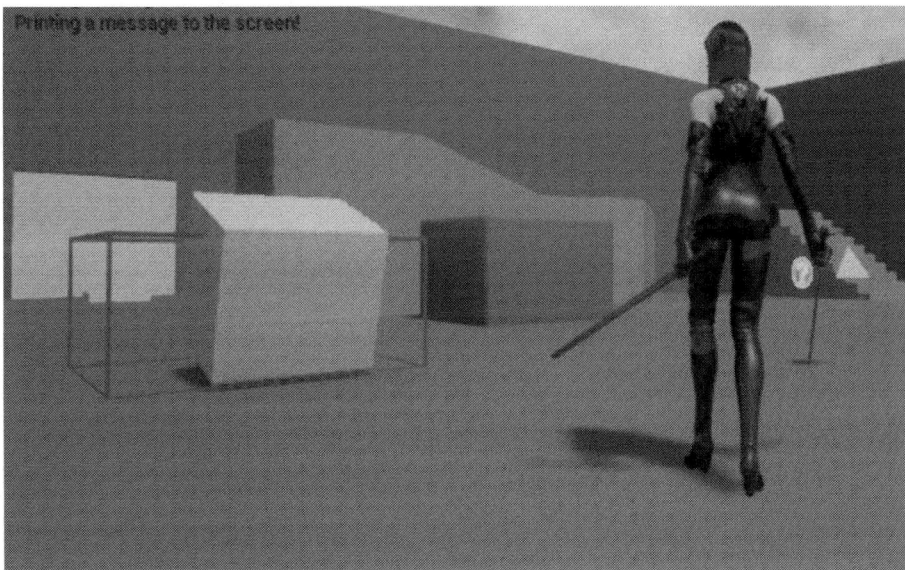

Figure 10.7: Printing a Message to the Screen

Now we will see the results of using a key value other than -1. Add the following to *MainCharacter.cpp*, in `Tick`:

```
if (GEngine)
```

```
        {
                FString Print = FString::Printf(TEXT("DeltaTime:
%f"), DeltaTime);
                GEngine->AddOnScreenDebugMessage(1, 1.5f,
FColor::Cyan, Print, false);

        }
```

Here, we create an FString called Print. Next, we use the static function Printf in FString to create an FString formatted with data using an escape sequence. We use a float, and pass in DeltaTime for its value. The result is a string containing the text "DeltaTime: " followed by the numerical value of DeltaTime converted to a string of characters. We pass this into AddOnScreenDebugMessage, using a key value of 1 and a color of Cyan. We use a value of 1.5f for the time, but this doesn't matter, because each new message will remove any previous messages with the key value of 1. Since this function will be called each frame, each message will be removed when it has been on the screen for the full 1.5 seconds. Compile and press **Play** and notice that we are given the value of DeltaTime for any given frame it is changing rapidly, as the value of DeltaTime varies each frame.

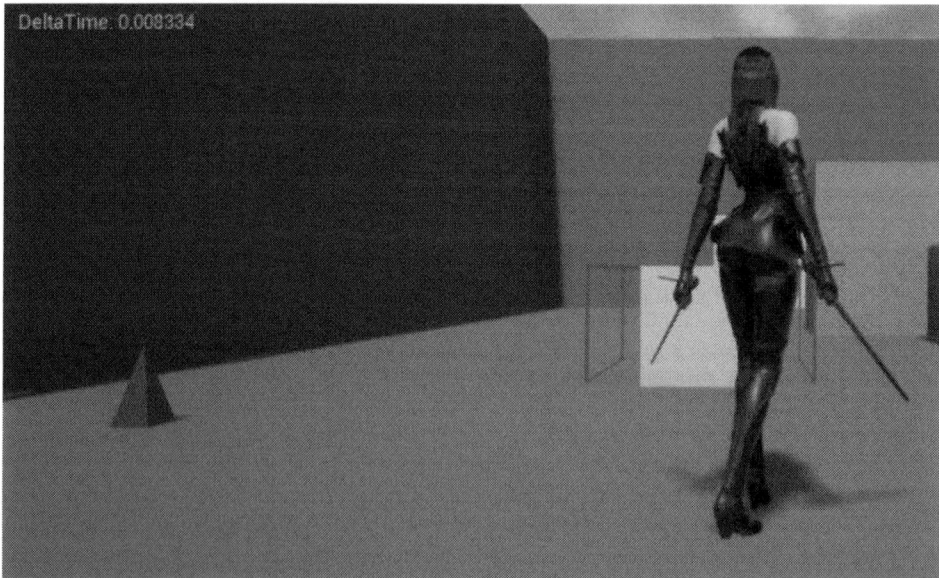

Figure 10.8: Printing DeltaTime each frame

Now we can look at how to create macros in order to provide ourselves with a way to print debug messages to the screen without the need to write so much code each time. Add the following to *FirstGame.h*:

```
#define print(Text) if (GEngine) GEngine-
>AddOnScreenDebugMessage(-1, 2.0f, FColor::White,
TEXT(Text), false)

#define print_k(Key, Text) if (GEngine) GEngine-
>AddOnScreenDebugMessage(Key, 2.0f, FColor::White,
TEXT(Text))

#define printf(Format, ...) if (GEngine) GEngine-
>AddOnScreenDebugMessage(-1, 2.0f, FColor::White,
FString::Printf(TEXT(Format), ##__VA_ARGS__), false)

#define printf_k(Key, Format, ...) if (GEngine) GEngine-
>AddOnScreenDebugMessage(Key, 1.5f, FColor::White,
FString::Printf(TEXT(Format), ##__VA_ARGS__))

#define warn(Text) if (GEngine) GEngine-
>AddOnScreenDebugMessage(-1, 2.0f, FColor::Yellow,
TEXT(Text), false)

#define warn_k(Key, Text) if (GEngine) GEngine-
>AddOnScreenDebugMessage(Key, 2.0f, FColor::Yellow,
TEXT(Text))

#define warnf(Format, ...) if (GEngine) GEngine-
>AddOnScreenDebugMessage(-1, 2.0f, FColor::Yellow,
FString::Printf(TEXT(Format), ##__VA_ARGS__), false)

#define warnf_k(Key, Format, ...) if (GEngine) GEngine-
>AddOnScreenDebugMessage(Key, 2.0f, FColor::Yellow,
FString::Printf(TEXT(Format), ##__VA_ARGS__))
```

These are just a few examples of how you can compact the code into a simple macro for ease of use. The first macro, `print`, takes a single argument called `Text`, which can be a simple string literal. It is passed into the `TEXT` macro, so this eliminates the need to even use TEXT while calling the print macro. AddOnScreenDebugMessage is passed -1 for the Key, 2.0f for the Time to Display, White for the Display Color, and false for allowing newer messages to appear on top.

The second macro, print_k, takes a Key argument first, allowing you to choose a value for the key.

In the third macro, printf, the first parameter is a formatted string, and the second is a variable number of arguments. Using an ellipsis for a variable number of macro arguments makes this a **Variadic Macro** – a macro with a variable number of arguments. When calling this function with multiple arguments, they must be passed in the form of a comma-separated list. Then, in the macro's definition, notice the presence of ##VA__ARGS__. This gets replaced with the comma-separated list of arguments when the macro is called.

Thus we can pass in a string using escape sequences, followed by the values used for those escape sequences, as will be seen in the following example.

Finally, printf_k is the same as printf, except it also takes a key.

The warn, warn_k, warnf, and warnf_k macros are identical to print, print_k, printf, and printf_k respectively in every way except in their color, which is Yellow.

Add the following to BeginPlay in *MainCharacter.cpp*:

```
print("Use of print macro");

print_k(2, "You will only see one of these print_k
messages!");
print_k(2, "You will only see one of these print_k
messages!");
print_k(2, "You will only see one of these print_k
messages!");
print_k(2, "You will only see one of these print_k
messages!");


printf("Formatting the string with Actor Name: %s",
*GetName());
```

And in Tick, replace the proper debug message code with the following:

```
printf_k(1, "DeltaTime: %f", DeltaTime);
```

Now compile and press **Play**. You should see something like the following:

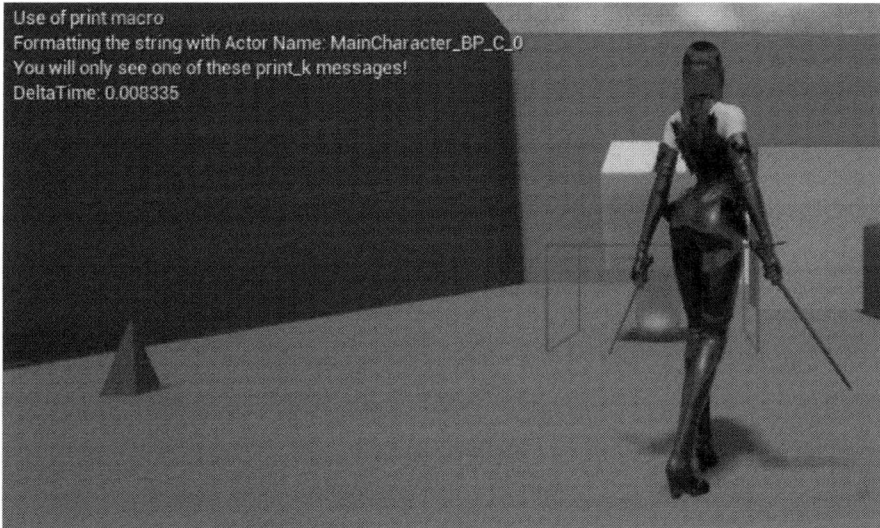

Figure 10.9: Using the Print Macros

Our first call to the `print` macro results in the top line in **Figure 10.9**. The call to `printf` results in the second line. Notice we only get one of the messages printing "You will only see one of these print_k messages!" because they all have the key value of 2, so each message with a value of 2 replaces any other on the screen with that key. And finally, the call to `printf_k` in `Tick` results in the fourth line, showing `DeltaTime`. Since we used a key value of 1, each frame the message is replaced by a new one showing the current value of `DeltaTime`. If the key had a value of -1, the messages would spam the screen rather than replace one another.

Using the warn macros is left as an exercise to the reader.

Now we have an understanding of debug messages, as well as how to create macros to make our lives easier when developing, reducing the amount of typing we need to do in order to print messages to the screen. But aside from messages, shapes can be extremely useful to show in our world. Next we will visit how to draw some debug shapes in 3D space, adding even more development tools to our toolbox!

Drawing Debug Shapes

The ability to draw debug shapes can come in handy when you wish to know when and where particular gameplay functionality occurs. In order to access debug drawing functions in Unreal Engine, we must include the following header:

```
#include "DrawDebugHelpers.h"
```

Now the debug drawing functions will be available for use.

Drawing a Debug Point

We will begin by drawing a single debug point. In *MainCharacter.cpp*, add the following to the `Tick` function:

```
DrawDebugPoint(GetWorld(), GetActorLocation() +
FVector(0.f, 0.f, 50.f), 5.f, FColor::Blue, false, 3.f);
```

`DrawDebugPoint` draws a single point in space.

- The first argument passed in is a `UWorld` object, which can be accessed via `GetWorld`.

- The next argument is the location at which you wish to draw the point. Here, we are passing in `GetActorLocation + FVector(0.f, 0.f, 50.f)` to get the location of the Character, plus 50 units in the Z direction to lift it up a bit (otherwise, we would pretty much be using the location of the Character's crotch).

- The next parameter is the size of the point. We passed in 5.f to create a decent-sized point.

- Next is the color, for which we used `FColor::Blue`.

- The next parameter is a Boolean for whether to drawn the point persistently. If `true`, the point will continue to be drawn to the screen each frame. If `false`, the point will disappear after a specified time.

- The final parameter we passed in is that time. We chose `3.f`, so the point will disappear after 3 seconds.

Compile and press **Play**, and run around in the world.

Figure 10:10: Debug Points Drawn at the Character's Location

See that the Character is followed by a trail of blue points being drawn each frame and disappearing after 3 seconds.

Drawing a Debug Line

Next, we will draw a line, rather than a single point. Add the following to `AMainCharacter`'s `Tick` function:

```
DrawDebugLine(GetWorld(), FVector(0.f, 0.f, 400.f),
GetActorLocation(), FColor::Red, false, -1.f);
```

- The first argument is the `UWorld` object, similarly to that in `DrawDebugPoint`.

- The second argument is the starting location for the line.

- The third argument is the ending location for the line. We start the line at the point `(0.f, 0.f, 400.f)` and we end it at the Character's location.

- The next argument is the color for the line. We chose red.

- Next we have the Boolean for whether we with the line to be drawn persistently or to disappear after a specified time.

- The last argument is the time to draw the line. A value of `−1.f` means the line will disappear after a single frame.

The final two parameters we entered actually have default values of `false` and `−1.f` in fact, so we could have omitted them.

Now press **Play** and notice that a line is drawn from `(0.f, 0.f, 400.f)` to the Character's location and updates each frame.

Drawing a Debug Circle

Say we would like to see a target at a particular pickup item location after we picked it up. We can easily do this by drawing a debug circle. Add the following to the top of *HealthPickup.cpp*:

```
#include "DrawDebugHelpers.h"
```

And add this in the `OnOverlapBegin` function:

```
DrawDebugCircle(GetWorld(), GetActorLocation(), 25,
50, FColor::Red, false, 5.f, 0, 1.f);
```

First, we pass in the `UWorld` object. Next, we pass in the location where we would like to see the circle. Here, we use the pickup's location using `GetActorLocation`. The third parameter is the circle radius, and we chose a radius of 25. Next is the number of segments for the circle. A lower number gives a more jagged circle. Next is the color, for which we chose red. Then we have the Boolean for whether we want persistent lines. We chose `false`, and next passed in the time for the circle to persist, for which we chose 5 seconds. The next is a Depth Priority number. This can place the render debug into a different priority for rendering. For example, placing one debug shape in 2 and another in 3 will result in the shape in 3 being seen in front of the one in 2. We can use 0 if we don't care about one shape being rendered with priority over any other.

Compile, press **Play**, then pick up some of the health pickups. Circles will be drawn in the locations where the pickups were.

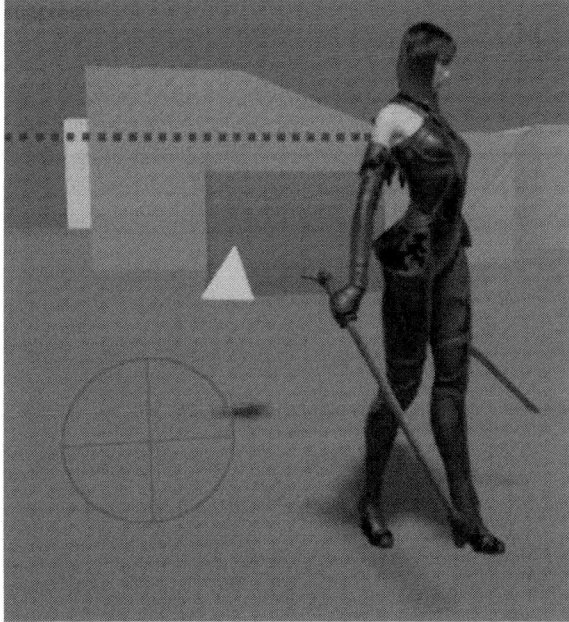

Figure 10.11: Drawing a Debug Circle

Circles are useful, but debug spheres can also be used, if a 3D shape is desired.

Drawing a Debug Sphere

Next, we will draw a debug sphere. We can place spheres where the hazard pickups are picked up, and circles where the health pickups are picked up, using a simple `if` check in `OnOverlapBegin` for *HealthPickup.cpp*:

```
if (HealingAmount >= 0.f)
{
        DrawDebugCircle(GetWorld(), GetActorLocation(),
25, 50, FColor::Red, false, 5.f, 0, 1.f);
}
else
{
```

```
        DrawDebugSphere(GetWorld(), GetActorLocation(),
25.f, 12, FColor::Red, false, 5.f, 0, 2.f);
    }
```

We check `HealingAmount`, and if it's positive, we draw a circle, and if it's negative, we draw a sphere. For `DrawDebugSphere`:

- The first argument, like the previous debug functions, is the `UWorld` object.

- The second is the location for the sphere, for which we used the Actor's location.

- The third is the radius of the sphere, for which we chose `25.f`.

- Next is the number of segments. We chose 12, but you can change this to get a more or less rounded sphere.

- Next is the color, for which we chose red.

- Then we have the persistent lines Boolean, which we set to `false`.

- We then have our time to draw the sphere, and we set this to 5 seconds.

- We set the Depth Priority to 0.

- Finally, our last argument is the line thickness. We chose 2, but you can experiment with this for thicker or thinner lines.

Press **Play** and pick up some health pickups and hazards and see the difference.

Figure 10.12: Drawing a Debug Sphere

In addition to drawing debug spheres, you can draw other shapes, such as cubes. When you type "DrawDebug..." in Visual Studio, the Intellisense feature will show you more functions that start with those characters.

Figure 10.13: Intellisense Showing Other Debug Functions

Drawing other debug shapes is left as an exercise to the reader.

Now we are able to draw debug shapes during our game. This can help us when developing code. Next, we are ready to learn about traces and how they can be used while developing.

Performing Ray Traces

The ability to line trace allows for various types of functionality in video games. Shooter games have used the line trace as a method to simulate gun shots. A line is fired from a location in a certain direction and if it hits anything, an explosion can occur, a bullet hole can appear, or blood effects can splatter at that location. Line traces are useful for developers, so we will learn how to trace lines and gather information if the line hits something.

Line Trace Single by Channel

One function built into Unreal Engine is `UWorld::LineTraceSingleByChannel`. This line trace shoots a ray into space and collides based on a chosen **Trace Channel**. Recall from *Chapter 8 – Collision* that you can select an Object Type for the object in its *Collision* settings in the **Details** panel. The default options are *WorldStatic*, *WorldDynamic*, *Pawn*, *PhysicsBody*, *Vehicle*, and *Destructible*.

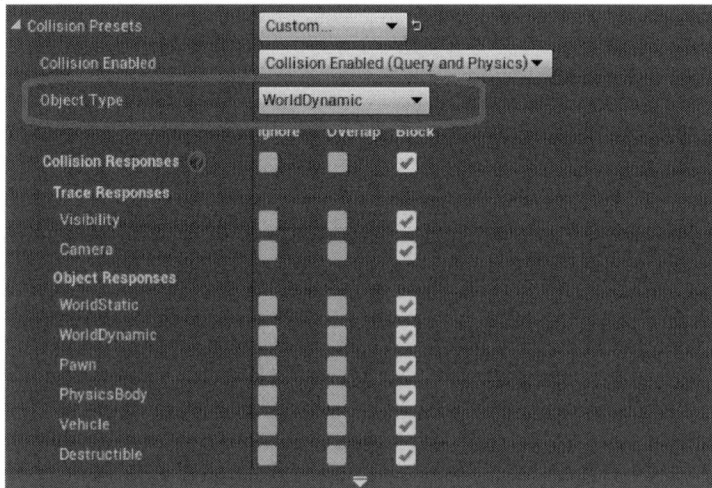

Figure 10.14: The Collision Channel

In C++, these are enum constants in the ECollisionChannel enum. When we perform a line trace, our ray will have a Collision Channel assigned to it. Then, we can have our individual objects in the world set to either ignore or block that channel depending on whether we want the trace to hit them. Since objects might be configured to ignore, overlap, or block other types of objects already, a special Trace Channel can be used (if you don't wish to use the others) called *Visibility*. We will use this channel with our line trace. In *MainCharacter.cpp*, add the following code to Tick:

```
FHitResult HitResult;
FVector Start = GetActorLocation() + FVector(0.f, 0.f,
75.f);
FVector End = Start + GetActorForwardVector() * 500.f;
FCollisionQueryParams CollisionQueryParams;
CollisionQueryParams.AddIgnoredActor(this);
GetWorld()->LineTraceSingleByChannel(HitResult, Start,
End, ECollisionChannel::ECC_Visibility,
CollisionQueryParams);

if (HitResult.bBlockingHit)
{
        DrawDebugSphere(GetWorld(), HitResult.Location,
15.f, 12, FColor::Red, false, 5.f);

}
```

Notice that the function LineTraceSingleByChannel takes several parameters. The first is of type FHitResult. Recall from *Chapter 8 – Collision* that the *FHitResult* struct can be used for Hit Events, storing data about the even such as the hit location and the hit Actor. We create an FHitResult called HitResult. We also create a Start and End vector to determine the starting and ending locations for the line trace. The function also takes an object of type FCollisionQueryParams as an optional parameter that can specify details about the collision query, such as Actors to ignore. We use its built-in function AddIgnoredActor, which can take a pointer to the Actor you wish for the query to ignore. The Unreal Engine documentation site shows the other functions belonging to this struct, including *AddIgnoredActors*, which allows you to supply a *TArray* of Actor pointers.

Next, we call `GetWorld` to get the `UWorld` object, then use it to call `LineTraceSingleByChannel`. We first pass in `HitResult`, then `Start`, `End`, the Collision Channel selection (we chose `ECC_Visibility`), and finally, `CollisionQueryParams`. Since we are calling this function in `Tick`, we will be performing the line trace every frame, shooting the ray outward from `Start` to `End`. If anything is hit, it must be set to block the `ECC_Visibility` Collision Channel, otherwise nothing will happen.

The `HitResult` has a Boolean called `bBlockingHit`, which we check in an `if` statement. This Boolean will only be `true` if a hit was achieved, which is why the function `DrawDebugSphere` is not being called when the line trace hits the second and third cubes.

We will test our code now.

In the Unreal Engine editor, in the **Content Browser**, in *Content -> StarterContent -> Shapes*, drag in three *Shape_Cubes*.

Figure 10.15: The Shape_Cubes

Select the first one and in the **Details** panel, under *Collision*, notice that the *Collision Response* for *Visibility* is set to *Block*. Select the second *Shape_Cube* and set the *Collision Response* for *Visibility* to *Overlap*. Select the third *Shape_Cube* and set the *Collision Response* for *Visibility* to *Ignore*.

Now, press **Play** and run up to the blocks and face them, one by one, with the Character. You will find that the line trace only works with the first *Shape_Cube*, which is set to block the *Visibility* channel.

Figure 10.16: Line Trace Hitting the First Cube Only

This is a good example of when being able to draw debug shapes comes in handy. If we weren't drawing the debug sphere, we would not know whether or not the trace hit was successful. We can also use debug lines to visualize the line trace as well.

Notice that when the Character faces one of the *Shape_Cube* objects that is set to either *Overlap* or *Ignore* the *Visibility* channel, there will be no successful hit.

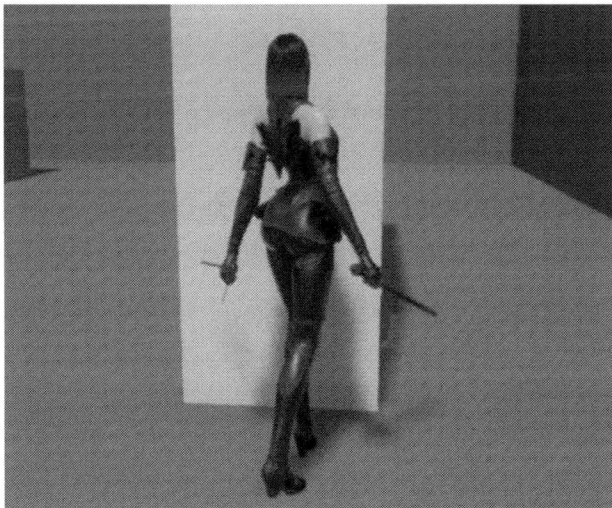

Figure 10.17: Line Trace Not Getting a Hit

This is because we are only doing a single trace, hence the name
`LineTraceSingleByChannel`. However, there exists a function that will continue
shooting a ray through objects until it hits an object set to block its channel. We will visit
this function now.

Line Trace Multi By Channel

This function will perform a line trace and if the first object hit is not set to trigger a hit,
the ray will continue firing through subsequent objects. The Hit Results will be stored in
a `TArray`. We will use this function now. First comment out the
`LineTraceSingleByChannel` function call:

```
//GetWorld()->LineTraceSingleByChannel(HitResult,
Start, End, ECollisionChannel::ECC_Visibility,
CollisionQueryParams);
```

And add the following in the `AMainCharacter` `Tick` function:

```
TArray<FHitResult> HitResults;
GetWorld()->LineTraceMultiByChannel(HitResults, Start,
End, ECollisionChannel::ECC_Visibility);
for (int32 i = 0; i < HitResults.Num(); i++)
{
    if (HitResults[i].bBlockingHit)
    {
        FString ActorName = HitResults[i].Actor-
>GetName();
        printf_k(i, "%d Actor Name: %s", i,
*ActorName);
    }
    else
    {
        printf_k(i, "%d Failed hit!", i);
    }
}
```

First, we create a `TArray` to hold `FHitResult` objects, called `HitResults`. Next,
we call `LineTraceMultiByChannel`, passing in this `TArray` as the first argument.
After the function call, it will be filled in with information. Next we pass in `Start`, `End`,
and the Trace Channel. Then, we create a `for` loop, looping through the number of

elements in `HitResults` by calling `TArray`'s `Num` function, which returns the number of elements in the array. For each element, we first check to see if its `bBlockingHit` Boolean is true. If it is, we create an `FString` called `ActorName`, then get the array element and access the hit `Actor`. We call the Actor function `GetName` to get that `Actor`'s name, and we store it in `ActorName`. We then use one of our debug macros we created earlier, `printf_k`. We supply a key, for which we use `i`, the current index for the array element. Then we provide a formatted string, using the escape sequence `%d`, to provide an integer, and `%s`, to provide a string. The integer is the array index, and the string is the `FString ActorName`, using the * overload, which returns a string of characters, which is what `printf_k` needs. The result will be that the hit Actor's name will be printed to the screen. Press **Play** and have the Character face the cubes from the side of the cube set to ignore the *Visibility* Trace Channel.

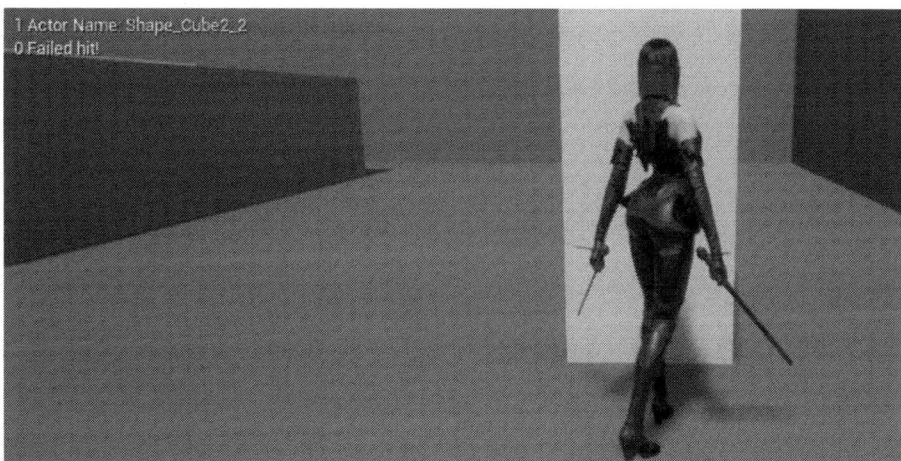

Figure 10.18: Tracing Through Objects

We see that the first element in the array, with index 0, was a failed hit. This is because the line trace is first hitting the cube set to ignore the *Visibility* Trace Channel. Then, we see that we get an Actor's name printed, *Shape_Cube2_2* (yours might be named differently). This is because the trace continued casting until it found something to hit (within the length of the line defined by `Start` and `End`). Now we see the usefulness of the `LineTraceMultiByChannel` function! We can detect whether or not failed hits have occurred, and can continue casting through objects until a successful hit was achieved.

There exist similar functions which trace for Object Types rather than Trace Channels. These can be found in the Unreal Engine documentation, and are called `LineTraceSingleForObjects` and `LineTraceMultiForObjects` and work similarly to the above functions, only they trace for Object Types. These are left as exercises for the reader if interested.

Not only can we use line traces to detect collisions, but we can also trace using shapes. We will visit this functionality now.

Traces of Various Shapes

A trace doesn't have to be a simple line. Sphere, capsule and box traces are also possible. We will begin with a box trace. This time, rather than tracing by channel, we will trace by Object Type to get some practice with that method.

Box Trace Single For Objects

When tracing for objects, we must supply a list of Object Types to trace for. For this purpose, there exists an `enum` called `EObjectTypeQuery`. There are 32 `enum` constants in this `enum` to choose from, and the majority are available to assign custom Object Types to. However the first few correspond to the Object Types that we are familiar with.

Comment out the line trace we did above:

```
//GetWorld()->LineTraceMultiByChannel(HitResults,
Start, End, ECollisionChannel::ECC_Visibility);
```

And add the following:

```
TArray<TEnumAsByte<EObjectTypeQuery>> ObjectTypes;
ObjectTypes.Add(EObjectTypeQuery::ObjectTypeQuery2);
TArray<AActor*> ActorsToIgnore;
ActorsToIgnore.Add(this);
FHitResult BoxTraceResult;
UKismetSystemLibrary::BoxTraceSingleForObjects(GetWorl
d(), Start, End, FVector(32.f, 32.f, 32.f), FRotator(),
```

```
ObjectTypes, true, ActorsToIgnore,
EDrawDebugTrace::ForOneFrame, BoxTraceResult, true,
FColor::Red, FColor::Blue);
    if (BoxTraceResult.bBlockingHit)
    {
        print_k(1, "Blocking Hit!");

    }
```

First, we create a TArray of Object Type Queries. Notice that we use TEnumAsByte, because this is the form the enum must be in for this function. There's no need to worry about converting an enum to a TEnumAsByte. Simply adding an enum constant to the TArray will suffice; the conversion is done implicitly. TEnumAsByte allows an enum constant to take up only a single byte of storage. We add an enum constant to our ObjectTypes array in this manner. Notice that the enum constants in EObjectTypeQuery aren't very descriptive. The Object Types of the first few enum constants correspond to the following Object Types:

- **ObjectTypeQuery1**: *World Static*

- **ObjectTypeQuery2**: *World Dynamic*

- **ObjectTypeQuery3**: *Pawn*

- **ObjectTypeQuery4**: *Physics Body*

- **ObjectTypeQuery5**: *Destructible*

- **ObjectTypeQuery6**: First Custom Object Type

- **ObjectTypeQuery7**: Second Custom Object Type...

We added ObjectTypeQuery2, which corresponds to *World Dynamic*. Thus our box trace will only trace for *World Dynamic* Object Types.

Next, we created a TArray<AAActor*> to specify Actors to ignore. We add the this pointer so that the trace will ignore our Character. We create an FHitResult called BoxHitResult for storing the result of a possible hit.

Next, we call the function
`UKismetSystemLibrary::BoxTraceSingleForObjects`.

- The first argument is the `UWorld` object.

- The second is the starting location for the trace. We simply use our `Start` variable, since we aren't concerned with the trace hitting our Character.

- Next is the end location of the trace, for which we use our `End` variable.

- Next is the Box Half Size. You can adjust these values to change the shape of the box.

- The next argument is an `FRotator`, which determines the orientation of the box. We simply supply the default `FRotator` constructor, which creates an `FRotator` with `0.f` for each component.

- Next is the Object Types array.

- After that comes a Boolean for whether or not to trace against complex geometry. We set it to true, meaning that the trace will be performed against the complex geometry of a mesh, rather than its collision hull.

- The next argument is the Actors to Ignore array.

- Then, we have an argument of type `EDrawDebugTrace`. This allows us to optionally draw a debug shape for our trace so that we can see it without needing to call any debug drawing functions. We used the `enum` constant `EDrawDebugTrace::ForOneFrame` to draw the trace for a single frame, since we are calling this function in `Tick`. The choices are: `ForOneFrame`, `ForDuration`, `None`, and `Persistent`. `ForDuration` enables the trace to persist for a specified time. `None` means no debug shapes will be drawn. `Persistent` means the debug shapes will persist in the world.

- Next we have the `BoxTraceResult`.

- The last two arguments are `FColors`. The first is the Trace Color, which will be used to draw the box. The next is the Trace Hit Color, used to show the point of the hit. There is an optional parameter for the time duration, but since we are drawing for a single frame, we can omit it and allow it to have its default value.

We check to see if we have a blocking hit, and if we do, we use our `print_k` function to print to the screen, indicating we have a hit.

Now we can press **Play** and watch our box trace hit objects in the world depending on their Object Type!

Figure 10.19: Box Tracing By Object

The other shape traces are done in the same way, and when filling in the parameters in the function call, Intellisense will remind you of all the parameters you need as well as their types.

```
bool BoxTraceSingleForObjects(UObject *WorldContextObject, const FVector Start, const FVector End, const FVector HalfSize,
        const FRotator Orientation, const TArray<TEnumAsByte<EObjectTypeQuery>> &ObjectTypes, bool bTraceComplex,
        const TArray<AActor *> &ActorsToIgnore, EDrawDebugTrace::Type DrawDebugType, FHitResult &OutHit, bool bIgnoreSelf,
        FLinearColor TraceColor = FLinearColor::Red, FLinearColor TraceHitColor = FLinearColor::Green, float DrawTime = (5.0F))
```

Figure 10.20: Intellisense Showing the Input Parameters for the Function

The remaining shape trace functions are left as exercises for the reader.

Summary

In this chapter, we gained some important skills that game developers use when creating video games. We learned about UE_LOG and the various levels of verbosity, and how they can be used to filter out logs based on their Verbosity Levels. We learned how to print debug messages to the screen and a useful way to create macros to shorten the amount of code necessary to call these functions. We learned how to draw debug shapes so that we can visualize when certain functions get called (or fail to get called). We learned about ray traces and how they can cast a straight line into the world and return information if an object is hit. We saw that traces can stop after hitting a single object or they can go through multiple objects until a successful hit was achieved. We then learned that traces can take the form of other shapes, and we examined this by using the box shape trace. We learned that we could trace for specific Object Types, and that the trace would ignore all other objects except the designated types.

This chapter has given us many tools that can be used to make sure our code is running correctly. Next, we will dive into Delegates and Interfaces – two coding techniques that allow us to communicate between classes in order to orchestrate more complex gameplay logic.

Chapter 11 – Delegates and Interfaces

In most video games, classes often need to communicate with one another. This is in fact true for most complicated programs in general. There are three main ways classes can communicate between one another in the game:

- **Direct Class Communication**: We discuss direct class communication. This occurs when an object of a class has a direct reference to another object and is able to call functions on it.

- **Delegates**: We learn what Delegates are and how they can be used to broadcast signals out which other objects can listen for and respond to.

- **Interfaces**: This third method of class communication involves the use of **multiple inheritance** – a class inheriting from more than one parent. We can create an Interface class with function declarations in it, and the class that inherits from it will inherit those functions, and be free to define them.

Each of these methods can be more useful depending on the situation.

Direct Class Communication

Direct Class Communication is perhaps the simplest way for classes to communicate with one another. In order to perform this type of communication, an object must have a reference to another in order to call functions on it or alter its variables. We can take advantage of Direct Class Communication by creating a class based on `Actor` that can have a function on it which we can call from our Character class.

Creating a Rotating Actor

We will create an Actor that will rotate when we want it to. In the **Content Browser**, in *Content*, create a new folder called *Chapter11*. Then in *C++ Classes -> FirstGame* create a new C++ class based on Actor called *RotatingActor*. In *RotatingActor.h*, just under the constructor, declare the following:

```
/** Base Mesh Component */
UPROPERTY(VisibleAnywhere, BlueprintReadWrite,
Category = "Item | Mesh")
class UStaticMeshComponent* Mesh;

/** Toggles on/off rotating */
UPROPERTY(EditAnywhere, BlueprintReadWrite, Category =
"Item | ItemProperties")
bool bRotate;

/** Rate at which the mesh should rotate */
UPROPERTY(EditAnywhere, BlueprintReadWrite, Category =
"Item | ItemProperties")
float RotationRate;
```

We declared a `UStaticMeshComponent` to give this class a mesh representation. We also gave this class a Boolean for rotating, and a `float` for the rotation rate, just like we did for the `Pickup` class. Add the following in the class's constructor in `RotatingActor.cpp`:

```
Mesh =
CreateDefaultSubobject<UStaticMeshComponent>(TEXT("Mesh"));
RootComponent = Cast<USceneComponent>(Mesh);

bRotate = false;

RotationRate = 45.f;
```

We set `Mesh` to be the `RootComponent`. `bRotate` has a default value of `false` and `RotationRate` is given a value of `45.f`. Next, add the following to the `Tick` function just under `Super::Tick(DeltaTime);`:

```
if (bRotate)
{
        FRotator Rotation = GetActorRotation();
```

```
Rotation.Yaw += DeltaTime * RotationRate;
SetActorRotation(Rotation);
}
```

Now we have an Actor that can rotate when its bRotate variable is set to true. In order to toggle the bRotate variable easily, let's create a function for doing so. In *RotatingActor.h*, just under the declaration for Tick, add:

```
void ToggleRotate();
```

And define it in *RotatingActor.cpp*:

```
void ARotatingActor::ToggleRotate()
{
    bRotate = !bRotate;
}
```

Now, let's create a Blueprint from this class in the Unreal Engine editor and give it a mesh. Open the editor, go to the *C++ Classes -> FirstGame* folder, right-click on *RotatingActor* and select *Create Blueprint Class based on RotatingActor*. Call it *RotatingActor_BP* and place it in the *Chapter11* folder. Open the Blueprint, give the *Static Mesh* property of *Mesh* the value *Shape_QuadPyramid* and a material *M_Metal_Chrome*. Now we have an Actor that can rotate if the bRotate variable is set to true. Place an instance of *RotatingActor_BP* in the world.

Figure 11.1: The RotatingActor Placed in the World

Now we can take advantage of direct class communication by calling ToggleRotate on the RotatingActor class.

Using Direct Class Communication

When communicating directly from one class to another, one class must have a reference to the other class. One way to get a reference to another class is to use `GetAllActorsOfClass`. This is a function in `UGameplayStatics`, so you'll need to make sure to include the appropriate header for it wherever you use it. We'll use it from within the `MainCharacter` class. In *MainCharacter.h*, just under the declaration for `LoadGame`, add the following:

```
UFUNCTION(BlueprintCallable)
void ToggleAllRotators();
```

We want this to be `BlueprintCallable` so we can easily test it from Blueprints. Next, in *MainCharacter.cpp*, define the function as follows:

```
void AMainCharacter::ToggleAllRotators()
{
    TSubclassOf<AActor> WorldClassObject =
ARotatingActor::StaticClass();
    TArray<AActor*> ActorsOfClass;
    UGameplayStatics::GetAllActorsOfClass(this,
WorldClassObject, ActorsOfClass);
    for (AActor* Actor : ActorsOfClass)
    {
        ARotatingActor* RotatingActor =
Cast<ARotatingActor>(Actor);
        if (RotatingActor)
        {
            RotatingActor->ToggleRotate();
        }
    }
}
```

Ror `UGameplayStatics::GetAllActorsOfClass`:

- A World Context Object is the first argument. We can use `this`, similarly to other functions that require a World Context Object.

- The second argument is of type `TSubclassOf<AActor>`. We created a local variable `WorldClassObject` of this type and used

`ARotatingActor::StaticClass` for it. This gives us a variable for the class we would like to get all Actors of.

- The third argument is an array of type `TArray<AActor*>` which will be filled in by the function. We created one of these called `ActorsOfClass` as a local variable.

After calling `GetAllActorsOfClass`, our `ActorsOfClass` array should contain pointers to all Actors in the world of the class type we specified. These are stored in the form of pointers to the `AActor` type. We then loop through all elements in `ActorsOfClass`, casting each one to the `ARotatingActor` type. We do this because we wish to access the `ToggleRotate` function, which is defined in the `ARotatingActor` class, not `AActor`. We check to see if the cast is successful, and if so, we call `ToggleRotate` on that object.

Compile this code, and in the Unreal Engine editor, open the *MainCharacter_BP* Blueprint. Add the following nodes to the **Event Graph**:

Figure 11.2: Calling ToggleAllRotators from Blueprints

This way, we can simply use the *R* key to call this function, which we made `BlueprintCallable` in C++. Now press **Play** and notice that the *RotatingActor_BP* in the world starts and stops rotating with the press of the *R* key. In fact, you can duplicate the *RotatingActors _BP* instance as many times as you like, and you will find that pressing R toggles the rotation of all of them, thanks to our use of `GetAllActorsOfClass`.

Direct Class Communication is useful and simple. However, functions like `GetAllActorsOfClass` can be inefficient, especially if there are hundreds or thousands of Actors of the class you are getting. There are more efficient ways to achieve class-to-class communication. Delegates are one such technique. We will dive into them now.

Communicating with Delegates

Delegates in Unreal Engine allow for one class to communicate with one or more other classes. The sender object will have a Delegate declared in its class, and the receiver will bind a function to that Delegate. There are three main categories of Delegates in Unreal Engine:

- **Delegates**: This the basic form of Delegate. The sender class has the Delegate, and a receiver class binds a function to that Delegate that will be called in response to the sender triggering the Delegate.

- **Dynamic Delegates**: These Delegates can have functions bound to them from within Blueprints. They can be triggered from the sender class in C++, and other classes can bind functions to them both in C++ and in Blueprints.

- **Multicast Delegates**: These can be have functions bound to them from multiple classes. A single sender can trigger the Delegate, resulting in multiple classes responding by calling their respective functions bound to the Delegate.

We will begin by creating a Delegate of the most basic category.

Binding Functions to Delegates

Instead of getting all Actors of a particular class and casting them to a specific Actor (as we did with the `ARotatingActor` class), we will now take advantage of Delegates. In *MainCharacter.h*, let's create a Delegate. Add the following code, just under the list of `#include`s, but just above `UCLASS()`:

```
DECLARE_DELEGATE(FRotateDelegate);
```

This macro declares the identifier `FRotateDelegate` to be a Delegate type. But we must actually create a variable of this type to have the Delegate on the `MainCharacter` class. Just under the declaration for `SetMaxHealth` (in a `public` section), add:

```
FRotateDelegate RotateDelegate;
```

Now a Delegate called `RotateDelegate` exists for this class. We must have a function in our `RotatingActor` class, which we would like to bind to this Delegate. We already have `ToggleRotate`, so we'll use that. In *RotatingActor.cpp*, in `BeginPlay`, add the following:

```
APawn* Pawn = UGameplayStatics::GetPlayerPawn(this,
0);
AMainCharacter* MainCharacter =
Cast<AMainCharacter>(Pawn);
if (MainCharacter)
{
    MainCharacter->RotateDelegate.BindUObject(this,
&ARotatingActor::ToggleRotate);

}
```

We use `UGameplayStatics::GetPlayerPawn`, passing in this for the World Context Object, and 0 for the player index. We then cast this value to `AMainCharacter` and store it in the local variable `MainCharacter`. After checking to see if this variable is valid, we then do the binding. We access the Character's `RotateDelegate` and call `BindUObject`, which binds a `UFunction`-based function to a Delegate. Since the function belongs to a `UObject` (`AActor` inherits from `UObject`), this is the appropriate function for binding this Delegate. `BindUObject` takes a User Object (which is the object doing the binding, so we pass in `this`), followed by the address of the function we would like to bind. We pass in the address of `ARotatingActor::ToggleRotate`, using the address-of operator (`&`). Notice the function name must be fully qualified with the `ARotatingActor::` prefix. In order for the above code to work, we must include the following at the top of *RotatingActor.cpp*:

```
#include "Kismet/GameplayStatics.h"
```

```
#include "MainCharacter.h"
```

We have created the Delegate and bound a function to it. Now we must actually trigger, or execute, the Delegate. In *MainCharacter.cpp*, in `ToggleAllRotators`, comment out the code we placed in there, and add the following:

```
RotateDelegate.ExecuteIfBound();
```

`ExecuteIfBound` will only execute the Delegate if a function is bound to it. There exists an `Execute` function, which performs no such check, so this one is safer. Now when we call `ToggleAllRotators`, this Delegate will simply execute and all functions bound to it will be called. Compile this code and in the Unreal Engine editor, press **Play** and use the *R* key to toggle the rotation of the rotating Actors.

This is the basic form of the Unreal Engine Delegate. Notice, however, that if you duplicate the Rotating Actor in the world, pressing the *R* key will only result in one of them toggling their rotation. This is because only one function can be bound to the basic Delegate. We will learn shortly how to bind multiple functions to the same Delegate. First, we will learn about the Dynamic Delegate.

Binding Functions with Dynamic Delegates

Dynamic Delegates are similar to regular Delegates. They are slightly slower than regular Delegates, they can be **serialized** – meaning they can be translated into a format that can be stored and transmitted and reconstructed later. Their functions can be found by name. At the top of *MainCharacter.h*, add the following:

```
DECLARE_DYNAMIC_DELEGATE_RetVal_OneParam(float,
FDynamicRotateDelegate, float, RotationSpeed);
```

This macro declares a Dynamic Delegate type, which we choose to call `FDynamicRotateDelegate`. Notice the `_OneParam` part. When typing this Delegate, Intellisense should reveal to you the other options for the Dynamic Delegate creation macros:

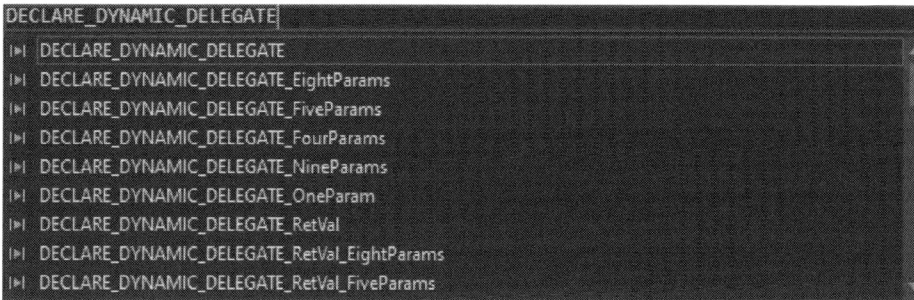

Figure 11.3: The Different Dynamic Delegate Macros

And the `_RetVal` part indicates that this Delegate is capable of binding a function with a return value. Notice also the Delegates with `Param` in the name. These are for creating Delegates which are capable allowing functions to be bound to them which have input parameters. For the macro `DECLARE_DYNAMIC_DELEGATE_RetVal_OneParam`, functions can be bound to this type of Delegate which return a value and have a single input parameter. For this macro, we have four arguments. First is the return type for the function that will be bound to this Delegate. Next is the name given to this Delegate. The second is the type of the parameter for functions that will bind to this Delegate, and the third is the name for this parameter.

In *MainCharacter.cpp*, just under the declaration for `FRotateDelegate`, add:

```
FDynamicRotateDelegate DynamicRotateDelegate;
```

Now, we will create a function to bind to this Delegate. In *RotatingActor.h*, declare:

```
UFUNCTION()

float SetRotationRate(float Rate);
```

And in *RotatingActor.cpp*, define:

```
float ARotatingActor::SetRotationRate(float Rate)
{
    float Temp = RotationRate;
    RotationRate = Rate;
    return Temp;
}
```

It is very important that `SetRotationRate` be marked with `UFUNCTION`. This is because Dynamic Delegates are designed to work with the reflection system, so the function must be exposed to the reflection system. Now we simply need to bind this function to the Delegate. In `BeginPlay`, change the code to include:

```
    APawn* Pawn = UGameplayStatics::GetPlayerPawn(this,
0);
    AMainCharacter* MainCharacter =
Cast<AMainCharacter>(Pawn);
    if (MainCharacter)
    {
        MainCharacter->RotateDelegate.BindUObject(this,
&ARotatingActor::ToggleRotate);
        MainCharacter-
>DynamicRotateDelegate.BindDynamic(this,
&ARotatingActor::SetRotationRate);

    }
```

Now we will create a function in `MainCharacter` to execute this Delegate. Add the following to *MainCharacter.h*:

```
    UPROPERTY(EditAnywhere, BlueprintReadWrite)
    float RotatingActorRotate;

    UFUNCTION(BlueprintCallable)

    void SetRotatingActorRates(float Rate);
```

And in *MainCharacter.cpp*, initialize `RotatingActorRate` in the constructor:

```
    RotatingActorRotate = 180.f;
```

Now define the function:

```
void AMainCharacter::SetRotatingActorRates(float Rate)
{
    float PreviousRotationRate =
DynamicRotateDelegate.Execute(Rate);
    printf("Previous Rotation Rate: %f",
PreviousRotationRate);

}
```

Notice we needed to pass in a `float` parameter, because this Delegate is designed for functions with a single `float` parameter. Because the callback function, `SetRotationRate`, returns a `float`, the call to `Execute` will return the value returned by the function. We store this in the local variable `PreviousRotationRate`, because this is what the callback function returns. We finally make use of our `printf` macro we created and added to *FirstGame.h* to print the previous rotation rate value to the screen. Compile this code, then in the Unreal Engine editor, add the following to the **Event Graph**:

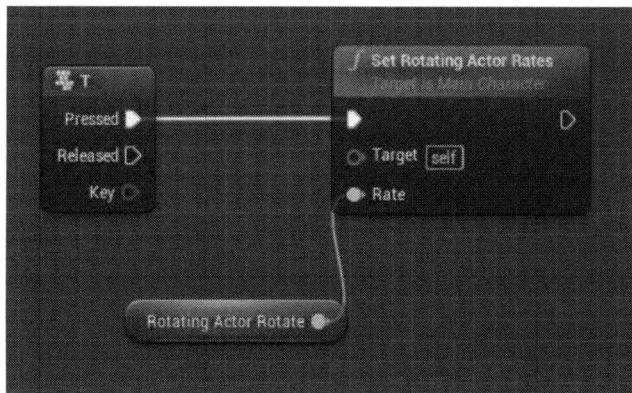

Figure 11.4: Calling SetRotatingActorRates

Now press **Play** and test out our code with the *T* key. The rotating Actor's rotation will speed up to 180 degrees per second. The previous value of 45.0 will be printed to the screen as well.

Dynamic Delegates are useful, but the most versatile (and slowest performing) type of Delegate is the Multicast Delegate.

Binding to Dynamic Multicast Delegates

While Dynamic Delegates can be saved/loaded in Blueprints and thus bound there, **Multicast Delegates** can have multiple functions bound to them. Executing them results in all the functions bound to them being called at the same time. We will create a Dynamic Multicast Delegate now. In *MainCharacter.h*, add:

```
DECLARE_DYNAMIC_MULTICAST_DELEGATE_OneParam(FDynamicMultica
stRotateDelegate, bool, bPlaySound);
```

We chose to create a Dynamic Multicast Delegate with _OneParam at the end so we can bind a function that takes a single parameter. Multicast Delegates cannot bind functions with a return value. This is because they can bind multiple functions from multiple classes, so there is no way to know which object's return value to use.

Now we must bind the function. Multicast Delegates can be bound in C++ using AddDynamic. If this sounds familiar, that's because we used AddDynamic to bind functions for overlap functionality. The OnComponentBeginOverlap Delegate is a Dynamic Multicast Delegate.

We will bind this Delegate from within Blueprints, however. In *RotatingActor_BP*, add the following to the **Event Graph**:

Figure 11.5: Accessing the Character from the RotatingActor

Now from the return value of the *Cast To MainCharacter_BP* node, drag off and search for "Bind Event to Dynamic Multicast Rotate Delegate" and choose *Bind Event to Dynamic Multicast Rotate Delegate*.

Click on the red square input pin on *Bind Event to Dynamic Multicast Rotate Delegate*, drag off, search for "custom event" and create a new Custom Event called *Respond To Rotate Delegate*. Connect the red square output pin on it to the red square input pin on the *Bind Event to Dynamic Multicast Rotate Delegate* node, as shown in the following figure.

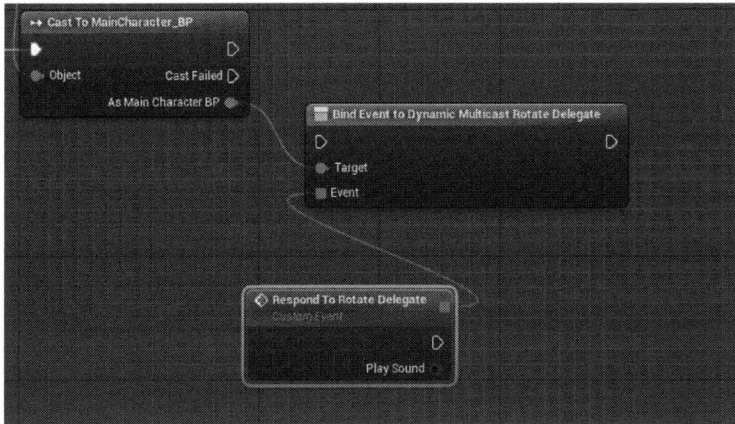

Figure 11.6: Binding an Event to the Delegate in Blueprints

Now any functionality that we implement for this event will be called when the Delegate is triggered. Don't forget to connect the output pin from the *Cast* node to the *Bind Event* node. Also notice that there is a red output pin on the event indicating that it returns a Boolean. This is because the Delegate is designed to bind functions that take a Boolean value. When we trigger the Delegate, we will be required to provide this Boolean value. Let's provide the logic for this event. Add the following Blueprint logic:

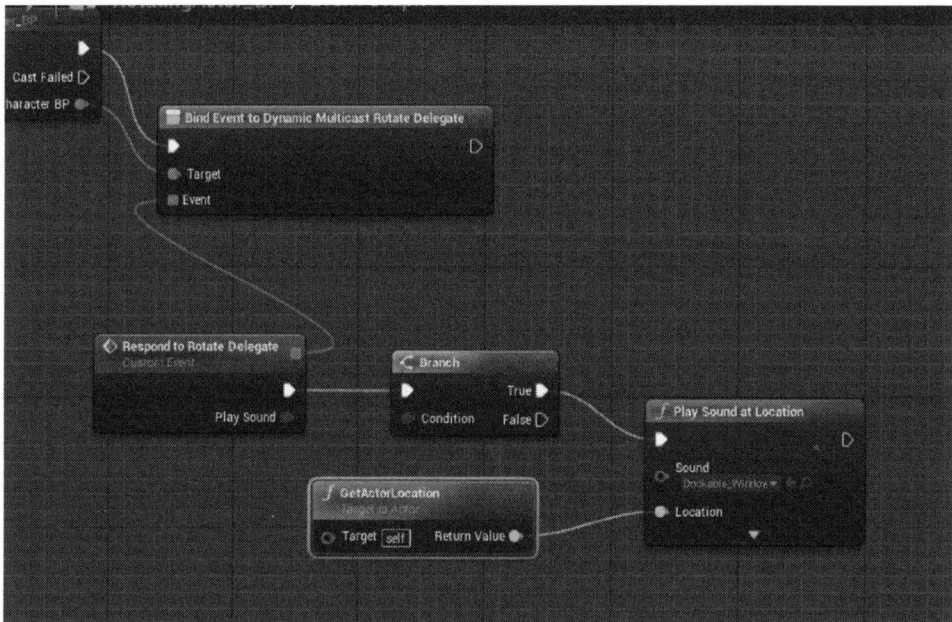

Figure 11.7: Logic for the Event Responding to the Delegate

We check the value of the Boolean, and if it's true, we use *Play Sound at Location*. This will play a sound at the location of the *RotatingActor*. For the sound, click the dropdown and select *Dockable_Window_Close*. The node takes a location, and we are using *GetActorLocation* and passing that value in. All that's left now is to actually trigger the event.

Add the following just under `FDynamicMulticastRotateDelegate DynamicMulticastRotateDelegate;`:

```
UPROPERTY(BlueprintReadWrite, EditAnywhere, Category =
"Delegates")
bool bShouldRotatorsPlaySound;
```

And initialize it in the constructor:

```
bShouldRotatorsPlaySound = true;
```

Now, create a Blueprint Callable function in *MainCharacter.h*:

```
UFUNCTION(BlueprintCallable)
void PlaySoundAtRotatingActors(bool PlaySound);
```

And implement it in *MainCharacter.cpp*:

```
void AMainCharacter::PlaySoundAtRotatingActors(bool
PlaySound)
{
        DynamicMulticastRotateDelegate.Broadcast(PlaySound);

}
```

For Dynamic Multicast Delegates, the `Broadcast` function will result in broadcasting a signal to all classes which have bound a function to the Delegate and trigger them to call their respective bound functions. We pass in the Boolean value which will be passed into all functions bound to this Delegate.

Finally, we can add the capability to call our Blueprint Callable function `PlaySoundAtRotatingActors` in the *MainCharacter_BP* **Event Graph**:

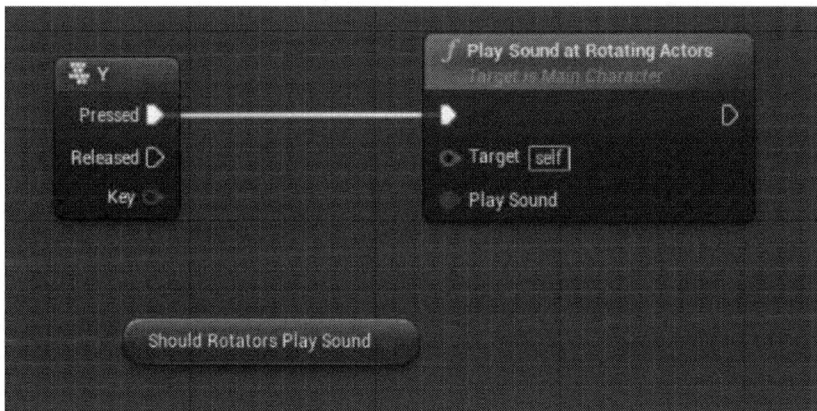

Figure 11.8: Calling the PlaySoundAtRotatingActors Function

Now press **Play** and hear the sounds emitted from each `RotatingActor` instance!

Delegates are useful for Class Communication. They can especially be useful when multiple objects of different class types need to respond to one object's actions. With Delegates, there is one sender who owns the Delegate (in our case, the Main Character) and one or more receivers who bind functions to those Delegates. So this type of communication is useful when the sender can be easily accessed. In our case, we accessed the Main Character relatively easily with `GetPlayerPawn`. There may, however, be cases where the sender isn't easily obtainable from the receiver, but the receiver is easily obtainable from the sender. In these cases, Interfaces are more appropriate.

Using Interfaces

Interfaces are special types of classes that are designed to be inherited from in order to inherit functions that are declared in them. It is not expected that the functions are defined in the Interface, but instead that they are defined in the classes that inherit them. This way, the function can have unique implementation in the class that inherits from the Interface. In Unreal Engine, classes which implement Interfaces inherit from them as well as their original parent class. This phenomenon is called **multiple inheritance**. A class that inherits from `Actor` class, for instance, and also inherits from some Interface class, is said to be both an `Actor` and a member of the Interface class from which it inherited.

We will use an Interface to create a generic Floor Switch that will be able to activate any number of items. Upon activation, those items can perform their own specialized functionality, and they need not even all be of the same class type.

To create a new Interface class, go to *C++ Classes -> FirstGame*, right-click, and choose *New C++ Class...* Scroll down until you see *Unreal Interface*.

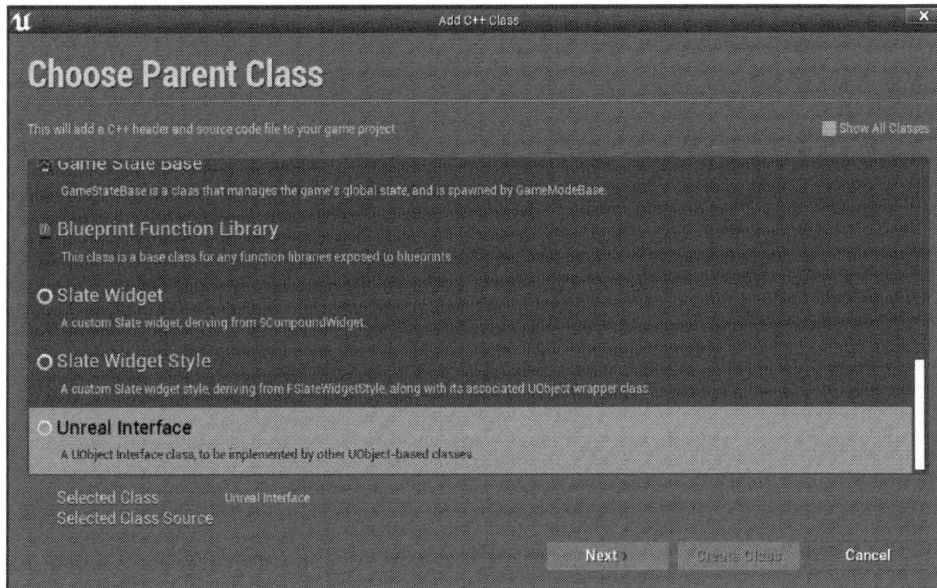

Figure 11.9: Creating an Unreal Interface

Choose this class, and name it *SwitchInterface*. In *SwitchInterface.h*, notice that there are two class declarations: one for `USwitchInterface`, inheriting from `UInterface`, and one for `ISwitchInterface`. Functions are to be declared in the `ISwitchInterface` class.

We will declare a function called `Activate`, which will be the function inherited by any class that implements this Interface. We will not define it in the `SwitchInterface` class, however. Add the following in the `public` section of *SwitchInterface.h*:

```
UFUNCTION(BlueprintNativeEvent, BlueprintCallable)
void Activate();
```

We made this function `BlueprintNativeEvent`, `BlueprintCallable`, and gave it the Category `Interfaces`.

Now we will create a class for items that will react to the Floor Switch. Create a new C++ class based on Actor called `SwitchTarget`.

Inheriting from the Switch Interface

The first thing we need to do in *SwitchTarget.h* is to inherit from the
`SwitchInterface` class.

1. Add the following to the line declaring the `ASwitchTarget` class:

```
class FIRSTGAME_API ASwitchTarget : public AActor, public
ISwitchInterface
```

Now we can add some variables to our `SwitchTarget` class.

2. Just beneath the declaration for the constructor, we'll add the following:

```
UPROPERTY (VisibleAnywhere)
class UStaticMeshComponent* TargetMesh;

FVector InitialLocation;

FRotator InitialRotation;
```

We declare a Static Mesh Component for our visual representation of the Switch Target
called `TargetMesh`. Then we have an `FVector` and an `FRotator` for the initial
location and rotation, respectively, called `InitialLocation` and
`InitialRotation`.

3. Just under the declaration for the `Tick` function, add:

```
virtual void Activate_Implementation() override;

UFUNCTION (BlueprintImplementableEvent, Category =
"Switch Target")
void ActivateSwitchTarget();

UFUNCTION (BlueprintCallable, Category = "Floor
Switch")
void UpdateSwitchLocation(float Location, float
Rotation);
```

First, we declare the `Activate` function which we are inheriting from the
`ISwitchInterface` class. Because this is a `BlueprintNativeEvent`, we must
append `_Implementation` to the name. The function is virtual and and override, so

we mark it as such. Next, we will create Blueprint Implementable Event `ActivateSwitchTarget` so we can call a function in C++ and trigger an action in Blueprints. We also have *UpdateFloorSwitchLocation* which takes a `float` called `Location`, which will be passed in to move the Switch Target Location. It also takes a `float` called `Rotation`, which will be passed in to change the Switch Target's Rotation. Now we can take care of the above code in *SwitchTarget.cpp*.

4. In the constructor, add:

```
    TargetMesh =
CreateDefaultSubobject<UStaticMeshComponent>(TEXT("TargetMe
sh"));

    RootComponent = Cast<USceneComponent>(TargetMesh);
```

We use `CreateDefaultSubobject` to construct the `TargetMesh` variable. After casting it to a `USceneComponent`, we set `RootComponent` to it. Now any changes to `TargetMesh` will affect the entire Actor.

5. Next, add the following to `BeginPlay`:

```
    InitialLocation = GetActorLocation();

    InitialRotation = GetActorRotation();
```

6. And finally, define `UpdateFloorSwitchLocation`:

```
void ASwitchTarget::UpdateSwitchLocation(float Location,
float Rotation)
{
    FVector NewLocation = InitialLocation;
    NewLocation.Z += Location;
    TargetMesh->SetWorldLocation(NewLocation);

    FRotator NewRotation = InitialRotation;
    NewRotation.Yaw += Rotation;
    TargetMesh->SetWorldRotation(NewRotation);

}
```

We use similar techniques to those used with the `FloorSwitch` class, except that we also update the rotation of the mesh as well.

7. We will also add the following implementation:

```
void ASwitchTarget::Activate_Implementation()
{
        ActivateSwitchTarget();

}
```

When the Interface function `Activate` gets called, we will simply call `ActivateSwitchTarget`, which we will shortly define in Blueprints.

8. Add the following to the top of *SwitchTarget.cpp*:

```
#include "Components/StaticMeshComponent.h"
```

9. And in order for the Switch Interface to be defined in the *SwitchTarget.h* file, add:

```
#include "SwitchInterface.h"
```

Keep in mind that the following line must be the last include:

```
#include "SwitchTarget.generated.h"
```

So make sure all other includes are above it.

10. Create a Blueprint based on `SwitchTarget` called *SwitchTarget_BP* and place it in the *Chapter11* folder. Select the *TargetMesh* component and choose *Shape_Cube* for the *Static Mesh*.

11. Next, in the **Event Graph**, add a node for *Event Activate Switch Target*. This is the Blueprint Implementable Event we declared in C++. From its output pin, create a *Timeline* and call it *SwitchTargetTimeline*. Double-click it to open it, and add a `float` track called *Location Track*. Add another `float` track called *Rotation Track*. In *Location Track*, add two points, at (0.0, 0.0) and (1.5, -200.0), respectively. In *Rotation Track*, add two points at (0.0, 0.0) and (1.5, 360.0), respectively. In *Location Track*, select both points, and right-click and select *Auto*

to make a smooth curve. Do the same in *Rotation Track*. Refer back to *Chapter 9 – Gameplay Mechanics* for more information on creating Timelines.

12. Back in the **Event Graph**, add a call to *Update Switch Location*.

This is the Blueprint Callable function we defined in C++ for updating both the rotation and location of the mesh. Hook up the *Location Track* and *Rotation Track* float outputs from the Timeline to the inputs for this function call. Make sure all your execution wires are connected as indicated in the following figure.

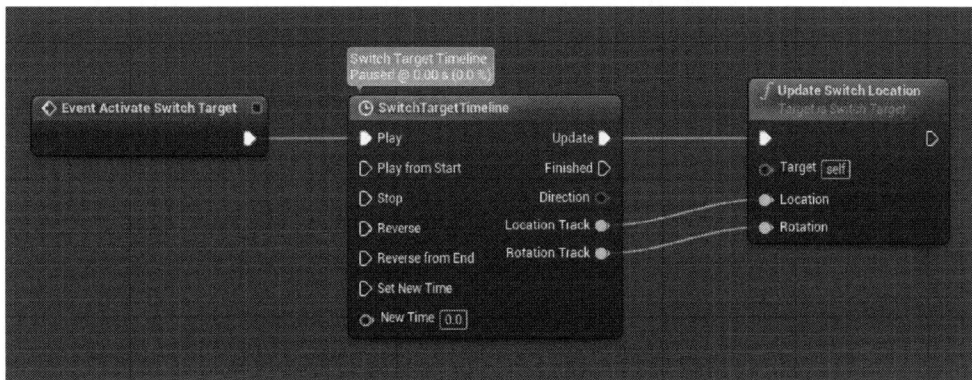

Figure 11.10: Activating the Timeline in Blueprints

Now we must figure out how to actually call the Interface function. We will do so from the FloorSwitch class.

13. In *FloorSwitch.h*, add the following, under class

```
AMainPlayerController* MainPlayerController;:

UPROPERTY(EditAnywhere, BlueprintReadOnly, Category =
"Switch")
TArray<class ASwitchTarget*> SwitchTargets;

UFUNCTION(BlueprintCallable)

void ActivateSwitchTargets();
```

We have created a `TArray` of pointers to the `AActor` class. We made this `EditAnywhere` so we can add elements to it from the **Details** panel. We made it `BlueprintReadOnly` in case we would like to access it from Blueprints, but we don't want it settable from Blueprints. We declared a Blueprint Callable function `ActivateSwitchTargets` which we would like to use to loop through the array of `SwitchTargets`.

14. Define it in *FloorSwitch.cpp* as follows:

```
void AFloorSwitch::ActivateSwitchTargets()
{
    for (ASwitchTarget* SwitchTarget : SwitchTargets)
    {
        ISwitchInterface* Interface =
Cast<ISwitchInterface>(SwitchTarget);
        if (Interface)
        {
            SwitchTarget->Activate_Implementation();
        }
    }
}
```

We loop through each item in `SwitchTargets`. Then we create a local variable of type `ISwitchInterface*` and populate it with the results from a cast to this type. If successful, we then use the `SwitchTarget` to call the `Activate_Implementation` function. It is important that we call the Interface function from the `SwitchTarget` variable and not the `Interface` variable, because from the Interface object, the function is not defined. This will result in the `Activate_Implementation` function being called, which is a Blueprint Native Event. The function will be called, in which we made a call to `ActivateSwitchTarget()`, a Blueprint Implementable Event which results in the starting of the Timeline in Blueprints.

15. Make sure the following are included in *FloorSwitch.cpp*:

```
#include "SwitchInterface.h"
#include "SwitchTarget.h"
```

The only thing left is to make sure the `TArray SwitchTargets` has items in it.

16. Back in the Unreal Engine editor, place a couple instances of *SwitchTarget_BP* next to the *FloorSwitch_BP*.

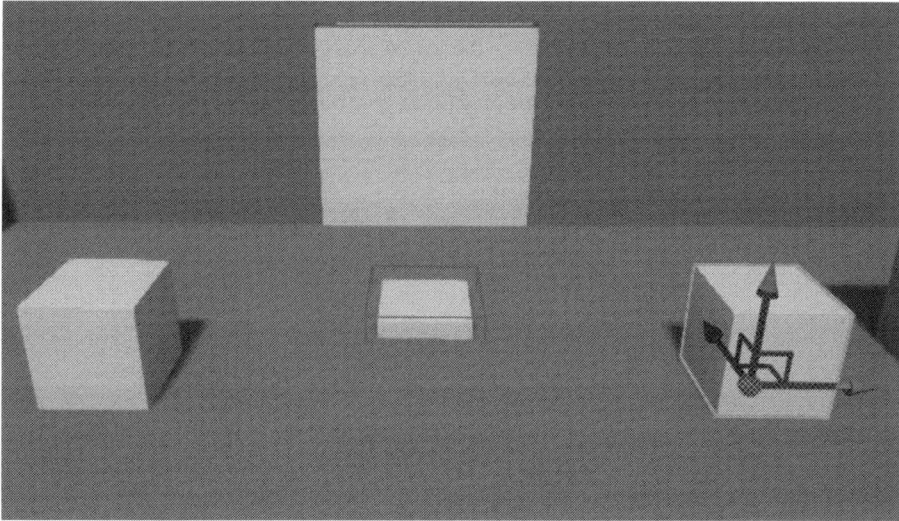

Figure 11.11: Placing Switch Targets near a FloorSwitch

17. Now, select the *FloorSwitch* instance, and in the **Details** panel, search for "switch targets" and notice the Switch Targets array:

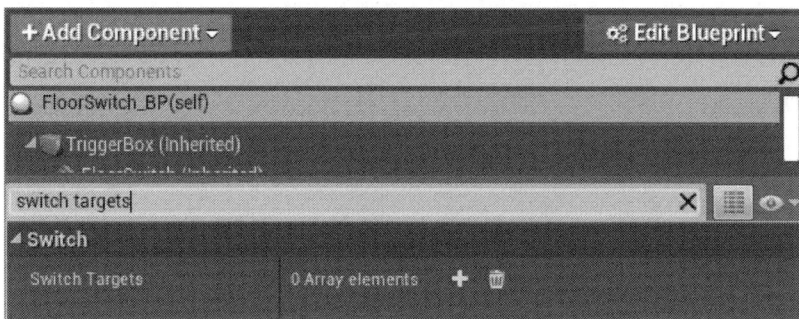

Figure 11.12: The Switch Targets Array

18. Add elements to this array manually by pressing the + icon next to *0 Array Elements*. On the new element, we can select the Dropper Tool, which will allow us to pick an object from inside the level in the **Viewport**.

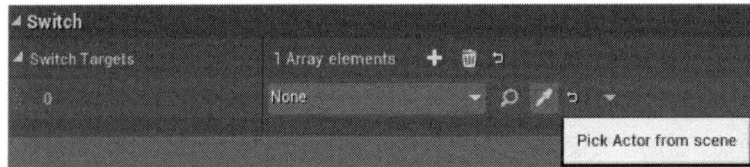

Figure 11.13: Selecting the Dropper Tool

19. With the Dropper Tool selected, left-click on one of the Switch Target objects in the level. Add another element to the array and use the same method to select the other Switch Target object.

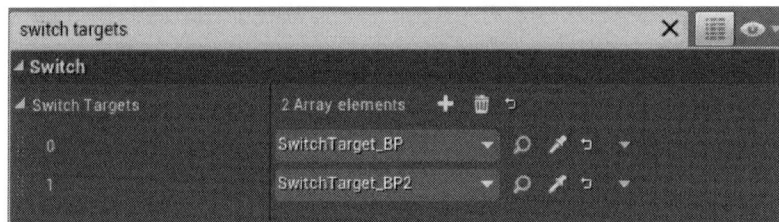

Figure 11.14: The Array with Two Elements

Now the Array has two elements in it, and our function `ActivateSwitchTargets` will loop through each of them.

Now with the code compiled, press **Play** and run over the Floor Switch and see the Switch Targets sink into the floor and rotate! We can also add as many elements to the array as we like. Additionally, we can create any number of classes in which we would like to implement the `SwitchInterface`. We could create our own unique functionality for the `Activate` function in them. If the class derives from `SwitchTarget`, it can be added to the Actor array in `FloorSwitch`. Creating a new class, implementing the `SwitchInterface` in it, and adding it to the array in an instance of `FloorSwitch` is left as an exercise for the reader.

Summary

We have seen that class communication can occur between classes directly, as long as one class has a reference to the other. We also learned about Delegates and how they involve a sender and a receiver of information. We learned that with Delegates, the receiver must have a reference to the sender in order to bind a function to the sender's Delegate. We learned about regular Delegates involving sending a message from one class to another. We then learned that Dynamic Delegates can be saved in Blueprints. We finally saw that Multicast Delegates can broadcast to multiple listeners. Finally, we learned that we could make Interfaces and inherit from them with an Actor, making use of multiple inheritance. We saw that classes that inherit from the Interface can implement their own version of Interface functions and that the sender of the information must have a reference to the receiver in order to call these functions.

Now that we have learned these important communication techniques, we are ready to dive into one of the most exciting aspects of game development: Artificial Intelligence! We will be diving into Behavior Trees and how they can be used to make AI fun and interesting in Unreal Engine. Soon we will have our own AI controlled Pawns in our level!

Chapter 12 – AI and Behavior Trees

Artificial Intelligence in games is the code that will determine how an **NPC** (non-player character) behaves in the game on its own as well as in response to actions by the player. This chapter is dedicated to creating artificially intelligent NPCs so that your games can be brought to life and your Character can have other entities to interact with. This chapter will cover the following topics:

- **Finding the Path to an Actor**: For an AI Character to be able to move to an Actor, it must be able to find the path to it.

- **Including the AI Module**: In order to use the AI classes, we must include the AI Module to our project so those types are recognized by the compiler.

- **The Different Components of Unreal Engine AI**: Unreal Engine contains a rich set of tools for creating AI. We go over them here and explain the purpose for each one.

- **The AI Character Class**: We learn how to create a `Character` class with AI functionality in mind.

- **The AIController Class**: We learn about the `AIController` class and how it differs from the regular `Controller` class.

- **Behavior Trees and Different Nodes**: We learn about the Behavior Tree and how it is used to create AI logic via the use of special nodes.

- **Creating a Working Behavior Tree**: We create an actual Behavior Tree for our AI Character.

- **Nav Mesh Generation Settings**: We explain the settings for a Nav Mesh and how to adjust them.

- **Nav Link Proxy**: We learn about the Nav Link Proxy and how it can connect gaps in a Nav Mesh.

- **Nav Modifier Volume**: We learn about how we can add volumes that modify the Nav Mesh.

- **Rebuilding Nav Mesh at Runtime:** We learn how to set the Nav Mesh to rebuild at runtime to accommodate for moving geometry in the game.

By the end of this chapter, we will have created a working AI non-player character. Let's get started!

Finding the Path to an Actor

Unreal Engine contains built-in functions designed to make Artificial Intelligence easier. One of the most fundamental AI capabilities is finding a path from one location to another. This may seem relatively simple when you think about the path from one object to another being a straight line. However, when obstacles exist between the two objects, a straight line from one object to the other isn't going to cut it. There needs to be a way for the path to go around the obstacle (otherwise the path would go straight through the obstacle). Algorithms designed to solve this problem are called **pathfinding algorithms** and they are well understood in computer science. Unreal Engine has pathfinding built-in and for game developers, finding a path from one object to another is as simple as understanding how to use these functions.

Adding a Nav Mesh Bounds Volume

In order for pathfinding to work in Unreal Engine, a **Nav Mesh** must be added – a volume placed in the level to designate an area for AI navigation.

1. Add a Nav Mesh Bounds Volume to the level by going to the **Modes** panel and searching for "nav" and dragging in a *Nav Mesh Bounds Volume*.

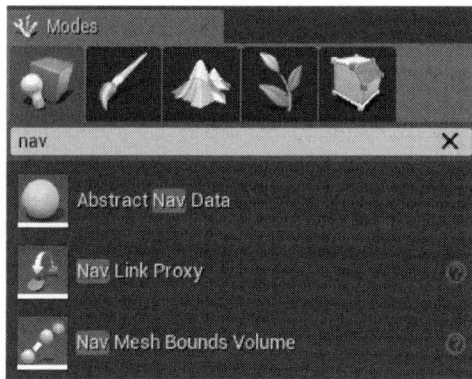

Figure 12.1: Searching for a Nav Mesh Bounds Volume in Modes

2. Once you have dragged in a Nav Mesh Bounds Volume, press *P* on your keyboard in order to activate visualization mode for the volume. You will see green within the navigation mesh box.

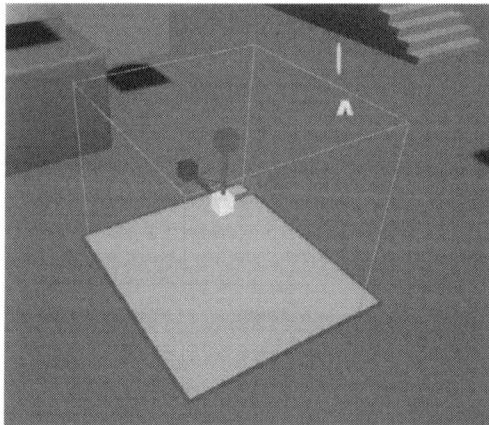

Figure 12.2: Visualizing the Navigation Mesh

3. Next, scale up the navigation mesh so that it covers the entire floor of the level.

If the green makes it difficult to see objects in the world, simply hit the *P* key again to toggle it on or off. You will see that objects in the world create holes in the navigation mesh, which effectively makes them obstacles for the pathfinding algorithms to work around.

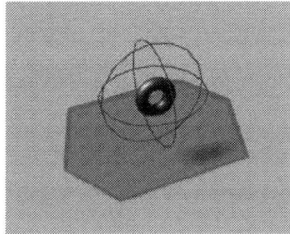

Figure 12.3: An Object Creating a Hole in the Navigation Mesh

Now that our map has a navigation mesh, we are ready to see Unreal Engine's pathfinding algorithms in action. First, we will need to add "NavigationSystem" to the PublicDependencyModuleNames in *FirstGame.Build.cs* in order to make the Navigation System code accessible to our project.

4. In the *.Build.cs* file for your project, make sure the

   PublicDependencyModuleNames line looks as follows:

```
PublicDependencyModuleNames.AddRange(new string[] { "Core",
"CoreUObject", "Engine", "InputCore", "HeadMountedDisplay",
"UMG", "NavigationSystem" });
```

Now we will be able to use the code in the NavigationSystem module. In *MainCharacter.cpp*, we will add some code to BeginPlay to observe how a pathfinding algorithm works. We will use the function FindPathToActorSynchronously, which will find the path to a given Actor in the world. Since we have created the class ARotatingActor and have an instance of this class in our world, we will use this object as our target for the pathfinding algorithm.

5. In BeginPlay, add the following code:

```
    TSubclassOf<AActor> WorldClassObject =
ARotatingActor::StaticClass();
    TArray<AActor*> ActorsOfClass;
    UGameplayStatics::GetAllActorsOfClass(this,
WorldClassObject, ActorsOfClass);
    if (ActorsOfClass.Num() > 0)
    {
```

```
        UNavigationPath* NavPath =
UNavigationSystemV1::FindPathToActorSynchronously(this,
GetActorLocation(), ActorsOfClass[0]);
        if (NavPath->PathPoints.Num() > 0)
        {
            for (auto pt : NavPath->PathPoints)
            {
                DrawDebugSphere(GetWorld(), pt, 20.f,
12, FColor::Red, true);
            }
        }

    }
```

First, we create a variable of type TSubclassOf<AActor> called
WorldClassObject. This allows us to have a UClass variable to use for the
GetAllActorsOfClass function (this is a UGameplayStatics function, so if you
don't have the correct header included, you must include it). We populate
WorldClassObject with ARotatingActor::StaticClass(). We then
create a TArray of AActor* type called ActorsOfClass and fill it by calling
GetAllActorsOfClass as we have done in previous chapters. All instances of the
ARotatingActor class in the world will now be stored in ActorsOfClass. We
check to see if this array has elements in it by using Num() which returns the number of
elements. If this number is not 0, we continue.

We then create a new variable of type UNavigationPath* called NavPath. This is
a data structure designed to hold path information for a navigation path generated by a
pathfinding algorithm. We then call the function
UNavigationSystemV1::FindPathToActorSynchronously which
generates the path for us.

- The first argument is a world context object, for which this will suffice.

- The second argument is the starting location for the path, and we pass in
  GetActorLocation so the path starts at the Character's location.

- The next argument is the Actor which will be the target for the pathfinding
  algorithm. We pass in the first element in the ActorsOfClass array, which is
  the first ARotatingActor object stored in it.

Once this function has been called, the object returned and stored in `NavPath` will contain path information. One item this variable contains is a list of points called `PathPoints`. We first check to make sure `PathPoints` contains elements in it, then we loop through it. Each element in `PathPoints` is an `FVector` for the location of that path point. Finally, to visualize these points, we use `DrawDebugSphere` to create a sphere at the location of each path point.

6. In *MainCharacter.cpp*, add the following includes:

```
#include "NavigationSystem.h"
#include "NavigationPath.h"
```

This will enable us to use the `UNavigationSystemV1` and `UNavigationPath` (the type for `NavPath`) types.

Now, compile this code and press **Play**. There should be red debug spheres starting at the Character's location and ending at the Rotating Actor. We will observe a key detail about the pathfinding algorithm used. First, drag the Rotating Actor to a spot in the world where there are no obstacles between it and the Character.

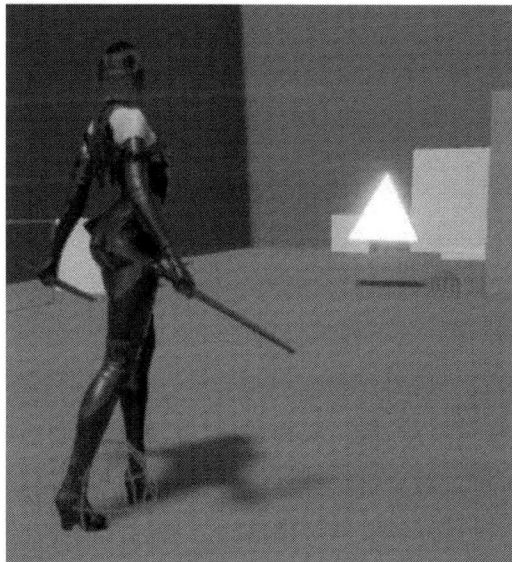

Figure 12.4: The Path Without Obstacles

You will notice that the path consist of relatively few points (in the case of the above figure, only two). This is because finding a path from one location to another without any obstacles is relatively simple and two points are sufficient to represent that path. Now, drag an object between the Character's starting location and the location of the Rotating Actor.

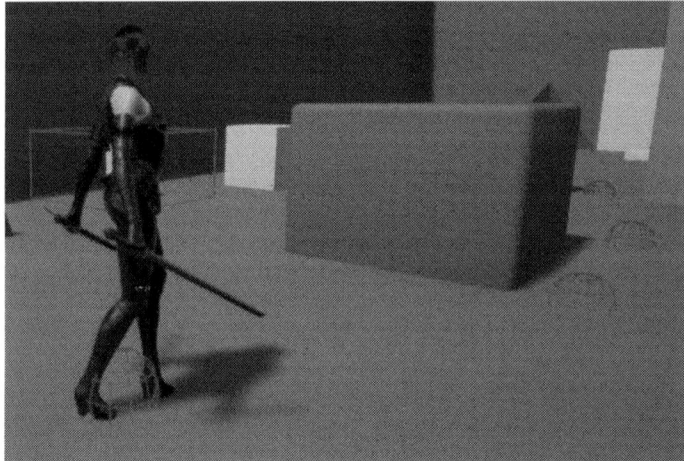

Figure 12.5: Path with an Obstacle in the Way

You will now see that the path contains more points and that they form a path around the obstacle. This is what makes pathfinding algorithms so valuable. An AI-driven Character can chase after a target and appear smart enough to move around obstacles rather than simply attempt to move straight through them.

Now that we have a taste of what pathfinding algorithms can do for us, it's time to learn how to create artificially intelligent Characters! We first must include the AI Module so that we have access to AI functions in Unreal Engine.

Including the AI Module

In *FirstGame.Build.cs*, add "AIModule" to `PublicDependencyModuleNames`. It should look like the following:

```
PublicDependencyModuleNames.AddRange(new string[] { "Core",
"CoreUObject", "Engine", "InputCore", "HeadMountedDisplay",
"UMG", "NavigationSystem", "AIModule" });
```

Now we will have AI functionality at our fingertips. Let's take a look at the different components that come together to make Unreal Engine's AI system work.

The Different Components of Unreal Engine AI

Unreal Engine AI involves several different components. Together, these come together to create functional AI. Here we go over the different elements in an high-level overview.

- **AI Characters**: AI Characters are simply Characters derived from the `Character` class, just like our `MainCharacter` class. The difference for AI Characters is that they use the `AAIController` for their `Controller` class.

- **AI Controller**: The `AIController` class is similar to the Controller class in that is handles movement for the Character. However, AI Controllers have additional functionality designated for AI Characters, such as causing the Character to move to a target given a navigation path.

- **Behavior Trees**: A **Behavior Tree** is a special system of nodes that determines how an AI Character behaves. It is different than the Blueprint nodes we are used to adding to an **Event Graph**. The Behavior Tree consists of AI-specific nodes designed to control the AI Character.

- **Blackboard**: A Blackboard allows variables to be accessed by all of the elements in an AI system. Think of it like an actual chalk board where all the pertinent variables to the AI Character are listed and any element in the system can look at and potentially change the values of the variables on the board.

- **Navigation Meshes**: As we have seen previously, the Navigation Mesh determines where in the level the pathfinding algorithms can work. Outside of the area of a Navigation Mesh, AI does not function.

These elements come together to form the AI system in Unreal Engine. We will be bringing these features together to create functional AI. Next, we will dive deeper into the `AIController` class.

The AI Character Class

We will need to create our own AI Character class in order to have an AI-controlled Character in our game. Create a new class based on `Character` and call it `Enemy`. Add the following just under the declaration for the constructor:

```
UPROPERTY(EditAnywhere, Category = "Pawn")
class UBehaviorTree* BehaviorTree;
```

Now we have a variable for storing the Behavior Tree in the `Enemy` class. Compile your code.

Next, in the Unreal Engine editor, in the **Content Browser**, just under *Content*, create a new folder called *Chapter12*. Create a Blueprint based on *Enemy* called *Enemy_BP* and place it in this new folder. Double-click it to open it.

Selecting a Mesh and Using the Countess AnimBP

The Countess Character came with several different versions of the Skeletal Mesh, each of which use the same skeleton asset. This means we can reuse the Animation Blueprint for the `Enemy` class. In the **Components** panel, select *Mesh* and in the **Details** panel, set *Skeletal Mesh* to *SM_Countess_Carnivale*. Rotate the mesh 90 degrees counterclockwise and bring it down in the *Z* direction by 80 units. Under the *Animation* section, set *Animation Mode* to *Use Animation Blueprint* and for *Anim Class* select *MainAnim_BP*.

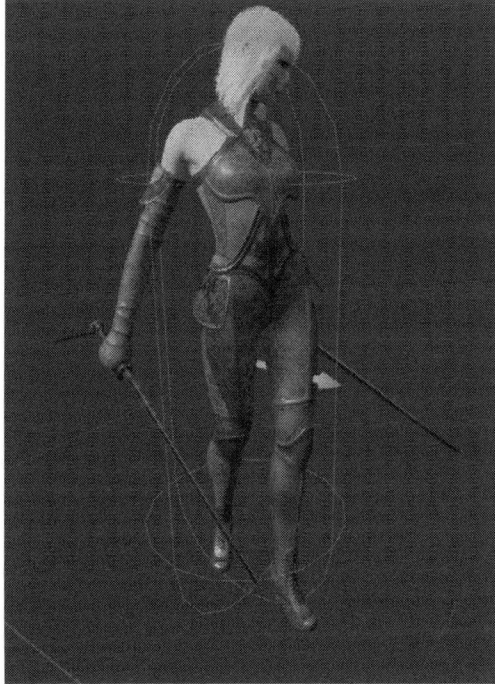

Figure 12.6: Adding a Mesh for the Enemy

Next we will create our AI Controller for the `Enemy` Character.

The AI Controller Class

The `AIController` is similar to the `PlayerController` class. It handles possessing the pawn it's meant to control. However, it contains additional functions designed for AI. For example, it has the ability to move to a particular location or Actor in the world. It also has a variable for storing a reference to the Blackboard. For these reasons, we will use an `AIController`.

Creating an AIController

We will now create an `AIController` class.

1. Create a new class based on `AIController`. You will need to check *Show All Classes* in the top right of the Unreal Engine Class Creation Wizard.

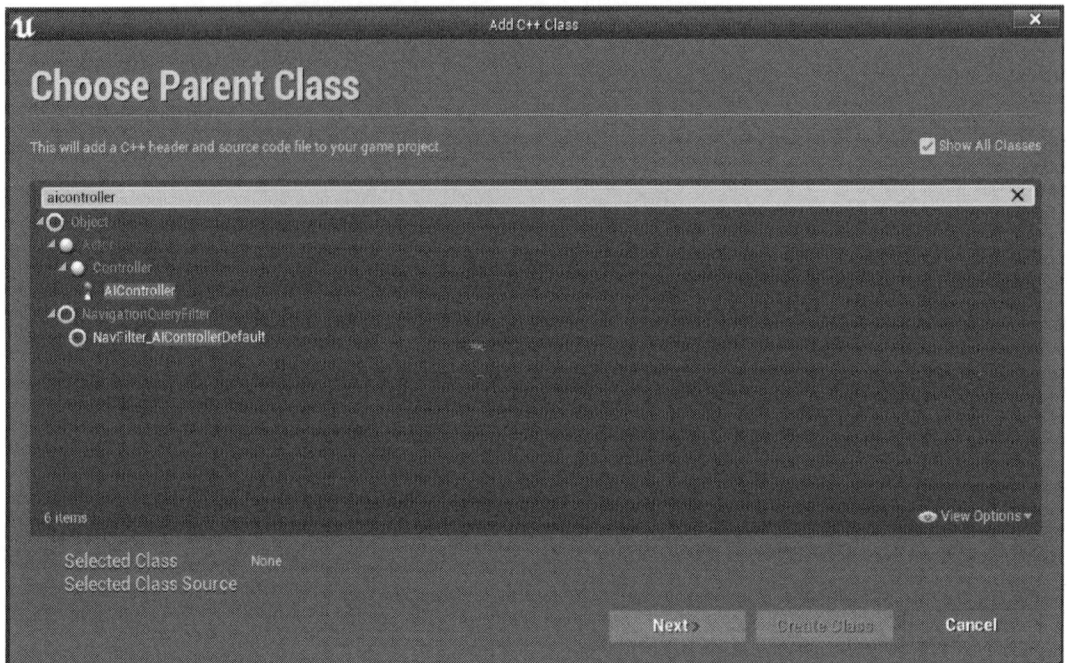

Figure 12.7: Creating a Class Based on AIController

2. Name this class `EnemyController`.

3. Just under `GENERATED_BODY()` in *EnemyController.h*, add:

```cpp
public:
    AEnemyController();

    virtual void OnPossess(APawn* InPawn) override;

    UBlackboardComponent* GetBlackboard();


protected:
    UPROPERTY(BlueprintReadWrite, Category = Behavior)
    class UBlackboardComponent* BlackboardComponent;
```

```
UPROPERTY(BlueprintReadWrite, Category = Behavior)
class UBehaviorTreeComponent* BehaviorTreeComponent;
```

We will be overriding the `OnPossess` function, which is called when the Controller possess the Pawn it is assigned to. We also are creating a `protected` section in which we declare two variables. The first is of type `UBlackboardComponent*` called `BlackboardComponent`, for storing the Blackboard Component for the Enemy. The second is of type `UBehaviorTreeComponent*` called `BehaviorTreeComponent` for storing the Behavior Tree Component. We mark these both with `UPROPERTY` and make them both `BlueprintReadWrite` so we can access and set their values from within Blueprints. We also created a getter for `BlackboardComponent` in the `public` section so we can easily access it.

4. Now, in *EnemyController.cpp* in the constructor, add the following:

```
BlackboardComponent =
CreateDefaultSubobject<UBlackboardComponent>(TEXT("Blackboa
rdComp"));
    check(BlackboardComponent);

    BehaviorTreeComponent =
CreateDefaultSubobject<UBehaviorTreeComponent>(TEXT("Behavi
orTreeComp"));
    check(BehaviorTreeComponent);
```

Here, we are using `CreateDefaultSubobject` to create a `UBlackboardComponent` and a `UBehaviorTreeComponent`. We also use the `check` macro to ensure these are valid and cause execution to halt if they are not valid.

5. Now, in *EnemyController.cpp*, provide the definition for the overridden function `OnPossess`:

```
void AEnemyController::OnPossess(APawn* InPawn)
{
    Super::OnPossess(InPawn);
    if (InPawn == nullptr)
    {
```

```
            return;
    }
    AEnemy* Enemy = Cast<AEnemy>(InPawn);
    if (Enemy)
    {
            if (Enemy->BehaviorTree)
            {
                BlackboardComponent-
>InitializeBlackboard(*(Enemy->BehaviorTree-
>BlackboardAsset));

                BehaviorTreeComponent->StartTree(*(Enemy-
>BehaviorTree));
            }
    }
}
```

6. And add these includes to the top of the file:

```
#include "Enemy.h"
#include "BehaviorTree/BlackboardComponent.h"
#include "BehaviorTree/BehaviorTree.h"
```

As soon as the Controller possesses its Pawn, we check the input parameter `InPawn` and cast it to an AEnemy. We store this in a local variable called Enemy, then check to see if the cast was successful. If so, we check to make sure `Enemy->BehaviorTree` is valid, then take `BlackboardComponent` and use `InitializeBlackboard`. This is how to assign a given Blackboard to this AI Controller. We access the `BehaviorTree` variable we added to the Enemy class and access its `BlackboardAsset` member variable. The Enemy's `BehaviorTree` variable will be set later in Blueprints. Since `BehaviorTree`'s member `BlackboardAsset` is a pointer, we must dereference it using the dereference operator (*) because `InitializeBlackboard` takes an argument of type `UBlackboardData`, not a pointer.

Next, we start our `BehaviorTreeComponent`. This gets the Behavior Tree to begin executing its logic (we haven't added any yet, but we will). This is done by calling `StartTree` on it, which takes an argument of type `UBehaviorTree`. Again, this is not a pointer, so after we access the variable `BehaviorTree` from `Enemy`, which is a pointer, we must dereference it.

7. Let's also define the getter for `BlackboardComponent`:

```
UBlackboardComponent* AEnemyController::GetBlackboard()
{
        return BlackboardComponent;
}
```

Now we are ready to create a Blueprint based on our `EnemyController` class. Create a Blueprint based on this class called *EnemyController_BP* and place it in the *Chapter12* folder.

Open *Enemy_BP* and in the **Details** panel, search for "AIController" and click on the dropdown for AI Controller Class. Select *EnemyController_BP*. We now have our AI Character class and AI Controller class set up. It's now time to take a look at Behavior Trees and see how the various types of nodes work so we can create some AI Logic to control our AI Character!

Behavior Trees and Different Nodes

The Behavior Tree contains nodes, like the **Event Graph** in an Actor's Blueprint. However, the nodes in a Behavior Tree function differently than the nodes in the **Event Graph**. Behavior Tree nodes are arranged in a hierarchical tree structure where child nodes are connected to parent nodes by branches. Each node is meant to attempt a specific task and it will either succeed or fail. The success or failure of a node is reported to its parent through the connecting branch. This results in different behavior depending on the parent node. The different types of Behavior Tree nodes are listed as follows:

- **Root Node**: Every Behavior Tree has a Root Node. The Root Node is where the Behavior Tree logic begins. When the tree fails, logic returns back to the Root Node and the execution of nodes is started over.

- **Task Nodes**: Tasks are simple actions that an AI can perform. Moving to an object is an example of an action performed via a Task.

- **Service Nodes**: A service node performs an action repeatedly. It can be set to fire off at a specific rate, for example, every second.

- **Selector Nodes**: A selector node is used to control the flow of logic in the Behavior Tree. A selector node can have child branches which it will attempt to execute. It will go through its child branches from left to right until one of them succeeds (if a child branch fails, the next child branch is executed). Once a success happens, the Selector Node reports a success to its parent. If all child branches fail, the Selector Node fails.

- **Sequence Nodes**: The Sequence node can have multiple child branches, like the Selector Node. The Sequence Node executes its child branches from left to right until one of them fails. If all child branches succeed, the Sequence node succeeds.

- **Simple Parallel Nodes**: A Simple Parallel node can have two child branches. One is a Task node and the other can be a complete subtree. The subtree is executed and the Task node fires, both simultaneously.

- **Decorators**: Decorators are attached to nodes (except for the Root Node) which provide the opportunity to make conditional checks (like `if` statements) and can affect the success or failure of the node.

Now that we have a high-level understanding of the Behavior Tree nodes, we can create our Behavior Tree.

Creating a Working Behavior Tree

The Behavior Tree will need to access variables that are pertinent to our AI functionality. For this reason, we need a Blackboard which will store a reference to the pertinent variables that we must access from the various elements in our AI system. We will first create a Blackboard, then we will create a Behavior Tree.

Creating a Blackboard

We will now create a Blackboard.

1. In the *Chapter12* folder, right-click and go to Artificial Intelligence -> Blackboard.

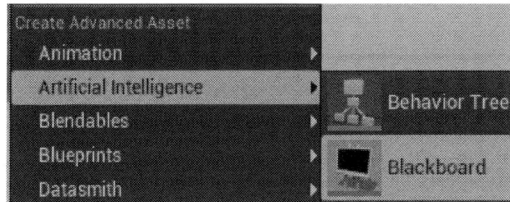

Figure 12.8: Creating a New Blackboard

2. Name the Blackboard *EnemyBlackboard*. Double-click it to open it. You will see that the Blackboard has two panels: The **Blackboard** panel and the **Blackboard Details** panel.

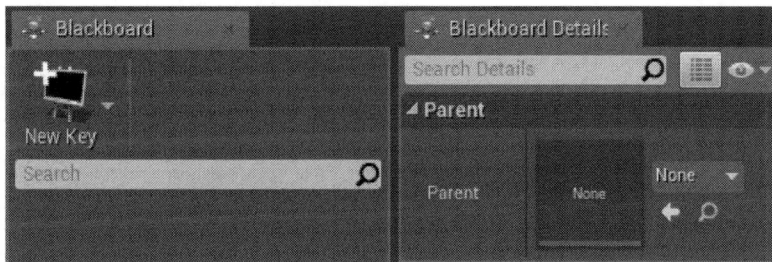

Figure 12.9: The Panels in the Blackboard

3. Click **New Key** to add a new **Blackboard Key** – a special type of variable unique to Blackboards.

The keys will be accessible from all elements in our AI system. Select *Vector* as the type and name this key *PatrolPoint1*. Add three more keys of type *Vector* and call them *PatrolPoint2*, *PatrolPoint3*, and *PatrolPoint4*. These will be locations for the enemy to walk to when it is not chasing the Main Character. Add a fifth key and this time select *Object* as the type and name it *TargetActor*. This key will hold the target Actor (which the Enemy will pursue). Add one more key of bool type called *InAttackRange*. We will use this to determine whether the AI Character is close enough to the Main Character to attack.

Now that we have a Blackboard, we can now create a Behavior Tree.

Creating a Behavior Tree

We will now create a Behavior Tree.

1. In the *Chapter12* folder, right-click and select *Artificial Intelligence -> Behavior Tree*.

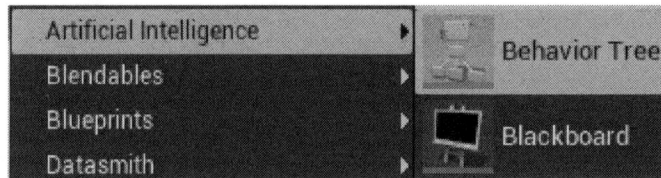

Figure 12.10: Creating a New Behavior Tree

Call it *EnemyBehaviorTree*.

2. Double-click it to open it. You will see in the **Behavior Tree** that there is a graph with a single node: the *Root* node.

Figure 12.11: The Root Node

This node is required and there can only be one. The gray bar at the bottom of the node is where we can drag off new branches and create new nodes. Optionally, the toolbar has several icons providing us with shortcuts for creating a few types of nodes as well:

Figure 12.12: The Behavior Tree Toolbar

In the **Details** panel, notice the *AI* section, in which there exists an item called Behavior Tree.

3. Select the dropdown next to this. You will see the *Blackboard Asset* variable, assigned with the value of *EnemyBlackboard*. If it is not assigned, ensure that it is assigned the value of *EnemyBlackboard*.

Figure 12.13: The Blackboard Asset

At the bottom-right of the screen, the **Blackboard** panel shows the Blackboard Keys that we set up in our Blackboard, and here is where the values of those keys can be checked during runtime for debugging purposes.

Figure 12.14: The Blackboard Panel

Recall that we added a `BehaviorTree` variable to the `Enemy` class. Open the *Enemy_BP* Blueprint and in the **Details** panel, in the **Pawn** section, find *Behavior Tree* and set it to *EnemyBehaviorTree*. This assigns a value to the `BehaviorTree` variable in the `AIEnemy` class.

Now that we have created a Behavior Tree, we are ready to set it up with logic.

Setting Up the Behavior Tree

Now that we have a behavior tree, it's time to start adding some nodes so that our Enemy will be able to perform actions.

Setting Up Patrolling Behavior

The first thing we will program our Enemy to do is to patrol.

1. In *EnemyBehaviorTree*, the **Behavior Tree** Graph, left-click and drag off of the bar at the bottom of the Root Node and release. Select *Sequence*.

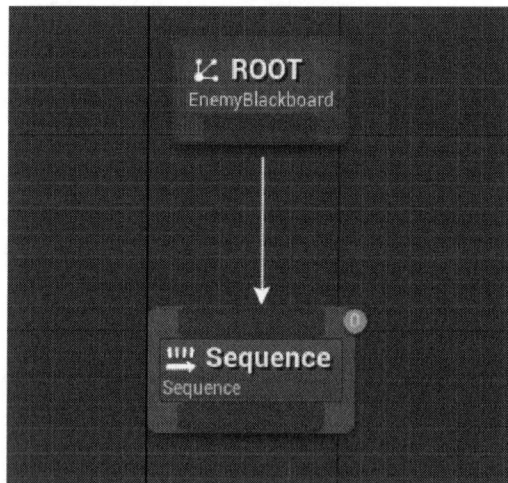

Figure 12.15: Adding a Sequence Node

Remember, Sequence nodes fire off child branches from left to right until one of them fails. Drag off of the bar at the bottom of the Selector node and click the dropdown next to *Tasks*. You will see that there is a list of pre-made Tasks that we can choose from. Remember, Tasks perform an action.

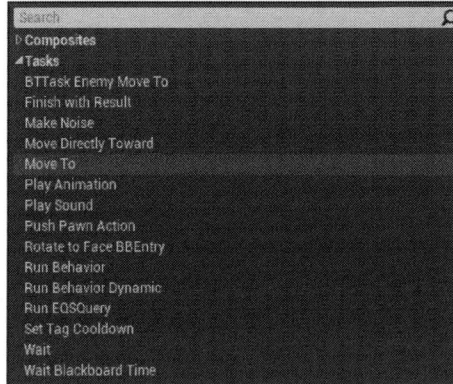

Figure 12.16: Selecting a Pre-Made Task

2. Choose the *MoveTo* Task.

3. Select the newly-created *MoveTo* Task node.

In the **Details** panel, notice that there are some parameters. In the *Node* section, notice the *Acceptance Radius*. This is how close the AI Character will come to the target before the Task is considered to be a success. In the *Blackboard* section, notice the *Blackboard Key* item. This is where we select the location for the AI Character to move to. We will choose *PatrolPoint1*.

4. Next, drag off of the *Sequence* node again and add another Task. From the list of pre-made Tasks, select *Wait*.

This task simply has the Character wait for a specified time. In the **Details** panel, in the *Wait* section, the *Wait Time* item is where we set the time for the AI Character to wait. *Random Deviation* allows for the wait time to deviate randomly by an amount less than the value specified here.

5. Set *Wait Time* to 1.5 and *Random Deviation* to 1.0. Continue to add *Wait* and *MoveTo* tasks until you have the following logic:

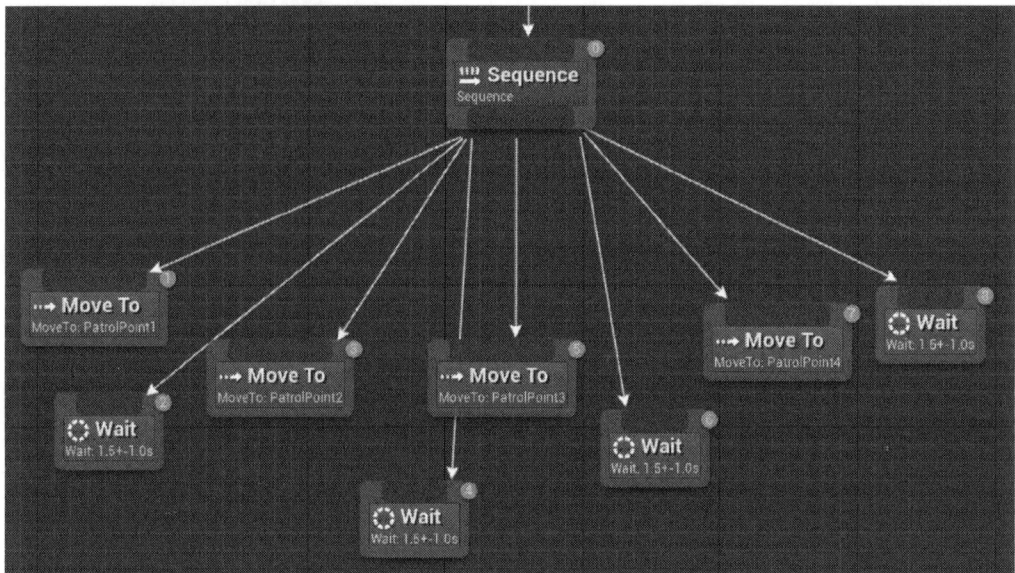

Figure 12.17: MoveTo and Wait Tasks

This Sequence will fire off child tasks one by one until one fails, then the tree will start over. The AI Character will move to *PatrolPoint1*, wait for 1.5 seconds (plus or minus 1.0 second, thanks to the random deviation), then move to *PatrolPoint2*, and so on, until it reaches *PatrolPoint4*. Notice the last *Wait* node. Without this, the AI Character would reach *PatrolPoint4* and immediately run back to *PatrolPoint1* without waiting.

Now we need a way to set the Patrol Points. Let's add four FVector variables to the Enemy class.

6. In *Enemy.h*, just under the declaration for BehaviorTree, add:

```
    UPROPERTY(EditAnywhere, Category = "BehaviorTree",
Meta = (MakeEditWidget = true))
    FVector PatrolPoint1;

    UPROPERTY(EditAnywhere, Category = "BehaviorTree",
Meta = (MakeEditWidget = true))
    FVector PatrolPoint2;

    UPROPERTY(EditAnywhere, Category = "BehaviorTree",
Meta = (MakeEditWidget = true))
```

```cpp
    FVector PatrolPoint3;

    UPROPERTY(EditAnywhere, Category = "BehaviorTree",
Meta = (MakeEditWidget = true))
    FVector PatrolPoint4;

    class AEnemyController* EnemyController;
```

We made these `FVector` variables `EditAnywhere` and gave them the Category "BehaviorTree". We also added `Meta = (MakeEditWidget = true))` which creates a 3D widget in the level that we can adjust in order to choose a location for each of these `FVectors`. One thing to keep in mind is that the location we choose in the world for these vector widgets will assign a value to each `FVector` variable **local** to the AI Character. For example, leaving the widgets at their starting locations (which is the location of the AI Character) will result in values of (0.0, 0.0, 0.0) since this is the location relative to the AI Character. We can easily convert the values for these `FVectors` to world space by adding the AI Character's world location to them.

We also created a variable of type `AEnemyController*` called `EnemyController`. This way, we have a stored reference to the Enemy Controller.

Next, we will want to set the values for the Blackboard Keys according to the locations of our `FVector` variables on the Enemy. We will do so in `BeginPlay`.

7. Add the following to `BeginPlay` in *Enemy.cpp*:

```cpp
    FVector Location = GetActorLocation();
    EnemyController =
Cast<AEnemyController>(GetController());
    EnemyController->GetBlackboard()-
>SetValueAsVector(TEXT("PatrolPoint1"), PatrolPoint1 +
Location);
    EnemyController->GetBlackboard()-
>SetValueAsVector(TEXT("PatrolPoint2"), PatrolPoint2 +
Location);
    EnemyController->GetBlackboard()-
>SetValueAsVector(TEXT("PatrolPoint3"), PatrolPoint3 +
Location);
```

```
    EnemyController->GetBlackboard()-
>SetValueAsVector(TEXT("PatrolPoint4"), PatrolPoint4 +
Location);
```

8. And add the following includes:

```
#include "EnemyController.h"

#include "BehaviorTree/BlackboardComponent.h"
```

First we get the location of the AI Character and store it in the local variable `Location`. We also call `GetController` which returns the `Controller` in the form of an `AController*`. In order to access the function `GetBlackboard` which we declared in the `AEnemyController` class, we must cast to `AEnemyController`. Next, we call `GetBlackboard` to get our `BlackboardComponent`. We use the function `SetValueAsVector` on the `BlackboardComponent` to set the value for the Blackboard Key. This function requires the name of the Blackboard Key in the form of an `FName`. We can simply provide the name as a string wrapped in a `TEXT` macro and it will be converted to an `FName` for us. The next parameter is the value to set the Blackboard Key to. Since the key is a *Vector*, we must provide an `FVector`. We use the value of `PatrolPoint1` with the AI Character's location added, since `PatrolPoint1` will be a value local to the AI Character (because we made it an editable widget). We do the same for `PatrolPoint2`, `PatrolPoint3`, and `PatrolPoint4`. The result is that the Blackboard Key values for the four Patrol Points will be set to these values.

9. Now return to the Unreal Engine editor and drag our `FVector` 3D Widgets to our desired patrol locations.

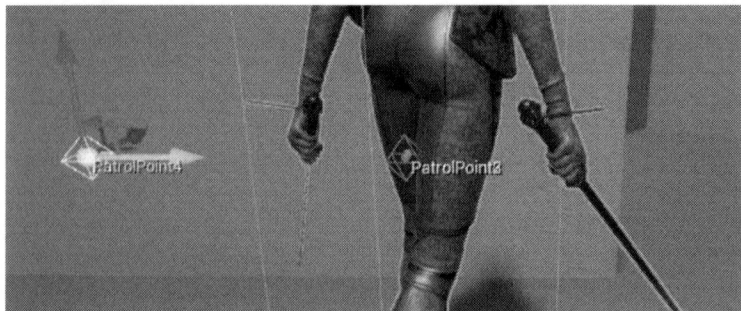

Figure 12.18: The Patrol Point Vector Widgets

Now we can compile and see the 3D Widgets for our Patrol Point vectors and we can set them at various locations in the level. Drag each one to a desired location. Now the AI Character will patrol between the various points in the world.

If you press **Play** however, you will notice that the AI Character doesn't look quite right when running. It starts the running animation, but it doesn't continue to run while moving. We can see the reason for this if we return to the **Content Browser** and open the *Chapter7* folder. Open *MainAnim_BP*. Click on the *AnimGraph* tab, then double-click the *GroundLocomotion* State Machine. Double-click on the transition rule between the *Run* and the *JogStop* States.

Figure 12.19: Transition Rule Between Run and JogStop

Recall that we are checking the *IsAccelerating* Boolean value and only entering the transition if this value is `false`. For the `MainCharacter` class, this value is updated in *MainAnimInstance.cpp*, in the `UpdateAnimationProperties` function. In this function, we have the following lines:

```
if (Main)
{
        if (Main->GetCharacterMovement()-
>GetCurrentAcceleration().Size() > 0)
        {
                bIsAccelerating = true;
        }
        else
        {
                bIsAccelerating = false;
        }
}
```

Here we are taking `Main`, a variable of type `AMainCharacter*`, and calling `GetCharacterMovement()->GetCurrentAcceleration().Size()` in order to get the magnitude of the Character's acceleration vector so we can see if it is greater than zero. Based on this result, we are setting the `MainAnimInstance`'s variable `bIsAccelerating` to `true` or `false`. With our AI Character, however, this will not work. We must figure out a different way to set the `bIsAccelerating` variable in the case that the Anim Instance's owning pawn is an `AEnemy` instead of an `AMainCharacter`. To do this, we will create a `bIsAccelerating` variable in the Enemy class.

10. In *Enemy.h*, in a `public` section, add:

```
UPROPERTY(BlueprintReadOnly)
bool bIsAccelerating;

UFUNCTION(BlueprintCallable)

void SetIsAccelerating(bool bAccelerating);
```

11. Now define `SetIsAccelerating` in *Enemy.cpp*:

```
void AEnemy::SetIsAccelerating(bool bAccelerating)
{
    bIsAccelerating = bAccelerating;

}
```

12. In *MainAnimInstance.h*, declare a variable of type `AEnemy` to store a reference to the Enemy if this anim instance is owned by an Enemy.

```
UPROPERTY(EditAnywhere, BlueprintReadOnly, Category =
Movement)
    class AEnemy* Enemy;
```

13. In *MainAnimInstance.cpp*, we must include:

```
#include "Enemy.h"
```

14. In order for this variable to hold the address of our Enemy, in the constructor, add the following inside the `if (Pawn)` check, just under `Main = Cast<ATestMainCharacter>(Pawn);`:

```
Enemy = Cast<AAIEnemy>(Pawn);
```

Now we have a Boolean on the Enemy class that we can check in *MainAnimInstance.cpp*.

15. In `UpdateAnimationProperties`, after the check `if (Main)` we mentioned earlier, place another check:

```
if (Enemy)
{
      bIsAccelerating = Enemy->bIsAccelerating;
}
else
{
      Enemy = Cast<AEnemy>(Pawn);
      if (Enemy)
      {
            bIsAccelerating = Enemy-
>bIsAccelerating;
      }
}
```

Now, if the Enemy variable is valid, we simply set the anim instance's `bIsAccelerating` variable to the value of the Enemy's `bIsAccelerating` variable. If, for any reason, Enemy is null, we cast Pawn to an AEnemy and store it in Enemy, then we set `bIsAccelerating` to the appropriate value.

Now the `bIsAccelerating` Boolean will be set to the value of the Enemy's `bIsAccelerating` variable. Now we must decide when to set it to `true` and when to set it to `false`. When our AI Character begins its *MoveTo* Task, this would be the perfect time to set the AI Character's `bIsAccelerating` variable to `true`. When it finishes the *MoveTo* task, we can set it back to false. This way, the transition rule checking this Boolean will result in not exiting the *Jog* animation State until the *MoveTo* task is complete.

In order to set the AI Character's `bIsAccelerating` Boolean when *MoveTo* is started, we will need to create our own custom version of the *MoveTo* Behavior Tree Task. We will do this now.

Creating a Custom Behavior Tree Task

To create a custom Behavior Tree Task, open the Behavior Tree and click the **New Task** icon in the Toolbar.

Figure 12.20: Creating a New Task

You will be prompted to choose a base class from which to derive the new Task. Choose *BTTask_BlueprintBase*.

Figure 12.21: Deriving from BTTask_BlueprintBase

The new Task will be given a default name. Go back to the *Chapter12* folder and rename it to *BTT_EnemyMoveToLocation* (BTT stands for Behavior Tree Task). Open the new custom Task.

The first thing we will need to do is have an entry point to our Task's logic. In the **My Blueprint** panel, hover your mouse over the *Functions* section.

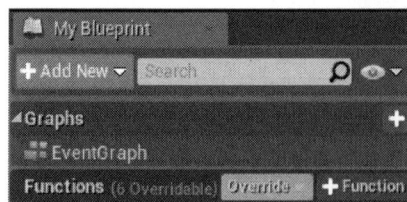

Figure 12.22: The Functions Section in the My Blueprint Panel

Notice the *Override* and *Function* icons appear. Click the *Override* icon and select *Receive Execute*. This creates an *Event Receive Execute* node in the **Event Graph** which will allow us to have a starting point for our logic.

We wish to achieve two main things in this custom Task: cause the AI Character to move to a Patrol Point location, and set the bIsAccelerating Boolean (which we declared in *Enemy.h*) value to `true` on the AI Character. In order to know which location to tell the AI Character to move to, we will need to access one of the Blackboard Keys. Thus we will add a variable of type *Blackboard Key Selector*.

In the **My Blueprint** panel, click the **+ Add New** icon and select *Variable*. For the type, choose *Blackboard Key Selector* and name this variable *PatrolPointKey*. In the **My Blueprint** panel, in the *Variables* section, click the eye icon next to our newly visible *PatrolPointKey* variable to make it *Editable* (this will make it visible and changeable from within the Behavior Tree.

Since we will also be causing the AI Character to move to a location, we will be calling the *MoveTo* function, which requires that we have a reference to the Enemy Controller that is controlling our AI Character. Thus we will create another variable, this time of type *EnemyController_BP*. Call this variable *EnemyController*.

The first thing we must do is check to see if the *EnemyController* variable is valid (the first time, it won't be) and if it isn't, we must access the Controller and store its value in this variable. Add the following nodes to the **Event Graph**:

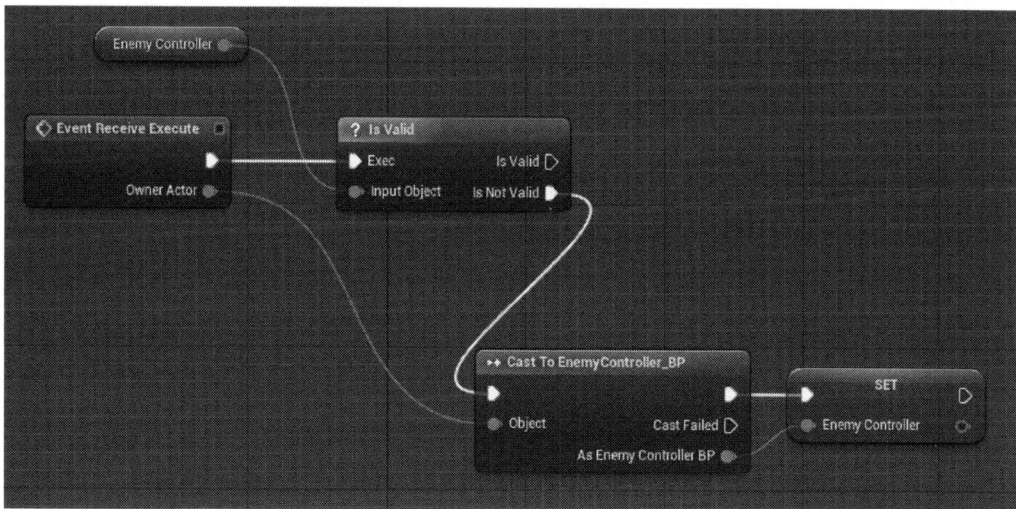

Figure 12.23: Storing a Reference to the Controller

449

Notice *Event Receive Execute* has a return value called *Owner Actor*. This is a reference to the Controller associated with this Behavior Tree. We cast it to *EnemyController_BP* and store it in our local variable *EnemyController*.

Next, we will be calling the *AI Move To* function, which is a function belonging to the Controller. Add the following nodes:

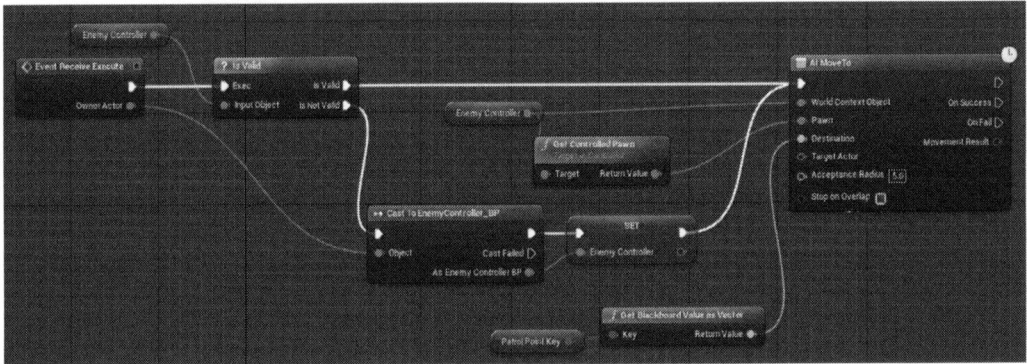

Figure 12.24: Adding a Call to AIMoveTo

We are accessing the *EnemyController* variable and calling *AI Move To*. *AIMoveTo* requires a Pawn, which we can get from *EnemyController* by calling *Get Controlled Pawn*. *AI Move To* requires either a *Target Actor* or a *Destination*. We are getting Patrol Point Key and calling *Get Blackboard Value as Vector* to get the value stored there. We then pass it into the *Destination* input for *AI Move To*. Whatever the value stored in the *Patrol Point Key* will be, that is where the AI Character will move.

Next, we wish to set the AI Character's `bIsAccelerating` Boolean to true. Add a new variable of type *Enemy_BP* called *Enemy*. After we ensure that we have a valid reference to the Controller stored in *EnemyController*, we will ensure that we have a valid reference to the AI Character stored in Enemy. Disconnect the wires going into *AI Move To* and add the following nodes:

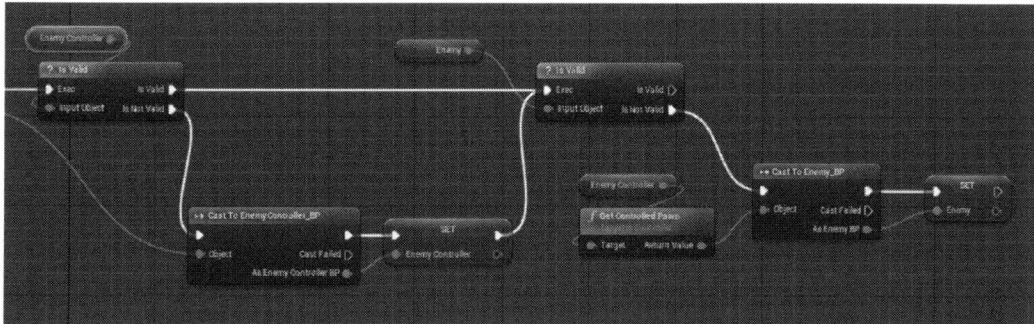

Figure 12.25: Storing a Valid Reference to the AI Character in Enemy

After we check to see if *EnemyController* is valid, we then check to see if *Enemy* is valid. We hook up the exit wires from the *IsValid* node (checking *EnemyController*) and the exit wire from the *Set EnemyController* node both up to the new *IsValid* node (checking *Enemy*). From there, if the *Enemy* variable is not valid, we call *Get Controlled Pawn* from the *EnemyController* variable, cast it to *Enemy_BP*, then set *Enemy*. After this, we will have valid references to both the Controller and the AI Character stored in *EnemyController* and *Enemy*, respectively.

Now that we have a reference to the AI Character, we can set the `bIsAccelerating` Boolean by calling our `BlueprintCallable` function `SetIsAccelerating`. Add the following nodes:

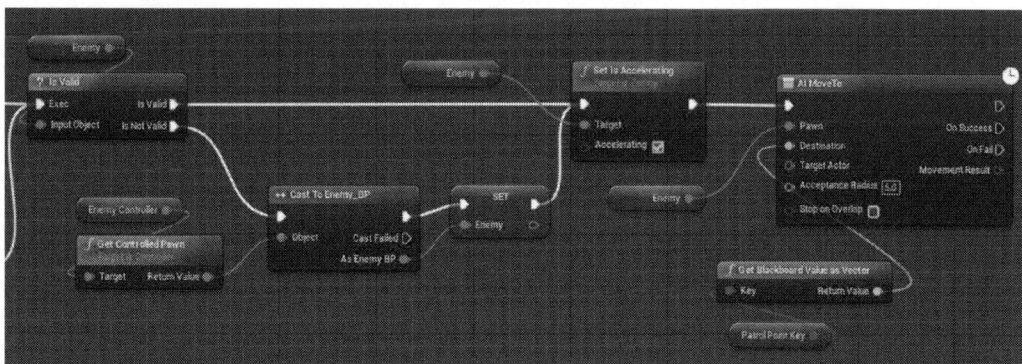

Figure 12.26: Calling SetIsAccelerating on Enemy

Now our AI Character's `bIsAccelerating` Boolean will be set to true. Don't forget to check the checkbox for Accelerating in the *Set Is Accelerating* node, otherwise we will be setting the boolean to `false`! Don't forget to plug in the *Enemy* for the *AI Move To Pawn* input parameter.

Finally, we must declare when this task is complete for the sake of the Behavior Tree. Remember, all nodes in a Behavior Tree either succeed or fail. We use the function *Finish Execute* to declare that this Task has completed. Add the following nodes after *AI Move To*.

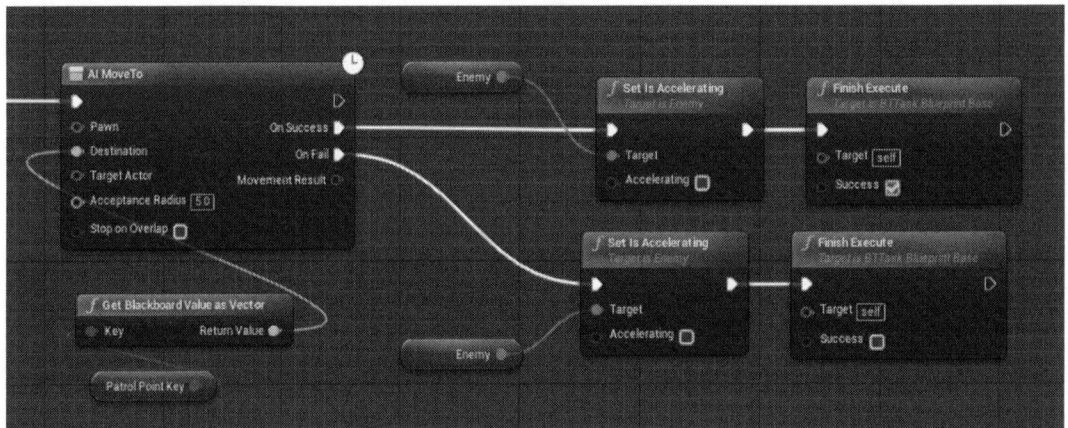

Figure 12.27: Calling Finish Execute

From the *On Success* exit pin in *AI Move To*, we first call *Set Is Accelerating*, setting the Boolean back to false, then we call *Finish Execute*, with the *Success* input checkbox checked so we can report the successful completion of the Task. We also add a call to Set Is Accelerating from the *On Fail* exit pin, followed by a call to *Finish Execute*, this time leaving the *Success* input unchecked, to report a failure. This way, when the AI Character finishes moving to its location, whether it succeeds or fails, either way the Task will be completed and the `bIsAccelerating` Boolean will be set back to `false`.

Now we can add calls to this custom Task in the Behavior tree.

Using a Custom Task in the Behavior Tree

In the *EnemyBehaviorTree*, replace the *MoveTo* Tasks with our custom Task *BTT_EnemyMoveToLocation*.

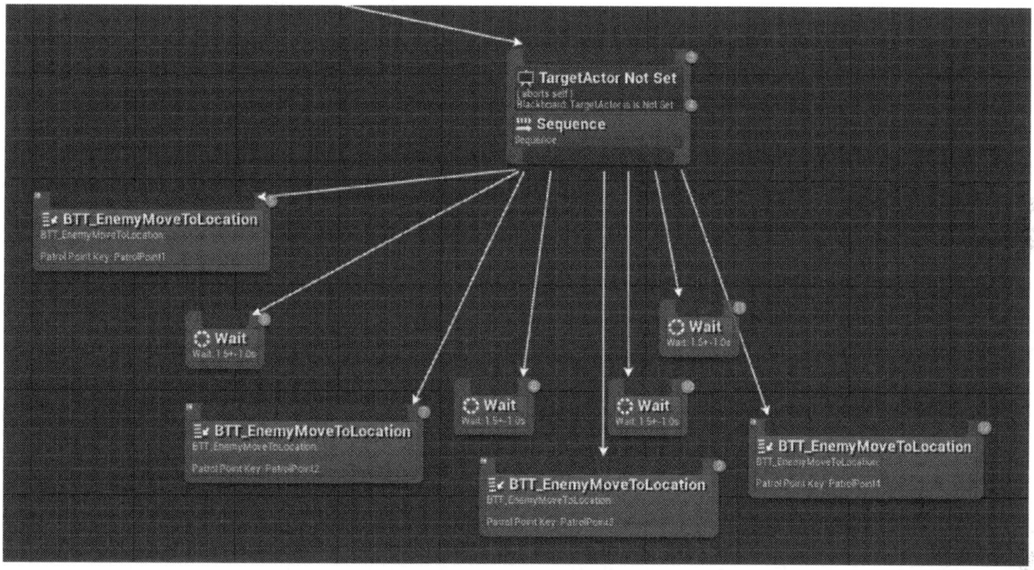

Figure 12.28: Using the Custom MoveTo Task

Notice that each node has a number on its top-right corner. This is a priority number that ranks each node. It determines the order in which the tasks are attempted, so make sure they increase in order from left to right. You may need to move the nodes around to make sure the correct values are assigned for these priorities.

Now press **Play** and watch the AI Character patrol to its four Patrol Points. It runs correctly because we are setting the `bIsAccelerating` Boolean at the appropriate times.

Setting Up Chasing Behavior

Now we would like the AI Character to chase the Main Character whenever the Main Character gets close. In addition, when the AI Character reaches the Main Character, we would like it to attack. In order to know when it's appropriate to chase the Character, we can add a collision sphere to the `Enemy` class. We will use this collision sphere to set the Blackboard Key *TargetActor*. We will also add a smaller collision sphere that will allow us to know when the Main Character is close enough to attack. We will use this collision sphere to set the Blackboard Key *InAttackRange*.

Adding Collision Spheres to Enemy

1. In *Enemy.h*, add the following:

```cpp
UPROPERTY(VisibleAnywhere, Category = "BehaviorTree")
class USphereComponent* AgroSphere;

UPROPERTY(VisibleAnywhere, Category = "BehaviorTree")
USphereComponent* AttackSphere;

UFUNCTION()
void AgroSphereBeginOverlap(UPrimitiveComponent*
OverlappedComponent, AActor* OtherActor,
UPrimitiveComponent* OtherComp, int32 OtherBodyIndex, bool
bFromSweep, const FHitResult & SweepResult);

UFUNCTION()
void AgroSphereEndOverlap(UPrimitiveComponent*
OverlappedComponent, AActor* OtherActor,
UPrimitiveComponent* OtherComp, int32 OtherBodyIndex);

UFUNCTION()
void AttackSphereBeginOverlap(UPrimitiveComponent*
OverlappedComponent, AActor* OtherActor,
UPrimitiveComponent* OtherComp, int32 OtherBodyIndex, bool
bFromSweep, const FHitResult & SweepResult);

UFUNCTION()

void AttackSphereEndOverlap(UPrimitiveComponent*
OverlappedComponent, AActor* OtherActor,
UPrimitiveComponent* OtherComp, int32 OtherBodyIndex);
```

First, we forward declare a USphereComponent called AgroSphere. We mark this UPROPERTY with VisibleAnywhere and give it a Category "BehaviorTree". Next, we declare a USphereComponent called AttackSphere. We don't need to forward declare this one because USphereComponent has already been forward declared in this file. We give it the same UPROPERTY settings as AgroSphere. Since we will be adding Overlap Events for these spheres, we declare `AgroSphereBeginOverlap` and `AgroSphereEndOverlap`, using the appropriate input parameter signature which can be seen in *PrimitiveComponent.h* where these are declared. We declare `AttackSphereBeginOverlap` and `AttackSphereEndOverlap` using the same input parameter signatures as well.

2. We will create these in the constructor:

```
AgroSphere =
CreateDefaultSubobject<USphereComponent>(TEXT("AgroSphere")
);
    AgroSphere->SetupAttachment(GetRootComponent());

    AttackSphere =
CreateDefaultSubobject<USphereComponent>(TEXT("AttackSphere
"));
    AttackSphere->SetupAttachment(GetRootComponent());
```

3. Our next step is to define the Overlap functions.

4. In *Enemy.cpp*, add:

```
void AEnemy::AgroSphereBeginOverlap(UPrimitiveComponent*
OverlappedComponent, AActor* OtherActor,
UPrimitiveComponent* OtherComp, int32 OtherBodyIndex, bool
bFromSweep, const FHitResult & SweepResult)
{
    if (OtherActor)
    {
        AMainCharacter* Main =
Cast<AMainCharacter>(OtherActor);
        if (Main)
        {
            if (EnemyController == nullptr)
            {
                EnemyController =
Cast<AEnemyController>(GetController());
            }
```

```
                    EnemyController->GetBlackboard()-
>SetValueAsObject(TEXT("TargetActor"), Main);
            }
        }
}
```

5. And add the following include:

```
#include "MainCharacter.h"
```

In `AgroSphereBeginOverlap`, we first check `OtherActor` to make sure it isn't null. We then cast `OtherActor` to `AMainCharacter`, create a local variable of type `AMainCharacter*` called `Main` and store this value in it. We check this variable, then check to make sure our `EnemyController` variable isn't null as well. If it is, we call `GetController`, cast its return value to an `AEnemyController` and store it in `EnemyController`. Finally, now that we know we have overlapped with the Main Character and that we have a valid `EnemyController`, we call the `EnemyController`'s `SetValueAsObject` function. This sets a Blackboard Key value for an Object Blackboard Key. We must pass in the name of the key, and since our Object Key in our Blackboard is called `TargetActor`, this is the name we supply. The second parameter is the value, and for this we use `Main`.

6. Let's define `AgroSphereBeginOverlap`:

```
void AEnemy::AgroSphereBeginOverlap(UPrimitiveComponent*
OverlappedComponent, AActor* OtherActor,
UPrimitiveComponent* OtherComp, int32 OtherBodyIndex, bool
bFromSweep, const FHitResult & SweepResult)
{
    if (OtherActor)
    {
        AMainCharacter* Main =
Cast<AMainCharacter>(OtherActor);
        if (Main)
        {
            if (EnemyController == nullptr)
            {
                EnemyController =
Cast<AEnemyController>(GetController());
            }
```

```
            EnemyController->GetBlackboard()-
>SetValueAsObject(TEXT("TargetActor"), Main);
        }
    }
}
```

We first check `OtherActor`. If not null, we cast it to `AMainCharacter` and store it in the local variable `Main`. If `EnemyController` is null, we get it with `GetController`, cast it to `AEnemyController`, then store it in our variable `EnemyController`. After this check, we call `GetBlackboard` on `EnemyController`. From this we call `SetValueAsObject`. This sets a Blackboard Key value, first by passing in the name of the key, then the value to set it to. We set the *TargetActor* Blackboard Key to the value stored in `Main`. This way, whenever the *AgroSphere* is overlapped, if the object that overlapped with it is the Main Character, the Blackboard Key *TargetActor* will hold a reference to the Main Character.

7. Define `AgroSphereEndOverlap`. The code for `AgroSphereEndOverlap` is identical to that in `AgroSphereBeginOverlap` except for one difference: instead of passing `Main` for `SetValueAsObject`'s second argument, we pass in `nullptr`. This way, when the Character stops overlapping with the `AgroSphere`, the Blackboard Key value will be null.

8. Define `AttackSphereOverlapBegin` and `AttackSphereOverlapEnd`. The function bodies for `AttackSphereOverlapBegin` and `AttackSphereOverlapEnd` will have the same code as `AgroSphereBeginOverlap` and `AgroSphereEndOverlap` for the `AgroSphere`, except for the line where the Blackboard Key is set. For `AttackSphereOverlapBegin`, this line is:

```
EnemyController->GetBlackboard()-
>SetValueAsBool(TEXT("InAttackRange"), true);
```

And for `AttackSphereOverlapEnd`, it is:

```
EnemyController->GetBlackboard()-
>SetValueAsBool(TEXT("InAttackRange"), false);
```

9. Finally, we need to bind our overlap functions to the Delegates on the Sphere Components. In *BeginPlay*, add the following:

```
    AgroSphere->OnComponentBeginOverlap.AddDynamic(this,
&AEnemy::AgroSphereBeginOverlap);
    AgroSphere->OnComponentEndOverlap.AddDynamic(this,
&AEnemy::AgroSphereEndOverlap);
    AttackSphere->OnComponentBeginOverlap.AddDynamic(this,
&AEnemy::AttackSphereBeginOverlap);

    AttackSphere->OnComponentEndOverlap.AddDynamic(this,
&AEnemy::AttackSphereEndOverlap);
```

10. And we must add the include:

```
#include "Components/SphereComponent.h"
```

Now when the Main Character overlaps with the AttackSphere, the *InAttackRange* bool Blackboard Key value will be set to true and when the Main Character stops overlapping with it, *InAttackRange* will be set to true. This will allow us to determine when it's an appropriate time for the AI Character to attack.

11. In the *Enemy_BP* Blueprint, set the AgroSphere radius to 600.0 and the AttackSphere radius to 90.0. These can be tweaked on the Blueprint, but these values are appropriate for now.

We now have two overlap spheres: the AgroSphere and the AttackSphere. When the Main Character walks inside the AgroSphere, the AI Character sets its Blackboard Key *TargetActor* to the Main Character, and when the Main Character steps out of this sphere, the *TargetActor* key gets cleared to null. When the Main Character gets even closer and steps into the AttackSphere, the *InAttackRange* Blackboard Key is set to true (remember, this key is of the Boolean type). Now that we are setting our Blackboard Keys, it's time to actually use them. Let's program our AI to chase the Character when it gets close.

Adding Chasing Behavior

Now we are ready to implement chasing behavior in the Behavior Tree.

In the Behavior Tree graph, hold *ALT* and left-click on the top bar of the *Sequence* node to disconnect the branch connecting it to the *Root Node*. Highlight the Sequence node and all of the nodes connected to it and drag them off to the right.

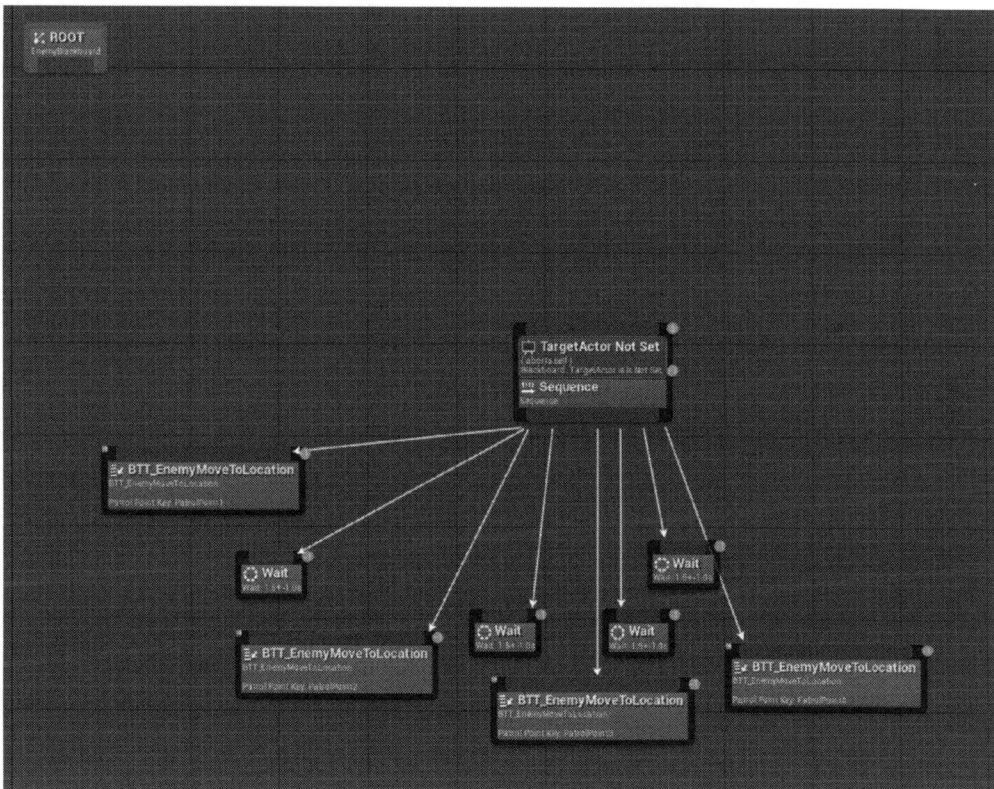

Figure 12.29: Detaching the Sequence Node and Moving It to the Right

Now, from the *Root* node, drag off from the bottom bar and select *Selector* to create a *Selector* node. Remember, a *Selector* node will execute its child branches from left to right until one succeeds. Once it succeeds, it reports the success up to its parent. From the selector, drag off to the left and create another *Selector* node. Drag off of the first (top) Selector and connect it to the *Sequence* node.

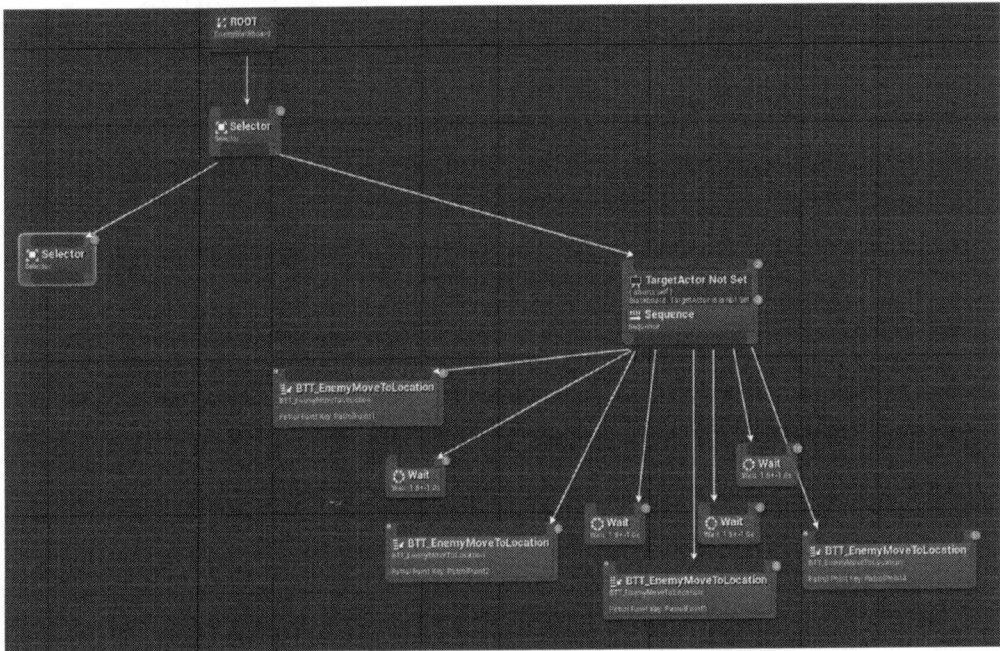

Figure 12.30: Splitting the Logic with a Selector Node

Now, since the Selector node executes child branches from left to right until one succeeds, the top *Selector* node will first attempt its leftmost child branch, and if it succeeds, the rightmost branch (with all of the patrolling code) will not even be executed. If the leftmost child branch fails, however, then the rightmost branch will be executed.

We can ensure that the top Selector's left and right child branches succeed or fail based on the values of our Blackboard Key values. For example, the Blackboard Key *TargetActor* will only be set once the Main Character overlaps with the AI Character's `AgroSphere`. When the Main Character stops overlapping with the `AgroSphere`, the Blackbaord Key *TargetActor* will not be set (because we set it to nullptr in `AgroSphereOverlapEnd`).

To place a condition on a particular Behavior Tree node to determine whether or not it should be executed, we have the *Decorator*.

Placing Decorators on Nodes

We only want the patrolling behavior to be executed if the *TargetActor* Blackboard Key has a value set. To ensure this, right-click on the *Sequence* node and select *Add Decorator -> Blackboard*. Now the Sequence node should appear as follows:

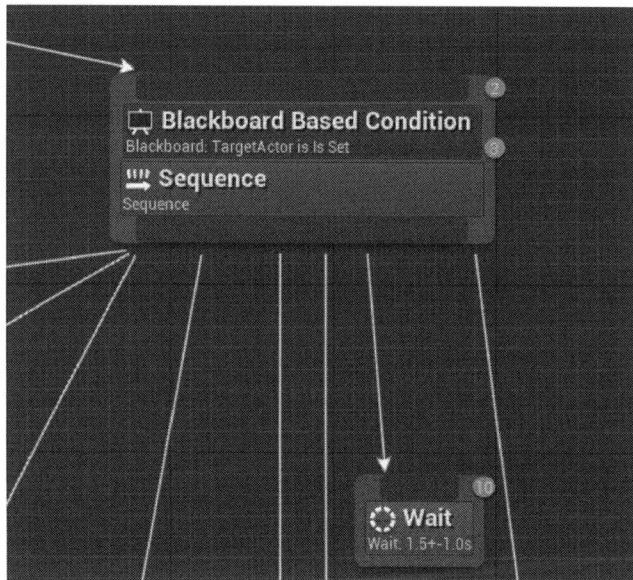

Figure 12.31: Adding a Decorator to the Sequence Node

Now left-click on the blue portion that says *Blackboard Based Condition*. We are now ready to configure our Decorator.

Configuring a Decorator

Decorators are sort of like `if` statements in C++. They can check conditions and determine the flow of logic in the tree.

1. With the Decorator selected, take a look at the **Details** panel. You will see the sections **Flow Control**, **Blackboard**, and **Description**.

2. The **Description** section has an item called *Node Name*, which is set to "Blackboard Based Condition" by default, can be changed. Change it to "TargetActor Not Set".

3. The **Blackboard** section determines what is being checked. The *Blackboard Key* item has a dropdown from which you can select which Blackboard Key value to check. Make sure this is set to *TargetActor*. The *Key Query* item can be set to *Is Set* or *Is Not Set*. Set it to *Is Not Set*. This way, if *TargetActor* is not set, the condition will succeed and the *Sequence* will be executed. If *TargetActor* is not set, the condition will fail and the Sequence will not be executed. As you can see, the Decorator behaved much like an `if` statement in C++. We want our AI Character to patrol when the *TargetActor* key is not set.

The **Flow Control** section has a couple of options that determine how the *Decorator* behaves. The *Observer Aborts* item can be set to *None, Self, Lower Priority*, or *Both*.

- Setting *Observer Aborts* to Self will cause the node to which the *Decorator* is attached to abort when the state of the *Decorator* changes. If the node aborts, none of its children will be executed. This also means that the node will fail.

- Setting *Observer Aborts* to *Lower Priority* will result in the nodes with higher ID numbers to fail. So if the Sequence node has an ID of 3 (the number at the top-right of the node) and its children have ID numbers that are higher than 3, all of the child nodes will fail.

- Setting *Observer Aborts* to *Both* will cause both the node to which the Decorator is attached and nodes with higher ID numbers to fail, and setting it to None doesn't cause anything to abort.

4. Choose *Self* so that the node will fail upon the evaluation of the condition.

The *Notify Observer* item determines how you would like to restart the node. If you would like to restart the node every time the Blackboard Key value changes (in this case, the *TargetActor*), set this item to *On Value Change*. To restart based on the result of the condition being evaluated, set this item to *On Result Change*.

5. We will choose *On Result Change* so the restart will occur when the condition check result is evaluated.

6. Next, we will place a *Decorator* on the bottom-left *Selector* Node, which is the left-most child of the top *Selector* node. Right-click on it and choose *Decorator -> Blackboard*.

7. In the **Description** Section, change the *Node Name* to "TargetActor is Set." The rest of the settings will be identical to those in the *TargetActor Not Set Decorator* except for the *Key Query* item, which will be set to *Is Set*. This way, the *Selector* will execute only if the *TargetActor* Blackboard Key value is set.

We now have a node that will execute when the *TargetActor* Blackboard Key is set. What do we want to do in this case? Well, if *TargetActor* is set, it means the Main Character is inside the `AgroSphere`. If the Main Character is not close enough to attack (it isn't inside the *AttackSphere*) the AI Character should chase the Main Character. But if the Main Character is close enough to attack, the AI Character should attack. Thus we must perform another check to see if the Main Character is inside the *AttackSphere*. If not, the AI Character should chase the Main Character. We will thus add another custom Task for making the AI Character move toward the Main Character while also setting the `bIsAccelerating` Boolean to the correct value. This will be similar to the *BTT_EnemyMoveToLocation* custom task we created in which we made the AI Character move to a location, except we will make the AI Character move to a target (the Main Character) instead of a static location in space.

Adding a Move To Target Behavior Tree Task

Our Move To Target Behavior Tree Task will be similar to *BTT_EnemyMoveToLocation*, except it will be designed to move the AI Character toward the Main Character, rather than to a static location.

1. Create a new Task based on *BTTask_BlueprintBase*. Call it *BTT_EnemyMoveToTarget*. Open this Task Blueprint. Add three new variables: A *Blackboard Key Selector* called *TargetActor*, an *EnemyController_BP* called

EnemyController, and an Enemy_BP called Enemy. Make sure to click the eye icon next to TargetActor to it will be visible and editable from within the BehaviorTree.

2. Just like we did in the BTT_EnemyMoveToLocation Task, we will be ensuring our EnemyController and Enemy variables have valid values:

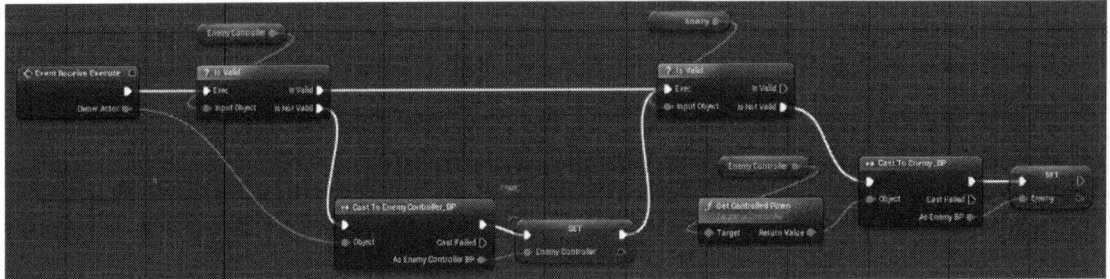

Figure 12.32: Setting the EnemyController and Enemy Variables

3. Drag Enemy out onto the graph from the Variables section in the **My Blueprint** panel to get Enemy, then call Set Is Accelerating. Check the box so we are setting the bIsAccelerating Boolean to true. Now, hook up the Is Valid pin from the IsValid node (checking Enemy) as well as the exit pin from the Set Enemy node both into the call to Set Is Accelerating.

Next, we will be calling AI Move To. The difference this time is that we won't be plugging in a value for the Destination input. Instead, we will be plugging in a value for the Target Actor input, as shown in the following figure.

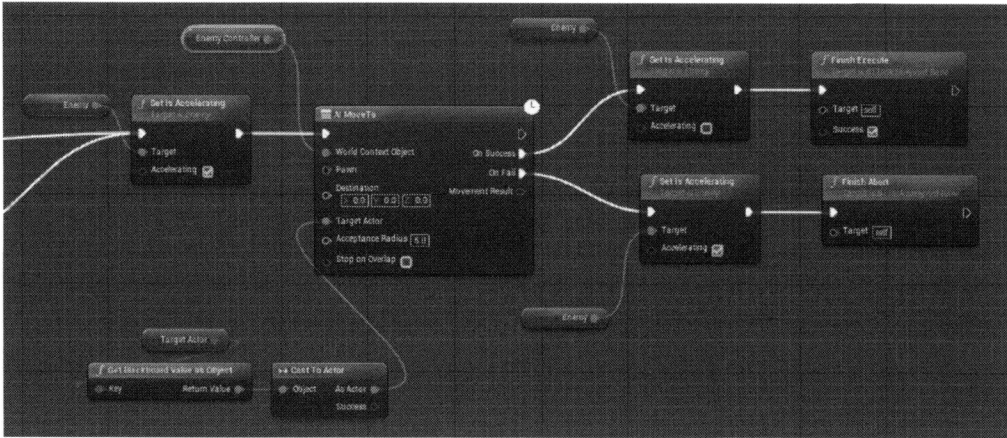

Figure 12.33: Calling AI Move To with a Target Actor Instead of a Destination Vector

4. Notice that we are getting the *TargetActor*, calling *Get Blackboard Value as Object* (instead of Vector) and casting it to Actor. Notice that the Cast node doesn't have input or output executing pins. This is called a BlueprintPure node. You can convert a regular Cast node to *BlueprintPure* by right-clicking on it and selecting *Convert to pure cast*. Do this with the Cast to Actor node. Connect its output *As Actor* value to the *Target Actor* input in *AI Move To*.

5. Finally, we have our *On Success* and *On Fail* exit pins hooked up to calls to *Set Is Accelerating*. For *On Success*, we have the checkbox for *Accelerating* unchecked, so the AI Character will not run. For *On Fail*, the checkbox for *Accelerating* is checked, so the AI Character will run. The success case is followed by a call to *Finish Execute*, passing in `true` for *Success*. The fail case, however, is hooked up to a *Finish Abort*. This way, we won't risk the *AI Move To* functionality triggering a success and setting *Is Accelerating* back to false. Make sure the Boolean checkboxes in these function inputs match those in the above figure. Compile and Save the Blueprint.

6. Now we are ready to use our new Task. In the Behavior tree, drag off of the bottom-left Selector with the *TargetActor is Set Decorator*, and choose *Tasks ->*

BTT Enemy Move to Target. Click on this node to select it and in the **Details** panel, make sure the *Target Key* item is set to *TargetActor*. This will ensure that the Blackboard Key Selector variable we added inside the *BTT_EnemyMoveToTarget* Blueprint is set to the actual Blackboard Key value. If you don't see it as an option, go back to the Blueprint and make sure the eye icon next to it is activated.

7. Next, we will place a decorator on the *BTT_EnemyMoveToTarget* Task to make sure the Main Character is not inside the `AttackSphere`. Add a Decorator just like we did with the Selector and Sequence nodes. The settings will be the same, except the Blackboard Key item will be set to *InAttackRange*, the *Node Name* will be changed to "Is Not in Attack Range" and the *Key Query* will be set to *Is Not Set*. This way, if the Main Character is not inside the `AttackSphere`, the AI Character will chase the Main Character!

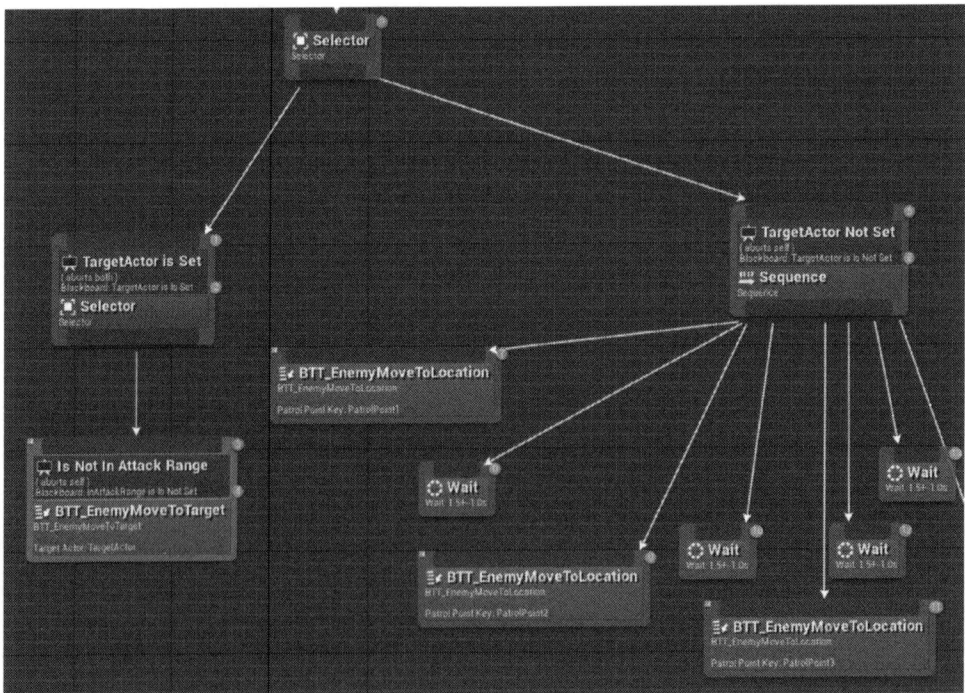

Figure 12.34: Adding a Decorator to BTT_EnemyMoveToTarget

Save all and press **Play**. The AI Character will be patrolling until the Main Character moves within the `AgroSphere`! As soon as the Main Character is within `AgroSphere`, the AI Character stops patrolling and chases the Main Character.

The only thing left now is combat. As soon as the AI Character is close enough to attack (InAttackRange is set to true) we want the AI Character to attack. We will implement this now.

Adding Attack Behavior

Now we are ready to add attacking behavior. We'll need to be able to know when our AI Character is able to attack (when the Character is within attack range) as well as when the AI Character is currently attacking.

1. Add the following to *Enemy.h*, in a `public` section:

```
UPROPERTY(BlueprintReadOnly)
bool bIsAttacking;

bool bAttackTimerStarted;
bool bInAttackRange;

UFUNCTION(BlueprintCallable)
void SetIsAttacking(bool Attacking);
```

We have a bool `bIsAttacking` for when the AI Character is attacking. We will be creating a timer so the AI Character waits for a period between attacks (that way, it doesn't spam the Character with attacks), so we created a bool for whether or not the attack timer has started, called `bAttackTimerStarted`. We also have the bool `bInAttackRange` for whether or not the Character is in the AI Character's attack range. Finally, we created a setter `SetIsAttacking` for setting the `bIsAttacking` bool, and we made it `BlueprintCallable` so we can call it from Blueprints. Its implementation in *Enemy.cpp* is simple:

```
void AEnemy::SetIsAttacking(bool Attacking)
{
        bIsAttacking = Attacking;
```

```
}
```

2. Now, to handle attacking, we will add the following variables to *Enemy.h*:

```
UPROPERTY(EditDefaultsOnly, BlueprintReadOnly,
Category = "Anims")
    class UAnimMontage* CountessAttackMontage;

UPROPERTY(EditAnywhere, BlueprintReadWrite, Category =
"Combat")
    float AttackMinTime;

UPROPERTY(EditAnywhere, BlueprintReadWrite, Category =
"Combat")
    float AttackMaxTime;

FTimerHandle AttackTimer;
```

The anim montage `CountessAttackMontage` is of type `UAnimMontage*`, and we will use the very same montage asset that we used with the Character *MainCharacter_BP*. We created `float` variables: `AttackMinTime` and `AttackMaxTime`, which we will use to place upper and lower bounds on the time between attacks, which we will randomize. Finally, we declare `AttackTimer`, an `FTimerHandle`. An `FTimerHandle` is used for setting timers and calling a callback function at the end of the time specified by the timer.

3. Next, let's give our variables default values in the `Enemy` constructor:

```
AttackMinTime = .5f;

AttackMaxTime = 1.5f;

bIsAttacking = false;

bAttackTimerStarted = false;

bInAttackRange = false;
```

We will let the delay between attacks range between 0.5 seconds and 1.5 seconds. The booleans `bIsAttacking`, `bAttackTimerStarted`, and `bInAttackRange` all start out `false` by default.

4. Now we must decide how to handle attacking. We will create a function to call in `Tick` called `StartAttack`. For actually playing the attack montage, we will create a function called `Attack`. Declare these in the `protected` section just under the declaration for `BeginPlay` in *Enemy.h*:

```
void StartAttack();

void Attack();
```

5. Now define them in *Enemy.cpp*:

```
void AEnemy::StartAttack()
{
    if (bIsAttacking)
    {
        if (!bAttackTimerStarted)
        {
            float AttackTime =
FMath::FRandRange(AttackMinTime, AttackMaxTime);

    GetWorldTimerManager().SetTimer(AttackTimer, this,
&AEnemy::Attack, AttackTime);
            bAttackTimerStarted = true;
        }
    }
    else
    {
        if (!bInAttackRange)
        {

    GetWorldTimerManager().ClearTimer(AttackTimer);
            bAttackTimerStarted = false;
        }
    }
}

void AEnemy::Attack()
{
```

```
    UAnimInstance* AnimInstance = GetMesh()-
>GetAnimInstance();
    if (AnimInstance && CountessAttackMontage)
    {
        AnimInstance->Montage_Play(CountessAttackMontage,
1.35f);
        AnimInstance-
>Montage_JumpToSection(FName("Attack"),
CountessAttackMontage);
    }
    bAttackTimerStarted = false;

}
```

First, in StartAttack, we check to see if the AI Character is currently attacking. If so, we then check to see if the attack timer has started. Only if it hasn't started yet, we calculate the attack time with FMath::FRandRange, which returns a random float within a range specified. We provide the low and high end for the range, then store the result in the local float variable AttackTime. Next, we get the World Timer Manager, which can be accessed via GetWorldTimerManager. This function returns an FTimerManager, which we use to call SetTimer.

There are a handful of overloads for SetTimer. In the overload we use:

- The first argument is an FTimerHandle, for which we supply AttackTimer.

- We then pass in a pointer to the class which will be using this timer handle, which is the AEnemy, so we pass in this.

- The next argument is the callback function that will be called when the timer has finished running. It must be a pointer to a function, so we use the address-of (&) operator, followed by the fully-qualified name of the function, AEnemy::Attack.

- The final argument we pass in is the time, for which we pass in AttackTime.

Finally, we set the bAttackTimerStarted to true. This way, the next frame, when Tick is called, thus calling StartAttack, this code will not run again (until bAttackTimerStarted is set to false again).

When `StartAttack` is called, if `bIsAttacking` is not set to true, we then check to see if `bInAttackRange` is not set to true. If it is not, then this means that the Character has moved outside of the `AttackSphere` and we no longer wish for the attack function to be called once the attack timer has finished. In fact, we can stop the timer by calling `ClearTimer` on the World Timer Manager. We do this, then we set `bAttackTimerStarted` to `false`.

When the timer does complete, it will call `Attack`. In `Attack`, we first use `GetMesh` to get the mesh of this AI Character, then we call `GetAnimInstance`. We store this in a local `UAnimInstance*` called `AnimInstance`. After checking to make sure this variable is not null along with `CountessAttackMontage`, we call `Montage_Play`, passing in `CountessAttackMontage`. We pass in a `float` value as a second parameter, indicating we would like the montage to play the animation at a 1.35 times the original animation speed. We then call `Montage_JumpToSection`, providing the name "`Attack`" for the montage section name. This function requires the montage to be passed in as well. Finally, we set `bAttackTimerStarted` back to `false`, so the next time we set `bIsAttacking` to `true`, we will be able to start the attack timer once again.

6. In order for the above code to work, we must add the following includes to the top of *Enemy.cpp*:

```
#include "TimerManager.h"
#include "Components/SkeletalMeshComponent.h"
#include "Animation/AnimInstance.h"
#include "Animation/AnimMontage.h"
```

7. Now we must know when to set `bIsAttacking` to true. A good place would be in `AttackSphereBeginOverlap`. This function is fired off once the Character comes into attacking range. Inside the check `if(Main)`, after the call to:

```
EnemyController->GetBlackboard()-
>SetValueAsBool(TEXT("InAttackRange"), true);
```

Add:

```
                bInAttackRange = true;

                bIsAttacking = true;
```

Now, in *AttackSphereEndOverlap*: just after `EnemyController->GetBlackboard()->SetValueAsBool(TEXT("InAttackRange"), false);`:

```
                bInAttackRange = false;

                bIsAttacking = false;
```

Now these Booleans will be set to `true` and/or `false` at the proper times.

We also must set `bIsAttacking` to `false` when the attack animation completes. We will use the Anim Notify that already exists in the anim montage for this. Compile the code.

8. In the Unreal Engine editor, open *MainAnim_BP*. In the **Event Graph**, add the following to *AnimNotify_AttackEnd*:

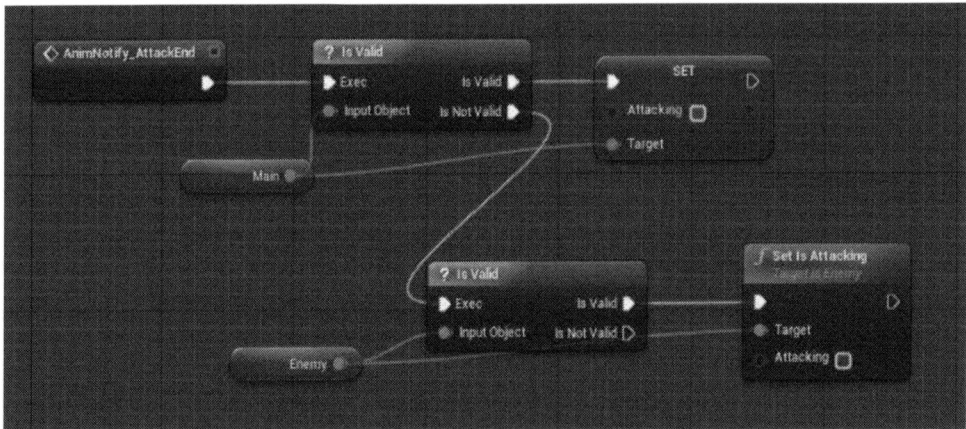

Figure 12.35: Setting IsAttacking to False with the AttackEnd Notify

Notice this additional logic only applies if the Main variable is not valid (we are the Enemy). Now that attacking is taken care of, we must make sure the AI Character doesn't move toward the Character while in attack range.

9. Open *EnemyBehaviorTree*, and make notice the bottom-leftmost Selector node with the following child branch:

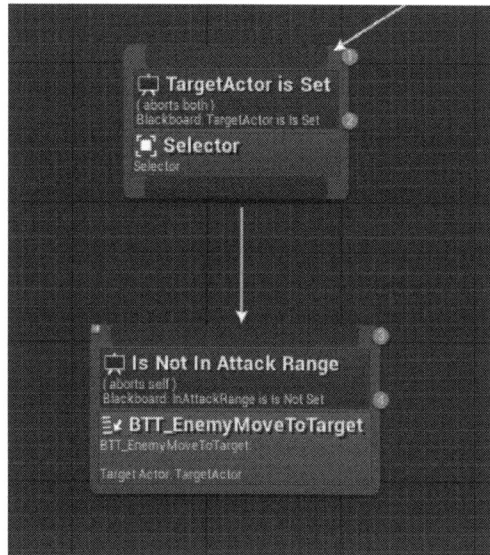

Figure 12.36: The Enemy Move To Target Node with a Decorator

We are using the custom *Task BTT_EnemyMoveToTarget*, with the Decorator added to check *InAttackRange*.

This way, if the Character is not in attack range, the AI Character will move to the target (this is of course assuming the target is set, as is checked in the Decorator attached to the selector above).

10. Once compiled, open the *Enemy_BP* Blueprint and notice in the **Details** panel that there is an **Anims** section and *Countess Attack Montage* exists there. Set it to the *CountessAttack* montage.

11. Now, `StartAttack` is designed to check `bIsAttacking` each frame. Thus we must call it each frame. In *Enemy.cpp*, in `Tick`, add the following call:

```
StartAttack();
```

Now press **Play** and enter the `AttackSphere` with the Character. Notice the AI Character chases the Character and once in attack range, the AI Character will attack in random intervals ranging between 0.5 seconds to 1.5 seconds apart.

We have the AI Character attacking, but no damage is done. We are now ready to add damaging capabilities to our Characters!

Adding Damage Capabilities

Our Main Character and our AI Character now can attack, however damage isn't occurring. In order to deal damage, we will need to set up some additional code. Because much of the attack and damage capabilities will be the same for both the `MainCharacter` class and the `Enemy` class, it will be convenient to create a common base class for both of them to inherit from. This way, we can place the code they will have in common in the base class, and both the `MainCharacter` and `Enemy` classes will inherit that code.

1. Create a new class based on `Character` called `BaseCharacter`.

2. In *MainCharacter.h*, change the line where the class AMainCharacter is declared to:

```
class FIRSTGAME_API AMainCharacter : public ABaseCharacter
```

Now `AMainCharacter` is based on `ABaseCharacter` (which is based on `ACharacter`). Go into *Enemy.h* and change the line where AEnemy is declared to:

```
class FIRSTGAME_API AEnemy : public ABaseCharacter
```

Now `AEnemy` is also based on `ABaseCharacter`. `AEnemy` and `AMainCharacter` will still inherit everything they previously inherited from `ACharacter`, but they will also inherit everything that we place in the `ABaseCharacter` class.

3. Replace the include:

```
#include "GameFramework/Character.h"
```

with:

```
#include "BaseCharacter.h"
```

because we are now deriving from this class rather than direcly from `Character`.

4. Repeat Step 3 for the `Enemy` class, since it will also inherit from `BaseCharacter`.

5. In *BaseCharacter.h*, declare the following items in the `public` section just under the constructor:

```cpp
UPROPERTY(VisibleAnywhere, Category = "Combat")
class UBoxComponent* SwordCollisionBox;

UPROPERTY(EditAnywhere, BlueprintReadWrite, Category =
"Combat")
class UParticleSystem* HitParticles;

UPROPERTY(EditAnywhere, BlueprintReadWrite, Category =
"Combat")
class USoundBase* HitSound;

/** Boolean for when the character is attacking */
UPROPERTY(VisibleAnywhere, BlueprintReadWrite,
Category = "Combat")
bool bAttacking;

UPROPERTY(EditDefaultsOnly, BlueprintReadOnly,
Category = "Anims")
class UAnimMontage* CountessAttackMontage;

UPROPERTY(EditAnywhere, BlueprintReadWrite, Category =
"Stats")
float Health;

UPROPERTY(EditDefaultsOnly, BlueprintReadOnly,
Category = "Stats")
float MaxHealth;

UPROPERTY(EditDefaultsOnly, BlueprintReadOnly,
Category = "Stats")
float Damage;

UPROPERTY(EditAnywhere, BlueprintReadWrite, Category =
"Combat")
TSubclassOf<UDamageType> DamageTypeClass;
```

475

```
      UPROPERTY(EditDefaultsOnly, BlueprintReadOnly,
Category = "Stats")
      int32 XP;
```

First, we declare a collision volume for when the sword strikes its target, called `SwordCollisionBox`. This is of the type `UBoxComponent*`, which we forward declare.

We will also be using a particle system to indicate where the sword strikes, so we forward declare a variable of type `UParticleSystem*`, called `HitParticles`.

To accompany our attack, we would like to play a sound as well, so we forward declare a variable of type `USoundBase*` called `HitSound`. We make the sound and particle system `EditAnywhere` so we can select the assets in the Blueprint for the Character and the Enemy.

6. Since there will be a `bAttacking` Boolean for both the `MainCharacter` class and the `Enemy` class, we will move the `bAttacking` variable here. Delete the declarations for `bAttacking` in *MainCharacter.h* and `bIsAttacking` *Enemy.h*. Since we called this variable `bIsAttacking` in the `Enemy` class, we will need to go into *Enemy.cpp* and change all instances of `bIsAttacking` to `bAttacking`.

Both classes also have an animation montage for attacking, so we also will be moving the `CountessAttackMontage` variable into this class.

7. Go into *Enemy.h* and *MainCharacter.h* and remove the declaration for `CountessAttackMontage`. They will now inherit this from `BaseCharacter`.

We also declared `float` variables `Health`, `MaxHealth`, and `Damage`. Both the `Character` and `Enemy` classes will inherit these for combat.

8. Go into *MainCharacter.h* and delete the declarations for `Health` and `MaxHealth`, since `MainCharacter` will now inherit these variables from `BaseCharacter`. These can still be set in the `MainCharacter` and `Enemy` constructors, where we will give them their own values.

9. In the constructor in *Enemy.cpp*, give the following variables default values:

```
Health = 20.f;
MaxHealth = 20.f;
XP = 10;
Damage = 20.f;
```

And give these variables default values in the constructor in *Character.cpp*:

```
Health = 85.f;
MaxHealth = 100.f;
XP = 0;
Damage = 10.f;
```

We start the Character with more health than the Enemy, as is typically done in most games.

Finally, we declare a `TSubclassOf<UDamageType>`. The `UDamageType` class allows for different behavior depending on the type of damage being dealt. `Enemy` and `MainCharacter` will inherit this variable as well.

10. In *BaseCharacter.h*, the second `public` section just under `SetupPlayerInputComponent`, add:

```
UFUNCTION()
virtual void SwordBoxBeginOverlap(UPrimitiveComponent*
OverlappedComponent, AActor* OtherActor,
UPrimitiveComponent* OtherComp, int32 OtherBodyIndex, bool
bFromSweep, const FHitResult & SweepResult);

UFUNCTION(BlueprintCallable)
void ActivateCollision();

UFUNCTION(BlueprintCallable)
void DeactivateCollision();

virtual float TakeDamage(float DamageAmount, struct
FDamageEvent const & DamageEvent, class AController *
EventInstigator, AActor * DamageCauser) override;
virtual void Die(AActor* Causer);
```

```
UFUNCTION(BlueprintCallable)
virtual void DeathEnd();

UFUNCTION(BlueprintCallable)
void SetIsAttacking(bool Attacking);
```

We declare the `SwordBoxBeginOverlap` callback for the sword collision box. Notice we are making this function as virtual so we can override it in the `MainCharacter` and `Enemy` classes.

We declare `ActivateCollision` and `DeactivateCollision`, and make them `BlueprintCallable`. These will be used to set the collision settings on the sword collision box so it doesn't trigger Overlap Events at inappropriate times.

We then override `TakeDamage`. This is a function inherited from the `Actor` class. This function is bound to a Delegate on the `Actor` class. We will see how this function works shortly.

Since both the `MainCharacter` and `Enemy` classes will involve death, we declare a virtual `Die` function to handle it, and we make it `BlueprintCallable`.

Next, we declare a virtual function called `DeathEnd`, which will be called when the death animation is finished playing. Since this will be different for the `Enemy` than for the `MainCharacter` class, we make it virtual so each can have their own unique overloads for it.

11. Finally, we declared `SetIsAttacking` and made it `BlueprintCallable` so we can set `bIsAttacking` from Blueprints. This function exists in the `Enemy` class as well as the `Character` class, so go into *Enemy.h* and delete its declaration, and go into *Enemy.cpp* and delete its definition. Do the same for the `Character` class.

12. Define `SetIsAttacking` in *BaseCharacter.cpp*:

```
void ABaseCharacter::SetIsAttacking(bool Attacking)
{
        bAttacking = Attacking;
}
```

13. Add the following to the `BaseCharacter` constructor in *BaseCharacter.cpp*:

```
// Create the sword collision box
SwordCollisionBox =
CreateDefaultSubobject<UBoxComponent>(TEXT("SwordCollisionB
ox"));
    SwordCollisionBox->SetupAttachment(GetMesh(),
FName("WeaponLSocket"));

    SwordCollisionBox-
>SetCollisionEnabled(ECollisionEnabled::NoCollision);
    SwordCollisionBox-
>SetCollisionObjectType(ECollisionChannel::ECC_WorldDynamic
);
    SwordCollisionBox-
>SetCollisionResponseToAllChannels(ECollisionResponse::ECR_
Ignore);

    SwordCollisionBox-
>SetCollisionResponseToChannel(ECollisionChannel::ECC_Pawn,
ECollisionResponse::ECR_Overlap);
```

And we will be using the following includes:

```
#include "Components/BoxComponent.h"
#include "Animation/AnimInstance.h"
#include "Components/CapsuleComponent.h"
```

We create the `SwordCollisionBox` and call `SetupAttachment` just as we have done with previous components. This time, however, we use an override of `SetupAttachment` that takes two arguments. For the first argument, we select the mesh component to attach this collision box to by passing in `GetMesh`. The second argument is an optional socket to attach the box to. This must be an `FName`, so we use the `FName` macro to convert the string literal "`WeaponLSocket`" to an `FName`.

14. Open Unreal Engine and in the **Content Browser**, go to *Content -> Chapter7* and open *MainAnim_BP*. In the top-right corner, click the *Skeleton* icon. In the **Skeleton Tree** panel, scroll down until you find the bone labeled *weapon_l*. Left-click on it to select it and select *Add Socket*. A new socket will appear called

weapon_lSocket. Left-click on it to select it, then right-click it and select *Rename Socket*. Rename it WeaponLSocket. Left-click the *weapon_l* bone again and add another socket. Name this one *WeaponBladeLSocket* and enter Translation Mode (either click on the rotation widget that shows up by default and hit *W*, or click on the translation icon at the top-right of the **Viewport**). Drag the socket about two-thirds of the way up the blade, as shown in the following figure:

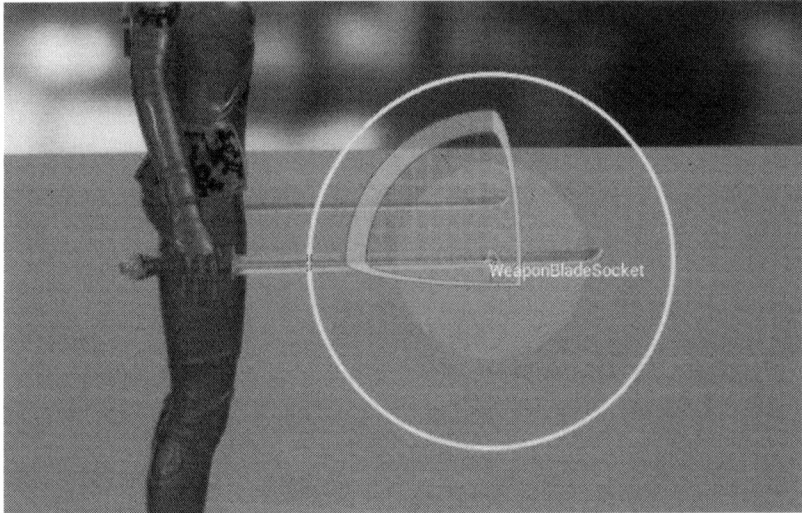

Figure 12.37: Dragging the WeaponBladeLSocket up the Blade

Now we have a socket to attach the box to as well as another socket we placed at a spot on the blade. We will use this socket shortly as a location at which to spawn the hit particles. Since the `Character` and the `Enemy` share the same skeleton, we only need to do this once.

15. Now we will define the above functions in *BaseCharacter.cpp*. First, add:

```
void ABaseCharacter::ActivateCollision()
{
    SwordCollisionBox-
>SetCollisionEnabled(ECollisionEnabled::QueryOnly);
}
```

```
void ABaseCharacter::DeactivateCollision()
{
     SwordCollisionBox-
>SetCollisionEnabled(ECollisionEnabled::NoCollision);

}
```

These functions simply set the Collision Enabled property for the Box Collision either to `QueryOnly` when collision should be activated, or `NoCollision` when it should be disabled.

16. Next, add:

```
float ABaseCharacter::TakeDamage(float DamageAmount, struct
FDamageEvent const & DamageEvent, class AController *
EventInstigator, AActor * DamageCauser)
{

     if (Health - DamageAmount <= 0.f)
     {
          Health = 0.f;
          Die(DamageCauser);
     }
     else
     {
          Health -= DamageAmount;
     }

     return DamageAmount;

}
```

This function has several parameters that get passed through whenever the Delegate is fired.

- The `float DamageAmount` is the most important, as it is the amount of damage done.

- An `FDamageEvent` is a `struct` that contains information specific to the event involving damage.

- The `EventInstigator` is the Controller of the Pawn that is doing the damage.

- `DamageCauser` is the Actor doing the damage. All this information is useable depending on what we wish to do. In our case, all we do is subtract `DamageAmount` from `Health` to see if the result is less than or equal to zero. If so, we set `Health` to 0.0, then call `Die`. We created `Die` with an input parameter of `AActor*` type so we can pass in the `DamageCauser`. If the damage amount does not put the `Health` at or below 0.0, we simply subtract `DamageAmount` from `Health`. This function has a `float` return type, so we simply return `DamageAmount`.

17. Next, we define:

```
void
ABaseCharacter::SwordBoxBeginOverlap(UPrimitiveComponent*
OverlappedComponent, AActor* OtherActor,
UPrimitiveComponent* OtherComp, int32 OtherBodyIndex, bool
bFromSweep, const FHitResult & SweepResult)
{


}
```

We don't need to add any code to the body of this function for now, since we will override it in the child classes and give it functionality there.

18. Next, add:

```
void ABaseCharacter::Die(AActor* Causer)
{
    UAnimInstance* AnimInstance = GetMesh()-
>GetAnimInstance();
    if (AnimInstance && CountessAttackMontage)
    {
        AnimInstance->Montage_Play(CountessAttackMontage,
1.0f);
```

```
        AnimInstance-
>Montage_JumpToSection(FName("Death"),
CountessAttackMontage);
    }

        SwordCollisionBox-
>SetCollisionEnabled(ECollisionEnabled::NoCollision);
    GetCapsuleComponent()-
>SetCollisionEnabled(ECollisionEnabled::NoCollision);

        bAttacking = false;

}
```

For the `Die` function, we access the skeletal mesh with `GetMesh` and call `GetAnimInstance` to get the Anim Instance. After checking to make sure it isn't null as well as the `CountessAttackMontage`, we call `Montage_Play`, passing in the `CountessAttackMontage`. We specify 1.0 for the animation speed. We also jump to the montage section for the death animation. Thus far, we only have the *Attack* montage section in the countess attack montage. We will be adding a *Death* section shortly.

Next, we set the Collision Enabled for both the `SwordCollisionBox` and the `CapsuleComponent` to `NoCollision`, since the Character will be dead and collision will no longer be appropriate.

We will add Death montage section.

19. In Unreal Engine, open the *CountessAttack* montage (in the *Chapter9* folder). In the **Asset Browser** at the bottom-right of the screen, search for the Death animation. Drag this animation onto the gray ribbon at the top of the Montage section. Right-click in the ribbon and select *New Montage Section*. Name this section *Death*. Make sure the green vertical line marking the beginning of the section is at the beginning of the *Death* animation (denoted by a green section on the ribbon) as in the following figure.

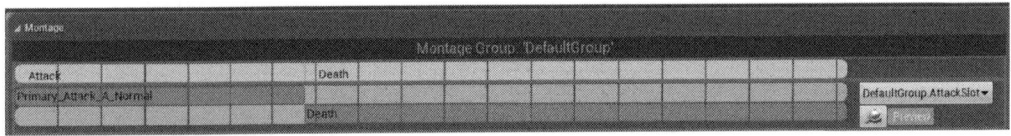

Figure 12.38: The Animation Sections in the Countess Attack Montage

Now our montage has two sections. Check the **Sections** section, and make sure there is only one animation per **Preview** bar. You can click on the green **X** icon next to one of the sections if there is more than one per **Preview** bar. This ensures that only one animation will play per section.

Figure 12.39: The Sections Section

Next, we will add Anim Notifies in the **Notifies** section. The gray **Notifies** bar has a **+** icon to the right. Click it to add a second bar. This allows us to have more room to work. At the beginning of the bar, in the **Attack** section, right-click and create a new notify called *EnableCollision*. Add another notify called *DisableCollision*. Use the red slider seen at the bottom of the screen in **Figure 12.40** to scrub through the animation and find the right spots to place these notifies. *EnableCollision* should be just before the sword swing, and *DisableCollision* should be just after it.

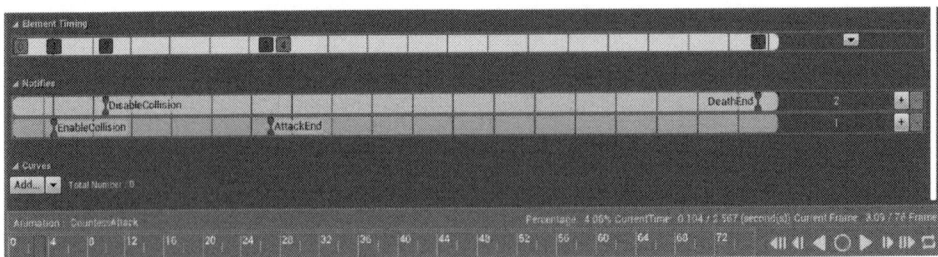

Figure 12.40: Adding Anim Notifies

As in the above figure, add another Anim Notify called *DeathEnd* near the end of the bar, in the *Death* section.

20. Now our montage is set up to call our anim notifies. Go to the **Event Graph** in the Animation Blueprint and add the following nodes:

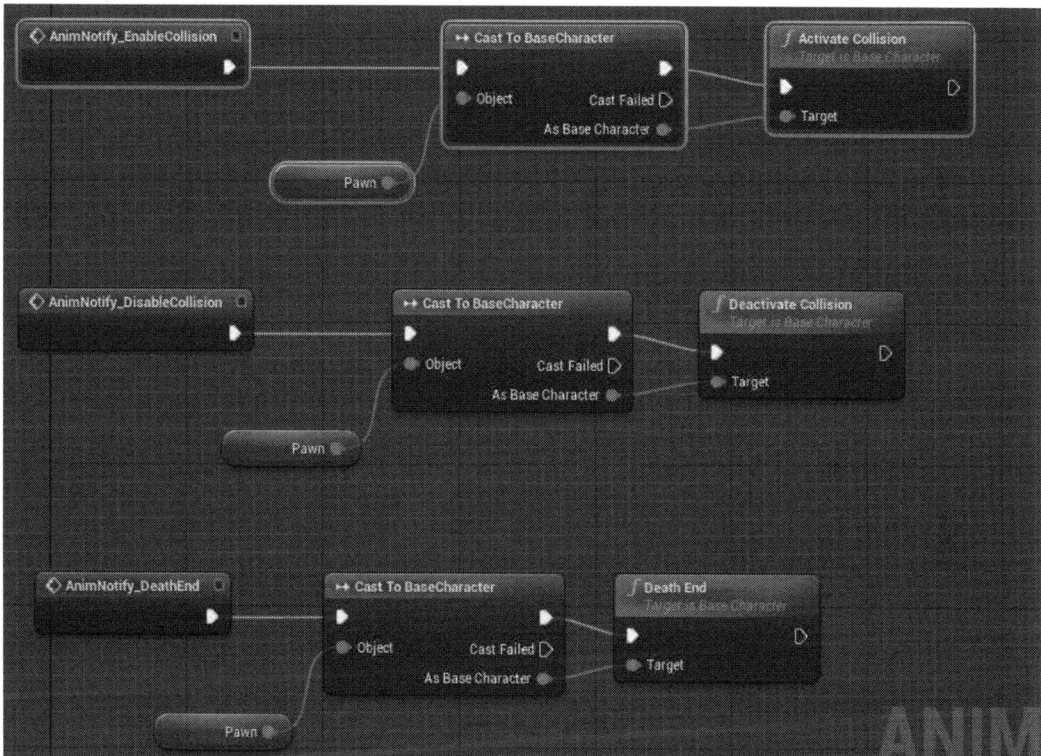

Figure 12.41: Adding Nodes for the Anim Notifies

We take the *Pawn* and cast it to BaseCharacter so we can call the BlueprintCallable functions ActivateCollision, DeactivateCollision, and DeathEnd corresponding to the anim notifies we created. Since both the MainCharacter and the Enemy class inherit these functions, they will be called regardless of which child the Animation Blueprint belongs to.

We can also change the implementation of the *AttackEnd* notify. Since both the Enemy and the Character inherit SetIsAttacking from the BaseCharacter now, we can simply cast the *Pawn* to BaseCharacter and call the function directly, as follows:

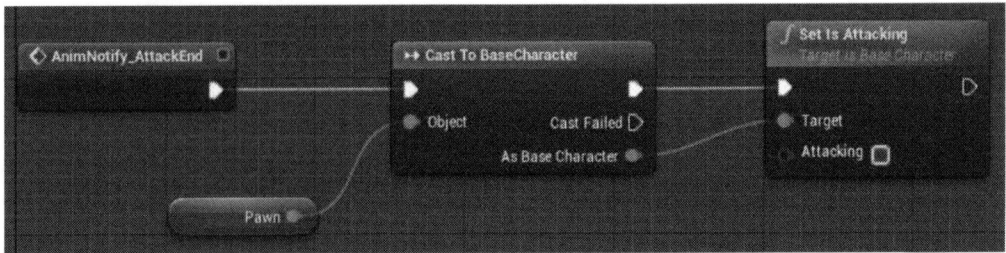

Figure 12.42: Calling Set Is Attacking on BaseCharacter

21. Now, back in *BaseCharacter.cpp*, add:

```
void ABaseCharacter::DeathEnd()
{

}
```

DeathEnd will be different for MainCharacter than for Enemy, so we will leave the function body empty here.

Now, we will be overriding some of these functions in the child classes to give them special functionality.

22. In *MainCharacter.h*, in the second public section, declare the following:

```
        virtual void SwordBoxBeginOverlap(UPrimitiveComponent*
OverlappedComponent, AActor* OtherActor,
UPrimitiveComponent* OtherComp, int32 OtherBodyIndex, bool
bFromSweep, const FHitResult & SweepResult) override;
```

Now define this function in *MainCharacter.cpp*:

```
void
AMainCharacter::SwordBoxBeginOverlap(UPrimitiveComponent*
OverlappedComponent, AActor* OtherActor,
UPrimitiveComponent* OtherComp, int32 OtherBodyIndex, bool
bFromSweep, const FHitResult & SweepResult)
{
        if (OtherActor)
        {
                AEnemy* Enemy = Cast<AEnemy>(OtherActor);
                if (Enemy)
```

```
            {
                    if (Enemy->HitParticles)
                    {
                            const USkeletalMeshSocket*
WeaponSocket = GetMesh()-
>GetSocketByName("WeaponBladeLSocket");
                            if (WeaponSocket)
                            {
                                    FVector SocketLocation =
WeaponSocket->GetSocketLocation(GetMesh());

        UGameplayStatics::SpawnEmitterAtLocation(GetWorld(),
Enemy->HitParticles, SocketLocation, FRotator(0.f), false);
                            }
                    }
                    if (Enemy->HitSound)
                    {
                            UGameplayStatics::PlaySound2D(this,
Enemy->HitSound);
                    }
                    if (DamageTypeClass)
                    {
                            UGameplayStatics::ApplyDamage(Enemy,
Damage, GetController(), this, DamageTypeClass);
                    }
            }
        }
}
```

And include these files:

```
#include "AIEnemy.h"
#include "Engine/SkeletalMeshSocket.h"
#include "Kismet/GameplayStatics.h" (if not already included)
```

We first ensure `OtherActor` is valid, then cast it to `AEnemy` and store it in local variable `Enemy`.

We check `Enemy`, then `Enemy->HitParticles`. If `HitParticles` is set, this `if` check will succeed.

We next want to access the socket that we placed about two-thirds of the way up the sword blade, which we called `WeaponBladeLSocket`. We access this by first calling `GetMesh` to get the skeletal mesh, then calling `GetSocketByName`, which takes the name of the socket. We pass in the string literal "`WeaponBladeLSocket`". This function returns a `UskeletalMeshSocket*`, so we store it in the local variable `WeaponSocket` of the same type. We make it `const` to ensure it isn't changed.

After checking to make sure the socket it valid, we call `GetSocketLocation` on the socket to get its location. `GetSocketLocation` requres the mesh to which the socket belongs, so again, we pass in the mesh returned by `GetMesh`. We store this location in a local `FVector` called `SocketLocation`.

Then we call the function `SpawnEmitterAtLocation`, which belongs to `UGameplayStatics`. This function spawns a particle emitter.

- The first argument is the World object, supplied via `GetWorld`.

- The next argument is the particle system. We access the Enemy's `HitParticles`. This way, we can have many different types of enemies, each with their own unique hit particles.

- The next argument is an `FVector` for the location at which to spawn the particle emitter.

- The next argument is an `FRotator` for the rotation, for which a simply zero rotator will suffice.

- The final argument is a Boolean for whether or not to automatically destroy the particle emitter. Our particle emitter will only play once, so we can use `false` here.

Next, we check Enemy's `HitSound`. If this is not null, we call `PlaySound2D`, another function that belongs to `UGameplayStatics`. The first argument is a world context object, for which we pass in `this`. Next is the sound, which is of type `USoundBase`. We pass in `Enemy->HitSound`. The result will be that the selected sound will be played. We simply must set this property in the Enemy Blueprint.

Finally, we check to make sure `DamageTypeClass` is set. We need a variable of type `DamageTypeClass` to pass into the `ApplyDamage` function, which we then call. `ApplyDamage` belongs to `UGameplayStatics`.

- This function first takes a damaged Actor as the first argument. We are damaging the `Enemy`, so we pass it in here.

- Next is the damage amount, for which we pass in `Damage`, which we are inheriting from `BaseCharacter`. Next is the instigator, which is the Controller of the damage causer. We simply pass in the value returned by `GetController`.

- Next is the actual damage causer, for which we pass in this.

- Finally, we pass in the `DamageTypeClass`.

23. Now open Unreal Engine and in the *Enemy_BP* Blueprint, set values for *HitParticles*, *HitSound*, and *DamageTypeClass*, as follows:

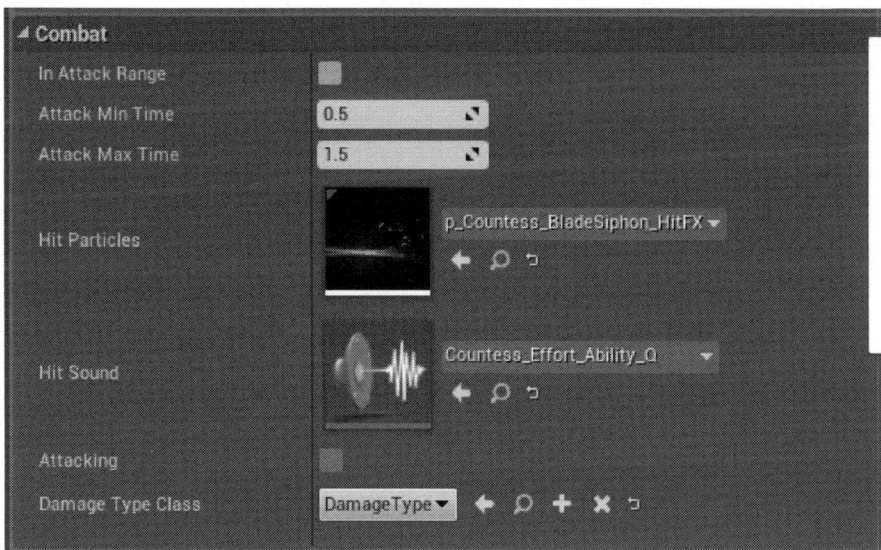

Figure 12.43: Setting Values for HitParticles, HitSound, and DamageTypeClass

For *HitParticles*, select *p_Countess_BladeSiphon_HitFX*. For *HitSound*, select *Countess_Effort_Ability_Q*. These come with the countess package that we downloaded for free from the Epic Marketplace. For *DamageTypeClass*, select *DamageType*, which is the basic damage type class. For more information on damage types, visit the Unreal Engine documentation.

24. For simplicity's sake, select the same assets for these items in the *MainCharacter_BP* Blueprint.

25. Next, in *MainCharacter.h*, declare:

```
virtual void DeathEnd() override;
```

We will be overriding this to give the `MainCharacter` unique dying abilities. Since the parent version on `BaseCharacter` is marked `UFUNCTION`, we do not need to mark it here as `UFUNCTION`. It will inherit the `UFUNCTION` quality, including being `BlueprintCallable`. Define them in *MainCharacter.cpp* as follows:

```
void AMainCharacter::DeathEnd()
{
    UKismetSystemLibrary::QuitGame(this,
Cast<APlayerController>(GetController()),
EQuitPreference::Quit, true);

}
```

We will simply use the function `QuitGame`, which belongs to `UKismetSystemLibrary`, to exit the game if the Main Character dies. The first argument is the Controller, for which we pass in `GetController`. Next is an enum constant of type `EQuitPreference`. Using `EQuitPreference::Quit` will simply result in the game session terminating.

26. Now we must override these functions in the `Enemy` class. Declare the following in *Enemy.h* in a `public` section:

```
virtual void SwordBoxBeginOverlap(UPrimitiveComponent*
OverlappedComponent, AActor* OtherActor,
UPrimitiveComponent* OtherComp, int32 OtherBodyIndex, bool
bFromSweep, const FHitResult & SweepResult) override;
```

```
virtual void Die(AActor* Causer) override;

virtual void DeathEnd() override;
```

27. Define them in *Enemy.cpp*, starting with:

```cpp
void AEnemy::SwordBoxBeginOverlap(UPrimitiveComponent*
OverlappedComponent, AActor* OtherActor,
UPrimitiveComponent* OtherComp, int32 OtherBodyIndex, bool
bFromSweep, const FHitResult & SweepResult)
{
    if (OtherActor)
    {
        AMainCharacter* Main =
Cast<AMainCharacter>(OtherActor);
        if (Main)
        {
            if (Main->HitParticles)
            {
                const USkeletalMeshSocket*
WeaponSocket = GetMesh()-
>GetSocketByName("WeaponBladeLSocket");
                if (WeaponSocket)
                {
                    FVector SocketLocation =
WeaponSocket->GetSocketLocation(GetMesh());

    UGameplayStatics::SpawnEmitterAtLocation(GetWorld(),
Main->HitParticles, SocketLocation, FRotator(0.f), false);
                }
            }
            if (Main->HitSound)
            {
                UGameplayStatics::PlaySound2D(this,
Main->HitSound);
            }
            if (DamageTypeClass)
            {
                UGameplayStatics::ApplyDamage(Main,
Damage, GetController(), this, DamageTypeClass);
```

```
                    }
               }
          }
     }
```

And include the following:

```
#include "MainCharacter.h"
#include "Engine/SkeletalMeshSocket.h"
#include "Kismet/GameplayStatics.h"
```

Notice that the implementation of this function for Enemy is the same as that for MainCharacter, except that we are casting OtherActor to AMain instead of AEnemy. Rather than using Enemy to access HitParticles and HitSound, we use Main.

28. Next we define our override for DeathEnd:

```
void AEnemy::DeathEnd()
{
     Destroy();
}
```

When the death animation for the Enemy is finished, we simply call Destroy, deleting the Enemy AI Character.

Next, we define Die for the Enemy:

```
void AEnemy::Die(AActor* Causer)
{
     Super::Die(Causer);

     AgroSphere-
>SetCollisionEnabled(ECollisionEnabled::NoCollision);
     AttackSphere-
>SetCollisionEnabled(ECollisionEnabled::NoCollision);

     AMainCharacter* Main = Cast<AMainCharacter>(Causer);
     if (Main)
     {
          Main->AddXP(XP);
     }
```

```
}
```

Notice that we call `Super::Die` in this function. This is because we want all of the code in the `Die` function in `BaseCharacter` to run, in addition to our extra code here. We didn't override this function in `MainCharacter` since the code in `BaseCharacter` is sufficient for the `MainCharacter` class.

In addition to that code, the Enemy also disables its `AgroSphere` and `AttackSphere` collision volumes. We also cast the damage causer to Main and if successful, we add to the Main Character's `XP` (experience points). We'll need to add this function to the `Character` class. Simply add the following to a `public` section of *Character.h*:

```
FORCEINLINE void AddXP(int32 AddedXP) { XP += AddedXP; }
```

Since the function is relatively simple, we can use `FORCEINLINE`.

29. Now, make sure the animation montages are set on both the *MainCharacter_BP* and *Enemy_BP*, along with their *HitParticles*, *HitSound*, and *DamageTypeClass*.

Next, we must scale the SwordCollisionBox so that it fits the shape of the sword.

30. In *Enemy_BP*, select *CapsuleComponent* and in the **Details** panel, in **Rendering**, uncheck *Visible*.

31. Do the same for *AgroSphere* and *AttackSphere*. Nowe we can see the *SwordCollisionBox* more clearly.

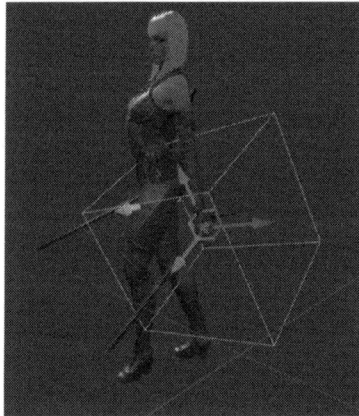

Figure 12.44: Showing Only SwordCollisionBox

32. Select the *Mesh* and in the **Details** panel, in the **Animation** section, check the *Pause Anims* checkbox. Now the Character will stop moving so we can position the collision box.

33. With the *SwordCollisionBox* selected, scale and position the box around the sword blade as in the following figure. You will likely want to turn off snapping.

34. Select the *Mesh* and uncheck *Pause Anims* in the **Details** panel. Check the *Visibility* checkboxes for the *CapsuleComponent*, the *AgroSphere*, and *AttackSphere*.

35. Repeat Steps 31 - 25 for *MainCharacter_BP*.

36. Finally, we must make sure our `SwordBoxBeginOverlap` function gets called in both our `Enemy` and `Character` classes. In *BaseCharacter.cpp*, add the following to the `BeginPlay` function:

```
SwordCollisionBox-
>OnComponentBeginOverlap.AddDynamic(this,
&ATestBaseCharacter::SwordBoxBeginOverlap);
```

We are now ready to test out damage! In the Unreal Engine editor, make sure all the variables have the proper values. If you aren't seeing any variables updating with their constructor-initialized values (`Health`, `Damage`, etc.) you may need to restart the editor, or in some cases actually delete the Blueprint and create a new one based on the proper class. If you don't want to go through all that, you can simply set these variable values on the Blueprint itself. This is the benefit of exposing variables to Bluepritnts!

Press **Play** and allow the Enemy to attack the Main Character. Notice that the Main Character's health bar goes down with each strike, and if it goes all the way down, the game session terminates. Notice also that after hitting the Enemy enough times, it will die and disappear. Allowing the Enemy to hit you until your life drains to 0 will also cause you to play the Death animation and the game will end. Hitting should also be accompanied by hit particles and sounds. We have conquered combat!

We are now ready to tweak our Navigation Mesh settings. This will allow us to make our AI behavior more tailored to our game, specifically.

Nav Mesh Generation Settings

Open the *ThirdPersonExampleMap*, and press *P* to enable the green visualization of the Navigation Mesh. Take a look at the stairs on in the middle of the level and notice that the Nav Mesh is broken here.

Figure 12.45: Broken Nav Mesh

Place an *Enemy_BP* in the level if you haven't already. If you agro the Enemy (step into its `AgroSphere` and make it chase you), if you run up the stairs, the Enemy will not be able to chase you if the Nav Mesh is broken there. We can alter some of the settings on the Nav Mesh to make sure we don't have this problem.

Go to *Edit -> Project Settings -> Navigation Mesh*. Scroll down to the **Generation** section. Set *Cell Height* to 20. This will bring the Nav Mesh up higher so it will encompass more area. *Agent Radius* and *Agent Height* refer to the capsule of the AI Pawn. These are already tailored to the approximate default size of the Capsule Component of the `Character` class, so we can leave them as they are. *Agent Max Slope* refers to the incline that the Nav Mesh will accommodate. It will not go above 90 degrees. Agent Max Step Height refers to the height of an obstacle on which the AI Pawn can step. Set this to 50. Now take a look at the Nav Mesh.

Figure 12.46: Nav Mesh Fixed

Now that the Nav Mesh accommodates for the stairs, you can press **Play** and make the AI Character chase you up the stairs and it will follow. However, if you jump down to the ground, the AI Character is not smart enough to jump down after you. For this, we must add a Nav Link Proxy. We will do so now.

Nav Link Proxy

In the **Modes** panel, search for **Nav Link Proxy**. This Actor allows for AI to cross through gaps in a Nav Mesh. Drag one into the world on the ramp. Make sure it is in the green Nav Mesh area.

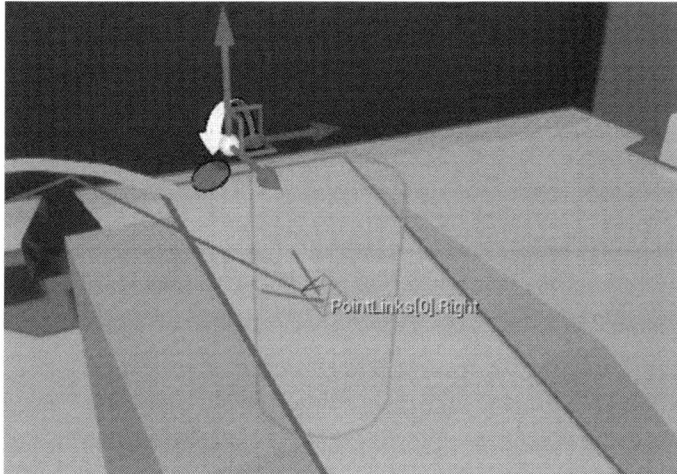

Figure 12.47: Dragging in a Nav Link Proxy

There are two vector widgets called *PointLinks[0].Left* and *PointLinks[0].Right*. Position one of these on the ramp and one on the ground. Make sure the cylinders representing their influence penetrates the green Nav Mesh.

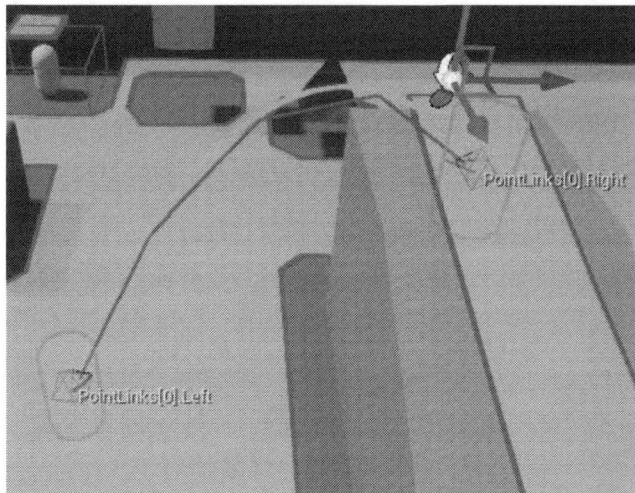

Figure 12.48: Setting up the Left and Right Points of the Nav Link Proxy

With the Nav Link Proxy selected, in the **Details** panel, find *Link Direction*. This can be set to *Left to Right*, *Right to Left*, or *Both Ways*. This determines which way the AI can go on the Nav Link Proxy. Set this to *Bboth Ways*. Now press **Play**, make the AI Character chase you, and jump down off the ramp. The AI Character will jump down from the ramp to the ground at the point of the Nav Link Proxy!

Nav Modifier Volume

There may be places in your level where you want the Nav Mesh to take on different properties. You can modify the Nav Mesh in specific areas with a Nav Modifier Volume. Search the **Modes** panel for Nav Modifier Volume and drag one in.

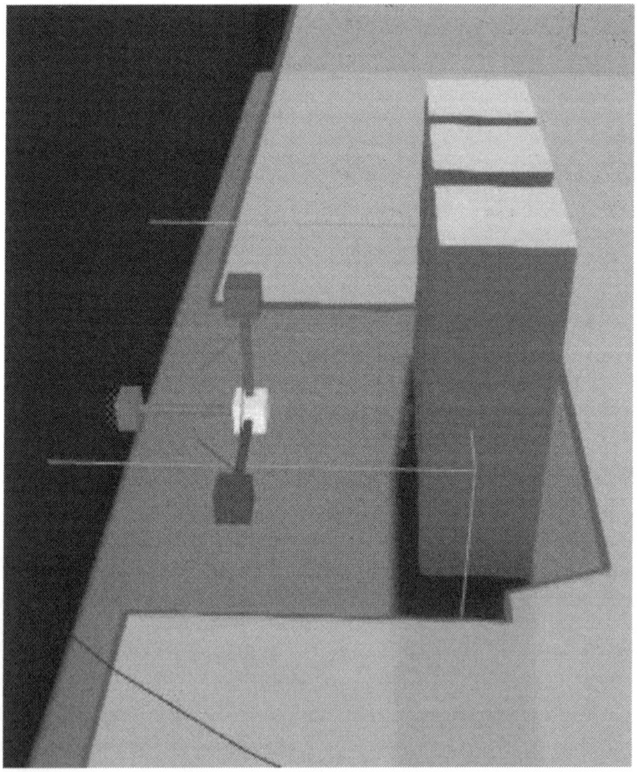

Figure 12.49: Placing a Nav Modifier Volume in the World

With the Nav Modifier Volume selected, in the **Details** panel, notice the *Area Class* item. Setting it to *NavArea_Null* actually puts a hole in the Nav Mesh where the volume is, so the AI Character cannot even traverse it.

You can also create a new Nav Area class by pressing the **+** icon next to *Area Class*. Do this. Call the new Area Class *CustomNavArea* and place it in the *Chapter12* folder. Open its Blueprint and notice in the **Details** panel that you can set *Default Cost*. This is the cost for AI to move through the area.

Fixed Area Entering Cost is how difficult it is for the AI to actually enter the Area. The *Draw Color* is the color that the area will appear on the Nav Mesh.

Set *Default Cost* and *Fixed Area Entering Cost* both to 10. Leave the *Draw Color* as is. Notice that the area now takes on the *Draw Color* in the map.

Drag in another Nav Modifier Volume and create a new custom *Nav Area* called *NavAreaHighCost*, as set both Default Cost and *Fixed Area Entering Cost* to 20. Change the color as well to red.

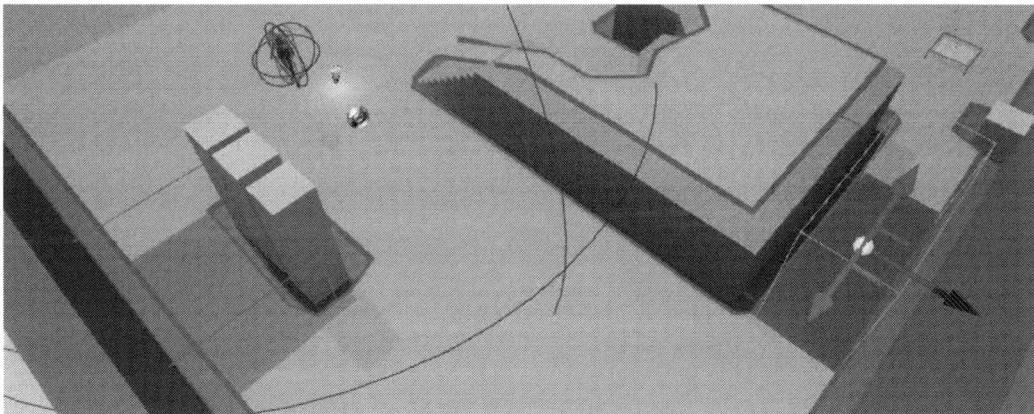

Figure 12.50: Two Custom Nav Areas with Different Costs

Now press **Play** and have the AI Character chase you through a nav area with a higher cost. The AI will attempt to take the cheapest path if one is available.

Rebuilding Nav Mesh at Runtime

Recall that we created a working door that opens and closes by pressing a floor switch. Well, that door blocks the Nav Mesh and even though we might open it at runtime, the Nav Mesh will still have a hole in it, as seen in the following figure.

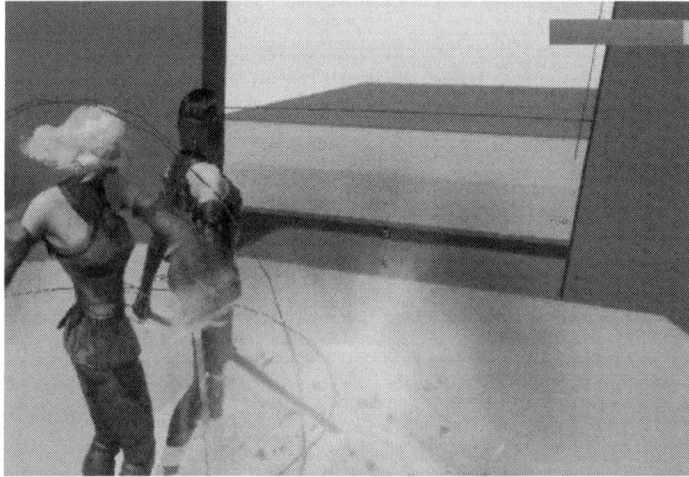

Figure 12.51: Hole in the Nav Mesh

To fix this, we can rebuild the Nav Mesh at runtime. Go to *Edit -> Project Settings -> Navigation Mesh -> Runtime*. Set *Runtime Generation* from *Static* to *Dynamic*. The *Observed Paths Tick Interval* item determines how often observed paths will be processed to rebuild the Nav Mesh.

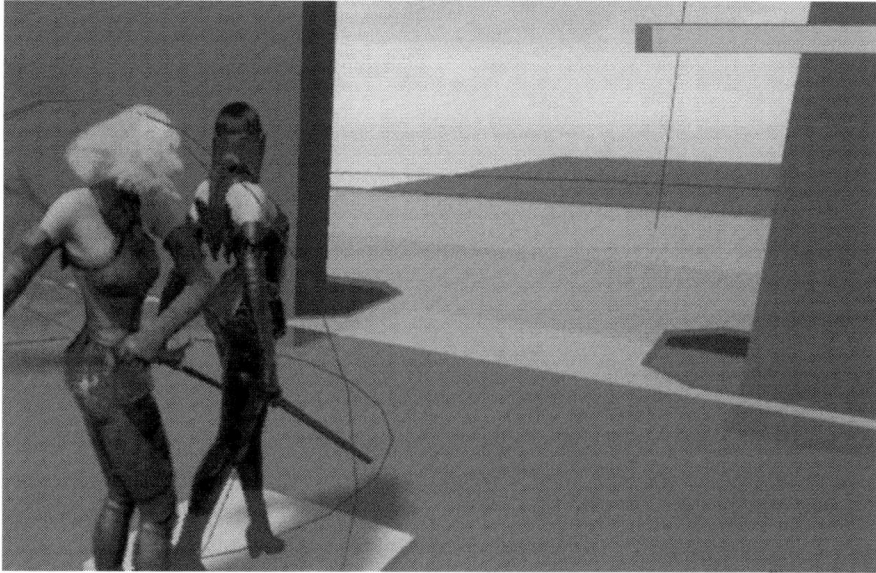

Figure 12.52: Regenerating the Nav Mesh at Runtime

Now the Nav Mesh will be complete and the AI will be able to chase the Main Character through an open door!

Summary

In this chapter, we have learned the fundamentals of AI in video games. We first saw that Unreal Engine has built-in pathfinding capabilities, or ways to find a path from one point to another, even with the presence of obstacles. We learned how to visualize the path point by drawing debug spheres at each point in a path. We saw that we needed to include the AI Module in our .*Build.cs* file in order to access the AI code in Unreal Engine. We then learned about the different components of Unreal Engine's AI system, including Blackboards and Behavior Trees. We created our own AI Character and AI Controller classes for a custom AI Character, which we called `Enemy`. We then created a Blackboard and a Behavior Tree for our AI Character, giving it the capability to patrol, chase the player, and even attack. We then implemented attack damage by making use of the `TakeDamage` function inherited from the Actor class, and we activated it by calling `ApplyDamage`, a function belonging to `UGameplayStatics`. We also learned how to adjust the parameters of the navigation mesh, allowing our AI to traverse more diverse terrain. We learned that a Nav Link Proxy can allow AI to move across gaps in the Nav Mesh, such as dropping down from the ramp in the ThirdPersonExampleMap. We learned how to make Nav Modifier Volumes in order to create sections in the Nav Mesh with different properties, such as difficulty for the AI to enter or cross. Finally we learned how to rebuild the Nav Mesh at runtime, so obstacles that move such as opening doors will not prevent AI from moving through those areas once the obstacles are moved away.

AI is a huge part of video game development, and now that you've conquered this chapter, you now know how to create AI-driven Characters for your own games! All that's left now is to finalize the game project and package it up into an executable file!

Chapter 13 – Downsizing the Project and Packaging Your Game

We are now ready to prepare our game project for packaging! By the end of this chapter, we will have a packaged executable file which can run the game. However, if we packaged the game project as-is, the game file would be quite large, as we have imported quite a few assets into our game project. Since we didn't use all of the assets in our project, our packaged game would be unnecessarily large. We will thus downsize our project so it only includes the assets we use. The chapter is broken into three sections:

- **Downsizing the Project – Migrating Levels**: We will create a project which only includes the assets we use in our game.

- **Copying the Config Files**: We will copy over the files that determine all the settings for our project, including the user inputs.

- **Packaging the Game**: We will package our game project into an executable file.

The heavy lifting has already been done, and we are now ready to finalize this project and turn it into an actual game! Let's get started.

Downsizing the Project – Migrating Levels

Finishing the Game

Before we downsize the project, let's make sure it's in the state we want to be in.

1. Go to *Edit -> Project Settings -> Maps & Modes -> Default Maps* and set both the *Editor Startup Map* and *Game Default Map* to *LV_Soul_Cave*.

2. First, we will need a Nav Mesh in this level. From the **Modes** panel, drag in a Nav Mesh Bounds Volume. Make sure it is large enough for the entire map. You

503

can change the camera speed to its maximum and zoom out to see the entire level from the sky and make sure the volume encompasses the entire level.

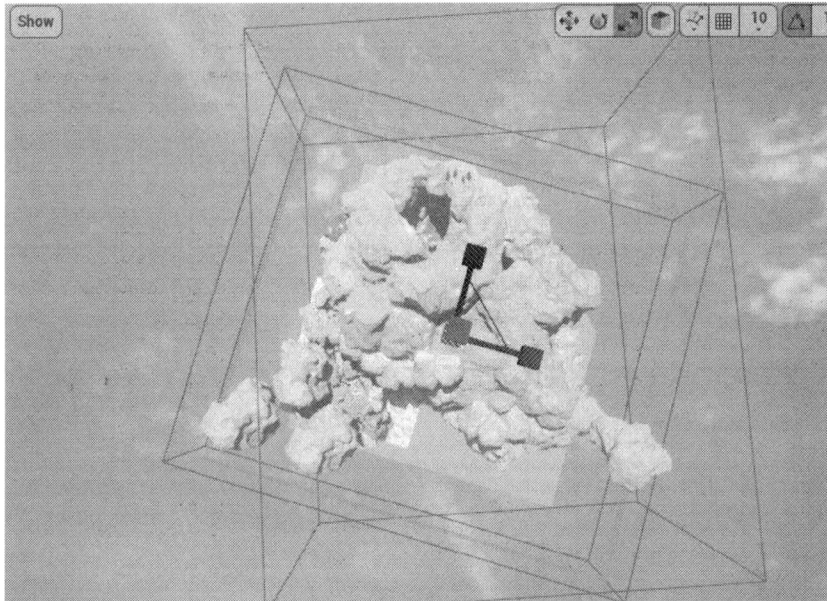

Figure 13.1: The Nav Mesh Bounds Volume Covering the Whole Map

3. Now, let's place some enemies throughout the level. From the *Chapter12* folder, drag in a few instances of *Enemy_BP*. Select the Vector widgets and move them to appropriate patrol points. You will need to make sure they are not in locations that the Enemy will not be able to reach due to obstacles it cannot get past (unless you place a Nav Link Proxy).

4. Place any number of obstacles, pickups, and hazards you would like to have in your game. For the mesh assets, you can easily replace them with assets that your game project contains. For example, open *FloorSwitch_BP* and select *Door*. Change the *Static Mesh* item from *Shape_Cube* to *SM_Slums_Wall_02k*, which came with the *Soul Cave* map. Select *FloorSwitch* and change the Static Mesh item from *Shape_Cube* to *SM_Cave_Rock_PillarTop*. You will need to drag it so that it sits at the correct position relative to the collision box.

Figure 13.2: Replacing the Shape_Cubes in FloorSwitch_BP

Depending on where you place the floor switch, you may need to select individual components and move or scale them as appropriate. Place as many of these game mechanics into the map as you desire.

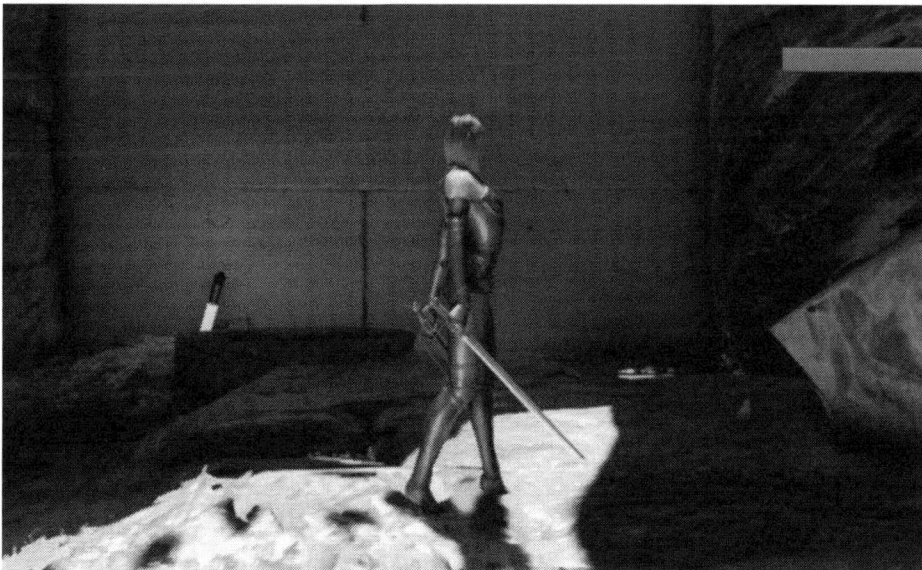

Figure 13.3: FloorSwitch in the Soul Cave

5. Replace the placeholder meshes on the other game mechanics as you see fit. For example, *SwitchTarget_BP* in the *Chapter11* folder has the *TargetMesh* component which can be replaced by a pillar, such as *SM_Cave_Rock_Pillar_Moss2* from the *Soul Cave* pack. As explained in *Chapter 11*, you can place these into the level and add them to the *FloorSwitch_BP's Switch Targets* array, using the dropper tool to select them.

Once you are satisfied with your level, it is now time to downsize the project.

Downsizing the Project

Having an Unreal Engine game project with only the assets you are using in the game can be useful. If you work with a team and need to share the project, having a smaller project cuts down on memory usage and file size. One way to downsize the project is to go through all of the folders and delete all assets you aren't using. Not only would this be time consuming, but you would run the risk of deleting assets you didn't know you were using. We will use a different method. We will create a new project and migrate the *Soul Cave* level into it.

Creating a New Unreal Engine Project

We must create a new project.

1. Open the Epic Games Launcher. Create a new C++ First Person Template based project. Select *Without Starter Content*. Select a location for this project and give it **the same name as your original project**. This will make it easier to copy all the C++ files over (you won't need to change names of variables due to having a different project name). In our case, the project will be called *FirstGame*.

Once the Visual Studio project has been generated, we will need to copy over the C++ files.

2. Close Visual Studio. Open the original project's folder. If you don't know where it is on your computer, open the Epic Games Launcher and find it in the *Library* section. Right-click on it and select *Show in Folder*. This will bring up the folder on your computer where your project is located. With this folder open, double-

click on the *Source* folder. There will be a *FirstGame* folder. Double-click on it. Inside, you will see all of the C++ files that belong to this project.

3. Now, find the folder which contains the newly-created, empty project. Find its *Source* folder. Copy all of the files from the *Source* folder of the original project and paste them into the *Source* folder of the new project. When prompted whether you wish to replace duplicate files or ignore them, replace them.

4. Now, in the folder which contains our new project, find *FirstGame.uasset*, right-click on it, and select *Generate Visual Studio Project Files*.

5. Now, open *FirstGame.sln* and notice that our newly-added C++ files are there. We must compile this project, because the Unreal Build Tool needs to generate all of the auto-generated content signaled by all the Unreal Engine-specific macros throughout our code. Compile the project.

If you get compile errors regarding the `AIController` class, include "AIModule" in the `PrivateDependencyModuleNames` as well as the `PublicDependencyModuleNames`.

Once complete, the project will contain all of the auto-generated code that aids the reflection system. We now must copy the Config files to our new project so all the settings and user inputs are configured.

Copying the Config Files

Copying the config files will allow us to get all our User Settings including inputs (Axis and Action Mappings) in our new project file without needing to set them up manually.

1. Open the original project folder and locate the *Config* folder. Select its contents and copy them. In the *Config* folder of the new project, past these contents. Opt to replace existing files. Now all of the configurations will exist in the new project including input mappings.

In the new project, you can prove this to yourself by going to *Edit -> Project Settings -> Input* and see all the configured input mappings.

Now we are ready to migrate all of the content we used in the original project to the new one.

Migrating Assets from the Old Project to the New Project

Open the old project. Find the Soul Cave level in the **Content Browser** under *Content -> SoulCave -> Maps*. Right-click on *LV_Soul_Cave* and select *Asset Actions… -> Migrate*. Click **Okay** and find the *Content* folder of the new project and select it.

When the migration is successful, the level will exist in the new project along with everything in it. This means any assets that weren't used will not be there.

We now have a working game project that only includes what we use. We are now ready to package the game!

Packaging the Game

Packaging a game in Unreal Engine is relatively straightforward. Go to *File -> Package Project -> Windows -> Windows 64 bit*.

Figure 13.4: Packaging the Project

You must choose a folder for the packaged project to be sent to. If your project exists in a path that has a long name, packaging might fail. If this happens, create a new folder close to your hard disk (for example in the C drive) and give it a short name. Send your packaged file there.

After packaging, there will be a folder called *WindowsNoEditor* in the folder you have chosen for your packaged build. Open it and inside there will be an executable with the name of your project; in our case, it is FirstGame. Double-click the executable and play your game!

Summary

We have learned in this chapter how to downsize our project by creating a new blank project and migrating our assets over to it. We saw that we needed to copy our C++ files from the *Source* folder, as well as the config files from the *Config* folder. Once we did that and compiled our project, we then learned how to migrate the level over to the new project. From there, we learned how to package the project into a working executable file.

You did it! You created a complete video game in Unreal Engine from scratch and packaged it into an executable file! This is a huge accomplishment and deserves congratulations. Keep this book and refer to it whenever you need a reference for the various nuances in the C++ programming language, the Unreal Engine C++ code base, and for general best practices when it comes to game development. With the skill set you have gained from this book, you now have the tools and knowledge necessary to create just about any type of video game you can fathom. I wish you the very best in your career as a game developer and hope that you can use Unreal Engine to bring your wildest dreams to life!

Unreal Engine C++ the Ultimate Developer's Handbook

Glossary

Made in the USA
Las Vegas, NV
19 December 2022

63611531R00293